Essays Metaphysical and Moral

Selected Philosophical Papers

J. J. C. Smart

D1381510

Basil Blackwell

Copyright © J. J. C. Smart 1987

First published 1987

Basil Blackwell Ltd
108 Cowley Road, Oxford, OX4 1JF, UK

Basil Blackwell Inc.
432 Park Avenue South, Suite 1503
New York, NY 10016, USA

British Library Cataloguing in Publication Data

Smart, J.J.C.
Essays metaphysical and moral : selected
philosophical papers.
1. Philosophy
I. Title
199'.94   B5704.S6

ISBN 0–631–15246–6

Library of Congress Cataloging in Publication Data

Essays metaphysical and moral.

Includes index.
1. Philosophy.   2. Ethics.   3. Utilitarianism.
I. Smart, J.J.C. (John Jamieson Carswell),
1920–
B29.E82   1987   100   86–19325
ISBN 0–631–15246–6

Typeset in 10 on 12pt Plantin
by Columns of Reading
Printed in Great Britain by
T J Press, Padstow, Cornwall

326776

Contents

Acknowledgements   vii

1   Introduction   1

PART 1   METHODOLOGY IN PHILOSOPHY AND SCIENCE   9
2   Philosophy and Scientific Plausibility (1966)   11
3   My Semantic Ascents and Descents (1975)   25
4   Ockham's Razor (1984)   38

PART 2   SPACE, TIME AND SPACE-TIME   49
5   Causal Theories of Time (1969)   51
6   Space-Time and Individuals (1972)   61
7   Time and Becoming (1980)   78
8   The Reality of the Future (1981)   91

PART 3   METAPHYSICS AND PHILOSOPHY OF SCIENCE   101
9   Ryle in Relation to Modern Science (1970)   103
10   Under the Form of Eternity (1976–7)   120
11   Difficulties for Realism in the Philosophy of Science (1982)   132
12   Sellars on Process (1982)   145
13   Laws of Nature and Cosmic Coincidences (1985)   158
14   Realism v. Idealism (1986)   169

PART 4   PHILOSOPHY OF MIND   187
15   Sensations and Brain Processes (1959, 1962)   189
16   Materialism (1963)   203
17   Further Thoughts on the Identity Theory (1972)   215
18   On Some Criticisms of a Physicalist Theory of Colours (1972)   229
19   The Revival of Materialism (1976)   240
20   Physicalism and Emergence (1982)   246

vi   *Contents*

PART 5   ETHICS   257
21   Extreme and Restricted Utilitarianism (1956, 1967)   259
22   Benevolence as an Over-Riding Attitude (1977)   272
23   Utilitarianism and Generalized Benevolence (1977)   283
24   Distributive Justice and Utilitarianism (1978)   292
Index   307

Acknowledgements

Permission to reproduce the essays in this book has been granted by the original publisher. The sources in which the essays first appeared are as follows:

'Philosophy and Scientific Plausibility' from Paul K. Feyerabend and Grover Maxwell (eds), *Mind, Matter and Method, Essays in Honor of Herbert Feigl* (Minneapolis: University of Minnesota Press, 1966) pp. 377–390. Copyright © 1966 by the University of Minnesota.

'My Semantic Ascents and Descents' from Charles J. Bontempo and S. Jack Odell (eds), *The Owl of Minerva, Philosophers on Philosophy* (New York: McGraw Hill, 1975), pp. 57–72.

'Ockham's Razor' from James H. Fetzer (ed.), *Principles of Philosophical Reasoning* (Totowa, New Jersey: Rowman & Allanheld, 1984) pp. 118–128.

'Causal Theories of Time' from *The Monist* 1969, vol. 53, pp. 385–395. Copyright © 1969, *The Monist*, La Salle, Illinois 61301. Reprinted by permission.

'Space-Time and Individuals' from *Logic and Art: Essays in Honor of Nelson Goodman*, edited by Richard Rudner and Israel Scheffler. New York: Macmillan Publishing Company, 1972, pp. 3–20.

'Time and Becoming' from Peter van Inwagen (ed.), *Time and Cause* (Dordrecht, Holland: D. Reidel, 1980), pp. 3–15.

'The Reality of the Future' from *Philosophia* 1981, vol. 10, pp. 141–150.

'Ryle in Relation to Modern Science' originally appeared in *Ryle: A Collection of Critical Essays* edited by Oscar P. Wood and George Pitcher. Copyright © 1970, by Doubleday & Company, Inc. Reprinted by permission of the publisher.

'Under the Form of Eternity' was given as the Seventh Walter and Eliza

Hall Institute Lecture, published in *The Walter and Eliza Hall Institute of Medical Research Annual Review* 1976–7, pp. 36–42.
'Difficulties for Realism in the Philosophy of Science' from L. Jonathan Cohen, Jerzy Łos, Helmut Pfeiffer and Klaus-Peter Podewski (eds), *Logic, Methodology and Philosophy of Science VI*, Proceedings of the Sixth International Congress of Logic, Methodology and Philosophy of Science, Hannover 1979 (Amsterdam: North-Holland Publishing Company, 1982), pp. 363–375.
'Sellars on Process' from *The Monist* 1982, vol. 65, pp. 302–314. Copyright © 1982, *The Monist*, La Salle, Illinois 61301. Reprinted by permission.
'Laws of Nature and Cosmic Coincidences' from *The Philosophical Quarterly* 1985, vol. 35, pp. 272–280.
'Realism v. Idealism' from *Philosophy* 1986, vol. 61, pp. 295–312.
'Sensations and Brain Processes' from *The Philosophical Review* 1959, vol. 68, pp. 141–156. Reprinted here with minor amendments as reprinted in V. C. Chappell (ed.), *The Philosophy of Mind* (Englewood Cliffs, New Jersey: Prentice-Hall Inc., 1962), pp. 160–172.
'Materialism' from *The Journal of Philosophy* 1963, vol. 60, pp. 651–662.
'Further Thoughts on the Identity Theory' from *The Monist* 1972, vol. 56, pp. 149–162. Copyright © 1972, *The Monist*, La Salle, Illinois 61301. Reprinted by permission.
'On Some Criticisms of a Physicalist Theory of Colours' from Chungying Cheng (ed.), *Philosophical Aspects of the Mind-Body Problem* (Honolulu, Hawaii: University of Hawaii Press, 1975) pp. 54–63.
'The Revival of Materialism' from *The Listener* April 1976, vol. 95, pp. 535–539.
'Physicalism and Emergence' copyright © International Brain Research Organization. Reprinted from *Neuroscience* 1981, vol. 6, pp. 109–113.
'Extreme and Restricted Utilitarianism' from *The Philosophical Quarterly* 1956, vol. 6, pp. 344–354. Reprinted here as in the revised version from Philippa Foot (ed.), *Theories of Ethics* (Oxford University Press, 1967) pp. 171–183.
'Benevolence as an Over-Riding Attitude' from *Australasian Journal of Philosophy* 1977, vol. 55, p. 127–135.
'Utilitarianism and Generalized Benevolence' from *Pacific Philosophical Quarterly* 1980, vol. 61, pp. 115–121.
'Distributive Justice and Utilitarianism' in *Justice and Economic Distribution*, John Arthur and William H. Shaw (eds), © 1978, pp. 103–115. Reprinted by permission of Prentice-Hall, Englewood Cliffs, New Jersey.

To Helen and Robert

1

Introduction

The essays in this volume were published over a thirty year period. The first twenty essays could be called 'metaphysical' and the last four 'moral'. There are two main concerns that chiefly have motivated me to do philosophy: (a) to attempt to speak clearly and plausibly about the nature of the universe (space, time, matter, mind, free will, the existence or non-existence of God, and so on) and (b) to try to speak clearly and benevolently about our practical decisions. In short, with what the world is like and what we should do about it; all this, however, at the abstract level at which I function best – I am no ornithologist or adviser of troubled citizens, much as I admire those who engage in these activities. I am a philosopher, not a scientist, and so I regret not having the intimate intellectual contact with nature that is enjoyed by even the most theoretical of my scientific friends, and if I were more practically minded I would equally regret not having the useful advisory skills of economists and other social scientists.[1]

In the ethical essays I defend utilitarianism as a normative theory. While I deny that a normative theory can be deduced from factual, scientific or metaphysical considerations I do hold that utilitarianism (as a normative theory) with its simplicity, generality and lack of anthropocentricity should be found congenial to the scientific temper. (This is of course compatible with ethics as a *descriptive* and sociological theory being quite properly anthropocentric.)

Some philosophers, such as my friend Hilary Putnam, would complain that my philosophical attitudes are 'scientistic' rather than 'scientific'. In return I am tempted to use the expression 'anti-scientistic' to apply to those philosophers who (sometimes despite their own notable scientific competence) want to give metaphysical prominence to non-scientific attitudes and ways of thinking. I have come to think that considerations of plausibility in the light of total science have an essential place in philosophical theorizing. The essay 'Philosophy and Scientific Plausibility' is an attempt to say why. At an earlier period I had accepted the neo-Wittgensteinian orthodoxy that philosophy is a purely conceptual investigation, but nevertheless I came to think even then that considerations of scientific plausibility had an important place, though in a merely heuristic way (see Smart 1957), much as plausible reasoning can be a heuristic for mathematicians (see Pólya 1954). This is because philosophical reasonings are often very tricky, and if a scientifically unplausible conclusion (such as mind–matter dualism) emerges from them we should look much harder at the reasonings. However, in the essay 'Philosophy and Scientific Plausibility' I go further and give plausibility considerations a place in metaphysical thinking which puts them far beyond being mere heuristic aids.

This attitude was reinforced when under the influence of W.V. Quine (especially his rejection of the analytic–synthetic distinction as an important philosophical tool) I came to reject a sharp line between metaphysics and science. Metaphysics is the more conceptual and relatively untestable end of science. Many scientific theories are only very indirectly testable and there is no sharp line between the testable and the untestable. I say more about this sort of thing in the essays 'My Semantic Ascents and Descents' and 'Ockham's Razor'. The latter essay modifies somewhat my position in the essay 'Sensations and Brain Processes', which was written at a time when I did think of metaphysics and science as more sharply distinct from one another.

In the essay 'My Semantic Ascents and Descents' I weave in a certain amount of intellectual autobiography and describe the influence of Gilbert Ryle and later of Quine on my conception of philosophy. I should like to record here my immense debt to U.T. Place and C.B. Martin, who were my colleagues in the philosophy department at the University of Adelaide in the 1950s. It was Place who converted me to the mind–brain identity theory. While Place was incubating his bold theory, which he published in his pioneering article 'Is Consciousness a Brain Process?' (Place 1956) he had many discussions with Martin and myself. The three of us wrote notes to each other on the subject, which we had typed out. (I have lost them now, but I remember sending some of them to Ryle.)

Ryle's behaviourism seemed to work pretty well in the case of mental dispositions, such as beliefs and desires, but experiences (for example having a toothache) seemed to resist behaviouristic analysis. I tried to counter Place's view by giving such a behaviourist account of experiences, eked out with some account of reports of experiences as 'avowals', which was a popular move in some quarters. It soon became clear that this was an unpromising line of attack, and also that the usual arguments against the identity theory were (as Place had seen) bad arguments. It seemed then that if Place's theory could not be refuted on considerations of plausibility it should be accepted. The penny belatedly dropped while I was giving a graduate class at Princeton on Ryle and Wittgenstein, and as a result I read a precursor of the essay 'Sensations and Brain Processes' at Cornell University. Because this article was published in a leading philosophical journal, while Place's pioneering one was published in a psychological journal, mine perhaps received too much attention from philosophers and Place's excellent article too little, or at any rate not so much as it so richly deserved. Fortunately Place's article was later reprinted in several philosophical anthologies.

At the time, and in the succeeding years, there was a feeling of missionary zeal in trying to get the materialist theory of mind taken seriously. After all, it was normal for first year undergraduates to be taught to reject it out of hand. It did fall on more fertile soil in the USA and in Australia, but in Oxford especially it had the initial obstacle of what I liked to call 'the argument of the raised eyebrow'. When my one time student B.H. Medlin was at Oxford he made valiant efforts to depress the eyebrow (see Medlin 1967 for a penetrating criticism of the anti-mechanistic strain in Ryle's thought). We were accused, no doubt, of crudity, but what our opponents seemed to see as sophistication we tended to see as fence sitting. Later the identity theory was worked out in a comprehensive way by D.M. Armstrong at Sydney, and in the USA it was well defended by David Lewis (1966, 1972, 1983, pp. 99–107, 130–2). (I am glad to say that it soon came to have very many other able defenders.)

When I wrote 'Sensations and Brain Processes' I was still struggling free from the unacknowledged but endemic residual verificationism which was characteristic of the neo-Wittgensteinian philosophy of the period. C.B. Martin did much to cure me of this and consequently to make it easier for me to reject the behaviourism to which I still clung in the case of mental states such as beliefs and desires. Armstrong (1968) extended the identity theory to cover such states and in the essay 'Further Thoughts on the Identity Theory' I followed him in this direction.

Perhaps the predominant view among philosophers of mind nowadays is functionalism, but I think that functionalists greatly exaggerate the difference between functionalism and the identity theory. One form of functionalism was put forward by Putnam (1975, pp. 408–28), who compared mental states with machine states of a Turing machine or computer. According to this view mental states are not concrete brain states but are abstract logical states. However, it is hard to suppose that an experience of toothache, say, is an abstract logical state, and even beliefs and desires are hardly abstract objects, because they cause actions.

A more plausible form of functionalism holds merely that mental states are described in an abstract way but are not themselves abstract objects. Compare the way in which a radio engineer might talk of 'a frequency changer' or 'an audio amplifier' which he or she might represent in a 'block diagram'. There might be different sorts of circuits and devices which concretely realize such entities. (The circuits need not be physically separable from one another. The army number 22 set of the Second World War was a transceiver, and so many of the same components could form part of both transmitter and receiver, whereas the Australian-made FS 6 had quite separate transmitter and receiver parts.) However, if it is just a matter of abstractness of description my 'topic neutral' formula in 'Sensations and Brain Processes' is pretty abstract too, and so the distinction between functionalism and the identity theory is not all that clear.

Identity theorists and functionalists agree that mental events and states have a neurological base. So the main bone of contention arises out of the stress that functionalists make on the possibility, or even probability, that the brain state or process corresponding to or identical with some mental state or process may be different from person to person, or perhaps from species to species, or from the terrestrial to the extra-terrestrial. The identity theorist would expect some abstract similarities, and in fact would be sure of them in the case of some properties of some experiences. The experience of having a toothache may wax and wane or be intermittent, and waxing and waning and being intermittent are part of a topic neutral description such as we are introspectively able to make. General statements of identity might be truly universal, merely terrestrial, merely species wide, or perhaps even restricted to the repeated mental processes and states of a single person. Even in the case of the single person there is some generality and a mere 'token token' identity does not seem plausible.[2] I should expect a good deal of similarity between even Alpha Centaurian brain processes and human ones when there was typical pain behaviour. If the Alpha Centaurian and human brains were discovered to be widely different then functionalist pressures notwithstanding we might choose to say that the Alpha Centaurians did not experience pain as we do and give a different name to their experiences (Lewis 1983, pp. 130–2).

I briefly discuss some other developments in the philosophy of mind in 'Further Thoughts on the Identity Theory' and 'The Revival of Materialism'. The essay 'On Some Criticisms of a Physicalist Theory of

Colours' deals with a modification of my previous account of colour concepts. This was necessitated by some criticisms of my former student and Adelaide colleague M.C. Bradley.

The essays in part 2 on space, time and space-time reflect another of my chief metaphysical interests. Even from when I was a second year undergraduate at Glasgow I have always been opposed to the notion of the passage or flow of time (Williams 1951). Not that I believe in space and time as such; modern physics should force one to accept a unitary theory of space-time, which ought anyway to have had antecedent appeal. (Nevertheless for expository reasons it is sometimes convenient to discuss space and time as though they were distinct from one another.) One topic that has much interested me is that of the so-called 'direction of time', or as I prefer to say 'the temporal asymmetry of the universe'. Adolf Grünbaum did much to develop my interest in this topic, which is one on which mathematical physicists have done much to contribute. This is eminently a field that illustrates the methodological contention that there is no sharp line between philosophy and science; indeed the question of temporal asymmetry is one in which we could say that the philosophers Reichenbach and Grünbaum (1973; see also Davies 1974) have done good physics just as many physicists have done good philosophy.

In the paper 'Time and Becoming' I am concerned to oppose the notion of time flow or absolute becoming, including a sophisticated theory of time flow due to my friend Storrs McCall. I have not been able to convince McCall – indeed when one is dialectically involved with a person of widely different methodological and substantive presuppositions this is hardly to be expected in the light of my considerations in the essays 'Philosophy and Scientific Plausibility' and 'My Semantic Ascents and Descents'. I think myself that it is easier to be convinced that the 'myth of passage' is indeed a myth than it is to explain how such a persistent conceptual illusion could have come about. I make a tentative suggestion towards a possible explanation. The title of the lecture 'Under the Form of Eternity' suggests a certain Spinozistic sympathy.[3] The lecture is in some sort a general philosophical manifesto, and it was given to a general audience mainly of high-powered research biologists and medical scientists. Similarly the essay 'Physicalism and Emergence' was largely written for a biological readership, and it could be of interest for a more general one.

Most of the papers in part 3 are mainly concerned with the defence of realism in metaphysics and science. An exception of course is the paper on 'Sellars on Process'. Despite a certain Kantian tendency in his thought Sellars has been a most influential and admirable defender of scientific realism. In some of the essays the main opponents are those who have expressed instrumentalist or phenomenalist points of view. The paper 'Realism v. Idealism' is concerned with the recent wave of 'anti-realism' of Michael Dummett and his followers and with Hilary Putnam's somewhat different arguments against 'metaphysical realism'. Rightly or wrongly I see this anti-realist wave of thinking as in some ways reminiscent of the neo-Hegelian idealism of F.H. Bradley and others.

In the ethical articles in part 5 I am concerned with 'act' as opposed to 'rule' utilitarianism. (My own terminology in the essay 'Extreme and Restricted Utilitarianism' was less felicitous than that of 'act' and 'rule' which was introduced by R.B. Brandt (1959) and which has become the usual one.) I think of utilitarian ethics as an expression of an over-riding attitude of generalized benevolence. However, I have recently been impressed by Donald Regan's 'cooperative utilitarianism' (Regan 1980; see also the 'generalized act utilitarianism' of Postow 1977). Cooperative utilitarianism is in the *spirit* of act utilitarianism and indeed reduces to it when cooperation is not in question. At least in the many person cooperative situation it seems to me at the moment that an independent pro-attitude to cooperation as such is needed to supplement generalized benevolence so as to produce maximal results. (In the two person situation the empirical evidence which on Regan's theory one would use to identify the other as a potential cooperator could be used in the act utilitarian manner as evidence of what the other person in fact will do, but it is not clear to me how this could be so in the n person situation – analogous to an n person Prisoner's Dilemma, especially in cases where n is very much greater than 2.)

Only since the book had gone to production did I notice that, at the time of writing most of the papers, I had been unaware of the desirability of observing gender neutrality in my prose. I hope that my feminist readers will forgive my past tendency to use the masculine pronoun and gender when neutrality would have been appropriate.

One can hardly do philosophy over the best part of a lifetime without some changes and modifications of views, and undetected inconsistencies are also far from impossible. I cannot claim that all the essays in this volume are completely consistent with one another, but I think that there is nevertheless a sufficient coherence of general outlook and of philosophical method.

NOTES

1 In an indirect way even abstruse metaphysics can be relevant to practical life. For example, a strong sense of the reality of the future, which I defend in the essay on that subject, may surely affect thinking on nuclear questions, if we reflect on the possible millions or even hundreds of millions of years of further evolution of sentience if we do not destroy ourselves now, and the vast potentialities for unimaginable future happiness.

2 Some remarks on these lines were made by U.T. Place in defence of 'type–type' identity in his 'Chairman's Comments' on a symposium between Colin McGinn and James Hopkins (1978, *Aristotelian Society Supplementary Volume*, 52, pp. 195–220). He kindly sent me a copy of these comments. Place thinks that James Hopkins is too conciliatory in his reply to McGinn, and he refers approvingly to some considerations put forward by Hopkins in support of a 'type–type' point of view, especially some evolutionary ones. Consider the way in which the identification of genes with DNA has come to have a far more than species wide force. It would not be appropriate for me to summarize Place's beautiful unpublished remarks, and it has been a source of regret to me that they have remained unpublished.

See also Place's 'comments' on Hilary Putnam's 'Psychological Predicates' in W.H. Capitan and D.D. Merrill (1967).

3 The sympathy is with Spinoza's rejection of anthropocentricity and indexicality in metaphysics. I do not of course go along with Spinoza's *a priori* rationalism. My sympathy with some of the seventeenth century rationalists on temporal matters goes back a long way. I remember reading a paper, as a second year undergraduate at the Glasgow University philosophy club, in which I used Leibnizean ideas to defend a Parmenidean (as opposed to a Heracleitean) view of time. I wish I had preserved it, as it would be fun to see how much I still agreed with it!

REFERENCES

Armstrong, D.M. 1968: *A Materialist Theory of the Mind*. London: Routledge and Kegan Paul.
Brandt, R.B. 1959: *Ethical Theory*. Englewood Cliffs, New Jersey: Prentice-Hall.
Davies, P.C.W. 1974: *The Physics of Time Asymmetry*. Surrey University Press.
Grünbaum, Adolf 1973: *Philosophical Problems of Space and Time*, 2nd edn. Dordrecht, Holland: D. Reidel.
Lewis, David 1966: An Argument for the Identity Theory. *Journal of Philosophy*, 63, 17–25.
—— 1972: Psychophysical and Theoretical Identifications. *Australasian Journal of Philosophy*, 50, 249–58.
—— 1983: *Philosophical Papers*, vol. 1. Oxford: Oxford University Press.
Medlin, B.H. 1967: Ryle and the Mechanical Hypothesis. In C.F. Presley (ed.), *The Identity Theory of Mind*, University of Queensland Press, 94–150.

Place, U.T. 1956: Is Consciousness a Brain Process? *British Journal of Psychology*, 47, 44–50. Reprinted 1962 in V.C. Chappell (ed.), *The Philosophy of Mind*, Englewood Cliffs, New Jersey: Prentice-Hall, 101–9.

—— 1967: Comments. In W.H. Capitan and D.D. Merrill (eds), *Art, Mind and Religion*, Proceedings of the 1965 Oberlin Colloquium, University of Pittsburgh Press, 55–68.

Pólya, G. 1954: *Mathematics and Plausible Reasoning*. Princeton University Press.

Postow, B.C. 1977: Generalized Act Utilitarianism. *Analysis*, 37, 49–52.

Putnam, Hilary 1975: *Mathematics, Matter and Method: Philosophical Papers*, vol. 2. Cambridge: Cambridge University Press.

Regan, Donald 1980: *Utilitarianism and Cooperation*. Oxford: Oxford University Press.

Smart, J.J.C. 1957: Plausible Reasoning in Philosophy, *Mind*, 66, 75–77.

Williams, Donald 1951: The Myth of Passage. *Journal of Philosophy*, 48, 457–72. Reprinted in *Principles of Empirical Reasoning*, Springfield, Illinois: Charles C. Thomas, 289–307.

PART 1
Methodology in Philosophy and Science

2

Philosophy and Scientific Plausibility

I

In the *Tractatus*, 4.1122, Wittgenstein said: 'Darwin's theory has no more to do with philosophy than any other hypothesis in natural science.' (1961, p. 49)[1] It is clear that Wittgenstein held that the results of scientific investigation have no bearing whatever on our philosophical investigations. On his view the sciences can be no more than the *object* of philosophical activity, which is the delimitation of sense from nonsense. This view of Wittgenstein's has become pretty orthodox in much contemporary philosophy, and I wish to challenge it in this paper. This seems an appropriate topic for a contribution to Professor Feigl's *Festschrift* since especially in his writings on the relations between mind and body he has shown a willingness to consider the bearings of contemporary science on his problems. Moreover I have found his conception of a 'nomological dangler' of great interest in the present connection, and in section II I intend to expatiate a little on this theme. In section III I shall use the philosophical problem of free will as an example to show that science is relevant to philosophy. Indeed, contrary to Wittgenstein's remark quoted above, I shall try to show that the Darwinian theory, or more properly the modern theory of evolution which combines the theory of natural selection with the ideas of recent genetics, is particularly relevant. In section IV I shall try to defend my position by arguing against a too narrow conception of philosophical method, such as, for example, relying on an analogy with mathematics.[2]

It is necessary first of all to clear up a possible misunderstanding. In appealing to modern scientific ideas I do not wish to imply that the body of our scientific knowledge is something inviolable and immune from drastic modifications, or that some such drastic modifications may not be inspired by philosophical speculation. The traffic between science and philosophy can go in both directions. In some of his recent papers P.K. Feyerabend (1962a, b, 1963) has spoken up against the self-perpetuating character of scientific orthodoxy, and in particular has argued persuasively for the legitimacy of such attempts as those of D. Bohm and J.P. Vigier to work out theories of microphysics alternative to those currently accepted. He has pointed out that dogmatic acceptance of a current theory may indeed make it impossible to discover facts which would refute it, since these facts could be satisfactorily understood only in the light of a novel and at present speculative theory. It is therefore important to work out *in detail* new theories which are capable of explaining all the facts which are explicable by the orthodox theory and which may lead us to new unascertained facts. While a theory is still in the metaphysical stage, that is, while it has no empirical advantage over the orthodox one, it is of course unknown whether it will ever be more than a merely speculative system. Perhaps it never will be, but we must not be afraid to try out new ideas.

While, however, we must remain alive to the possibility of radical changes in our scientific outlook, we must not exaggrate this possibility either. Consider a corridor which gives access to a number of rooms, in each of which there is a scientist engaged in fundamental research. In room number one there is a nuclear physicist, in room number two an atomic physicist, in room number three a classical physicist. In room number four there is a physical chemist and in room number five there is an inorganic or an organic chemist. In room number six there is a biochemist, in room number seven a cytologist, and in room number eight there is a physiologist. It is likely that revolutionary changes made in room n will usually have very little practical effect on room $n + 1$, and will probably have no practical effect at all on rooms $n + 2, n + 3$, etc.[3] (I say practical effect, because I do not wish to deny that the changes in earlier rooms may have some effect on how the scientists in later rooms look at the world.) This relative independence of the various rooms from one another obtains because it is usually only the approximate correctness of the results got in room n that are needed by the man in room $n + 1$, and an approximation to the results got in room n will pretty certainly be enough for the man in room $n + 2$. Now a revolutionary theory will clearly have to predict, within the limits of exerimental error, the results which constitute the evidence for the theory that it is meant to replace. Consider, for example, the general theory of relativity in its relation to the Newtonian theory of gravitation. Only in exceptional cases will the two theories predict different results, over and above the limits of experimental error. Most of the results that the man in room $n + 1$ wants from the man in room n can be got from a rather old-fashioned theory on the n level, and in the case of room $n + 2$ it is probable that all can. Still more is this so with rooms $n + 3$, $n + 4$, etc. It is, for example, extremely unlikely that revolutionary discoveries in nuclear physics will lead to any substantial modification of our beliefs about the physiology of respiration.

In any case I hope to make it plausible that the bare possibility of radical changes in our scientific beliefs does not furnish any reason for ignoring these beliefs, such as they are, in dealing with philosophical problems.

II

As I have mentioned above, Professor Feigl has introduced a particularly important concept, that of a 'nomological dangler.' As he defines it, a nomological dangler is a law which purports to 'connect intersubjectively confirmable events with events which *ex hypothesi* are in principle not intersubjectively and independently confirmable.'[4] There are perhaps difficulties in this definition, but it is implied in it that nomological danglers would have to be ultimate laws, which are not further explicable, and which nevertheless have a minimal explanatory function. At best a nomological dangler would merely subsume a lot of As that are associated with Bs under the generalization 'All As are Bs.' The reason for this is that the nomological danglers would be laws purporting to connect physical events, in fact neurophysiological ones, with allegedly non-physical ones, conscious experiences. These laws would therefore be ultimate ones, not explicable within neurophysiology or any other physical science. (There is the bare logical possibility that they might be deducible from the laws of some very general science which straddled the physical and nonphysical, but this does not, in the present state of our knowledge, seem to be one that we can take very seriously.) It is supposed to be just a fact, inexplicable by neurophysiology or any other science, that when a certain complex neurophysiological event occurs there also occurs a certain psychical event, such as the having of a green sense datum.

I wish now to point out that these nomological danglers have a further property which should make us view them with very great suspicion. This is that they purport to relate very complex neurophysiological processes to other things, which may or may not be simple, namely conscious experiences, and they relate those two classes of events in respect of the *fine structure* of the neurophysiological processes. For it is known that, in virtue of rather subtle differences between them, two neurophysiological processes which are roughly comparable in their complexity may be related to quite different experiences. Perhaps something of the order 10^{10} neurons are importantly involved in the having of a green sense datum. (This is an uninformed guess on my part, but if the number is 10^7 or even 10^5 that is still a big enough number.) Moreover if these neurons had been hooked up together in a different way there would not have been the experience. For example, however, the neurons in the auditory area of the brain are stimulated there will not be a visual experience. It is clear, therefore, that a law which relates a neural process to the having of a green sense datum must take account of the structure of the visual area of the brain which distinguishes it from the auditory area. Indeed it will have to go much further than this: it will have to take account of the fine structure of a visual neural process which ensures that it goes with the experience of having a green sense datum and not with, say, that of having a red sense datum. I wish now to suggest that since a nomological dangler has this feature, that of relating to something very complex in terms of its fine structure, then it is a bad candidate for an ultimate law of nature. In science as it has developed hitherto there has been a tendency for the more complex to be explained in terms of the more simple.

For some purposes, of course, the human brain can be regarded as a simple entity. For example, a brain might be dropped from an aeroplane and we might calculate the velocity with which it hit the earth. There would be no more difficulty in calculating the velocity of the brain than there would be in the case of a stone. We could treat the brain as a homogeneous solid to which the laws of gravity and air resistance could be applied. (Even so, the law of gravity in the first instance applies to particles or point masses and has to be applied to sizable bodies by integration. It was in fact this problem of integration that held Newton up for some time.) The unacceptable thing about the nomological danglers which purport to relate neurological events to psychical ones is that they would be ultimate laws and yet would have to be stated in terms of complex and nonhomogeneous fine structure.

Various writers, including Herbert Feigl (1958, 1960, 1964), U.T. Place (1956, 1959, 1960), and myself (1960, 1961, 1962 and 'Sensations and Brain Processes' in the present volume) have recently tried to argue for the view that experiences just *are* brain processes. The arguments largely consist in attempts to rebut philosophical arguments which are commonly thought to put such a view quite out of court. For if such arguments can be refuted the brain-process theory enables us to do without the suspect nomological danglers. Even so it would still be *logically* possible that the danglers and the purely psychical experiences should exist. The dualist simply says that there are two entities that always occur together, where the physicalist says that there is only one entity. No observation or experiment could, I think, refute the dualist. In the absence of positive reason to the contrary, this should not go to support dualism. Equally it is logically possible that the world should have begun ten minutes ago just as it was ten minutes ago, and no experiment or observation could refute this hypothesis (see Russell 1921, pp. 159–60). (Only the most hardened positivist can deny that there is a difference in meaning between the sentences 'The universe began ten minutes ago' and 'The universe has existed for many thousands of millions of years.') The ten-minutes-ago hypothesis is much too much an *ad hoc* one, leaving countless facts (describing how the world was ten minutes ago) as quite inexplicable. In short it is an unnecessarily untidy and complex hypothesis. Similarly if the view that experiences just are brain processes can be defended against *a priori* objections it should be preferred, as against dualism, as a more simple, elegant, and economical hypothesis.

It is worth noting how widespread are the forms of dualism of which I am suggesting we should be wary. My objections do not apply only to full-fledged Cartesian dualism. Even so restrained a dualism as that of Strawson in his recent book (1959) will be affected. For according to Strawson's account, conscious experiences are ontologically distinguishable from bodies, even though they are epistemologically dependent on them. This is made obvious by Strawson's contention that disembodied existence is consistent with his point of view. In the case of ordinary, not disembodied persons we therefore have brain events on the one hand and experiences on the other hand. No less than Descartes, Strawson surely needs nomological danglers.

III

In case the foregoing illustration of the relevance of scientific plausibility to philosophy is not found convincing, I shall try to drive home my point by means of another one. Directly contrary to Wittgenstein's remark which was quoted at the beginning of this paper, I wish to consider the relevance of the theory of evolution to a philosophical problem – the problem of free will.

Modern evolutionary theory is extremely mechanistic. In the case of bisexual organisms the variety on which natural selection gets to work is achieved partly through recombination and crossing over of chromosomes. These, however, merely shuffle the pool of genes in a species, and radical innovation is dependent on mutations, or changes in the genes themselves. The genes are thought to be DNA molecules. These are very stable self-replicating macromolecules. In spite of this great stability there will very occasionally be a change in the structure of a gene, perhaps on account of heat or of ionizing radiation. For our present purposes it is not important to speculate on exactly how such changes occur. The important thing to notice is that it would be a wonder if they did not occur and that they occur by chance: perhaps an alpha particle happens to bump into a certain part of a DNA molecule. The genes are believed to determine the production of enzymes, or organic catalysts, and hence the development of the organism. A mutation is therefore nearly always deleterious: the cell in which a mutated gene occurs, or the organism from which the cell develops, will nearly always fail to be viable or will be less able to cope with its environment. (There are more ways of spoiling a mechanism than of improving it.) Very occasionally, however, a mutation will be advantageous, and as the generations pass the process of natural selection will increase the proportion of members of the species in question which carry the mutated gene.

In the lights of these ideas, of which only a rough and crude outline has been given, let us take a look at the libertarian theory of free will. The libertarian believes that there is a 'self' or 'will' which is capable of 'contra-causal freedom' (Campbell 1951) and which is able to interfere with the usual processes in the central nervous system. How is it possible to reconcile this with the mechanistic conceptions of modern biology? It is quite possible to see how mutations may cause radical new types of neuronal hookup to occur: the 'wiring diagram' of the brain is determined by the biochemical processes in the cells of the embryo, and these themselves are determined by the chemistry of the genes. A change in the brain, such as the increase of the visual areas, could well come about in this sort of way. But how could there come about, not just a change in circuitry or perhaps a change in the structure or biochemistry of the individual neurons themselves, but the production of a contracausal 'self' or 'will'? Such a thing could not be explained in terms of biochemistry. Yet somewhere or other a 'self' or 'will' must have emerged; it would be fantastic to attribute such a thing to an amoeba, and still more fantastic to attribute it to the complex systems of organic molecules which presumably preceded true living cells. In any case any sort of 'self' or 'will' would apparently have to depend on special psychophysical laws, which would be nomological danglers. This would also be the case if the libertarian did not think of the self or will as a separate non-physical entity but nevertheless thought of the brain as itself operating in accordance with non-physical or 'vitalistic' laws. The emergence of such laws would be quite inexplicable within any mechanistic account of evolution in terms of changes in the chemistry of the nucleic acids.

The notion of emergence used to be supported by an analogy which the development of science has shown to be based on an error. It used to be said, for example, that however much we knew of the properties of sodium and however much we knew of the properties of chlorine, we could not predict the properties of salt (sodium chloride). To find out the chemical properties of salt, it was said, we should have to experiment with salt itself, and the properties we should find would therefore be emergent, not deducible from those of sodium and chlorine taken separately. By this it was meant not simply that the chemical properties of salt could not be deduced from the physical properties of the elements because the calculation would be too difficult, but that it was in principle impossible that there should be any such calculation. It was then commonly suggested that just as chemical properties were supposed to be emergent relative to physical ones, so there were properties of life and mind which were emergent relative to the chemical and the physical. This analogical argument, however, contains a false premise. In fact it is, in simple cases, quite possible to deduce the chemical properties (the chemical bonds) from purely physical (spectroscopically ascertained) properties of the elements. This is done by means of the quantum theory of the chemical bond. In cases where this can not be done in practice, the failure can be put down partly to plain ignorance of the physical assumptions that would be needed and partly to the complexities of the calculations that would have to be carried out. Simplifying assumptions have to be made, and these can easily lead to gross inaccuracies in prediction. Such difficulties do not in themselves lend support to a doctrine of emergent laws.

There is, of course, a trivial sense in which new qualities emerge when we move toward more complex structures. Consider a number of point masses, such as were envisaged by Boscovich. A cloud of such point masses could have a shape, roughly spherical or cubical, say. Four such point masses could determine a tetrahedron. In this context the properties of shape and of determining a tetrahedron could be said to be emergent, in the sense that they could not belong to individual point masses. This *trivial* sense of 'emergence' is clearly quite compatible with the most completely mechanistic of theories. Again, consider a wireless set. If you like to say that the property of being able to receive wireless signals is an emergent property of the set, since it is not possessed by the individual components of the apparatus, then you can. Nevertheless, if you do say this, then you must by no means imply that from a knowledge of the parts and the way they are put together we cannot deduce the behavior of the hookup as a whole.[5]

In spite of its evolutionary inspiration, the metaphysical idea of emergent evolution is in spirit alien to the modern genetical theory of natural selection. About all they have in common is the word 'evolution'.

There is no mystery about the fact that genes mutate, incomplete though our knowledge of what happens may be in detail. Then, since the biochemistry of the cells of an embryo is determined in part by the genes and in part by the topographical relationship between the cells, a change in the chemical structure of a gene or genes may lead to a snub nose instead of a straight one or to a more complex piece of neurophysiological circuitry. But how could such chemical changes lead to a nonphysical self or will, or even to vitalistic laws of functioning?

In science we sometimes come across a certain type of irresponsibility. For example, consider some of those writers who think that they see difficulties in special relativity and the clock paradox, and in consequence try to establish a new and non-relativistic kinematics. In some cases, though not always, such writers do not seem to recognize an obligation to show how their unorthodox ideas can be worked out in such a way as to deal with various secure and important branches of physics, e.g. electromagnetism and the study of fast-moving particles in microphysics. Unless they recognize this obligation and show that they can fulfill it in an *acceptable* way there is clearly no hope of their unorthodox kinematics being taken very seriously, especially since most physicists, in my opinion rightly, see no difficulties in orthodox relativistic ideas. In short, in physics a new theory not only must work in a limited field but must be shown to work in as many fields as does the orthodox theory which it is supposed to replace. This obligation to consider the wider ramifications of a physical theory has, I suggest, its parallel in philosophy. It is not at all satisfactory to produce a libertarian theory of free will as a solution to a limited set of puzzles and paradoxes if one cannot show how it can be reconciled with our biological knowledge.

In this respect the libertarian is in a worse position than his rivals. Those philosophers, such as David Hume, R.E. Hobart and P.H. Nowell-Smith (to name but three), who maintain that free will is perfectly compatible with determinism (with or without a bit of pure chance thrown in at the quantum-mechanical level) have no such problem. Their position is patently quite compatible with mechanistic biology. The libertarian is in a much more difficult position since, as I have suggested, his position is hard to reconcile with the modern biological picture of man. Libertarians have a responsibility to consider how such a synthesis of ideas could be carried out, but they commonly fail to discuss the matter adequately. Usually their interest lies in quite another direction. For example, Sir Isaiah Berlin, in his *Historical Inevitability* (1954, especially pp. 30–4), holds that determinism would entail a drastic change in our ordinary moral concepts. Berlin seems to think that this contention, that determinism is incompatible with our ordinary moral notions, provides a good reason for coming down on the libertarian side. Berlin is thinking here not of moral judgements themselves but of the common-sense metaphysical beliefs on which these moral judgements are (partly) based. (If a philosopher were to argue directly from moral judgements themselves to a metaphysical conclusion we could accuse him of committing the naturalistic fallacy in reverse.) Now when Berlin says that determinism would entail a drastic change in our common moral thinking he does so on slight grounds and without sufficiently considering the arguments of R.E. Hobart and others to the contrary. I myself would argue that determinism (with or without a bit of pure chance thrown in) does entail a slight modificaton in our ordinary moral thinking, but not a drastic one such as Berlin envisages. But even if it did, why be so solicitous of common sense, which especially in matters relating to human conduct is heavily loaded with archaic traditional and theological ideas? What evidential value can such an appeal to common-sense beliefs have?

IV

I have tried to argue that considerations of scientific plausibility are relevant to philosophy. It may be said in reply that they can be so in at best a heuristic way.[6] That is, they may lead us to re-examine philosophical arguments, for example those for psychophysical dualism, to see whether they are as cogent as they have hitherto seemed, but if we do examine them carefully we may have to recognize their validity, however implausible their conclusions may be. (I do not admit that the philosophical arguments for psychophysical dualism or for libertarianism are able to survive close examination, but let us for the sake of argument grant that they do.) It may be said that to pit considerations of plausibility against philosophical reasonings is like trying to cut glass with paper. Philosophical reasoning, it will be said, is either demonstrative or nothing, and no considerations of plausibility can affect a demonstrative argument.

This objection confuses demonstrability with certainty. A theorem in mathematics may be demonstrable and indeed demonstrated, but I may not be sure that I have not made a slip in checking the validity of the proof. Even in adding a column of figures I may be uncertain whether I have got the right answer, and even if I get some of my friends to check too there is the faint possibility that we may all have made the same slip. Of course in practice I am quite reassured when my calculations check with those of others, but this sort of reassurance is not so easily got in philosophy, since philosophical arguments are notoriously slippery, and philosophers are rarely unanimous. It therefore seems to me to be optimistic of philosophers to suppose that their a priori arguments give a higher order of certainty than do considerations of scientific plausibility. Even if we ourselves have so far not perceived any fault in our apparently demonstrative arguments, we can be pretty sure that some other philosophers will, though of course we may continue to disagree with their diagnoses.

In any case can we be sure that a philosophical argument can ever give the sort of demonstrative certainty that we can get in mathematics? Mathematicians commonly agree with one another on their assumptions and on the rules of proof. The difficulty in mathematical proof lies in the discovery of the appropriate chains of sentences which yield proofs; there is usually agreement on whether or not such a chain of sentences constitutes a correct proof. Sometimes, however, mathematicians do disagree on the methods of proof which are acceptable to them. The most important case is the disagreement between those who do and those who do not accept nonconstructive methods of proof. The majority of mathematicians accept such methods, mainly, I suppose, because they can do so much more with them, but a minority reject these methods as not sufficiently perspicuous. Other mathematicians again adopt a neutralist attitude and are interested in seeing both what can be and what can not be got by constructive and non-constructive methods. If there is a serious controversy between constructivists and non-constructivists it takes on all the undecidability of a philosophical dispute. It follows that an analogy between philosophy and mathematics will not necessarily lead us to suppose that philosophy can yield unquestionable demonstrations.

Someone who has been much influenced by Wittgenstein may wish to say that philosophical disputes are due to lack of clarity about the functioning of our language, and that if we work hard enough we shall resolve our disputes. The last part of this contention seems to be either a tautology or an empirical falsehood. If 'hard enough' means 'hard enough to resolve our disputes,' then it is a tautology to say that if we work hard enough we shall resolve our disputes. The question still remains whether it is possible to work hard enough in this sense. On any other criterion of 'hard enough' it is probably an empirical falsehood that if we work hard enough we shall resolve our disputes, since there is scarcely a philosophical issue on which all competent philosophers agree. There is therefore no adequate empirical evidence that all, or even many, philosophical issues are simply a matter of 'showing the fly the way out of the fly bottle', to use Wittgenstein's metaphor.

Our Wittgensteinian philosopher may now say that he or she has no theory of philosophical method; he just gets on with the job. The way in which he gets on with the job is by drawing attention to similarities and dissimilarities in the ways in which words are used. This sort of investigation of 'logical grammar' is a very good way of getting on with philosophy, and I should be one of the last to decry it. But what I do want to say at this stage is that if you do not lay claim to a theory of philosophical method then you are not in a position to object to me when I use considerations of scientific plausibility as part of my philosophical armoury.

After all, there will be some philosophers who will resist the procedures of the logical grammarian even in those cases where most of us believe them to be fruitful. A philosopher may object to the whole way of thinking about language which is implicit in this approach. For example, he may assert that meanings are apprehended by means of intellectual intuition. It is partly because a philosopher may question anything, including the theory of meaning and the psychology of knowledge, that it is always possible that he may be able to evade any contradiction in which you may think you have trapped him. Another difficulty is that one philosophical controversy may lead on to another, and this to yet another, and so on, without prospect of reaching finality. Thus in the dispute about free will we may give the libertarian two mutually exclusive alternatives: acting in a deterministic way and acting by pure chance. We point out that neither of these are what the libertarian wants. The libertarian may reply by questioning our assumption that determinism and pure chance are contradictories (see Acworth 1963; Campbell 1963). He may argue that we have here begged the question, and that a subspecies of what we call 'pure chance' is 'free action', and that he can give a sense, perhaps by appealing to inner experience, which distinguishes free action from what he is willing to call 'pure chance'. This will pretty certainly shift the issue to yet another philosophical controversy, and it does not seem to be evident that a really determined libertarian need ever allow himself to be finally caught. That at any rate is borne out by the seemingly interminable literature on the subject. Even what seems to one lot of philosophers to be an absolutely knockdown argument does not seem to be so to another lot of philosophers. There is, even so, another way in which our philosophical opponent may be attacked. He may be committed to a far less simple system of total science than we are. For example, it is the difficulty of fitting intellectual intuitions into our biological and psychological conceptual schemes which makes them unacceptable to some of us, even though talk about them should perhaps be rendered free from contradiction. Of course our opponent may question this approach too: he may repudiate the ideal of simplicity and economy of explanation. Philosophical disputes may still be intractable. Nevertheless, the appeal to scientific plausibility may carry weight with those who accept the ideals of simplicity and economy of explanation, and if so it may help to settle some arguments among some philosophers.

I hope that I have done something in this paper to support the contention that considerations of scientific plausibility have some part to play in philosophy. It is true of course that what appears to be a plausible conceptual scheme may in future turn out to be false, and an implausible one may after all be true. We must certainly not discourage the production of metaphysical speculations which may foreshadow the testable science of the future. Nevertheless, if we want to find out what, on our present knowledge, is the most probable view about some philosophical question, such as that of free will or of the relations between mind and body, then we should be foolish to neglect the direction in which our present scientific knowledge points. Indeed, part of this paper may be looked at in another light, not so much as an attempt to discourage the speculations of the dualist or of the libertarian, but as itself part of a speculative attempt to advocate a materialist or a physicalist metaphysics. In doing this we need not be dogmatic, for we can recognize fully that our present scientific beliefs have always to be tested against the facts, and so may have to be replaced by other beliefs in the future. In this way, therefore, I hope that I can avoid the suggestion that this essay is, to use the title of one of Professor Feigl's recent papers (1961), no more than a dogmatic and undesirable 'philosophical tangent of science'.

NOTES

1   Since writing the first draft of this article I have seen that Ernest Gellner opens his review of T.A. Goudge's *Ascent of Life* (1962) with this same quotation from Wittgenstein, and like me he rejects Wittgenstein's point of view here.

2   I should like to thank Professor D.A.T. Gasking of the University of Melbourne, who read an earlier draft of this paper and made helpful comments, without which it would have been very much worse than it is.

3   I think that this vivid example of the rooms along the corridor was suggested to me in conversation by Professor C.A. Hurst, of the mathematical physics department of the University of Adelaide.

4   See Feigl (1958, especially p. 428). In 'Sensations and Brain Processes' I made use of Feigl's concept, but inadvertently used the term 'nomological dangler' for the psychical entity that is supposed to dangle from the psychophysical law rather than for the psychophysical law itself. In this paper I have reverted to Feigl's usage.

5   For criticism of the notion of emergence, see Berenda (1953) and Nagel (1961, pp. 366–80).

6   In a note (Smart 1957) I argued for the heuristic importance of plausible considerations. I now wish to go further than this.

REFERENCES

Acworth, Richard 1963: Smart on Free Will. *Mind*, 72, 271–2.
Berenda, C.W. 1953: On Emergence and Prediction. *Journal of Philosophy*, 50, 269–74.
Berlin, Isaiah 1954: *Historical Inevitability*. London: Oxford University Press.
Campbell, C.A. 1951: Is 'Free Will' a Pseudo-Problem? *Mind*, 60, 441–65.
—— 1963: Professor Smart on Free-Will, Praise and Blame: A Reply. *Mind*, 72, 400–5.
Feigl, Herbert 1958: The 'Mental' and the 'Physical'. In Herbert Feigl, Michael Scriven and Grover Maxwell (eds), *Minnesota Studies in the Philosophy of Science*, vol. 2, Minneapolis: University of Minnesota Press, 370–497.
—— 1960: Mind-Body, *Not* a Pseudoproblem. In Sidney Hook (ed.), *Dimensions of Mind*, New York: New York University Press, 24–36.
—— 1961: Philosophical Tangents of Science. In Herbert Feigl and Grover Maxwell (eds), *Current Issues in the Philosophy of Science*, New York: Holt, Rinehart and Winston, 1–17.
—— 1964: Physicalism, Unity of Science and the Foundations of Psychology. In Paul Arthur Schilpp (ed.), *The Philosophy of Rudolf Carnap*, La Salle, Illinois: Open Court, 227–67.
Feyerabend, Paul K. 1962a: Explanation, Reduction, and Empiricism. In Herbert Feigl and Grover Maxwell (eds), *Minnesota Studies in the Philosophy of Science*, vol. 3, Minneapolis: University of Minnesota Press, 28–97.
—— 1962b: Problems of Microphysics. In R.G. Colodny (ed.), *Frontiers of Science and Philosophy*, Pittsburgh: University of Pittsburgh Press, 189–283.
—— 1963: How to Be a Good Empiricist – A Plea for Tolerance in Matters Epistemological. In Bernard Baumrin (ed.), *Philosophy of Science: The Delaware Seminar*, vol. 2, New York: Interscience, 3–39.
Gellner, Ernest 1962: Review of T.A. Goudge's *Ascent of Life*. *Inquiry*, 5, 85–90.
Nagel, Ernest 1961: *The Structure of Science*. New York: Harcourt, Brace and World.
Place, U.T. 1956: Is Consciousness a Brain Process? *British Journal of Psychology*, 47, 44–50.
—— 1959: The 'Phenomenological Fallacy': a Reply to J.R. Smythies. *British Journal of Psychology*, 50, 72–3.
—— 1960: Materialism as a Scientific Hypothesis. *Philosophical Review*, 69, 101–4.
Russell, Bertrand 1921: *Analysis of Mind*. London: Allen and Unwin.
Smart, J.J.C. 1957: Plausible Reasoning in Philosophy. *Mind*, 66, 75–8.
—— 1960: Sensations and Brain Processes, A Rejoinder to Dr Pitcher and Mr Joske. *Australasian Journal of Philosophy*, 38, 252–4.

—— 1961: Further Remarks on Sensations and Brain Processes. *Philosophical Review*, 70, 406–7.

—— 1962: Brain Processes and Incorrigibility. *Australasian Journal of Philosophy*, 40, 68–70.

Strawson, P.F. 1959: *Individuals*. London: Macmillan.

Wittgenstein, Ludwig 1961: *Tractatus Logico-Philosophicus*. Translation by D.F.Pears and B.F. McGuiness. London: Routledge and Kegan Paul.

3

My Semantic Ascents and Descents

It seems clear that the concept of philosophy is a family resemblance one, so that no general definition of it can be given. However, one important characteristic of the family is that of being in some sense a *conceptual* inquiry, and so a science can be thought of as bordering on philosophy to the extent to which it raises within itself problems of a conceptual nature. Consider a typical meeting of a university philosophy club. It will be unusual to find an organic chemist in the audience. Organic chemists do not talk much with philosophers because although their problems may be difficult and in certain ways sophisticated ones, the conceptual guidelines of their science are pretty well agreed upon. Contrast mathematical physicists, who come up against such questions as the following one.

With one experimental arrangement you can determine the position of an electron. With another experimental arrangement you can determine the momentum of an electron. There is no experimental arrangement by which you can determine both the position and momentum of an electron. This is no mere practical impossibility. The mathematics of the theory shows that a contradiction would arise if we supposed that the electron had at one and the same time both a determinate momentum and a determinate position (even though we could not in fact measure both of them). Hence there naturally arises the so-called Copenhagen interpretation of quantum mechanics, whereby the states of a particle are relations to experimental arrangements. Thus the position of the electron is a relation to an experimental arrangement of one sort, and the momentum of the electron is a relation to an experimental arrangement of another sort. However, we get into an infinite regress if we suppose that the properties of the experimental arrangement (or the particles making it up) are themselves relations between the experimental arrangement and yet other experimental arrangements. That is, the positions and momenta of the components of the experimental arrangement have to be positions and momenta as in classical physics. This reliance upon classical physics for the theory of the experimental arrangement is embraced by adherents of the Copenhagen interpretation, but by others it may be seen as a serious weakness in quantum mechanics. Surely a physical theory ought to be a theory of everything in the universe, including the measuring instruments which are needed to test the theory. Or again, like P.K. Feyerabend (1962, 1969) in an important recent paper, a person may feel this uneasiness while yet conceding that the Copenhagen interpretation of quantum mechanics is the only viable one which has been produced, and that, indeed, to get an interpretation which did not produce this sort of uneasiness in us, a radically new theory of microphysics would have to be discovered.

This brief excursus into the interpretation of quantum mechanics shows the way in which theoretical physicists are brought up against conceptual questions, questions about the general structure of their theories. They get into debates about what sorts of theories are intellectually satisfactory. Where the organic chemist debates about whether a particular theory is a good one or not, the theoretical physicist is drawn into a debate about what it is for a theory to be a good one. Is inability to provide within itself a theory of measuring instruments to be regarded as a defect in existing quantum mechanics? To ask this question is to get involved in issues, such as that between realism and instrumentalism, which are typically philosophical, i.e. part of the stock in trade of people who are normally called 'philosophers'.

It should be noted, however, that the conceptual investigations undertaken by physicists are not done merely for their own sakes. When the physicist discusses and compares various sorts of physical theory he does so because he wishes to know which sort of theory it would be best to adopt, or which sort of theory should be viewed with suspicion (even despite undoubted success in predicting empirical facts). So in the last resort his conceptual investigation is done in the interests of finding out what the universe is like. Conceptual issues need not be factually neutral. W.V. Quine (1969) has drawn attention to the phenomenon of semantic ascent, in which we go from debate about things to debate about our talk about things. This is especially valuable when it is not agreed as to whether the ostensible objects of our discourse exist. (Whether or not we believe in phlogiston, we can discuss the role of the word 'phlogiston' in a chemical theory.) Semantic ascent implies also the possibility of semantic descent: the settling of conceptual questions can influence our beliefs about what the world in fact is like.

I have argued that activities which most of us would regard as 'philosophical' occur in mathematical physics. Since mathematical physics is generally regarded as a highly respectable subject, this suggests that philosophy is a respectable subject. However, when we look at the profession of philosophy itself, we may begin to doubt this supposed respectability. This is because there do not seem to be any agreed standards in philosophy. Consider the writings of a certain sort of phenomenologist or existentialist. To many philosophers, including myself, they seem to be not only incomprehensible but to be utter bosh. Whether such writings really are bosh or not, it does seem to be an empirical fact that there are groups within the philosophy profession between whom dialogue does not seem to be possible. It almost seems, sometimes, that though phenomenologists, existentialists, and a certain sort of Thomist are interested in concepts, their interest is often not so much to clarify concepts as to muddy them up. Perhaps muddy reflection on concepts produces certain emotions, such as *angst*, which are prized by some of these philosophers. (It is odd that *angst* should be prized. Contrast David Hume's short autobiography, in which he expresses his calm and cheerful reflections on his own imminent death. He was singularly free of *angst*, which I should have thought was good both for him and for his friends and for those of us who read his words.) No doubt the reason why the purveyors of *angst* are thought of as falling under the family resemblance concept *philosopher* is that they are, in their own strange way, engaged with concepts and interested in the nature of the universe.

I cannot, however, disguise the fact that this division and lack of communication between parts of the philosophy profession does worry me. Surely if philosophy were a respectable subject, there would be general agreement as to what is and is not bosh, at least among those who are paid large sums of money to teach it at prestigious universities. Compare the situation in mathematical physics. There may be disagreement over the goodness or badness of the Copenhagen interpretation of quantum mechanics. Nevertheless there is a very definite way in which those who so disagree do speak the same language. They have a great body of techniques in common. They can handle matrices and differential equations, they play around with Hilbert space, they write down bras and kets, they understand how sophisticated experiments are done, and so on. There is a body of expertise which gives them *discipline*. This common discipline prevents their seeming to one another as mad or beyond the reach of reason, however much they may differ on fundamental issues. The trouble about philosophy is not that we get disagreement about fundamental issues. Such disagreement occurs healthily in science. It is that we get something like *total* disagreement or even total incomprehension.

A similar background of discipline is building up among professional philosophers. In order for a student to understand a great deal of current philosophy, it is necessary for him to familiarize himself with quantification theory, Gödel's and Church's theorems, Tarski's definition of truth, and so on. Consider, as a somewhat random example, the sort of background needed for reading such an article as W.V. Quine's 'Implicit Definition Sustained' (1966). This background of shared discipline can do much to prevent the sort of philosophy which we teach our students from degenerating into either verbalistic triviality or mad speculation. A generation or two ago a background of discipline in the form of Greek scholarship performed a similar function for Oxford philosophy. However, in this case the discipline was more adventitious. Except in so far as Plato and Aristotle could be regarded as mines for arguments which could be applied in contemporary contexts – and surely before long the mines would be worked out – Greek scholarship was not a tool for philosophers in the way in which contemporary logic, recursive function theory, and semantics are. Another background of shared discipline which has also prevented a large group of philosophers from disintegrating too much into different factions has been familiarity with a certain corpus of philosophical writing, e.g. Locke, Hume, Moore, Russell, Wittgenstein, Carnap (to mention only philosophers who are no longer alive). However, since the purveyors of *angst* can point to their own more literary and dark corpus of philosophers (Hegel, Kierkegaard, Nietzsche, Husserl, Heidegger, et al.), it is dangerous to rely on any purely philosophical corpus as the disciplinary backbone. It is better to stress logic, semantics and the like – disciplines which are mathematical or scientific rather than philosophical, but which provide tools for philosophical disputation or results which are of philosophical interest. I have moments of despair about philosophy when I think of how so much phenomenological and existentialist philosophy seems such sheer bosh that I cannot even begin to read it, and I wonder whether philosophy is a proper subject. In such moments I tend to cheer myself up by reflecting that if the student reads Quine's philosophy he at least learns some logic, and if he reads Adolf Grünbaum's he at least learns some physics! However, this is rather a last line of defence.

I wish now to pass on to a more domestic sort of disagreement about philosophical method: a disagreement with philosophers with whom I can still do business and who are not separated from me by a vast gulf as are the purveyors of *angst*. Since this more domestic disagreement can be illustrated by comparing different temporal segments of myself, I can perhaps best illustrate it by engaging in some mild autobiography.

When I was a boy I read such books as Eddington's *Nature of the Physical World* (1928), which I now recognize to be partly philosophical, though when I tried to read G.E. Moore's *Ethics* (1912), I was quite baffled. Indeed Moore was a friend of my parents in Cambridge, and all that I then knew about philosophy was that it was whatever it was that Moore did for a living! We moved to Glasgow when my father was appointed Regius Professor of Astronomy there, and I entered Glasgow University to do mathematics and physics (or 'natural philosophy' as it was called there). It was necessary to do two other subjects for one year, and I picked on what was then called 'logic' because it seemed to be the most mathematical non-mathematical subject. 'Logic' in Glasgow really meant 'philosophy' (though moral philosophy had a separate department), and the professor was C.A. Campbell. I got enthusiastic about philosophy and went on with it, so that mathematics took second place. I was able to see how Campbell out-Bradleyed F.H. Bradley. When war service took me to India, this adventitious circumstance got me reading the *Upanishads* and *Bhagavad Gītā* in translation, as well as accounts of the Advaita Vedānta, and I recognized in the Advaitin's Brahman or Atman the suprarational absolute of C.A. Campbell. I was interested to try to find self-referential inconsistencies in this sort of position. Whether or not I succeeded is another matter. In reacting against this sort of idealist philosophy I was much influenced by D.R. Cousin, who (with Miss Levett) represented empiricism in the department at Glasgow. I found it harder to get puzzled about problems of ethics; when I read *Principia Ethica* (Moore 1903) it seemed to give all the answers, and I thought it a fine thing to devote myself to increasing the amount of the non-natural quality, goodness, in the world. This now seems rather an odd thought, though with the metaphysics taken out of it I still think that this sort of utilitarianism provides an attractive basis for ethics.

It can be seen therefore that when I went to Oxford to do postgraduate work in philosophy I was groping my way in a metaphysical fog, and the sort of account of philosophy which was being purveyed by Gilbert Ryle came as a liberation. According to this account philosophy was a second-order activity, 'talk about talk' as Ryle put it, or as he put it in an early paper, 'the detection of the sources in linguistic idioms of recurrent misconstructions and absurd theories' (Ryle 1951). There seemed to be two good things about this. In the first place, it seemed to make philosophy secure as a profession. Philosophy seemed to have acquired a respectable place in the republic of letters as a second-order activity, so that it would not all hive off into special sciences in the way in which psychology had recently done. And this secure place could be seen not to depend on the existence of intuitive, transcendental, or otherwise mysteriously non-scientific modes of knowing. In the second place, the Rylean philosophy pleasingly exorcised a lot of mysterious and ghostly entities. When I was an inexperienced student at Glasgow I saw a review

of Brand Blanshard's *Nature of Thought* (1939) and thought to myself:
'What a clever chap Blanshard must be. What a queer stuff thought must
be! Is it some sort of fluid? How does one find out about it? I know how
to do experiments with electricity, but how does one do them with
thought?' Of course when I looked at the book it turned out unexcitingly
to be just another (however excellent) book of idealist philosophy. How
good it was to get to Oxford and to find the mind vanishing into
behaviour dispositions! All seemed clear for a physicalist world view,
with cybernetics one day explaining the dispositions. Of course in the
intellectual climate of Oxford at that time one would not ever admit
explicitly that there were 'world views', but to me the appeal of Ryle's
talk about talk was nevertheless that it cleared a lot of lumber away and
did in fact give rise to a certain implicit way of looking at the world.

Besides being influenced by Ryle, I was also much impressed by
F. Waismann and G.A. Paul, and by the sort of second-hand Wittgensteinianism which was in the air generally. This second-hand
Wittgensteinianism was partly characterized by talk of 'this is the
language game' and by a certain unacknowledged verificationism.
Unacknowledged and even consciously denied presuppositions are of
course the most insidious ones. This sort of Wittgensteinianism helped
me to avoid facing certain important issues for some time, and in
particular the question of whether I could honestly continue the practice
of religion, to which I was emotionally very drawn despite the fact that
another side of my nature craved an austerer metaphysics. What finally
made me break with religion was getting interested in biology, largely
because of the excellent biological discussion group which centred on the
zoology department of the University of Adelaide. When one comes to
see man as a zoological species, a lot of the Christian story seems most
unplausibly anthropocentric. Moreover, how can one think biologically
of immortality and of prayer? Could there be an information-flow model
of prayer? Such questions could no longer be blocked by evasive
Wittgensteinian talk about language games.

This made it clear to me how much more potent then neo-
Wittgensteinian philosophical analysis were considerations of scientific
plausibility. At first I had felt that these considerations were merely part
of philosophical heuristics; that is, if philosophical analysis in the Rylean
or neo-Wittgensteinian manner suggested a conclusion which was
scientifically unplausible, then we should consider that there was
probably an undetected fallacy in the philosophical arguments (Smart
1957). For example, Oxford philosophers were rejecting Rylean
behaviourism, and they thought of materialism as even beyond the pale
of serious discussion. If their arguments were correct, then these
philosophers were surely committed to irreducible psychical entities

which did not seem to fit in happily with physics and biology. This suggested to me that we should look again at the arguments against behaviourism and materialism. At this stage, however, I still thought of philosophy as an autonomous *a priori* discipline, so that these colnsiderations of scientific plausibility could be heuristic only. I drew the analogy with G. Pólya's well-known heuristics for mathematics. (Pólya 1954). He made use of inductive and plausible arguments which could not belong to the corpus of mathematics itself, which is a system of rigorous proof in accordance with the rules of deductive logic.

However, I later came to think that the plausible reasoning in philosophy which I had advocated could not be merely heuristic. Despite all the brave words of the neo-Wittgensteinians, conceptual problems were not being resolved to the satisfaction of all concerned; there was nothing analogous to the agreement which mathematicians reached by means of their proofs. The neo-Wittgensteinians had of course themselves stressed certain differences between philosophical arguments and mathematical proofs, but nevertheless they did think that their methods would lead to assured results in an *a priori* manner. The empirical fact unfortunately was that philosophers continued to disagree as they had always done in the past, and the fly often remains obdurately within the fly bottle (Wittgenstein 1953). It therefore began to look as though there was something wrong with the neo-Wittgensteinian conception of philosophy. I began to think that considerations of scientific plausibility had their own rightful place in settling philosophical disputes, and that they were not mere heuristics paving the way for future proofs. Indeed they appeared more convincing than merely *a priori* or analytic philosophical argument could be on its own (see my essay 'Philosophy and Scientific Plausibility' in this volume).

This can be illustrated by a controversy in which once more I engaged in friendly debate with my old mentor C.A. Campbell. When not concerned with his suprarational absolute (which, of necessity, was most of the time), Campbell argued for many philosophical theses about the phenomenal (as opposed to noumenal) world. In particular he defended a libertarian theory of free will. I thought that I had a knockdown argument against such a theory. I gave a Laplacean definition of determinism and defined pure chance as the negation of determinism. These definitions seemed to be natural ones, and they implied that an action had to be either determined or a matter of pure chance, so that no third possibility (acting from Campbellian free will) was left open (Smart 1961). However, in discussion with various philosophers it soon became apparent that libertarians (including Campbell (1963) himself) were not willing to accept my definition of 'pure chance', but within the field demarcated by me as 'pure chance' they distinguished two possibilities,

(a) pure chance and (b) free action. Of course such philosophers then have the problem of explaining what they mean by 'free will' and 'pure chance', since neither can now be defined as the negation of determinism. This pushes the libertarian into problems about meaning, and so I still think that the original argument does good, in bringing to light difficulties in the libertarian's position. However, it is manifestly not an apodeictic refutation. In the end the strategy is to force the libertarian into adopting more and more unplausible assumptions. Of course what is thought plausible depends on the person in question; for example, one man may judge theology in the light of scientific plausibility, while another may judge science in the light of theological plausibility. However, those libertarians who prize scientific plausibility may be brought to feel doubts about their theory when they are asked to reflect on how a libertarian free will can be explained in terms of mechanistic biology. How could mutations in DNA molecules lead to the existence of such a transcendent entity?

This all too sketchy account of a philosophical controversy has been intended to illustrate the thesis that you cannot refute another philosopher merely by *a priori* argument, but you may use argument in order to push him into having to rely on premises which he (or others) may feel to be unplausible in the light of total science. This account of philosophy as dependent on considerations of scientific plausibility explains why philosophers need to engage in conceptual investigations, but it implies that these conceptual investigations do not have the sort of autonomy and independence of scientific theories which the neo-Wittgensteinians have held that they have. The view of philosophy to which I have come is not very different from Quine's, since Quine has been concerned to work out a canonical notation in which to express total science (Quine 1960). This is no accident. Quine's criticisms of the analytic-synthetic distinction (Quine 1961) broke down the distinction between the conceptual and the factual, and hence shed doubt on the autonomy of philosophy as a second-order activity. Also Quine's writings stimulate reflection on different formulations of set theory. This reminds us that what is ruled out as ungrammatical or nonsensical according to one form of theory may turn out as simply unprovable (or even provably false) in another formulation. This helps to break down the Rylean notion of a *category mistake* as something different in kind from ordinary factual error (Smart 1966). Unfortunately this breaking down of the sense–nonsense versus true–false dichotomy implies that I cannot give a *clear* account of what I have meant when earlier in this essay I have said that some subjects are more concerned with 'conceptual matters' than are others. The best I have been able to do is to illustrate the notion of *being more concerned with conceptual matters* by giving examples.

When one adopts the criterion of scientific plausibility one tends to get a certain way of looking at the universe, which is to see it *sub specie aeternitatis*. The phrase of course comes from Spinoza, and in Spinoza's philosophy to see something *sub specie aeternitatis* implies seeing it as occurring by something like logical necessity. Of course I do not wish to include this as part of the connotation of the phrase as I use it. To see the world *sub specie aeternitatis* is to see it apart from any particular or human perspective. Theoretical language of science facilitates this vision of the world because it contains no indexical words like 'I', 'you', 'here', 'now', 'past', 'present' and 'future', and its laws can be expressed in tenseless language. Moreover, it contains no words for secondary qualities, such as colours, which though in a sense perfectly objective are of interest only because of the specific structures of the perceptual mechanisms of *Homo sapiens*. Other attitudes are of course possible. Some may prefer to see the world in perspective, so that, as F.P. Ramsey put it, 'The foreground is occupied by human beings and the stars are all as small as threepenny bits' (Ramsey 1931). So far this is a matter of taste, but in the case of Ramsey there was surely also intellectual error (in the shape of phenomenalism), since he went on to say, 'I don't really believe in astronomy, except as a complicated description of part of the course of human and possibly animal sensation.' Apart from the usual neo-Wittgensteinian arguments which have been brought against it we may surely reject phenomenalism as quite unplausible. It is too much to believe that the world should consist of sequences of sensations which are just *as if* they were caused by enduring physical objects. The implausibility of phenomenalism is quite closely related to its anthropocentricity (or at any rate sentience centredness).

My interest in seeing the world *sub specie aeternitatis* is not shared by some influential contemporary philosophers who are primarily interested in man's ordinary common-sense picture of the world.[1] A few years ago there were some discussions by philosophers of the question of whether there could be disparate spaces and times (Quinton 1962; Skillen 1964–5; Swinburne 1964–5; Hollis 1967). The details do not matter here, but what worried me about these discussions was that much of the argument was carried on by considering what certain tribes would say if certain strange things happened in their experience, or what we should say if certain strange things happened in our experience. The turn the discussion took perhaps depended on a neo-Kantian shift (rather characteristic of some recent Oxford philosophy) from talking about X to talking about *our experience* of X. That is, the discussion was often almost anthropological, whereas in reply I suggested that it was more relevant to argue mathematically, for example, to point out that two disparate four-spaces (space-times) can be embedded in a five-dimensional space (Smart

1967). Of course denizens of four-space might know nothing of the other four-spaces, and so they might not need to use the concept of disparate four-spaces. However, I slightly adapted a speculation by the physicist F.R. Stannard (1966) to show how a hypothesis about disparate space-times might even come to have some tenuous relationship with observation. This, then, illustrates a divergence in philosophical method between myself and some of my contemporaries. It is, however, not a really wide one, as is the divergence between both myself and these contemporaries on the one hand and the purveyors of *angst* on the other hand!

So far I have not said much about ethics. Ethics is part of philosophy not only for obvious historical reasons (because Plato, Aristotle, et al., wrote about it) but also because it gives rise to many conceptual problems. Suffice to say that I have been interested to defend act utilitarianism, which has the sort of universality and generality which can appeal to one who is concerned with the world *sub specie aeternitatis*. Its supreme principle would be as applicable if we had to deal with beings from Alpha Centauri as it is in dealing with members of *Homo sapiens*, as well as horses, dogs, etc. Act utilitarianism appeals as a possible 'cosmic ethics'. (It is, of course, not necessarily the only system of ethics that does so.)

Another branch of study which has traditionally been regarded as part of philosophy is political philosophy. Once more this may be for the historical reason that many great metaphysicians and epistemologists have also written about politics. Of course they have often written about mathematics and physics too, but the fact that these require special mathematical and experimental techniques and expertise may partly explain why they are not taught within philosophy departments. Another reason, no doubt, is the high proportion of conceptual questions which arise in the writings of traditional philosophers who have discussed political theory. However, my own opinion (for what it is worth) is that on the whole there is not much new conceptual work to be done in this area, and what there is can be done with quite an elementary knowledge of general philosophy. Political philosophy is concerned with the best ways of organizing human society and requires empirical more than conceptual ability, and I tend to think that it is probably best done within politics departments of universities. However, this preference is a practical and undogmatic one: there certainly are political philosophers who are fun to have around, and I do not wish to lose their company if they happen to be in my own department! Another reason why I do not want to be too dogmatic about whether political philosophy should be regarded as philosophy proper is that the extension of the term 'philosopher' is one of the things which philosophers do not agree about.

I have no more academic right to object to a philosophical colleague lecturing about politics than he has to object to me if I encroach on physics. My proposal is pragmatic only and in accordance with a general view that tight departmental boundaries are unjustifiable.

At present we live in a very politically conscious age, and my feeling that political philosophy is best not done in philosophy departments will not meet with approval from those who wish philosophy to be 'socially relevant'. In reply I should like to make two points.

First of all, it is a shame that philosophers should be persecuted so much with demands for social relevance. No doubt some of the radical young may feel this way even about subjects like topology, botany and mechanical engineering, but they do tend to scream at philosophers more than at most other people. One of the worst features of the demand for social relevance is that it is frequently coupled with a contempt for intellectual curiosity as such. Let me put the denigrator of intellectual curiosity on the horns of a dilemma. Consider the arms race. This is a positive feedback process which we all deplore but which is very hard to stop. Now either it can be stopped or it cannot be stopped. If it cannot be stopped, we are all doomed, and to satisfy intellectual curiosity can do no harm and will give us some pleasure during the period before the final catastrophe. Alternatively it can be stopped. But if it can be stopped, it will require much high-powered thought to discover *how* to stop it. Probably many highly abstract intellectual tools, such as the theory of games, will be needed. These intellectual tools tend to be acquired only by those students who have enough intellectual curiosity to enjoy the hard and difficult work of acquiring them. So once more intellectual curiosity is a good thing. The antiscientific young often blame science for our present troubles (overpopulation, pollution, destructive weapons). They perhaps have too rosy a picture of earlier ages when babies died young, few people had meat to eat, teeth had to be removed without anaesthetics, and all sorts of horrible diseases flourished. However, let us concede that science may have made the world a worse place in which to live. It is still fallacious to go on to say that we should give up thinking in a scientific way. If science has got us into this fix, it will be nothing less than science which will get us out of it again. (This is not to deny that other conditions may be needed too, such as a change of heart.) And if science will not get us out of our fix and we really are doomed, is this a reason for forgoing the higher intellectual activities in the time which remains to us? If a ship is sinking, the passengers need not revert to barbarism.

The second point which I wish to make about the social relevance of philosophy follows on naturally from the first point. If intellectual sophistication really is needed to get us out of our present troubles, then a really tough sophisticated philosophical education is a good thing. Those philosophers who prefer to lecture on topical themes of immediately obvious social concern do so at the cost of not lecturing on abstract, sophisticated tough philosophical questions. In their courses they may deal with certain rather elementary conceptual confusions, but there is so much empirical content in their courses that the student does not get scope for really advanced conceptual work, as he does when discussing, say, Quine on the indeterminacy of translation. So the students do not get the really sophisticated conceptual training which they can apply later in other fields, perhaps socially relevant ones. In other words, philosophy can be most socially relevant by being true to itself and not setting out directly to be socially relevant.

NOTE

1 For an advocacy of anthropocentricity in philosophy see the remarks by P.F. Strawson (Magee 1971, p. 141).

REFERENCES

Blanshard, Brand 1939: *The Nature of Thought*. London: George Allen & Unwin.
Campbell, C.A. 1963: Professor Smart on Free-Will, Praise and Blame. *Mind*, 72, 400–5.
Eddington, A.S. 1928: *The Nature of the Physical World*. London: Cambridge University Press.
Feyerabend, Paul K. 1968: On a Recent Critique of Complementarity, part 1. *Philosophy of Science*, 35, 309–31.
—— 1969: On a Recent Critique of Complementarity, part 2. *Philosophy of Science*, 36, 82–105.
Hollis, Martin 1967: Box and Cox. *Philosophy*, 42, 75–8.
Magee, Bryan 1971: *Modern British Philosophy*. London: Secker and Warburg.
Moore, G.E. 1903: *Principia Ethica*. London: Cambridge University Press.
—— 1912: *Ethics*. London: Williams and Norgate.
Pólya, G. 1954: *Mathematics and Plausible Reasoning*. Princeton, New Jersey: Princeton University Press.
Quine, W.V. 1960: *Word and Object*. Cambridge, Massachusetts: MIT Press, 270–6.
—— 1961: *From a Logical Point of View*, 2nd edn. New York: Harper & Row, chapter 2.
—— 1966: Implicit Definition Sustained. In *The Ways of Paradox*, New York: Random House.
Quinton, Anthony 1962: Spaces and Times. *Philosophy*, 37, 130–47.
Ramsey, F.P. 1931: *The Foundations of Mathematics*. London: Kegan Paul, 291.
Ryle, G. 1951: Systematically Misleading Expressions. In A.G.N. Flew (ed.),

Logic and Language, 1st series, Oxford: Basil Blackwell & Mott.

Skillen, A. 1964–5: The Myth of Temporal Division. *Analysis*, 25, 44–7.

Smart, J.J.C. 1957: Plausible Reasoning in Philosophy. *Mind*, 66, 75–8.

—— 1961: Free-Will, Praise and Blame. *Mind*, 70, 291–306.

—— 1966: Nonsense. In W.H. Capitan and D.D. Merrill (eds), *Metaphysics and Explanation*, Pittsburgh: University of Pittsburgh Press.

—— 1967: The Unity of Space-Time: Mathematics versus Myth-Making. *Australasian Journal of Philosophy*, 45, 214–17.

Stannard, F.R. 1966: Symmetry of the Time-Axis. *Nature*, 211, 693–5.

Swinburne, R.G. 1964–5: Times. *Analysis*, 25, 47–50.

Wittgenstein, L. 1953: *Philosophical Investigations*. Oxford: Basil Blackwell & Mott, section 309.

4

Ockham's Razor

In the past ('Sensations and Brain Processes' this volume; Smart 1963, 1967), I have invoked Ockham's Razor in connection with the defence of physicalism, but how Ockham's Razor really came into the matter is less clear to me now. I was thinking of the Razor in the version '*Entia non sunt multiplicanda praeter necessitatem*'. It seems that this formula is a seventeenth century invention, and is nowhere to be found in the extant writings of William of Ockham. In this and subsequent historical remarks, I shall be generally relying on W.M. Thorburn's very interesting paper 'The Myth of Occam's Razor' (Thorburn 1918). However, Ockham did use a formula to very much the same effect, '*Frustra fit per plura quod potest fieri per pauciora*', that is, it is in vain to do by many what can be done by fewer. We can take the 'many' and 'fewer' here to be explanatory propositions, and in many cases these will be existential propositions. So Ockham's Razor counsels us against an unnecessary luxuriance of principles or laws or statements of existence. Putting it in this way enables us to avoid a certain infelicity[1] in the post-medieval formula. A philosopher cannot multiply the fundamental entities or sorts of entities that there are in the universe: all he can multiply is existential hypotheses. The infelicity in the post-medieval formula smacks of a use–mention confusion, but it is so obvious a one that it should not mislead anyone. Despite the title of Nelson Goodman's *Ways of Worldmaking* (1978), we cannot fill up or empty the universe by our mere philosophical discourse. More congenial is Goodman's earlier very witty remark that though there may be more things in heaven and earth than there are dreamt of in our philosophy, he is concerned that there should not be more things dreamt of in his philosophy than there are in heaven and earth (Goodman 1973, p. 34). This is very much in the spirit of the Razor.

This term 'the Razor' seems to derive from Condillac who used the phrase '*Rasoir des nominaux*,' and the Latin version of this '*Novaculum Nominalium*,' came into vogue. The English phrase 'Ockham's (or Occam's) Razor' comes from the Scottish philosopher Sir William Hamilton (1853) who regarded this as tantamount to what he called 'The Law of Parcimony' (thus spelt), according to which 'Nature never works by more complex instruments than are necessary'. J.S. Mill objected to this ontological formulation: how do we know this alleged fact about nature? (Mill 1979.) Indeed, he said, we know that nature often proceeds in a very complex manner to produce various effects, and we cannot be confident that such effects could not have been produced in a simpler manner. According to Mill 'The Law of Parcimony' is a rule of methodology, that we should not believe anything for which we have no evidence. Thus he claims that defense of the Razor requires no assumptions about the ways of nature. Even if the ways of nature were the reverse of what we now believe them to be, it would still be improper, Mill said, for us to assume a proposition about nature without our having evidence for it.

The Razor suggests, reasonably enough, that if we have a choice between a theory of the form p on the one hand and one of the form p & q on the other hand, then if we have no antecedent reason to believe q, and if the explanatory force of p & q is not superior to that of p, then we should assert only p. Of course, if p & q had more explanatory force than p, this would raise the antecedent probability of q. (I am here taking it that p and q could be conjunctions of quite complex propositions.) However, in the developed sciences it is not usual for choices to be between theories of the forms p and p & q respectively.

Usually in pure science when a conjunction of propositions is needed to explain some facts, each conjunct separately will not even be a candidate for being a plausible *explanans*. However, in medicine and technology, the situation may be quite common. Thus if my lawn mower fails to start, I may consider the hypothesis that this is due *both* to a blocked carburettor *and* to a defective spark plug, but if I find that the spark plug has oiled up, I accept the simple hypothesis that this is the cause of the trouble, not that the cause is also the blocked carburettor. In pure science the choice is more likely to be between a hypothesis of the form p' & q and one of the form p, where p' is some non-trivial modification of p. The scientist does not compare the merits of p & q with those of p but rather those of p' & q with those of p. The hypothesis p' may have epistemic advantages over p sufficient to justify us in taking on the extra baggage q. The principle of Ockham's Razor, as literally construed, needs to be replaced simply by the principle that other things being equal, we should prefer more simple theories to more complex ones.

I have noted earlier that J.S. Mill cast doubt on this principle, because of the fact that nature often works in more complex ways than are necessary. Certainly we find this in natural history. The locomotive mechanism involved in walking is far more complex than is that of a vehicle on wheels. Nevertheless this consideration does not tell against the principle of simplicity. If an explorer discovers a new animal, he or she does not expect it to run on wheels. There is no simple or even remotely plausible explanation of how locomation on wheels would fit into the palaeontological story of animal evolution. Motion on legs may be more complex than motion on wheels, but a theory of how animal motion on legs might have evolved may be much more simple than a theory of how animal motion on wheels might have evolved.

One thing that is needed is some theory of simplicity whereby we could show that if p is simpler than q then p has the epistemic advantages over q that it has over p & r, even though q can not be decomposed into p & r. Though a good deal of progress has been made in the theory of simplicity (for example, in Sober 1975, 1981), I suspect that it is not possible fully to justify the idea that simple theories are objectively more likely to be true than are complex ones or even that they contain fewer arbitrary elements. For those who wish, as I do, to regard science as metaphysics, as telling us what the universe really contains and is really like, and not as a mere instrument for prediction of our experiences, the ability to justify our beliefs objectively is what is wanted from Ockham's Razor and analogous principles of parsimony. It is not that we prefer simpler theories because they are more congenial and easy for our intellects. The sort of simplicity achieved by quantum mechanics or general relativity is not a matter of easiness of comprehension or of application.

The sort of simplicity I am after is an objective simplicity, hard though it is to explicate this notion. Scientists do often seem to take simplicity as a sign of truth. Until recently, at any rate, the tests of the general theory of relativity were rather few and beset by controversy. Nevertheless the theory tended to be believed because of its beauty, a sort of simplicity, for example in its explanation of gravitation in terms of geodesics in curved space-time, which is a sort of generalization of Newton's first law of motion. Admittedly a space-time of variable curvature is less simple than a space-time of zero or constant curvature, but it is still something of the same general kind, and its postulation explains mysteries – for example, the proportionality of gravitational and inertial mass. The theory was certainly not accepted because of its practical utility: it was impossible to use it to calculate the nautical almanac, for example. Nevertheless the theory explained the approximate truth of Newton's theory, which could then be used as before to compute the nautical almanac, predict the paths of space rockets, and so on.

There is a tendency, then, for us to take simplicity, in some obscure objective sense, as a guide to metaphysical truth. Perhaps this tendency derives from earlier theological notions: we expect God to have created a beautiful universe. But what is beauty? Partly symmetry, which is a form of simplicity. Why do we love simplicity? Perhaps there is an evolutionary explanation: simplicity is merely a reflection of innate cognitive mechanisms that have proved successful during the evolution of the human species. But if this is all there is to it, we would have no reason to expect these innate mechanisms to be a good guide to theories of quantum mechanics or general relativity, which hitherto at least have had no immediate relevance to everyday practical living, still less to the needs of predators or hunter-gatherers. The evolutionary argument is that our tastes in theories (our feelings for simplicity) must be adapted to the real world. This is no good for *justifying* (though it could *explain*) our appeal to simplicity in sophisticated twentieth-century physics. Tastes suitable for such sophisticated theories as quantum mechanics and relativity would have had no selective advantage for early humans or their ancestors. Nor is an inductive argument from the success of simple theories in the past to the success of simple theories in the future at all convincing. Such a meta-induction would be one by simple enumeration, and we have reason to think that heuristic strategies that worked in the past might well be as inapplicable to future theories (or even contemporary ones) as are the lessons of past wars for possible future nuclear wars. In such cases we indeed have good reason for thinking that the future will *not* be like the past. Furthermore, such a meta-induction may seem less cogent if we remember simple theories, such as that of Boscovich, which have been unsuccessful as compared with less simple and aesthetically pleasing theories. However, perhaps Boscovich's theory, if it is put in the wider context of physics, turns out to be less simple than it seems. As Schlesinger has argued, when we try to make a false theory accord with the facts, we encumber it more and more with *ad hoc* hypotheses and complications (Schlesinger 1963, p. 44).

I have been tempted to throw in the towel here and say that just as induction, the principle that the future will be like the past, can neither be validated nor vindicated (to use Herbert Feigl's terminology, Feigl 1950), and yet must be accepted if we are to believe anything at all about the universe, so the principle of simplicity must be accepted, even though it cannot be validated or vindicated either. I think, however, that this would be too pessimistic. A vindication of induction does not now seem to be out of the question, because I think that John Clendinnen has at least got pretty close to it (Clendinnen 1982). A vindication of induction would not show that inductive policies are successful (as a validation would), but it would show why it is reasonable to use induction rather than any alternative. Clendinnen argues that any non-inductive policy is irrational because it would involve arbitrary decisions and be no better than mere guessing. (Guessing can be rational, if a person's ability to guess rightly is inductively warranted, but this is not *mere* guessing.) And it is interesting that Clendinnen's argument makes the principle of simplicity part and parcel of the principle of induction. Clendinnen connects the principle of induction and the principle of simplicity together as a matter of not being arbitrary. I think that he does indeed vindicate the principle of simplicity in this way, but more is needed for my purposes in order to vindicate our preference in sophisticated science for certain more simple theories as compared with certain more complex ones. The more complex theory may not be related to the less complex one as p & q is related to p. In these cases the difference between the less complex and the more complex does not seem to be obviously reducible to a matter of arbitrariness. So I shall have to shelve this matter for the purposes of this paper and merely draw attention to the promise of Clendinnen's work.[2]

Kent E. Holsinger, in an interesting discussion paper (Holsinger 1981), has remarked that it is not often the case that two hypotheses account for the facts equally well but that one is simpler than the other. One case in which Holsinger holds that the principle of simplicity was legitimately applied is that of the issue between the Copernican heliocentric theory of planetary motion as contrasted with the geocentric theory that prevailed in Copernicus's time. However, it is a matter of debate among historians of science as to whether at the time in question the Copernican system *was* simpler.[3] Nevertheless it lended itself to transformation into Kepler's theory, and then to explanation by the laws of Newtonian mechanics, so that even if it was not more simple in what Schlesinger has called a 'static' sense, it did have greater 'dynamic' simplicity (Schlesinger 1963, pp. 36ff). A system may not be simpler in the form in which it was put forward, but it may appear simpler to us in retrospect, because of the greater simplicity of later theories into which simple modifications of it were incorporated. It is hard to see how the geocentric hypothesis could have been integrated with the Newtonian theory of dynamics and of gravitation, or could have been used, as by Adams and Leverrier, to predict from anomalies in the motion of Uranus the existence and position of Neptune. It is to be expected that it is in cosmology and metaphysics, whose ties with experience are indirect and tenuous, that the true locus of simplicity, as an autonomous or nearly autonomous principle, is to be found.

Not surprisingly, therefore, a particularly good example of the principle is to be found in the writings of William of Ockham himself.

Holsinger, in the aforementioned discussion note, fastens on a passage in which Ockham asserts his '*Frustra fit per plura quod potest fieri per pauciora.*' A translation of this passage from Ockham's *Summa Totius Logicae* is given and discussed in Moody (1965, pp. 49–50). Ockham seems to have believed that thought proceeds by means of 'natural signs'. He wanted to argue against the theory that the actual sign was some concept constructed in the mind and distinct from an 'act of understanding'. Ockham suggested that this act of understanding itself could be a natural sign (stand for or signify an object) just as well as could some intermediate constructed mental entity. Therefore we might as well dispense with belief in such intermediate mental entities. But even here the application of the Razor seems to have temporary usefulness only. Ockham's question was posed in terms of thought signifying objects, and modern ideas of semantics and of the mind make Ockham's question unclear. We now have quite different theories about the relationship between thought and the world.

As I remarked at the outset of this essay, I myself have brandished what I referred to as Ockham's Razor. But now that I have thought more about the nature of Ockham's Razor (and considerations of simplicity in general), I begin to think that what I was brandishing was not Ockham's Razor at all. As Holsinger pointed out against M.J. Dunbar (Dunbar 1980), Ockham's Razor does not imply that we should accept simpler theories at all costs. The Razor is a method for deciding between two theories that equally account for the agreed-upon facts. I was using it to defend physicalism and to attack dualism in the philosophy of mind. The dualist would, of course, not agree that the physicalist *does* account for all the facts. The dualist thinks that he is immediately aware of non-physical items of experience. When I brandished Ockham's Razor, or rather what I carelessly took to be Ockham's Razor, I was merely drawing attention to unpleasant complexities in the dualist theory, which made it implausible to me. The dualist would reply that if his theory is complex or implausible looking, that is just too bad, because he thinks that to deny it would be to deny obvious facts of experience. Entities should not be multiplied beyond necessity, he might agree, but according to him his non-physical entities do not lie beyond necessity.

It begins to look as though my principle is not so much 'Entities should not be multiplied beyond necessity,' but rather 'Entities should not be multiplied beyond what I want' ('*Entia non sunt multiplicanda praeter voluntatem meam*'???). I was in particular concerned to avoid the 'multiplication of entities' that would arise from the postulation of brain processes on the one hand and associated non-physical entities (sensations) on the other hand. The latter seemed to me to be excrescences on the face of science. In particular they would seem to imply the existence of laws connecting them to their associated brain processes, and these would be, as Feigl put it, 'nomological danglers' (Feigl 1958). That is, they would stick out or dangle from the nomological net of science. Moreover they would be laws of a most peculiar kind, since they would not relate simple or relevantly homogeneous entities. Thus, though a non-physical sensation of blue, say, might or might not be a simple, it would have to be connected by a law to a very complex and idiosyncratic type of brain process, involving perhaps hundreds of millions of neurons, all connected together in very special ways. And yet it would have to be an ultimate law, not derivable from laws relating to simple or homogeneous entities.

I held, therefore, that it is highly implausible that there should be such nomological danglers or the entities that would hang down from them. And I still think this. But if I was using Ockham's Razor, I was misapplying it. 'Entities must not be multiplied beyond necessity.' If it is not necessary to postulate non-physical mental entities, then they ought not to be postulated. (Instead, sensations should be identified with brain processes.) We might apply the principle as *modus ponens*: 'If it is not necessary to postulate non-physical sensations, then non-physical sensations ought not to be postulated; it is not necessary; therefore we ought not to postulate non-physical sensations.' But to apply the principle in this way, we would need to possess ourselves of the minor premise, which in the present case is the very point at issue. Was I not therefore thinking in terms of an affirmation of the consequent, and hence of an invalid argument? In other words my considerations about the horrors of nomological danglers suggest that we should not hold that sensations are non-physical. One may be tempted to use the Ockhamist principle to deduce 'It is not necessary to hold that there are non-physical sensations.' But if one did so, one would be affirming the consequent.

It therefore looks as though these considerations about the horrors of nomological danglers are heuristic only. The vital *philosophical* argument comes when we argue that it is *not* necessary to believe that sensations are non-physical. Indeed we do not need to prove apodeictically that there are no non-physical mental events. We can make it plausible that there is no good reason to postulate Xs by examining all the reasons the philosophers have given for supposing that there are Xs, and by showing that these reasons are bad ones. Of course, it may be that there are better reasons that someone may discover later, and perhaps there may be good reasons that no one has thought of or will think of. However, the mere *possibility* of this does not matter: one could not accept even a well-tested scientific theory if one were prevented by the mere possibility that an unknown experimental refutation of it exists.

Following   U.T. Place   (Place   1956)   and   in   agreement   with
D.M. Armstrong (Armstrong 1968, 1981) and others, my way of getting
rid of the nomological danglers was to argue that sensations are *identical*
with brain processes and are not extra-psychical entities merely *correlated*
with brain processes. Mental events are individuated by their typical
environmental causes and their typical behavioural effects. But brain
processes have these environmental causes and behavioural effects. And
so far, then, it would seem to be a simple and uncontroversial use of
Ockham's Razor to chop off the non-physical and simply *identify* the
mental with the physical. But if we let it go at that, the real work has not
been done and the dualist will not be convinced.

There is indeed an obstacle to using Ockham's Razor to deny the
existence of *X*s if it seems that we are immediately aware of *X*s. We need
to give reasons for thinking that when people report an apparent
awareness of the non-physical, they are in some way deceived. In the
case of perception of the external world, we can often give scientific
reasons for thinking that a supposed perception of putative entities is no
such thing: these reasons will contain an explanation of how the mistake
is brought about by normal physical and physiological causes. Consider,
for example, the optical explanation of mirages. Sometimes the
explanation will be psychological (in a sense compatible with physicalism) rather than, say, optical. This would be the case, presumably, with
an explanation of the headless woman illusion, which has been discussed
by D.M. Armstrong (Armstrong 1968–9). He argues that the apparent
phenomenology of consciousness as non-physical comes from an illusion
analogous to that of the headless woman. The headless woman illusion is
achieved by placing black cloth over the woman's head and by
illuminating the woman's body against a black background. Spectators,
not seeing that the woman has a head, jump to the conclusion that the
woman has no head. (Not seeing that *p* gets confused with seeing that not
p.) Similarly, it can be argued that the properties that are presented in
inner sense are neutral ones that could be possessed alike by physical and
non-physical entities, and so our inner sense is not an awareness of things
as having *specifically* physical properties. Just as with the headless
woman, we jump from this to an unwarranted negative judgement: we
are not aware that our inner experiences are neurological processes and
we jump to the concusion that they are *not* neurological processes.
Armstrong does concede that the consideration about the headless
woman illusion will not completely satisfy the objector who relies on the
phenomenology of inner experience, so that more needs to be said.

However, I find it very hard to put much weight on such
phenomenological objections. The neutral properties do seem to be the
ones of which I am aware in inner sense. It is up to the philosopher who

appeals to phenomenology to tell us more and I do not think that he succeeds.

Of course, if sense data and mental images were part of the world, they would be things with phenomenological properties, such as blueness, for example. A sense datum cannot be identified with a neurophysiological process, since such a process presumably cannot be blue. However, I hold that there are no sense data or images as such, but only the havings of them, and the having of a blue sense datum is not itself blue. Of course, I do have to give a physicalist account of the blueness of physical objects, for example, cornflowers. (See 'On Some Criticisms of a Physicalist Theory of Colours', this volume, which replaces the also physicalist account in Smart 1963.)

The pattern of my argument is therefore as follows. I use plausibility considerations of simplicity, in an attempt to soften up the dualist, by getting him to wonder whether the arguments against the materialist theory of mind are as good as he thought they were. If he can be convinced that they are not good arguments, then it is only a mere uncontroversial application of Ockham's Razor to chop away the immaterially mental, since it is then agreed that there is no necessity to suppose that it exists. But my plausibility arguments came *before* the argument that the immaterially mental was *praeter necessitatem*. Are my plausibility arguments heuristic only? What I have said so far suggests that the answer to this question is in the affirmative. In conclusion I should like to suggest (contrarily to the position I have taken up earlier in this paper) that a case could be made out that plausibility arguments can have a more than heuristic role. Perhaps we should have more faith metaphysically in considerations of plausibility in the light of total science than we have in attempts at apodeictic argument. Philosophical arguments are notoriously slippery. If they lead us to conclusions that do not fit in well with our scientific picture of the world, then we should distrust them. Since a philosopher can question anything whatever, complete apodeictic refutation of a philosophical position is hardly possible. Philosophical arguments can be got around, though at the cost of perhaps implausible extra premises. So it could be that plausibility in the light of total science is the best touchstone of metaphysical truth, and that formal philosophical arguments and clarifications play a somewhat ancillary (though necessary) part. But all this is another story ('Philosophy and Scientific Plausibility', this volume[4]).[5]

NOTES

1 The infelicity was noted in Routley (1980, p. 412).
2 Lewis S. Feuer has argued that the principle of Ockham's Razor is part and parcel of scientific method since it counsels the rejection of unverifiable and hence arbitrary elements. (Feuer 1957, 1959. However, see also the discussion of this in Schlesinger 1963, pp. 20–3.) In Schlesinger (1974, ch. 2), there is an argument that without appeal to a principle of simplicity, the inductive method would not enable us to pick out a unique hypothesis and so we would be completely paralysed in choosing between them.
3 For a striking illustration of a similarity in complexity between Copernicus's system and the geocentric one, see the illustrations on pp. xii–xiii in de Santillana (1953). I am indebted to the reference in Lakatos (1978, p. 174, n. 8).
4 In part this essay looks forward to 'Sensations and Brain Processes' and 'On Some Criticisms of a Physicalist Theory of Colours', in this volume.
5 I should like to thank my friends D.M. Armstrong, K.K. Campbell, F.J. Clendinnen, F.C. Jackson, P.N. Pettit, and H. Price, who read an earlier draft of this paper and made useful comments.

REFERENCES

Armstrong, D.M. 1968: *A Materialist Theory of the Mind*. London: Routledge and Kegan Paul.
—— 1968–9: The Headless Woman and the Defence of Materialism. *Analysis*, 29, 48–9.
—— 1981: *The Nature of Mind and Other Essays*. Brighton: Harvester Press.
Clendinnen, F.J. 1982: Rational Expectation and Simplicity. In R. McLaughlin (ed.), *What? Where? When? Why?* Dordrecht, Holland: D. Reidel, 1–25.
Dunbar, M.H.J. 1980: The Blunting of Occam's Razor, or to Hell with Parsimony. *Canadian Journal of Zoology*, 58, 123–8.
Feigl, H. 1950: De principiis Non Disputandum . . . ? In M. Black (ed.), *Philosophical Analysis*, Cornell University Press, 119–56.
—— 1958: The 'Mental' and the 'Physical'. *Minnesota Studies in the Philosophy of Science*, 2, 3–36.
Feuer, L.S. 1957: The Principle of Simplicity. *Philosophy of Science*, 24, 109–22.
—— 1959: Rejoinder on the Principle of Simplicity. *Philosophy of Science*, 26, 43–5.
Goodman, N. 1973: *Fact, Fiction and Forecast*, 3rd edn. Indianapolis: Bobbs-Merrill.
—— 1978: *Ways of Worldmaking*. Brighton: Harvester.
Hamilton, W. 1853: *Discussions on Philosophy and Literature*, 2nd edn. London: Longman, Brown, Green and Longmans.
Holsinger, K. 1981: Comment: The Blunting of Occam's Razor, or to Hell with Parsimony. *Canadian Journal of Zoology*, 59, 144–6.

Lakatos, I. 1978: *The Methodology of Scientific Research Programmes: Philosophical Papers*, vol. 1. Cambridge: Cambridge University Press.

Mill, J.S. 1979: *Examination of Sir William Hamilton's Philosophy*, edited by J. Robson, London: Routledge and Kegan Paul.

Moody, E.A. 1965: *The Logic of William of Ockham*. New York: Russell & Russell.

Place, U.T. 1966: Is Consciousness a Brain Process? *British Journal of Psychology*, 47, 44–50.

Routley, R. 1980: *Exploring Meinong's Jungle and Beyond*. Canberra: Department of Philosophy, Research School of Social Sciences, The Australian National University.

Santillana, G. de 1955: Historical Introduction to Galileo. *Dialogue on the Great World Systems*. Chicago: Chicago University Press.

Schlesinger, G. 1963: *Method in the Physical Sciences*. London: Routledge and Kegan Paul.

—— 1974: *Confirmation and Confirmability*. Oxford: Clarendon Press.

Smart, J.J.C. 1963: *Philosophy and Scientific Realism*. London: Routledge and Kegan Paul.

—— 1967: Comments on the Papers. In C.F. Presley (ed.), *The Identity Theory of Mind*, St Lucia, Queensland: University of Queensland Press, 84–93.

Sober, E. *Simplicity*. Oxford: Clarendon Press.

—— 1981: The Principle of Parsimony. *British Journal for the Philosophy of Science*, 32, 145–56.

Thorburn, W.M. 1918: The Myth of Occam's Razor. *Mind*, 27, 345–53.

PART 2
Space, Time and Space-Time

5

Causal Theories of Time

There is a family of theories of time which attempt to construct the structure (or at least the topology) of space-time on the basis of the notion of causality, or of some notion closely related to that of causality. In the last fifty years or so such attempts have been inspired by the special theory of relativity. Consider a point A in space-time. All light signals arriving at or departing from A lie along generators of the four-dimensional analogue of a double cone, which may be called the 'light cone' of A. Then it is a consequence of the special theory of relativity that any event which is causally connected with A must lie within the double light cone. No event outside the light cone is causally connected with A. This suggests the possibility that there is some deep connection between causality and the structure of space-time, and even that the former may be used to explain some or all features of the latter.

In the last paragraph I have been using the words 'causality' and 'causally connected' in a fairly loose manner. The proposition that in special relativity causal influences lie only within light cones is almost trivial, in the sense that it is assumed that any causal influence is explained physically by a physics which conforms to the kinematics of special relativity. The proposition is saved from triviality by the tacit assumption that physics which conforms to relativity is the only physics that there is (or ought to be). This assumption has plenty of empirical evidence to support it.

If we know that an event C is the cause of an event E, then we know that there exists at least one light cone, such that C lies in its earlier half and E lies in its later half. It thus looks easy to define a relation of earlier and later in terms of that of cause and effect. This was the basis of Reichenbach's construction in his book *The Philosophy of Space and Time* (Reichenbach 1958). Reichenbach's construction runs up against certain difficulties, which have been pointed out by Henryk Mehlberg in his 'Essai sur la Théorie Causale du Temps' (Mehlberg 1935, 1937) and by Adolf Grünbaum (1963a, chapter VII). In the absence of a prior notion of earlier and later how can we distinguish cause from effect, especially in view of the time-symmetry of the laws of nature? (If we may neglect the recent discovery of a rather recondite violation of time-symmetry in physics, the 2π decay of the K_2° meson.) Reichenbach attempted to answer the objection by means of his so-called mark method, which is essentially an appeal to irreversible causal processes. This is objectionable, because it is desirable to separate the discussion of the topology of space-time from the question of the directionality of physical processes, since (as Reichenbach himself has argued) this directionality apparently depends on statistical considerations. I shall not reiterate the detailed objections to Reichenbach's mark method: these have been well made by Mehlberg and lucidly recapitulated by Grünbaum.

Grünbaum's version of the causal theory of time (like Mehlberg's) makes use of a symmetrical concept of causal connectedness ('k-connectedness'), instead of an asymmetrical concept of cause and effect. His construction therefore avoids the circularity which might arise from the fact that the concepts of cause and effect already presuppose those of earlier and later.

How do we deal with points of space-time which are not occupied by causes or effects? One way which probably will not do is to use for our construction not the concept of causal connectedness but the concept of causal connectibility. This is because of the modal nature of the concept of connectibility: the notion obviously depends on that of physical possibility, which in turn refers back to the laws of nature. If these laws of nature themselves presuppose the very structure of space-time which we are seeking to elucidate by means of the notion of causal connectibility we are clearly involved in a vicious circularity. Grünbaum therefore seems to be quite right in basing his construction on the notion of connectedness, not that of connectibility. The question about points of space-time which are not occupied by causes or effects can perhaps be answered from a deterministic point of view by saying that we need not consider such points: on a relational theory of space-time we need analyse only spatio-temporal statements which are about actual events. It is difficult, however, to see how to deal with points of space-time which are occupied by events which are neither effects nor causes of other events. Surely, even on a relational theory of space-time, such an event has to be located somehow (supposing that there are such events). Alternatively, we might, as Mehlberg (1935, pp. 163–4) does, take it that there will be events everywhere, for example the event of the gravitational field (or the electrical field) taking a certain value.

Let us concede, then, that causal connectedness, though not causal connectibility, will do the trick. Nevertheless my chief complaint against the causal theory of time still stands, because even the notion of causal connectedness would appear to be a disguisedly modal one, or at least an intensional one. Does it not, on the face of it, seem to be very odd to want to reduce a geometrical concept (and hence presumably one whose axiomatisation can be carried out in an extensional language) to a philosophically questionable (and probably at bottom intensional or modal) notion like that of causality? Surely space-time need be no less transparent to the intellect than is geometry. Is not geometry a respectable mathematical business, with no need of dubious metaphysical notions like that of causality? To this a proponent of the causal theory of time may reply that my objection neglects the difference between pure geometry and applied geometry, and it is the purpose of the causal theory of time to provide correspondence rules which tie down pure geometry (or perhaps at least its non-metrical part) to reality, thus converting it to a physical geometry.

An additional consideration might be put forward by a proponent of the causal theory of time. He might wonder why I should be squeamish about using causal connectedness as a primitive in a physical geometry. It might be said that the notion of causal connectedness is no more objectionably modal than is the operator 'it is a law of nature that . . .', and that it is necessary to retain this operator in the special theory of relativity, whose chief principle is the assertion that the laws of nature retain the same form under transformations from one set of inertial axes to another. However, I prefer to take the view that the principle of the invariance of the laws of nature under Lorentz transformations is a heuristic maxim for construction of the theory rather than an axiom of the theory itself. Alternatively it can be interpreted as a metatheoretical statement (a statement *about* the theory, not *of* the theory). Thus Maxwell's equations can easily be seen to be Lorentz invariant, and Lorentz invariance guided Einstein's search for the relativistic laws of mechanics which replace Newton's laws. Maxwell's equations and the relativistic laws of mechanics do not themselves contain the expression 'it is a law of nature that . . .' or any equivalent expression. It would indeed be odd if a physical theory could not be stated without the help of the apparently *metalinguistic* concept of 'law of nature'.

Similarly, one should hope that any physical theory can be formalized without strong conditionals or the notion of natural necessity. On the view which I should support, statements of natural necessity are disguised metalinguistic statements to the effect that certain truth-functional conditionals follow from fairly fundamental laws of nature. Trivially, then, we may say that any *fundamental* law of nature expresses a natural necessity because the law is of course deducible from itself. Even 'merely empirical' generalizations may sometimes be said to express a natural necessity in the sense that we hope or believe that they may one day be shown to follow from some suitable theory. Thus physical necessity is a metatheoretical notion, not a theoretical notion of physics.

As against this view of natural necessity it is sometimes contended that strong conditionals are essential to science, and are not disguised metalinguistic statements. Thus Newton's first law of motion (that if any body is not acted on by a force it moves with uniform velocity in a straight line) is probably no more than trivially true if it is interpreted in the sense of the weak conditional, because probably there are no bodies in the universe which are acted on by no force at all. The reply to this is that Newton's first law of motion is a dispensable luxury, because it is a special case of the second law, which is true in a non-trivial way. Moreover even if a law should be trivially true it is then at least *true*, and so it can do no harm to the theory. (No falsehood can be deduced from a truth.) It is true that Newton's first law does seem to occur in a non-trivial way in some presentations of special relativity. In Newtonian mechanics we can define an inertial system as one according to which the components of momenta of mutually attracting bodies balance out, but in special relativity this is not possible, because of the arbitrariness of simultaneity of spatially distant events. It might therefore be thought necessary to define an inertial system by reference to Newton's first law, expressed as a strong conditional. However, in principle this course can be avoided by defining an inertial system by reference to collision phenomena. In practice, of course, this method is too unwieldy: it would be too bad for humanity if in celestial mechanics collisions between the heavenly bodies occurred often enough for this purpose. And so in practice we will have to specify an inertial system by taking a Newtonian one as a first approximation. Nevertheless this method does not require an appeal to natural necessity or the use of strong conditionals.

My position, then, is that a physical theory should be based on a purely extensional language, and the predicates '. . . is necessary' and '. . . is necessary for . . .' should not occur in it. (For detailed support of this philosophical stance, let me refer to the work of Quine, especially his *Word and Object*, 1960.) Now if we look at Grünbaum's exposition of the causal theory of time, we find that he does make use of the concept of necessity. This is notwithstanding the fact that his theory is based on the notion of causal connectedness and not on the obviously modal notion of connectibility, which he rightly rejects. He recognizes, moreover, that causal connectedness can not be defined in terms of necessary and sufficient conditions for the occurrence of events, for reasons similar to those which are familiar from Nelson Goodman's work on subjunctive conditionals. (See Grünbaum's remarks on p. 609 of his paper 'Carnap on the Foundations of Geometry', pp. 545–684, and his reference to Goodman's *Fact, Fiction and Forecast*.) (I myself would be happy to elucidate causal connectedness metalinguistically, as suggested earlier in this article, but clearly what Grünbaum needs is an intratheoretic, not a metatheoretic, concept of causal connectedness.) Grünbaum therefore introduces the concept of causal connectedness as a *primitive*. So far (perhaps) so good. But he does need the concepts of 'necessary' and 'sufficient' in his definition of 'n-quadruplet'. This last notion is introduced for the purpose of defining the notions of betweeness and separation closure. Thus the quadruplet of events ELE′M is said by Grünbaum to be an n-quadruplet if and only if, 'given the actual occurrence of E and E′, it is necessary that either L or M occur in order that E and E′ be k-connected, L and M being genidentical with E and E′, . . .' (Grünbaum 1963a, p. 194).

Mehlberg (1935, p. 153) defines the notion of one event 'acting on' another in a more apparently extensional fashion. According to him, an event A acts immediately on an event B if for every event A' which is intrinsically similar to A there corresponds an event B' which has the same intrinsic properties as B and the event B' coincides partially with A'. Here the intensionality resides in the notion of one thing's being intrinsically similar to another and in the notion of an intrinsic property: this can be checked by consulting Mehlberg's definitions of these notions. It is also not clear to me that Mehlberg's definition of 'immediately acts on' avoid Goodman-like objections. However, I have to confess that my understanding of Mehlberg's complex theory of decompositions of events is as yet defective. It does seem to me, however, that his concept of an event is an implicitly intensional one. Let me now, however, pass on to discuss another type of objection to certain causal theories of time.

Following Reichenbach, who derived it from K. Lewin (Reichenbach 1958, p. 142, footnote), Grünbaum speaks of causal chains of events as 'genidetical'. He goes on to 'utilise the property of causal continuity possessed by genidentical causal chains' (Grünbaum 1963a, p. 194) and asserts that associated with any two genidentically related events there are certain classes of events which are genidentical with these first events, and that these classes have the cardinality of the continuum. It is not necessary here to go into the full details of Grünbaum's assertion, which is a little bit complicated because of his laudable desire to avoid prejudging the question of whether time is topologically open (like a Euclidean straight line) or closed (like a great circle on a sphere). However, one of the classes of events in question is the class of events which, in the case of the topological openness of time, could be said to be *between* the two originally given events.

Now it seems to me to be a defect in a theory of time that it should have to depend on the assumption of continuous classes of events. Certainly according to classical physics there will be a continuous set of genidentical events between any two genidentical events, but it is hard to make much sense of this in the context of quantum mechanics (unless a value of the ψ-function perhaps counts as an event).[1] In saying this I do *not* want to fall into the error, so well castigated by Grünbaum (1967, pp. 109–14), of supposing that quantum mechanics allows of a discrete space-time. Quantum mechanics uses continuous mathematics and a continuous geometry, like any classical theory. Indeed it is not at all clear what a physical geometry based on a discrete space-time would look like, especially in view of the well known incommensurability of certain geometrical ratios and in view of Zeno's paradox of the stadium. Fully allowing Grünbaum's point here, I wish only to query how the postulation of a continuous set of genidentical events would work out in the context of quantum theory. An obvious difficulty comes from the breakdown of causal connectedness in quantum mechanics. The difficulty shows itself in the absence of definite trajectories, which is evidence of an uncertainty as to just what is supposed to be the set of events which would make up a genidentical causal chain. Perhaps Grünbaum is offering the causal theory of time as a construction which works within the context of classical physics (as modified by special relativity). However, we may well doubt the utility of a construction which works only for classical physics.

The general theory of relativity also would seem to make big trouble for the causal theory of time. This is because the causal theory of time is a form of the relational theory of time: it defines betweeness relations (or separation closure relations) only for quadruplets of actual events. However, the question of whether or not a relational theory of time will work for general relativity boils down to the question of whether relativistic cosmologies can accommodate Mach's principle, and this is a rather open question. (Grünbaum has indeed himself argued to this effect (1963a, chapter XIV).) The above objection is probably not valid against Mehlberg's version of the causal theory of time, because for him there are events everywhere, though it is hard to see how he could accept the complete geometrisation of the gravitational field and the theoretical possibility (in some cosmologies) of a universe devoid of matter and yet with a certain space-time structure. In fact Mehlberg has conceded this sort of point in a later paper, in which he rejects the causal theory of time (see Mehlberg 1966, especially pp. 484–6).

As we remarked earlier, modern attempts at a causal theory of time derive their inspiration from special relativity, which rejects action at a distance and implies that all causal influences (all world lines, all signals)

lie within light cones. This implication is, however, extratheoretical
rather than intratheoretical. If it is not a heuristic maxim it is a theorem
in the metalanguage of physics. It is instructive to consider two space-
time objects, $B'AB$ and $C'AC$, as in figure 5.1, such that the former lies
entirely within the light cone whose vortex is A and the latter lies (except
for the point A) entirely outside the light cone. Clearly we should allow
$B'AB$ to determine a world line, whereas we must not regard $C'AC$ as
lying along a world line but must interpret it as a brief but widely
occurring disturbance. The structure of classical physics is such that a
sufficiently detailed knowledge of a sufficiently large 'time slice' through
B' (say $P'B'P$) would enable an infinite intelligence to deduce the event
B, whereas no amount of knowledge of however large a 'space slice'
through C', such as $Q'C'Q$ in the figure would enable the event C to be
deduced. This is what the causal grain of the world, as determined by
world lines, comes to. These are the insights which give rise to the causal
theory of time and they can be preserved, in the present *metatheoretical*
form, by a physics which postulates space-time independently of the
notion of causal connectedness.[2]

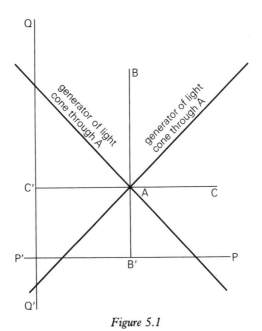

Figure 5.1

The insights which give rise to a causal theory of time can then be
preserved by a philosophy of science which simply postulates a structure
of space-time, and then together with the associated physics and its

metatheory deduces causal relations between events in the world. In postulating that events are related as in accordance with such and such a geometry we can even keep the options open as between a relational and an absolute interpretation of this geometry. In the case of an absolute theory of space-time the spatio-temporal relations will directly relate not events but space-time points, which will have the status of theoretical entities of physics. In the case of a relational theory the spatio-temporal relations will relate events in the world directly. The primitives of such a geometry might perhaps be those of conical order, as in the theory of A.A. Robb (1914), and would not involve the notion of causal connectedness.

In this way, instead of 'constructing' the (non-metrical) structure of space-time from a relation of causal connectedness we deduce relations of causal connectedness and non-connectedness from the theory (including the associated physics and its metatheory). We can also deduce spatio-temporal relations from relations of causal connectedness or non-connectedness. In view of the preceding remarks this might look like the fallacy of affirming the consequent. This is not so, however. We deduce that if E and E' are causally connected then one of them lies within the light cone of the other by transposition of the proposition (which may be deduced from the theory plus its metatheory) that if one of E and E' does *not* lie within the light cone of the other then they are *not* causally connected. In this way, though spatio-temporal relations are logically prior to causal ones, we can indeed deduce certain spatio-temporal relations from certain causal ones. This, once more, is the grain of truth in a causal theory of time.

To conclude, then, my main qualms about the causal theory of time are as follows:

1　To elucidate the concept of space-time in terms of the concept of causal connectedness seems to be to elucidate the comparatively clear by reference to the comparatively unclear.

2　Even if causal connectedness is itself taken as a primitive, causal theories of time seem to need modal or intensional concepts somewhere or other.

3　It is difficult to see how the causal theory of time is applicable to theories which allow for the existence of events which are neither causes nor effects of other events.

It at least *seems* to me that I can consistently envisage a universe of purely random events spread out through space-time. The objection that only if such events were causes or effects of other events could they in fact be located ought, I think, to be dismissed as too verificationist. On p. 88 of his 'Reply to Hilary Putnam' Grünbaum (1968) remarks that 'spatially separated events can sustain physical relations of one kind or another only because of the presence or the absence of their actual or at least physically possible connectibility'. It seems to me that if 'physical relations' here means 'causal relations' Grünbaum's assertion is doubtful, or at least dependent on certain philosophical assumptions. It can not be used as a premiss with which to refute someone who does not accept a causal theory, because such a person could say that some physical relations (namely spatio-temporal ones) could exist even in the absence of causal connectibility. Finally, I do not think that I have conclusively *disproved* any causal theories of time. I would claim only to have expressed certain qualms about causal theories of time and doubts about the motivation for such theories. For example I have by no means adequately discussed Mehlberg's stimulating and detailed treatment of the subject. It is quite possible that the qualms I feel about causal theories of time are due more to defects in my own thinking than to defects in the theories. Even so, since I suspect that others may be liable to feel similar qualms, I hope that it has been of some value to have ventilated the matter, however unsatisfactorily.[3]

NOTES

1 A difficulty here is that the ψ-function relates to points of a many-dimensioned Hilbert space, whose coordinates are given by complex numbers, and not to our ordinary space-time.

2 Of course we could not deduce. Presumably God could. I now prefer a model-theoretic account in terms of logical and set theoretic consequence. This semantic (as opposed to syntactic) approach gets round obvious difficulties, including the one that in order to determine the state $P'B'P$ we would have to disturb it.

3 See also a paper by Hugh M. Lacey (1968) which appeared since the present one was originally submitted for publication.

REFERENCES

Goodman, Nelson 1955: *Fact, Fiction and Forecast*. Cambridge, Massachusetts: Harvard University Press.

Grünbaum, Adolf 1963a: *Philosophical Problems of Space and Time*. New York: Knopf.

—— 1963b: Carnap on the Foundations of Geometry. In P.A. Schilpp (ed.), *The Philosophy of Rudolf Carnap*, La Salle, Illinois: Open Court.

—— 1967: *Modern Science and Zeno's Paradoxes*. Middletown: Wesleyan University Press.

—— 1968: Reply to Hilary Putnam. In R.S. Cohen and M.W. Wartofsky (eds),

Boston Studies in the Philosophy of Science, vol. 5, Dordrecht, Holland: D. Reidel.

Lacey, Hugh M. 1968: The Causal Theory of Time, A Critique of Grünbaum's Version. *Philosophy of Science*, 35, 332–54.

Mehlberg, Henryk 1935: Essai sur la Théorie Causale du Temps, part 1. *Studia Philosophica*, 1, 119–258.

—— 1937: Essai sur la Théorie Causale du Temps, part 2. *Studia Philosophica*, 2, 111–231.

—— 1966: Relativity and the Atom. In Paul Feyeraband and Grover Maxwell (eds), *Mind, Matter and Method, Essays in Philosophy and Science in Honor of Herbert Feigl*, Minneapolis: University of Minnesota Press.

Quine, W.V. 1960: *Word and Object*. Cambridge, Massachusetts: MIT Press.

Reichenbach, Hans 1958: *The Philosophy of Space and Time*. New York: Dover. Originally published in German in 1928 under the title *Philosophie der Raum-Zeit-Lehre*.

Robb, A.A. 1914: *A Theory of Time and Space*. Cambridge: Cambridge University Press.

6

Space-Time and Individuals

Since Minkowski it has been customary to think of the physical world as a four-dimensional space-time manifold. When we think in this way, the Lorentz transformations of special relativity are seen to be merely a matter of rotation of axes in space-time: the space-time manifold is itself independent of our particular space-time axes (or spatial and temporal frames of reference). The four-dimensional way of thinking was of course available prior to the special theory of relativity, and it is possible that as metaphysicians we ought to have regarded it as a good thing even then. However, the non-invariance in special relativity of lengths and periods of time, as well as of many dynamical quantities, seems to make the four-dimensional point of view more imperative. It is the purpose of this paper to defend the four-dimensional picture of the world as (in the present state of knowledge) giving us the best clue to the metaphysical truth.[1]

The ordinary, or common sense, or, as I shall call it for convenience, the 'Strawsono-Aristotelian' or 'SA', view of the world differs from the four-dimensional 'Minkowskian' view in that a physical object, such as an orange, is a *three*-dimensional thing that *endures* through time. However, this enduring through time is not thought of as implying that the thing has a temporal dimension. To be *at* a time is to have a certain temporal *property*, just as being red is to have a certain colour quality. The orange does not extend through time: it is the *whole* orange, not just a temporal 'slice' of the orange, that is at a given time. Again, according to the SA scheme, the *whole* orange can be spherical at one time and ellipsoidal at another time, and can move from one place to another. An SA object thus does not have purely three-dimensional properties such as being spherical or ellipsoidal: it has more complex properties, such as being *spherical at such and such a time*. (For if it had the simpler properties, it would have incompatible ones, such as being both spherical and ellipsoidal.) On the Minkowskian view objects (such as temporal parts or 'time-slices' of oranges) can have the simpler properties, such as being spherical. Considerations of this sort can lead one to view the SA picture, with its resolute desire not to treat objects as temporally extended, as a theoretically awkward one. Our common-sense conceptual scheme, viewed from a Minkowskian vantage point, can seem to be a rather odd one.

Other philosophers, however, obviously feel very differently. For them it is the four-dimensional world view that is the odd one. Thus in his introduction to his collection of British Academy lectures, P.F. Strawson refers to the four-dimensional way of thinking as 'fanciful philosophical theorizing', though it claims 'to derive respectability from physics' (Strawson 1968, p. 5).

Perhaps neither way of talking is 'fanciful': perhaps the two ways are inter-translatable. Thus when the Strawsono-Aristotelian might say that the orange changed at about midday from being spherical to being ellipsoidal, the Minkowskian could say that time-slices of the orange$_4$ before about midday are (tenselessly) spherical and time-slices of the orange$_4$ after about midday are (tenselessly) ellipsoidal. I have put a subscript '4' below the word 'orange' in the latter part of the sentence to show that the word 'orange' in Minkowskian is not quite the same as the word 'orange' in SA terminology. In fact it would seem that 'orange' cannot to be defined in terms of 'orange$_4$', though complete SA sentences containing 'orange' are perhaps inter-translatable with complete Minkowskian sentences containing 'orange$_4$'. For example oranges are correctly said to move or to be at rest, whereas it is nonsense to talk of four-dimensional space-time objects as moving or as at rest. When in SA language we say that the two oranges are at rest with respect to one another, in Minkowskian we say that two oranges$_4$ are parallel to one another (lie along parallel world lines). Similarly, to say that one orange is moving relatively to another is equivalent to saying, in Minkowskian, that appropriate segments of their world lines are inclined to one another. In this paper I shall sometimes put the subscript '4' under words that take on a 'four-dimensional' sense in the way that 'orange' does, so as to avoid objections such as that oranges are the sorts of things that can be at a point of time, as a whole, and so are not four-dimensional solids. On other occasions, when it seems too inelegant to put them in, I shall leave the reader to imagine the subscripts when he feels the need.

One is tempted, then, to ask what is the relationship between the SA orange and the Minkowskian orange$_4$. However, this would be very misleading. Someone who, like myself, is inclined to believe physics in a realist way, would be inclined to see the world in terms of Minkowskian objects, and to deny the existence of the SA ones. Now even though sentences ostensibly about SA objects could be mapped on to sentences ostensibly about Minkowskian objects, we do not need to acquiesce in an ontology that contains *both* sorts of objects. From the Minkowskian perspective, SA objects are like the virtual classes of chapter 1 of W.V. Quine's *Set Theory and its Logic* (1963), at least in so far as talk ostensibly of SA objects can be translated away in terms of talk about the Minkowskian ones. (Compare the way in which sentences ostensibly about virtual classes can be translated into sentences containing predicates instead of class expressions.)

From the SA perspective, of course, it may go the other way: it will be the Minkowskian sentences that are like the sentences ostensibly about virtual classes. However, to take this line would seem to be to reject the explanatory power that comes from taking Minkowski's interpretation of special relativity in a *realist* way. From the point of view of a realist philosophy of science, we must surely agree with Minkowski that 'henceforth space by itself and time by itself, are doomed to fade away into mere shadows, and only a kind of union of the two will preserve an independent reality' (Minkowski 1924, p. 75). The only way to avoid this would be to have a merely *instrumentalist* interpretation of special relativity, much in the spirit of Einstein's pre-Minkowski paper 'On the Electrodynamics of Moving Bodies', which was rather operationist in tone, and was written at a time when (as he indicated in his autobiography) Einstein was much influenced by Hume and Mach (Schilpp 1959, p. 53). It is no part of my intention in the present paper to go into the defence of scientific realism against operationism or instrumentalism, and the correctness of a *realist* interpretation of special relativity must be taken as a presupposition of my general argument. However, I wish to point out one difficulty that special relativity seems to pose for the SA conceptual scheme, and that perhaps applies even when this is allied to instrumentalism.

We have noted that an SA object is not (say) spherical *tout court*, but is spherical *at a time*. Thus the SA scheme is tied to the notion of a present instant at which the whole SA object possesses certain properties. Since the advent of special relativity, however, it has become clear that there is no absolute simultaneity. Two parts of an extensive SA object might, for example, simultaneously have the same colour with respect to one set of axes and have different colours with respect to a different set of axes. (Looking at the matter Minkowski-wise, points A and B in figure 6.1 on a space-time object might be simultaneous with respect to one set of axes, and A and C might be simultaneous with respect to another set of axes. Let A be red, B red, C green.)

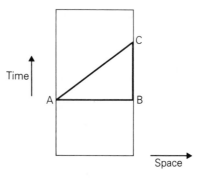

Figure 6.1

So with respect to what axes must the Strawsono-Aristotelian think of an object as being 'all at once'? A natural answer might be: a set of axes with respect to which the object is at rest. This would appear at first sight to remove ambiguity. However, what about an extensive Strawsono-Aristotelian object rotating rapidly on its axis? And what about a complex of SA objects all moving at different velocities relative to one another?

Well, then, to echo Strawson's disparaging comment, what is 'fanciful' about the metaphysics of the physical world as a four-dimensional manifold? Let us see what arguments can be put on the other side, and in particular, let us look at the arguments of P.T. Geach (1968) in a paper alluded to by Strawson, and which are directed against the view of the world as a four-dimensional manifold.

'Some of the arguments used in its favour are distinctly odd', says Geach. Well, maybe they are, but so long as *some* arguments are good we do not need to worry about rejecting the bad ones. Thus I would agree with Geach that the mere fact that 'we can represent local motion in a graph with axes representing space and time' (Geach 1968, p. 176) does not prove anything much. But Minkowski does not use this weak argument, and I do not wish to use it either. It is true that in popular exposition Minkowski says, 'We will try to visualize the state of things by the graphic method. . . . With this most valiant piece of chalk I might project upon the blackboard four world axes . . .' (Minkowski 1924, p. 76) and so on. But his *argument* is not the analogy with graphs. His argument is that only space-time entities are invariant and their laws covariant: one cannot get invariance or covariance by taking space and time separately. And it is sensible to take invariance and covariance as a touchstone of reality (see Born 1953).

Another argument, which Geach says is 'odd', is Quine's, from an apparent consilience between quantificational logic and space-time physics. I would agree with Geach that Quine goes too far when he says that 'the four-dimensional view of space-time is part and parcel of the use of modern formal logic' (Quine 1966, p. 145), since, as Geach points out, Quine elsewhere shows how quantification theory can be applied to the analysis of arguments in ordinary language, and even (if due caution is exercised) to some of those arguments that contain tenses and other indicator or egocentric expressions. Nevertheless, it is very natural to see a consilience between quantification theory, with its tenseless 'is' in 'there is a . . .' or '∃x' on the one hand, and Minkowski-type physics on the other hand.

Of course besides the 'modern logic' mentioned by Quine, there have recently arisen systems of 'tense-logic'. In accordance with these, I suppose that the friends of tenses might use a tensed 'is' of quantification, which of course would not be the present tense but would be the universal tense 'was, is or will be' (or else, as Prior does, they might use 'there is a' in a present tensed way, and then introduce the notion 'it was, is, or will be the case that there is a . . .'). However, this seems to me to be an unnatural way of going on. This is partly because I see no reason why temporal matters should be imported into logic. To turn one of Geach's arguments against Quine against Geach himself, could we not conceive of a physics of the future in which not only space and time but also space-time was shown to be one of the myths of primitive twentieth-century science and metaphysics? And might not *logic* still survive? Moreover, logic has most importantly been used to formalize such subjects as number theory and set theory, in which a tenseless idiom seems appropriate. Hence those who wish logic to be applicable to *all* subject-matters, whether temporal or atemporal, will not wish for temporality to be imported into the very structure of logic. The reason why tense logicians wish to import time into logic seems to be that they correctly see the connection between logic and the concept of truth, and they also espouse the ancient and mediaeval notion of a proposition as something whose truth-value can vary with time. However, this argument can be reversed. We can argue from the inappropriateness of of bringing a special subject matter like time into logic to the necessity to reject this ancient concept of a proposition and of truth.[2] What is needed to avoid this ancient philosophy of logic is to recognize tenses as token-reflexive or egocentric expressions.[3]

We do not need to claim that the tensed interpretation of the quantifier is actually incompatible with special relativity, though tense logic does need modification to take account of it. (A.N. Prior has mentioned postulates for relativistic tense logic due to N.B. Cocchiarella.)[4] But the simplest course in formalizing the Minkowski theory would seem to be to avail oneself of ordinary quantification theory in which the 'there is a . . .' is tenseless. But be this as it may, we do not have to depend on the argument that the four-dimensional world view is forced upon us by modern logic: the best reasons for accepting it are reasons of physics.

Geach proceeds to attack another view which he alleges is part of the Minkowski way of thinking. He attributes to the Minkowskian the view (a) that change is an illusion and (b) that it is a changing illusion. Hence he has no difficulty in convicting his opponent of contradiction. Now the Minkowskian *can* accommodate the facts of change. Thus when the Strawsono-Aristotelian may say 'the orange changes from spherical to ellipsoidal', the Minkowskian can say: 'an earlier time-slice of the orange$_4$ is round and a later time-slice of the orange$_4$ is ellipsoidal'. The Minkowskian is *not* asserting the existence of a 'static world': he would have to say, of what the Strawsono-Aristotelian would call 'a static world', that all time-slices of it were exactly similar. Consider another form of change, namely what the Strawsono-Aristotelian would call the 'propagation' of a signal from place P at time t to place P' at time t'. (Remember that the four-dimensional counterpart of an SA place is not the neighbourhood of a point but of a line.) The Minkowskian would describe this 'propagation' in different terms, namely as the *lying* of a four-dimensional object (whether a photon or a message stick$_4$) along the world line joining (P, t) to (P', t'). (In the case of the photon we have the curious fact that the space-time interval between (P, t) and (P', t') is zero.) The signal is not *propagated through* space-time since motion through space-time would have to be with respect to a hyper-time. The signal *is* (tenselessly) along a line in space-time. It is true that many books and articles use the misleading term 'propagate' even in a four-dimensional context. However, such locutions can nearly always be rendered harmless by appropriate mental adjustments on the part of a clear-headed reader, such as by interpreting 'propagated from . . . to . . .' in the four-dimensional context as meaning no more than 'lying between . . . and. . .'. What is *not* so good is when advocates of the Minkowski world mix in dualistic metaphysics, illegitimate notions of time travel and of 'consciousness crawling up world lines'. Consider the remark by H. Weyl: 'We travel along the world line of our body with "screened off consciousness"' (Weyl 1949, p. 194). But no such bad metaphysics should be foisted onto other philosophers who wish to defend the space-time world picture. All Weyl needed to say was the aseptic remark that any perceptual awareness or memory (which I myself would identify with a space-time chunk of a brain$_4$) is an awareness of earlier space-time entities. If one thinks consistently in the four-dimensional manner one comes to *reject* loose talk of movement of consciousness or of time travel of consciousness. Now most people do seem to be subject to the metaphysical illusion of an absurdity (flow of time, advance through time), perhaps because of a misunderstanding of egocentricity, token-reflexiveness, tenses, etc. However, the description of this absurdity need not itself be done absurdly: the illusion of the septic sort of change may involve change, but this need only be aseptic change, i.e. the sort of change that can be described four-dimensionally in terms of non-similarities of time-slices of the brain of the metaphysician who has the illusion of time flow.[5]

Geach seems to me to be even more unfair when he suggests that the four-dimensional view implies fatalism. He refers to one of John Buchan's novels, in which the characters 'get a glimpse of the future, with no power to change it'. If fatalism is the view that we cannot change the future, then it seems to be either trivial or absurd (according as to whether we interpret 'we change the future' as contradictory or nonsensical). Suppose that I decide to do *A* rather than *B*. Then *whatever* our metaphysics, whether SA or Minkowskian, we ought to agree that *A* was our future. Our future was *never B*, because *A* was what we eventually did. To talk of changing the future is as silly as to talk of changing the past. But *ordinarily* fatalism is the view that what we do does not have any causal effect on what happens. This view is obviously false, and is so just as much from a Minkowskian perspective as from an SA one. Causal rules can relate space-time chunks to one another just as well as they can relate SA events. The fatalistic soldier believes that he will be killed, or not killed, no matter what he does. His view is false, because if he does pop his head out of a slit trench and gets his head shot off, his death *is* caused by his action of popping his head out. In space-time language, his world line and that of the bullet intersect, whereas if his world line were to coincide a bit longer with that of the deep interior of the slit trench it would be a longer one thereafter![6]

Geach, as might be expected in so subtle a philosophical logician, is more interesting when he goes on to attack the Minkowskian way of talking as involving 'an erroneous analysis of propositions into subject and predicate' (Geach 1968, p. 182). Geach proposes to analyse 'while' not as a temporal predicate but as a sentential connective. He considers some examples such as 'McTaggart in 1901 was a philosopher holding Hegel's dialectic to be valid, and McTaggart in 1921 was a philosopher not holding Hegel's dialectic to be valid' (Geach 1968, p. 183). He then goes on to say that if we regard 'McTaggart in 1901' and 'McTaggart in 1921' as designating two individuals, 'then we must say that they designate two philosophers: one philosopher believing Hegel's dialectic to be valid, and another philosopher believing Hegel's dialectic not to be valid'. I do not agree that the Minkowskian need talk like this. Surely the most natural way to interpret 'philosopher' four-dimensionally is as the whole four-dimensional individual from birth to death, and then McTaggart in 1901 and McTaggart in 1921 would not be two different philosophers but two different temporal parts of one philosopher$_4$ (philosopher stages, in Quine's terminology; Quine 1960, p. 51). Then we can say that 'believing Hegel's dialectic to be valid' and 'believing Hegel's dialectic not to be valid' could be construed as dispositional predicates applicable to different temporal parts of McTaggart, just as 'magnetized' and 'unmagnetized' can be construed four-dimensionally as dispositional predicates applicable to different temporal parts (iron bar stages) of the same iron bar. Of course Geach's example is 'a philosopher believing that Hegel's dialectic is valid', and as Geach says, only a philosopher, not a temporal slice of a philosopher can be a philosopher believing that Hegel's dialectic is valid. But, despite Geach's refusal to allow us to amend the predicates (perhaps to 'is a temporal stage of a philosopher believing that . . .'), I do not myself see why we should not take such a liberty. Geach says, 'The whole ground for treating, for example, "McTaggart in 1901" and "McTaggart in 1921" as designating two different individuals was that we seemed to find predicates true of the one and false of the other'. This reason seems to be unconvincing, because a sensible Minkowskian will claim that he or she has grounds which are quite other than those mentioned by Geach, namely consilience with the space-time world of special relativity, and besides that, a metaphysically neat picture, epitomized perhaps in Nelson Goodman's (1966, pp. 46–61) calculus of individuals.

I might mention yet another way which is open to the Minkowskian when construing the proposition about McTaggart. Instead of taking 'McTaggart in 1901' and 'McTaggart in 1921' as designating two individuals, let us have two predicates 'believes in 1901 . . .' and 'believes in 1921 . . .' applicable to the one four-dimensional individual McTaggart. (To believe in 1901 is of course to have a certain dispositional state of its 'around 1901' part.) Indeed ultimately *all* distinctions should be made by means of predicates, if we have a Quinean language that has *no* designating expressions, but only variables, quantifiers and predicates. We can agree with Geach that temporal predicates which contain mention of dates are dispensable. (Geach considers the example of people on a cloud-bound planet who are not able to keep dates or tell the time.) What is in question is merely the *topology* of space-time, and thereby some (perhaps wholly non-metrical) notion of earlier and later.

According to Geach, the statement that one event is simultaneous with another is not to be analysed as saying that the two events are at the same time as another. For, he argues, we could not introduce ways of telling the time unless we already had a concept of simultaneity. 'A physicist', says Geach, 'may protest that he simply cannot understand "at the same time" except via elaborate stipulations about observing instruments', and Geach continues, 'his protest may be dismissed out of hand, for he could not describe the apparatus, except by certain conditions' having to be fulfilled *together*, i.e. simultaneously, by the parts of the apparatus' (Geach 1968, p. 185). Geach holds that the basic notion of simultaneity is that of 'while', which is a sentential connective, not a relation word. The study of 'while', he argues, belongs to *logic*, and a physicist who casts doubt upon such a notion is sawing off the branch upon which he is sitting.

But this branch sawing is going on all the time in science, and scientists are very adroit in not sitting on the branch just when it is sawn. They sit on a higher branch. Thus from the vantage point of special relativity we can see that, strictly speaking, no two spatially separated events are simultaneous with one another independently of a frame of reference, though our ordinary common sense notion of simultaneity is workable, within the limits of observational error, when either distances or relative velocities are fairly small, for example in the observation of laboratory instruments.

The Minkowskian would wish to disentangle a temporal function of the word 'while' from a conjunctive function of the word. He would say not, for example, 'he runs while I walk' but 'he runs and I walk and his running is simultaneous with my walking'. Here the conjunctive function of 'while' is taken over by the first 'and', and the simultaneity asserting function is taken over by 'is simultaneous with'. 'His running' could be taken here as referring to a certain running stage of the four-dimensional he$_4$ and 'my walking' could be taken as referring to a certain walking stage of the four-dimensional me$_4$. That is, we replace talk of SA *processes* by talk of four-dimensional chunks of things, and let 'is running' be a predicate applicable to just those four-dimensional chunks that are the four-dimensional equivalents of the things in process (people running).

Geach, of course, will have none of this, because he holds that 'we need to get events expressed in a propositional style, rather than by using name-like phrases'. He suggests therefore, that we should say 'Wellington fought Napoleon after George III first went mad', and not 'George III's first attack of madness is earlier than the battle of Waterloo'. This is indeed an interesting suggestion, but I see no reason for the Minkowskian to accept it: indeed the Minkowskian had better *not* accept it, or Geach is very likely to have him properly on the hook. The Minkowskian must use something like Goodman's calculus of individuals, in which simultaneity, or being earlier or later than (if necessary with respect to some frame of reference), relates four-dimensional entities. Thus to say that my army service is earlier than my career as a teacher of philosophy is to say that the army serving chunk of me is earlier than the philosophy teaching chunk of me. I see no difficulty in adapting my talk in this sort of way, even though it may be at some cost to literary elegance. I suggest that talk of processes gets replaced by talk of four-dimensional chunks, and that talk of events gets replaced by talk of boundaries between different temporal chunks: thus the event of my demobilization is four-dimensionally to be thought of as a boundary between an army serving chunk of me and a later non-military chunk of me. Some events may be vaguely defined borders, of course. Thus the event that is my becoming grey haired is the rather vaguely defined boundary between a (now far distant) dark haired chunk of me and a later grey haired chunk of me. There is no more difficulty about vaguely defined temporal boundaries then there is about vaguely defined spatial boundaries, such as the boundary between arid and non-arid regions of a country. Also there is in special relativity a sense of 'event' in which an event is more like a point than a boundary, as when we talk of the space-time *interval* between two events. Here 'event' could be construed as an arbitrarily small four-dimensional part of a thing, much as in Newtonian mechanics a particle is an arbitrarily small bit of a three-dimensional thing.

Being a materialist, I hold that all processes, even, for example processes of thought, are four-dimensional, and that all events, even, for example, acts of thought, are boundaries between four-dimensional chunks, or perhaps, alternatively, are arbitrarily small four-dimensional chunks. But dualists can readily adapt this for their own purposes, and construe processes of thought as *one*-dimensional segments and acts of thought as boundaries between these one-dimensional segments.

Clearly, then, if 'earlier than', etc., are predicates relating space-time entities, these cannot relate events in the sense in which an event expression, as Geach puts it, 'goes proxy for a clause'. I do not deny that Geach is right in saying that in ordinary language there is such a sense of 'event': for example he points out that in 1918 we might assert or deny or doubt the Kaiser's death, *i.e. that* the Kaiser is dead.

Geach concludes his paper with some more peripheral matters, which I shall not discuss. I have suggested that we regard a process four-dimensionally as a space-time individual (usually part of a larger, more extensive individual, of course). I am here using 'individual' in the sense of Goodman, not of Strawson. Thus consider the following very simple example. A rubber ball is bouncing on an elastic floor. Looked at four-dimensionally, the process is as in figure 6.2. Looked at four-dimensionally, again, a brain process might be thought of as a vast cat's cradle of world lines ('world lines' meaning here not geometrical lines

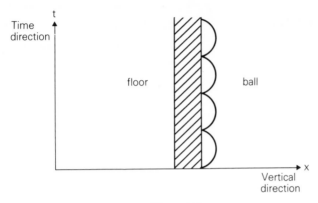

Figure 6.2

but the thin four-dimensional wormlike solids which are particles). Here I am permitting myself to think classically: the quantum mechanical picture would of course be less picturable. Since quantum mechanics has to be Lorentz invariant, it also supports the Minkowski point of view, unless perhaps the difficulties of giving a realist interpretation of quantum mechanics lead us to espouse an instrumentalist philosophy.

We cannot, of course, expect brain physiologists, for example, to talk in terms of Minkowski space-time. They talk in the language and with the grammar that comes naturally to them, which they have learned as children. There is no reason why scientists and philosophers should not follow Berkeley, and frequently 'think with the learned, and speak with the vulgar' (Berkeley 1710, section 51). Let me take some sentences from books on brain physiology and the like.

1 'There are neurons at all depths within the cortex that give rise to axons leaving the cortex' (Sholl 1956, p. 59). This requires practically no translation at all. Minkowski-wise we must of course think of the axons not as approximately lines in three-dimensional space but as planes in four-dimensional space. 'Give rise to' has to be interpreted in a tenseless and non-causal manner, but this is no problem.
2 'The ten-per-second cycle of the alpha rhythm . . . ceases when the subject opens his eyes' (Sholl 1956, p. 94). Something like this might do: 'Shut eye stages of a person have ten alpha rhythm peaks per second and open eye stages have no alpha rhythm peaks'.
3 'The surface membrane of muscle fibres is certainly permeable to chloride ions' (Katz 1955, p. 239). Here the translation is

again very easy: 'Chloride ions sometimes *intersect* surface membranes of muscle fibres', where the chloride ions and the surface membranes are four-dimensional solids.

Problems in physics are commonly stated in SA terminology, even when the solution is worked out Minkowski-wise. Consider this problem, from a text book:

> An excited atom, of total mass m, is at rest in a given frame. It emits a photon and thereby loses internal energy ΔE. Calculate the exact frequency of the photon, making due allowance for the recoil of the atom.
>
> (Rindler 1960, p. 108)

We might say, pedantically in Minkowskian language, something like the following:

AB is an early atom stage, every time-slice of which has mass m and it lies parallel to the Ot axis of a given frame. BC is a later time-slice of the atom stage. The difference between the internal energy of a time-slice of AB and that of a time-slice of BC *is* ΔE. BP is a photon stage, connected to AB at B, so that angle $ABP = 1\frac{1}{2}$ right angles. (I here assume the unit of time to be such that the velocity of light is equal to unity.) Calculate the frequency of the photon stage, making due allowances for the fact that angle PBC is slightly greater than half a right angle

The advantages of 'talking with the vulgar' are obvious, but these cut no metaphysical ice: a sufficiently pedantic philosopher can translate into Minkowskian if he wants to. To take another example, we sometimes find problems in relativity theory about rotating fly wheels. According to the Minkowskian, a rotating fly wheel is a helical sheaf of particles.

I think that the problem of replacing SA talk in the biological sciences by Minkowskian language is often very difficult and awkward, leading to artificial constructions. But equally, it would hardly be possible to calculate the nautical almanac using the general theory of relativity. It is known, however, that Newtonian mechanics provides a pragmatically more convenient and sufficiently accurate approximation in most cases (the perihelion of Mercury aside). But no one who accepted general relativity (and here I am not of course wishing necessarily to imply that it *should* be accepted since general relativity is so much less well tested than is special relativity) would regard the pragmatic convenience of Newtonian methods as in any way impugning the superior *metaphysical* truth of general relativity. (The contrast between truth and pragmatic convenience is one that has been stressed by Paul Feyerabend in many of his writings.)

Perhaps it is going too far to say that the SA conceptual scheme is essentially *false*. A lot depends on how much we import into it. If the conceptual scheme implies that there are events that are absolutely simultaneous with one another, then it does imply a falsehood. As I indicated earlier, I suspect that the reason why the SA scheme might have to be rejected is its apparent reliance on a notion of absolute simultaneity, when it is implied that even an extensive object can be given to us 'all at once' at a moment of time. According to special relativity, only events at the same point of space can be absolutely simultaneous. However, let us suppose that an austere SA language might be all right, because translatable into Minkowskian. Thus, 'this orange will become more elliptical' translates into 'later time-slices of the orange$_4$ are (tenseless) more elliptical than earlier ones, some of which are (tenseless) later than this utterance'. Even if the translations can always be carried out, we may still be inclined to think of the SA scheme as metaphysically false. Compare the way in which statements ostensibly about 'virtual classes', but Platonistically construed, would be regarded as false by a nominalist, even though he would agree that statements about virtual classes could be mapped on to statements employing only quantifiers, variables, predicates, and truth functional operators. Again, let us suppose that many statements ostensibly about witches could be 'translated' into statements about schizophrenia. Truth of the latter would not, in a sense, confer truth on the former. We might ask what is the relation between a witch and a schizophrenic. In a sense, there is no relation, because there are no witches. In another sense, it is of course identity: that is, the very same objective situation that *causes* a believer in witches to say 'that's a witch' may be what causes a believer in schizophrenia to say 'that's a schizophrenic'. (Here it will be obvious to many readers how much I have been influenced by some of Paul Feyerabend's writings.) Similarly, an SA object *A* may be the same as a four-dimensional Minkowskian object *B* in the sense that the very same objective situation that causes a Strawsono-Aristotelian to report the existence of an *A* may cause the Minkowskian to report the existence of a *B*. This is without prejudice to the metaphysical questions of whether *A*s, or *B*s, or both, or neither, really exist.

It may well be that the ordinary conceptual scheme of the permanent-in-change, which partitions reality into space and time separately, a space that somehow *endures* through time, is *in practice* inescapable to us. Evolution by natural selection can well have programmed our brains so that we have an innate tendency to perceive the world in this way. After all, it is the *local present* that is of paramount importance to an animal that is about to leap on to its prey, and the brains of animals are very largely computers to organize leaping on to prey and plucking of fruits, and so on. That is, they have evolved as decision-making devices, not as organs of scientific contemplation. No wonder the (local) present seems in the forefront of consciousness, since (almost by definition) it is the local present that is involved in decision and action. (One might ask whether brains might not have evolved rather differently, however, if we had been animals moving with near-light velocities, and perhaps signalling to one another in practically important ways.) So *perhaps* scientists will always, in their laboratories, have to talk in terms of the common sense conceptual scheme (or 'the manifest image' of Wilfrid Sellars 1963, chapter 1) even though what they say has also (by a sort of double vision) to be thought of four-dimensionally (in what Sellars calls 'the scientific image'). I do not know whether this view that the manifest image is inescapable is true or not, but even if it is true, it is compatible with the *metaphysical* correctness of the four-dimensional view. It is quite possible that we have been programmed by natural selection to a false but useful way of perceiving the world, and that it is only in our studies, when we read Minkowski, and so on, that we can overcome this sort of original sin. The example of Newtonian mechanics and the nautical almanac shows that truth and pragmatic value need not go together, and it is pragmatic value for which natural selection selects. Alternatively, it is possible that one day, even in their homes and laboratories, scientists will not only think but also talk Minkowski-wise, and say such things as 'at (x, y, z, t) approximately a time-slice of John Smith perceives (tenseless) a time-slice of Mary Jones'. It depends on which hypothesis is true: the Sellarsian hypothesis that (roughly speaking) we have been programmed with original sin, or the Feyerabendian one that we have merely been indoctrinated into error by nannies, Oxford philosophers, and the like. (See my remarks in my paper 'Conflicting Views about Explanation', 1965, especially pp. 168–9; also see Feyerabend 1965, top half of p. 235, pp. 246–51.) But even if the answer favours Sellars, it has no more bearing on the question of what the world is really like than has the fact that within special domains it is convenient to use false theories when it is known that they enable us to predict phenomena in these restricted domains to a sufficiently high degree of approximation.

NOTES

1 Part of an earlier version of this paper was read to the Conference of the Australasian Association of Philosophy, August 1969, as the first part of a symposium with Professor Bernard Williams. I am indebted to Professor Williams for his comments, some of which have made the present paper less bad than it was, even though I have not come round to agree entirely with his

general point of view. I am also indebted to Professor A.N. Prior for some comments that he made in correspondence, after reading the earlier version, and that led me to expunge some erroneous passages about tense logic.

2   To future generations it may well seem as odd that time distinctions were once imported into grammar (via tenses) as now seems to modern eyes the interesting phenomenon of periphrastic verbs in certain Australian aboriginal languages. Thus in Aranda, by means of repetitions and suffixes, verb forms may be modified so as to express extremely complicated ideas. In his *Aranda Phonetics and Grammar* 1942, pp. 108–9), T.G.H. Strehlow gives the example of descriptions of a mountain kangaroo eating. Various modifications of the verb 'to eat' give, respectively, 'descended eating', 'descended-slowly-eating-all-the-while', 'wandered-on-away-from-us-eating-on-its-way', and several even more complex variants on the verb 'to eat'. In a way this is more sensible than tenses (which Aranda also has) because to descend-slowly-eating-all-the-while is to do a unitary sort of action, different from just eating, whereas to eat tomorrow is to do the same sort of thing as to eat yesterday. However, when in English we say 'eating while slowly descending', we are doing something rather analogous to a Fourier analysis, and the scientific advantages of this are obvious. One day, perhaps, the scientific advantages of getting time distinctions out of verbs will seem equally obvious.

3   It is not necessary for the present purposes to decide what the best account of these is, so long as it is agreed that there is no particular mystery about an utterance's being able to refer to itself. Reichenbach's theory (in his *Elements of Symbolic Logic*) has been influential, but has certain weaknesses, of which I have learned from Mr Dene Barnett of the Flinders University of South Australia. Barnett has devised an ingenious account, which interprets the body of the speaker as a part of the total symbol of which the word 'I' forms another part. There is no mystery that a complex consisting of the letter 'I' plus your body should be a different symbol (and refer to a different person) from a complex symbol consisting of the letter 'I' plus my body. Compare the case of a word in inverted commas. In a quotation expression the inverted commas do not themselves denote, but together with another expression they denote that other expression. Similarly, according to Barnett, the word 'I' does not denote, but taken together with another nearby object, the speaker's body, it denotes that other object, namely the speaker's body. In line with Barnett's theory, we might make our basic egocentric expression 'I now', of which a time-slice of my body, at the time of the utterance, forms a constituent. Then 'past' can be rendered as 'earlier than I now', 'future' as 'later than I now', and so on. In his *Past, Present and Future* (1967, pp. 12–15), A.N. Prior has pointed out that for certain tenses, such as future perfects, more than one 'reference point' is needed, but perhaps these could be handled in terms of 'the first reference point referred to by me now', 'the second reference point referred to by me now', etc. I would now prefer Donald Davidson's method of giving truth conditions for tensed language (indeed for indexical language in general) in a non-indexical metalanguage.

4   See A.N. Prior (1967, p. 177). It is perhaps worth commenting that if tense

logic is modified in order to fit relativity theory, this distorts common sense language and makes tense logic less useful for *another* of its purposes, which is to formalize the *grammar* of ordinary tensed discourse.

5   I am assuming materialism. A dualist could describe it in terms of non-similarities of time-slices of the one-dimensional entity which is the 'soul' of the metaphysician.

6   Bernard Williams has suggested that what the person who confusedly says 'we can change the future but not the past' is trying to express is that causal chains run from past to future. This brings us to the so-called problem of 'the Arrow of Time', which I think is less misleadingly described as that of the temporal asymmetry of the world, or at least of our cosmic epoch of it. I see no reason why this should not be considered within the context of the four-dimensional world picture: indeed if it is, as I believe it is, a deep problem of theoretical physics, it had *better* be so considered.

REFERENCES

Berkeley, George 1710: *Principles of Human Knowledge*.
Born, Max 1953: Physical Reality. *Philosophical Quarterly*, 3, 139–50.
Feyerabend, Paul K. 1965: Comments. In Robert S. Cohen and Marx W. Wartofsky (eds), *Boston Studies in the Philosophy of Science*, vol. 2, 223–61.
Geach, P.T. 1968: Some Problems about Time. In P.F. Strawson (ed.), *Studies in the Philosophy of Thought and Action*. Oxford: Clarendon Press.
Goodman, Nelson 1966: *The Structure of Appearance*, 2nd edn. Indianapolis: Bobbs-Merrill.
Katz, Bernard 1955: Nerve Impulse. In *The Physics and Chemistry of Life*, a *Scientific American* book. New York: Simon and Schuster.
Minkowski, H. 1924: Space and Time. In H.A. Lorentz, A. Einstein, H. Minkowski and H. Weyl, *The Principle of Relativity, A Collection of Original Memoirs on the Special and General Theories of Relativity*, New York: Dover.
Prior, A.N. 1967: *Past, Present and Future*. Oxford University Press.
Quine, W.V. 1960: *Word and Object*. Cambridge, Massachusetts: MIT Press/New York: John Wiley.
—— 1963: *Set Theory and its Logic*. Cambridge, Massachusetts: Harvard University Press.
—— 1966: Mr Strawson on Logical Theory. In *The Ways of Paradox and Other Essays*, New York: Random House.
Rindler, W. 1960: *Special Relativity*. Edinburgh: Oliver and Boyd.
Schilpp, P.A. (ed.) 1959: *Albert Einstein, Philosopher Scientist*. New York: Harper Torchbooks.
Sellars, Wilfrid 1963: *Science, Perception and Reality*. London: Routledge and Kegan Paul.
Scholl, D.A. 1956: *The Organization of the Cerebral Cortex*. London: Methuen.
Smart, J.J.C. 1965: Conflicting Views about Explanation. In Robert S. Cohen

and Marx W. Wartofsky (eds), *Boston Studies in the Philosophy of Science*, vol. 2, 157–69.

Strawson, P.F. (ed.) 1968: *Studies in the Philosophy of Thought and Action*. Oxford: Clarendon Press.

Strehlow, T.G.H. 1942: Aranda Phonetics and Grammar. In *Oceania Monographs No. 7*, Australian National Research Council.

Weyl, H. 1949: *Philosophy of Mathematics and Natural Science*. Princeton, New Jersey: Princeton University Press.

7

Time and Becoming

Richard Taylor[1] has made valuable contributions to the discussion of many central questions of philosophy. Of particular interest to me has been his work on the philosophy of time. I agree with some of his conclusions and disagree with others, but whether his conclusions are true or false his arguments are always challenging. I find Taylor's arguments for similarities between time and space particularly good, as in his fine papers 'Spatial and Temporal Analogies and the Concept of Identity' (1955) and 'Moving About in Time' (1959). On the other hand I do not agree with certain views which Taylor has held about an alleged difference between time and space, namely that there is a passage or movement of time, an irreducible *pure becoming*. I refer here in particular to chapter 8 of the second edition of Taylor's *Metaphysics* (1974). In this paper I intend to argue for a contrary view, namely that the alleged passage of time or pure becoming is an illusion. Certainly we *feel* that time flows, but I want to say (contrary to Taylor) that this feeling arises out of metaphysical confusion. It is easier, in my opinion, to argue for the illusoriness of temporal passage or of pure becoming than it is to give a plausible diagnosis of the cause of the illusion, but I shall try to make some suggestions about this toward the end of this paper. In defending the ideas of passage and pure becoming Taylor has ranged himself alongside many other philosophers, and I shall be concerned with this tradition in general, and not only with Taylor's own particular version of it. It should be noted that Taylor is himself quite aware of the sorts of arguments which I shall put forward, but he is more impressed than I am by the apparent 'datum', as he calls it, of our experience of time as apparently involving a pure becoming or passage.

It is undeniable that we do commonly talk of the passage or flow of time. We thus think of time as like a river bearing us inexorably into the future toward the big waterfall which is our death. Alternatively we can think of time as like a river flowing past us, while we sit on its bank, so that events are born down from the future toward us, and then recede away from us downstream into the past. When we think in either of these ways we think of the passage or flow of time as an objective feature of the universe, which would occur whether or not we were conscious of it. As Newton said, 'Absolute, true and mathematical time, of itself, and from its own nature, flows equably without relation to anything external' (Cajori 1960, see the 'Scholium to the Definitions'). Other writers treat passage as the movement of our consciousness through time, so that on this view events are just there in time (or rather space-time) and our consciousness just comes across them in its advance into the future (see Eddington 1959, p. 51). According to this view the movement or passage belongs to consciousness, not to anything in the physical world. I find the notion of the movement of our consciousness just as incoherent as the movement of time itself (or of events in time). Even if I did not I would find a further difficulty in this treatment of passage as the passage of our consciousness through a non-changing physical world, because I hold that there is no separation between the physical and the mental anyway. I hold that mental processes are just physical processes in the brain, and so if passage were passage of something mental it would still be a physical phenomenon.

If the passage of time is supposed to be literally a motion, whether of time, or of events in time, or of our consciousness through time (or space-time), then there is *prima facie* a simple objection to the idea. Motion is rate of change of spatial position with respect to temporal position. What then could be meant by the motion of time itself or of motion through time? Would this motion be at the rate of one second per second? Admittedly A.N. Prior (1958) has seemed happy with this answer. However, what is wrong with it can perhaps be brought out by reminding ourselves about what motion through space is. If you and I are moving with respect to one another, then your world line and mine are inclined at an angle to one another in space-time. If you and I are at rest with respect to one another then our world lines are parallel. But how on earth would one represent a movement of one second per second? It is true, as Prior points out, that after one second I have got older by a second. But equally one could say that a ruler gets larger in a left to right direction (say) by one centimetre per centimetre. There is no notion of 'flow' or 'passage' here.

If one believes, then, in the flow or passage of time, one has to take 'flow' or 'passage' in some metaphorical sense. Indeed what one has to do is to concentrate on what seems to be left out in the notion of 'getting older by a second per second' if this is taken in the sense in which a ruler gets larger by a centimetre per centimetre. What is allegedly left out is 'becoming'. But even this word 'becoming' has to be taken in a non-standard sense. C.D. Broad (1949, chapter 2) has used the term 'absolute becoming' and Richard Taylor has the term 'pure becoming' (Taylor 1974, chapter 8). The question is whether one can make any clearer sense of this than one can of passage or flow as simple motion.

Understanding the word 'becoming' as it is ordinarily used does not take us very far toward understanding the notion of 'pure' or 'absolute' becoming. Broad, in his *Scientific Thought* (1949), talked of 'events becoming', and 'become' here is evidently used as a monadic predicate. Normally we talk of something becoming something or other, as when we say that a man has become fat, or his hair has become grey. In the pure becoming of an event, what does the event become? Perhaps we can restore syntactic parity with ordinary becoming by saying that the event becomes present. Still, this does not seem very helpful, since every event becomes present at some time or other. So the notion of becoming present seems a pretty empty notion, and this is even more obvious when we recognize the indexical nature of words like 'present', 'past', and 'future'.[2] When a person P utters at a time t the sentence 'Event E is present' the assertion is true if and only if E is at t. More trivially, when P says at t 'time t is now' his assertion is true if and only if t is at t, so that if P says at t 't is now' his assertion is thereby true.

Richard Taylor tries to bring out the distinction between pure becoming and ordinary becoming by contrasting two senses of 'becoming older' (Taylor 1974, p. 83ff). Sometimes when we say that someone has become older, or has aged, we mean to convey that he has become more decrepit, that his skin has become wrinkled, that his hair has become grey, and so on. That is, we imply that a certain sort of change has occurred in the person. Taylor contrasts this with the sense in which something gets older even though it suffers no change whatever. Suppose that a crystal remains quite unchanged for ten years, or at any rate suffers no deterioration. It is still true, however, that the crystal has become ten years older: the crystal after ten years is ten years older than it was ten years before. But where has the notion of passage got to? Consider a north-going highway at milestone 100. The highway here is ten miles more northerly than it is at milestone 90. There is no suggestion of 'passage' or 'pure becoming' in this case. It is not clear that getting older implies passage or pure becoming either. The notion of pure becoming itself remains as elusive to me as ever.

If a person gets older in the sense that his or her hair has become grey and so on, this means simply that a later temporal stage of him is different in various particular respects, such as hair colour, from an earlier temporal stage of him. In the other sense of 'getting older' whereby the mere fact of the so-called passage of time makes a person 'get older', there is also a difference of a sort, apart from the mere difference of temporal position and relations to changing things elsewhere in the universe. This difference, so far as I can see, is simply the difference of identity: the later temporal stage is not identical with the earlier temporal stage. However, the relation of identity is a queer or degenerate sort of relation, and the predicate 'is identical with' has good claims to being regarded as belonging to pure first-order logic. Indeed in a first-order language with finitely many predicates the identity predicate is eliminable (see Quine 1970, pp. 63–4).

The notion of pure becoming is connected with that of events receding into the past and of events in the future coming back from the future to meet us. This notion seems to me to be unintelligible. What is the 'us' or 'me'? It is not the whole person from birth to death, the total space-time entity. Nor is it any particular temporal stage of the person. A temporal stage for which an event E is future is a different temporal stage from one for which event E is present or past. Nor is the change of E from future through present to past a genuine change. To think that it is a genuine change is to treat the indexical expressions 'past', 'present' and 'future' as though they were non-indexical predicates like 'is red' or 'runs'. Nor do I think that introspection of our temporal experience (which is of course all our experience) can give meaning to such expressions as 'pure becoming' or 'the transitory aspect of temporal facts' (Broad 1938, vol. 2, pt. 1). A concept has to be a public concept or no concept at all: if there is no intersubjective way of singling out the concept of pure becoming, how on earth can I know the aspect of inner experience to which I am supposed to apply the concept?

The elusiveness of the notion of temporal becoming can be brought out if we consider a recent attempt by Storrs McCall to explicate the notion of temporal passage, in his article 'Objective Time Flow' (1976). In this paper McCall argues that objective time flow is connected with irreducible contingency in the world, so that in a deterministic world there would be no time flow.[3] He compares his view of the universe with the theory of branching universes which is apparently implied by Hugh Everett III's interpretation of quantum mechanics (see DeWitt and Graham 1973; for some cautions see Skyrms 1976). Consider the situation of Schrödinger's cat paradox. There is an animal trapped in a box together with a device which will trigger off a gun which shoots the cat if and only if some radioactive material decays within a certain time, the probability of the decay being one half. The wave function for the system is a superposition of wave functions giving 'cat dead' and 'cat alive'; on the usual interpretation a 'measurement' (which in this case would be the shooting or non-shooting of the cat) leads to a collapse of the wave function into one or other of the two states. On the Everett interpretation the wave function does not suffer the discontinuous collapse but proceeds deterministically; however, the *universe* splits into two branches, one containing a live cat and one a dead cat. Indeed on this view the universe is suffering innumerable such splittings all the time. We can compare the universe to a shrub with many branches, each branch itself having many branches, and so on. McCall's picture of the universe is a modification and elaboration of this sort of thing. He holds that at time t the space-time universe is in a state which contains all the branches after t but only the trunk before t. As time proceeds there is a continual lopping-off of branches on the lower part of the shrub, so as to leave a single trunk. Any branch can become part of a later trunk, and so we can envisage grotesquely bent trunks (see McCall 1976, p. 343, bottom diagram). It is this continual change of the whole space-time universe which according to McCall constitutes the objective flow of time.

This seems to imply a proliferation not only of branches of the shrub but also a proliferation of shrubs. After all a given shrub either has or has not branches on a certain lower part (from ground level upward) of its trunk. A single space-time universe surely either has branches before t or it does not have branches before t. We must suppose therefore a vast multiplicity of universes, one for each value of t. Think of a universe with branches after t but none before t as a card with a shrub drawn on it. Then McCall's picture suggests to me that there is a super-universe which is like a pack of continuum-many cards, one above the other, cards higher in the pack portraying a longer unbranched 'trunk' than those lower in the pack. Indeed McCall has to complicate his theory in order to deal with special relativity, because of the relativity of simultaneity: the universe branches 'now', let us suppose, but there is no unique 'now'. So we must (to continue our analogy) have continuum-many piles of continuum-many cards, each pile corresponding to a different time direction (or set of inertial axes). There is a super-universe consisting of continuum-many arrays of continuum-many branched super-universes.[4] I think that McCall does not want to commit himself to this huge ontology. He says that 'the analogy with a three-dimensional tree, which grows and changes in time, should not be carried too far', and goes on to say that we can 'deny that every entity which is different at different times changes', or alternatively that we can say that 'the progressive falling away of future branches on the universe-tree does not "take" time, but instead "generates" time' (McCall 1976, p. 348). It is unclear to me how the first alternative helps, and the second one seems to me to be quite obscure, and so I can not see how McCall can avoid the huge ontology. However, it may be the case that a 'Heracleitean' will find things quite intelligible which are quite obscure to a 'Parmenidean' like me.[5]

In correspondence McCall has kindly commented on my interpretation of him, and has said that in one important respect it misses the spirit of what he intended to convey. He holds that the universe at time t is not a slice of some super-universe, something analogous to a card in a deck. The universe at time t consists of just the universe at t, and the universe at t', where t' is earlier or later than at t, does not exist at all. My worry is this: if the universe *now* is an entity, how can the universe at some other time be a non-entity? After all, McCall seems to be able to say things about it.

McCall further remarks that the deck of cards could not include a card for (say) a time in 1999, since nothing now indicates which branches of the universe should be lopped off. From my point of view this is too verificationist. We may not be able to tell what branches would be going to be lopped off, but the ones which would be lopped off are the ones which would be lopped off! What will be will be! No doubt once more, I am too Parmenidean to understand the Heracleitean point of view. I can approximate to doing so only by a theory of a super-universe which the Heracleitean McCall naturally rejects. I must leave it to the reader to judge whether this rejection is intelligible.

In our ordinary theory of space-time, change is a matter of one time slice or temporal stage of the space-time universe being different from an earlier time slice. McCall's theory is concerned to explicate the queer sort of change which is implied by time flow. As far as I can see this would be a matter of one 'super-universe slice' being different from another 'super-universe slice', or, on our analogy, one card on a pile being different from another card on the pile.

The lopping-off of branches with time is supposed to do justice to something which McCall and others have thought characteristic of the flow of time. The flow of time is supposed to reduce alternative possibilities to one. At a given time there is only one past but there are alternative futures. Thus there are no branches coming from the past. Branches in the future are supposed to imply a real contingency in the universe. If the universe were fully deterministic then there would be only a single future, just as there is only a single past.

Thus according to McCall's theory, if the universe were strictly deterministic there could be no objective time flow. Now if McCall's theory is mainly to explain our tendency to think that time flows, this is very odd. The human brain probably works fairly nearly as a deterministic machine, because neurons (and even protein molecules and the like) are macroscopic objects as far as quantum mechanics is concerned. It is hard to see how the question of physical determinism or otherwise can affect our subjective feelings about time. Thus it seems to me that we would have the same sort of illusion (as I think it is) of the flow of time even in a deterministic universe. I do not therefore see how McCall's theory of time flow as real and objective (but dependent on contingency) could provide a plausible explanation of this puzzling feature of our temporal experience.

If we confine ourselves to asserting only that an ordinary non-branching space-time exists, we can of course still accept contingency. To say that the universe is not deterministic is to say that the laws of nature do not connect an event E with some time-slice of the universe earlier than E. The event E of course exists determinately in the future, even though no conceivable knowledge about the present would enable even an infinitely powerful calculator to predict E.

McCall's theory makes the future *bigger* than we commonly believe it is. (It has all those branches.) And of course the whole super-universe, as I have described it in order to make sense of it, consists of continuum-many sets of continuum-many sets of such branched universes. Considerations of parsimony surely make the theory very implausible. It may be instructive to compare McCall's theory with an earlier theory due to C.D. Broad in his *Scientific Thought* (1949). In this theory (one of several theories of time which Broad held during his life) the future is *less* big than I think it is. Indeed according to this theory of Broad's, the future is empty and the world increases in size as time passes and more and more layers of the present get added to it. The past keeps pushing up into the emptiness of the future. At a time t_2 there is *more* universe than there is at an earlier time t_1. The incoherence in Broad's theory comes out when we reflect that this accretion through time of the contents of the universe cannot be a process in time, because this would once more bring us back to the idea of a rate of change of time with respect to time itself. Would the universe get bigger by one second per second, in any sense other than that in which a ruler gets longer by one centimetre per centimetre? Later in his life Broad himself came to reject the notion of temporal flow as motion (Broad 1959, especially pp. 766–7) but he gives no clear idea of what else he thought it might be. One objection which he then made to his theory of accretion of existence was that it suggested that past stages of the universe 'coexist' with present ones. This seems to be a mistaken objection. If 'coexist' means 'coexist *now*' then we can reply that past and present stages do not coexist *now* but they coexist (using this verb tenselessly) and of course they coexist at different times. However, according to Broad's theory there would have to be *a* sense in which events at times earlier than now would have to coexist now. Just as I interpreted McCall's theory as implying that there would have to be a super-universe consisting of continuum-many branched universes, 'later' branched universes having longer unbranched parts of their 'trunks' than earlier ones, so I must interpret Broad's picture as a whole continuum-many array of universes so that 'later' ones have more content than 'earlier' ones. Indeed if we modified Broad's theory so as to take account of the relativity of simultaneity, it would consist of continuum-many stacks of continuum-many such worlds, just as in attempting to interpret McCall we thought of the super-universe as analogous to continuum-many stacks of continuum-many cards. So though if we take only *one* of the worlds I have attributed to McCall and one of Broad's then McCall's theory seems to make the universe too big and Broad's makes the universe too small (by leaving out the future); in fact Broad's theory nevertheless ends up (as I interpret it anyway) by implying that there are many worlds and so foists on us a bloated super-universe. It is rather like David K. Lewis's realistic interpretation of possible worlds (Lewis 1973, pp. 84–91). In order to make sense of a dubious notion of modality we end up with an unacceptable metaphysics. (This is not to say that all modal notions are unclear: sometimes a metalinguistic account or something of the sort will do the trick.) Similarly, in order to make sense of a dubious notion of pure becoming we end up by postulating a bloated universe. We would do better to reject this dubious notion of modality and the dubious notion of pure becoming.

Nevertheless it does *seem* that time passes. When we are bored it seems to pass very slowly. For a criminal awaiting execution it no doubt seems to pass very quickly. Richard Taylor (1974, p. 86) remarks that the criminal's terror at the thought of the rapid diminution of what little is left of his life would hardly be relieved by metaphysical arguments about the absurdity of this sort of change. Perhaps, however, an opponent of the notion of pure becoming could give *some* rational basis to the criminal's terror: he has at t_2 less of his life to make plans about than he has at t_1, where t_2 is later than t_1, and we have a strong biologically explicable propensity to plan for the future. Frustration of this propensity is upsetting to us. Still, no doubt this gives only *part* of the explanation of the criminal's terror.

If the passage of time is an illusion it is a strange and intellectually worrying one. It would be good if we could not only give reasons for thinking that it *is* an illusion (as I have tried to do) but also if we could give some sort of explanation of how this illusion arises. The difficulty is that it seems to be the illusion of an absurdity. A straight stick may look bent, but there is nothing absurd about a bent stick. Perhaps the case is more like that of those impossible pictures which have been drawn by M.C. Escher. In the case of an impossible picture we have the following situation. One part of the picture is a two-dimensional pattern which can be interpreted by the rules of perspective as representing a certain three-dimensional entity. An adjoining part of the picture can be interpreted as representing another three-dimensional entity. Unfortunately one single interpretation of the two-dimensional pattern will not do for both parts: the two parts cannot be fitted together so that the whole two-dimensional pattern represents a single three-dimensional entity. In the middle part of the pattern, where the two parts come together we are forced into trying two inconsistent interpretations at once. Is there anything analogous to this in the genesis of the idea of temporal passage or pure becoming?

Many years ago (Smart 1949) I held that the illusion of the flow of time came from confusion about indexical expressions such as 'past', 'present', 'future', 'now' and tensed verbs. If we forget the indexical character of the words 'past', 'present' and 'future' we may think that events really change in respect of being future and then present and then past. If a man says in his youth in 1755 'It is ten years since the '45 rebellion' and then in his old age in 1805 he says 'tis sixty years since'[6] he may be tempted to think that there has been a real change of the '45, a recession into the past, whereas all there really is to the matter is the relations of being ten years earlier than one of his utterances and being sixty years earlier than another of his utterances. The events have not changed as a continuant changes: we do not mean that one later temporal stage of the event is different from an earlier temporal stage of it. Indeed we may be tempted to think of even a momentary event as changing from being future to being past, and a momentary event has no distinct earlier and later stages. So the trouble may come from trying to talk of events in terms appropriate only to continuants, and from talking of words like 'future', 'past' and the tenses as though they were non-indexical predicates. Taylor's criticisms of 'the attempts to expurgate pure becoming' (Taylor 1974, pp. 87ff) seem to me to turn on the impossibility of translating indexical expressions, such as tenses, into non-indexical ones. I agree on the impossiblity, but I challenge its metaphysical significance, since the semantics of indexical expressions can be expressed in a tenseless metalanguage.

However, I have become less sure of this 'linguistic' explanation of the source of the notion of the illusion of passage.[7] The very etymology of the word 'past' suggests that our concepts of past and future are already infected with the notion of passage, rather than the other way round. Of course etymology is a dubious guide in philosophy. Indeed tenses alone are enough to set up the idea of passage: 'was, is, and will be' serves as well as 'was future, is present, and will be past'. Nevertheless it is natural to wonder whether an exotic people who spoke a tenseless language with no indexicals, or perhaps with the single indexical 'this utterance',[8] would not have the feeling that time passes. There are of course obscurities here. There are obvious problems about radical translation of the exotic language. If Quine is right about the indeterminacy of translation there might be alternative translations of an exotic sentence, in the first place as 'time flows', and in the second place as something metaphysically harmless. In which case there might be no 'fact of the matter', as Quine might put it, as to whether or not the exotic people felt that time passes. It is also worth considering whether a person with no language at all could feel that time flows. As Wittgenstein said, 'Can a dog hope?' Incidentally the case of our exotic people is one in which the linguistic principle of charity need not be applied: in the case of a widespread human illusion it might be better, though uncharitable, to attribute the illusion to the exotic people too. It might even be that the exotic metaphysicians could be most plausibly interpreted (in the process of radical translation) as espousing a philosophy like Bergson's, and this would give us additional reason for translating some of their sentences as 'time flows' and the like.

Let us now explore the possibility of non-linguistic explanations of the illusion of passage. Remember Broad's theory of the universe getting bigger all the time, as more and more events come into existence. The theory is objectionable, not only because, as I suggested, it involves the notion of movement through time, but also because it makes an unjustified ontological distinction between future and past. Just as a past event E *did* exist, so a future event F *will* exist. Still, it is an empirical fact that people often confuse Xs with our experience of Xs. Some works on time perception by psychologists have seemed to me to suffer from this defect. So if we say that we feel that time passes perhaps we misdescribe our feeling. Perhaps our feeling is that our *experience* changes. It is not that at t_2 there is more of the *world* than there is at t_1. It is that at t_2 there is more of our *experience* recorded in our memories than there is at t_1. In other words the stock of our memories is continually increasing. At the age of fifty a man has more memories than he has at the age of forty.

But then why do we feel that the world is getting bigger with time rather than getting smaller? In one time direction the stock of our memories is increasing, whereas in the other time direction it is decreasing. It is true that there is a temporal asymmetry about memory. We remember only our previous experiences, whereas we have only theoretical knowledge of our future experiences. Thus I know immediately at 11.00 a.m. that I have memories which I did not have at 10.50 a.m., but I do not know immediately (by memory) that I will have experiences at 11.10 a.m. that I have not had at 11.00 a.m. What I do believe about my experiences at some future time is based on rather general grounds, and is on the assumption that I will not drop dead or become unconscious before 11.10 a.m. But it is hard to see how this temporal asymmetry explains why we feel that the flow of time is in the direction of the increasing stock of our memories.

Another difficulty in the idea that the feeling of the flow of time arises from the increase in our memories comes out if we consider the case of a very old man, who might be losing memories faster than he is gaining them. (We can think here of his long-term memories: presumably information would be going into and coming out of his short-term memory at about the same rate.) I write in ignorance of any psychological literature on the subject, but it seems to me that such a case might well exist, and I would conjecture that nevertheless the old man would still feel that time flows in the same direction in which we feel it does. This throws doubt on the hypothesis that the feeling of the flow of time does after all depend on the increase of our memories.

Adolf Grünbaum has suggested another way in which memory may explain our feeling of the passage of time. He has remarked that 'The flux of time consists in the *instantaneous awareness* of *both* the temporal order *and* the *diversity* of the set of the membership of the remembered (recorded) or forgotten events, awareness in each of which the instant of its own occurrence constitutes a *distinguished element*' (Grünbaum 1963, p. 663; 1973, p. 325). Grünbaum also makes Kant's point that such an awareness is an awareness of succession, not just a succession of awarenesses. But the problem still arises why this should give a feeling not just of a directed temporal order but also one of a temporal *flow* or *passage*. Consider a nested set of arrows, each pointing to the right. If we contemplate it this does not give us a feeling of spatial flow.

Henry Krips has ingeniously pointed out to me, in discussion, another way in which our memories might explain our feeling of temporal passage. If we are floating down a river on a raft we have memories of the places which are upstream from us but not of things which are downstream from us. So 'past' feels a bit like 'upstream', and 'future' feels a bit like 'downstream'.

I am myself inclined to favor yet another suggestion. This is that we are aware of the flow of information through our short-term memories and we confuse this with a flow of time itself. This conjecture is perhaps supported by empirical evidence according to which the greater the number of stimuli that there are in a given temporal interval the greater is the subjective estimate of the length of that interval. It also might be further supported by some more equivocal evidence which suggests that estimation of the length of an interval depends in the same way on the complexity ov the stimuli (see Ornstein 1969, chapter 4). However, it is still obscure to me how such a flux of information should be misperceived as a flux of time itself.

1 This paper was for a *Festschrift* for Richard Taylor.
2 For the semantics of indexical expressions see Donald Davidson (1967), especially the remarks on pp. 319–20.
3 I apologise to McCall if I have misunderstood him, as it is quite likely in my view of my own inability to make sense of theories of time flow. At least I am trying to say what his theory comes to, to the extent that I can make sense of it to myself.
4 Taking a future universe to consist of one particular path upwards along branches of the shrub, there will be 2^c of them, where c is the cardinality of the continuum. See McCall (1970).
5 See also McCall (1984) for a more recent discussion.
6 The alternative title of Sir Walter Scott's *Waverley*.
7 Recently Ferrel Christensen, in his paper 'The Source of the River of Time', (1976), has defended a linguistic explanation of the metaphor of passage. He holds that predicates like 'past' and 'future' are parasitic on adverbial ones and treats tenses as adverbs; that there are in the ordinary sense no temporal relations, so that 'and then' does not signify such a relation. This seems to me to be wrong. I think that ordinary adverbs should be understood in terms of predicates of events, as has been suggested by Donald Davidson. Tenses should be handled differently, by means of a tenseless metalanguage – see Donald Davidson (1967). 'And then' should be handled by ordinary conjunction and the predicate 'earlier than'. Nevertheless, even if I am right about these points of disagreement with Christensen, the article is of interest for the way in which it aims to trace 'the river of time' to a linguistic source.
8 So that instead of 'here', 'now', 'you' and 'will be', for example, they would have 'near this utterance', 'simultaneous with this utterance', 'the person to whom this utterance is addressed' and 'is later than this utterance'.

REFERENCES

Broad, C.D. 1938: *An Examination of McTaggart's Philosophy*. Cambridge: Cambridge University Press.
—— 1949: *Scientific Thought*. London: Routledge and Kegan Paul.
—— 1959: Broad's reply to his critics. In P.A. Schilpp (ed.), *The Philosophy of C.D. Broad*, La Salle, Illinois: Open Court.
Cajori, F. (ed.) 1960: *Sir Isaac Newton's Mathematical Principles of Natural Philosophy and His System of the World*. Berkeley: University of California Press.
Christensen, Ferrel 1976: The Source of the River of Time. *Ratio*, 18, 131–44.
Davidson, Donald 1967: Truth and Meaning. *Synthese*, 17, 304–23. Reprinted 1984 in *Essays on Truth and Interpretation*. Oxford: Clarendon Press.
DeWitt, Bryce and Graham, Neill (eds) 1973: *The Many-Worlds Interpretation of Quantum Mechanics*. Princeton, New Jersey: Princeton University Press.

Eddington, A.S. 1959: *Space, Time and Gravitation*. New York: Harper.

Grünbaum, Adolf 1963: Carnap's Views on the Foundations of Geometry. In P.A. Schilpp (ed.), *The Philosophy of Rudolf Carnap*, La Salle, Illinois: Open Court.

—— 1973: *Philosophical Problems of Space and Time*, 2nd edn. Dordrecht, Holland: D. Reidel.

Lewis, David K. 1973: *Counterfactuals*. Oxford: Blackwell.

McCall, Storrs 1970: The Cardinality of Possible Futures (abstract). *Journal of Symbolic Logic*, 35, 363.

—— 1976: Objective Time Flow. *Philosophy of Science*, 43, 337–62.

—— 1984: A Dynamic Model of Temporal Becoming. *Analysis*, 44, 172–6.

Ornstein, Robert E. 1969: *On the Experience of Time*. Harmondsworth: Penguin.

Prior, A.N. 1958: Time After Time. *Mind*, 67, 244–6.

Quine, W.V. 1970: *Philosophy of Logic*. Englewood Cliffs, New Jersey: Prentice-Hall.

Skyrms, Brian 1976: Possible Worlds, Physics and Metaphysics. *Philosophical Studies*, 30, 323–32.

Smart, J.J.C. 1949: The River of Time. *Mind*, 58, 483–94.

Taylor, Richard 1955: Spatial and Temporal Analogies and the Concept of Identity. *Journal of Philosophy*, 52, 599–612.

—— 1959: Moving About in Time. *Philosophical Quarterly*, 9, 289–301.

—— 1974: *Metaphysics*, 2nd edn. Englewood Cliffs, New Jersey: Prentice-Hall.

8

The Reality of the Future

It is a pleasure and an honour to be invited to contribute an article to a volume of good wishes to Sir Peter Strawson. My article is not one of those which directly concerns itself with Strawson's own work, but as considerations to do with reference are central to it, I hope that Strawson, who has done so much to illuminate our thoughts on this topic, may find it of interest. I hope that he will not mind if I have in general talked in a Quinean rather than a Strawsonian idiom, for example parsing proper names as predicates, but I do not think that anything of great metaphysical importance rests on this difference. I think of Quinean canonical notation as something for scientific and metaphysical theorizing to which we must ascend via the living language which works rather in ways which Strawson has so well investigated, with his emphasis on contextual and presuppositional considerations.

The genesis of this paper comes from the fact that I have come to discover, in philosophical discourse with those who are not professional philosophers, that it is very common for people to doubt the reality of the future, and it is very hard to convince them that the future is real. The denial of the reality of the future seems to me to be quite preposterous, and we are used to the idea that a statement may be so preposterous that only a philosopher could make it. But preposterousness is in fact often a product of the lay philosophical mind, not that of the professional philosopher's. It seems to me that a sort of subjectivism comes very naturally to the (philosophically) lay mind when it comes to discussing metaphysical issues. It can be hard to disentangle theses of epistemology from those of ontology. Yet despite much discussion, I find it hard to get clear in my own mind what the considerations are which impel people to deny the reality of the future. No doubt these considerations are multivarious, and those which impel the lay mind may be different from those which must have weighed with a philosopher like Arthur Prior. I have spoken of the natural bent towards subjectivism. There is a tendency to confuse knowledge of X and the concept of X with X itself. Consider some (not all) articles with titles like 'The Genesis of Time' or 'The Evolution of Time', where what has genesis or evolves is clearly not time itself but our concept of time. The same confusion may be partly at the back of the verification principle and of the logical positivist thesis that statements about historical events are really statements about our present evidence for these events. I suppose 'evidence' here has to be taken in a Pickwickian sense, because normally 'evidence' implies a contrast between itself and what it is evidence for. The logical positivists of course paid some attention to this contrast, but the 'evidence for' would be cashed out in terms of further sense data, further 'evidence'. The whole theory is probably incoherent, but if not incoherent it is at least preposterous. Imagine a Roman soldier, cold, wet, miserable and suffering from dysentery, and some prophet telling him that in the twentieth century AD there would be philosophers who would say that he and his dysentery were just a matter of certain marks on paper or inscriptions on stones and coins existing in the twentieth century AD.

Analogously conceive of a soldier in the twenty-first century likewise cold, miserable and suffering from dysentery, and being told that some twentieth century philosophers and non-philosophers had held that the future was unreal. He might have some choice things to say, and if he were at all interested in abstract thought, I doubt if he would be mollified by the view that his sufferings were real then, but not real now (in the twentieth century). If so, I think that his philosophical instincts would be right. Reality is not a property which anything can acquire. To be real is to be part of the universe, and if the universe in the twenty-first century contains a certain thing or event then that thing or event is surely real. To say 'an F is real' is just to say '$(\exists x)\ Fx$' with tenseless 'Fx'. (It is of course the case also that the quantifier 'there is an x' has to be read tenselessly.)

There is another reason why reality is not a property which something can acquire. This is simply that reality is not a property of any sort. 'Exists' is not a predicate. If an object acquired reality, there would have to be a time at which it lacked reality and a time at which it possessed reality. But to lack reality (or to have any other property) it would have to exist, i.e. be real, which is a manifest contradiction. On the other hand *coming into* existence is a property. (In so far as we allow that there *are* such things as properties, which in a more extended treatment of our present problem I might want to deny.) The Sydney Harbour Bridge came into existence: i.e. it had an earliest time slice. Or to get over the problem about exactly *when* the Sydney Harbour Bridge came into existence (was it when the last rivet was knocked in or the last girder was put into position or somewhat earlier than that?), we can say that a thing comes into existence if and only if there is a time before the times of any of its time slices. (In the light of special relativity, where there is no separation of space-time into an objective space and time, the talk of earlier times would have to be rephrased in an obvious way in terms of nestings of light cones, but I shall not bother with this refinement at the moment.) To have come into existence is a property of the Sydney Harbour Bridge. God, if he were either sempiternal or eternal, would lack this property.

In his paper 'Beginning and Ceasing to Exist', William Godfrey-Smith (1977) rightly rejects the view that beginning to exist is the acquisition of a property. He thinks however that 'it must be accepted that starting to exist is an inescapably stark phenomenon' (1977, p. 399). His worry is that '*A* did not exist' seems to imply that before *A* existed there was nothing (presumably it would have to be *A*) 'for there to be any facts about' (1977, p. 398). He rejects the idea that we could analyse 'someone ceased to exist between t_1 and t_2' as '$(\exists x)$ (x is a man at t_1 and it is not the case that x is a man at t_2)'. Godfrey-Smith says that all this says is that someone ceased to be a *man* between t_1 and t_2. I think that my formulation in terms of time-slices gets over this objection and the time-slices can be specified as being 'of a man'. If 'stark' means 'irreducible', then we should not agree with Godfrey-Smith about the starkness of coming into existence.

Part of Godfrey-Smith's worries have to do with naming. He holds, perhaps rightly, that one can not *name* a wholly future entity. As a result, Godfrey-Smith (1978), in agreement with Ryle (1954, p. 27) holds that predictions about wholly future entities are general. He does allow, as against Ryle, that we can make predictions about particulars if the particular has already begun to exist and so is nameable. (Godfrey-Smith follows Kripke in denying that a name can be identified with a description or set of descriptions.) Since wholly future entities are not nameable, he holds that there are no particular facts about wholly future entities; indeed he claims that there are no such entities for the facts to be about.

I suspect that there is a notion of substitutional quantification behind all this, and indeed there is at least a hint of adherence to substitutional quantification in Godfrey-Smith's remarks in the top paragraph of p. 394 of his 'Beginning and Ceasing to Exist' (1977). The worry here appears to be that there are no names of wholly future individuals which can be substituted for the variables of quantified propositions. But if one accepts *objectual* quantification, as surely one must, then there is no problem about particular truths about the future. We can say something of the form '$G(ıx)Fx$'. and if we are fortunate, or have chosen our 'F' well, there is a unique individual x such that Fx. Indeed for metaphysical purposes there is no need for names as such, since following Quine one can parse names as predicates, so that 'Socrates' becomes '$(ıx)x$ socratises'. Objectual quantification makes the variable the bearer of reference. Unless one *already* has reason to deny the reality of the future, one will hold that the variables range over all entities, whether spatio-temporal (past, present, or future) or non-temporal (e.g. numbers). I conclude that even if we concede to Godfrey-Smith a causal theory of naming which somehow implies the 'in principle' non-nameability of wholly future entities, this provides no argument against either the reality of future entities or our ability to refer to them (even if we can't name them).

The expansion of '$G(ıx)Fx$' is '$(\exists x)(y)((Fy \equiv x=y).Gx)$' and since this contains no name but has an existential and universal quantifier, I suppose that we must concede that '$G(ıx)Fx$' is a 'general' rather than a particular truth. Also even though happily there should be a unique x such that Fx, nevertheless the statement is in a sense not particularly 'about' this unique x. Or at least the notion of 'being about' is not all that clear. One feels some inclination to say that '$G(ıx)Fx$' is about the unique x, such that Fx, if there is one such, but since the variable ranges over all objects in the universe, one might also feel an inclination to say that '$G(ıx)Fx$' is about everything. But this has nothing to do with the question of the reality of the unique x such that Fx. Even if we concede a causal theory of names such that future events are unnameable (because there is no or little backward causation) this does not at all support a thesis that the future is unreal. If one has objectual quantification (and there are good arguments why we *must* have objectual quantification) nameability is unimportant.

The view of the universe as a four-dimensional manifold is of course familiar from the Minkowski interpretation of special relativity and from the extension of this geometrical approach into the general theory of relativity. Even if Newtonian mechanics had still held the field, I think that the four-dimensional world view would be inescapable. However, special relativity poses *extra* problems for those who want to say that the future is unreal. Given infinite space, there will be events which are as far in the future as you like relative to an inertial frame A but which are in the past relative to another inertial frame B. Consider two metaphysicians McDonald and Campbell who inhabit fast space ships which have a considerable velocity relative to one another. (Perhaps they are even approaching one another head on: it may be that McDonald in a suicidal way desires to avenge the massacre of Glencoe!) We may suppose that each uses the words 'past', 'present' and 'future', as well as tenses, as relative to the inertial frame at which he is at rest. (This would be a non-arbitrary way in which we could modify our tensed language to suit an interstellar future. Of course we might have the good sense to reject tensed language altogether, though we could retain some indexical expressions such as 'here-and-now' and 'this'.) Then given infinite space, there will be distant events which are as far in the future as you like relative to McDonald's inertial frame, but which will be in the past relative to Campbell's, and vice versa. Now if McDonald and Campbell each claim that the future is unreal we get a curious situation. Consider a thing or an event X which is in McDonald's future but Campbell's past. Then McDonald will claim that X is unreal, but Campbell will claim that it is real.

An argument on these lines was put forward by Hilary Putnam (1967), and in an article which discussed Putnam's argument (as well as an argument by C.W. Rietdijk), Howard Stein (1968) has claimed that Putnam was illegitimately making use of notions foreign to the special theory of relativity. Stein holds that special relativity should be stated in terms of four-vectors, without the reliance that Minkowski put on the notion of a coordinate system. Properly speaking since the notion of 'present' or 'future' is relative to a coordinate system (inertial frame) it does not belong to the theory. All that belongs are the notions of 'absolute future' and 'absolute past' of a single event or space-time point. Consider an event E which takes place at a certain space-time point P. The absolute future of E is the upward part of the double light cone whose vertex is P, and the absolute past of E is the downward part of the double light cone. Events outside the light cone are simply neither absolutely later than E nor absolutely earlier than E.

Independently of relativity there was a problem about the alleged unreality of the future. The idea was that if t is the present time all events later than t are unreal. That is, $\sim(\exists x)(x$ later than $t)$. But any event is earlier than t, for some t, and later than t for some other t. So E would seem to be both real and not real. Perhaps it may be suggested that we should not talk in terms of 'real' and 'unreal' but in terms of 'real at t' and 'unreal at t'. The trouble with this last notion is that reality and unreality are not relative notions in this way. There is of course a harmless sense in which we can say that an F is real at t. What we mean, I suggest, is that an F at t is real. We have only a non-relative 'real'.

Stein, who discusses a further ingenious argument of Putnam's which I shall not examine here, argues that instead of going in the direction of a non-relative sort of reality or existence, so that all events, everywhere and everywhen are real, we might save the spirit of the thesis of the unreality of the future, by relativizing 'real' not to 'now' but to 'here-now'. If I understand Stein rightly (and I have rather loosely paraphrased him) we should not talk of 'real at t', because in special relativity there is no space or time taken separately, but we should talk of 'real at P', where P is a space-time point. Only events in the lower half of the double light cone whose vertex is at P are real at P. Stein holds that special relativity forces us to give up the notion of 'temporal evolution as the development of the word *in time*' (Stein 1968, pp. 15–16). He says that we have to consider 'the more complicated structure constituted by, so to speak, the "chronological perspective" of each space-time point'.

Now I am unclear what Stein is really claiming here. If all he means is that the universe has a certain causal structure which can be understood in terms of the double light cones, then he is quite right. (Appropriate modifications to the description of causal structure will be needed if there are tachyons.) But he appears to be holding that Putnam has been somehow incorrect in thinking that he had soundly refuted the doctrine of the unreality of the future. So presumably he is taking 'development of the world' in some stronger sense, which is unclear to me, but which presumably has some analogy to the notion of the future being unreal, i.e. in the sense that one can say that events in the upward half of the light cone whose vertex is P are 'unreal at P'. But perhaps I am misinterpreting Stein here and exaggerating his disagreement with Putnam.

Notice how hard it is even to state this notion of the unreality of the future. Presumably even the upward half of the light cone itself would have to be unreal at P. After all, it is one of those things which is inside itself. In order to state the notion of 'real at P' we need to fall back (perhaps in a metalanguage) on a notion of 'real' *simpliciter*. And this is what one should expect, because the notion of 'real' is fundamentally just that of existence, and of the existential quantifier, expressed by 'there is a . . .' with tenseless 'is'.

Now with this tenseless quantifier, objectually understood, I see no problem about reference to things or events, wherever they may occur in space-time or outside it (whether in the lower or upper parts of the double light cone whose vertex is at our place-time of utterance, or whether elsewhere in space-time, or even whether – like numbers – outside space-time altogether). As I suggested earlier, even an inability to *name* a future thing or event does not matter: with objectual quantification reference is carried by the variable, and reference can be done quite generally.

Suppose then that we have the tenseless quantifier or expression 'is real'. ('Fs are real' with tenseless 'are' is just an idiomatic way of saying '$(\exists x)Fx$'.) With this fundamental notion of 'real' we can define a rather pointless notion of 'real at t' (in Newtonian kinematics) or of 'real at space-time point P' (in kinematics of special relativity). I want to emphasize that these notions which I am about to define *are* pointless, but they are all I can concede to those who in some sense or other want to deny the reality of the future. However, these notions of course are defined in terms of a notion which presupposes the reality of the future.

We could, rather pointlessly, define 'real at t' (in Newtonian kinematics) as 'exists at or prior to t', and then we could modify this in the light of special relativity to the notion of 'real at space-time point P', i.e. as 'existing at P or in the lower half of the double light cone whose vertex is P'. But though we can define the expressions which are needed by the people who deny the reality of the future, we are of course begging the question against them. This is because we are defining 'real at t' or 'real at P' in terms of the notion of reality whereby everything in the universe, past, present or future or even eternal, is real. But it is only by thus begging the question that I can make sense to myself of the locutions of those against whom I am arguing. The pointlessness of the notion of 'real at t' or 'real at P' can be seen if we consider how we could define other notions. We could define an F as being real at femininity if and only if $(\exists x)(Fx$ and x is female); we could define it as being real at yellowness if and only if $(\exists x)(Fx.$ yellow $x)$: and we could define being real at latitude θ as existing south of latitude θ. And so on. The very artificiality and pointlessness of 'real at t' or 'real at P' is apparent.

Why, then, is the notion of the unreality of the future more seductive than that of the unreality of non-feminine, non-yellow or non-southerly things? There are of course the old verificationist reasons. We can not know the future in detail as we know the past. But to make an ontological point out of this is surely to confuse ontology and epistemology. In any case our lack of knowledge of the future can be over emphasized. Astronomers know a lot about future positions of planets, about the future evolution of stars, and so on. Admittedly because of the causal grain of the universe we do not have the knowledge of the future which is of the sort which depends on traces, the sort of knowledge of the past which historians have. In spite of this, it can sometimes be easier to know the future than the past, as when one might compute the position of a recently launched space satellite a month hence, even though we had no idea where (on earth) it was a month ago. There is also the worry that we cannot name the future. I have examined this matter earlier in this paper, and have pointed out that with objectual quantification we can have reference without naming.

Still, even if we have *no* knowledge of particular future facts, this would not show that the future events in question were not real. Why should there not be things of which at present we can have no knowledge? There is a paradox, perhaps, in saying that there are events of which we know *absolutely* nothing. If we not only *say* this but *know* this, then we know about these events that we know nothing about them, a palpable contradiction. Without paradox, a man could claim that he knew almost nothing about the future. But if he did claim this, he would have no justification for denying the *reality* of the future.

It may be suggested that the view that the future is unreal is somehow theological.

'The Moving Finger writes, and having writ,
Moves on: nor all thy Piety or Wit
Shall lure it back to cancel half a Line . . .'.
                    (Edward Fitzgerald, *The Rubá'iyát of Omar Khayyám*)

Now if the book which the Moving Finger writes is supposed to be the universe itself, then the metaphor is misleading because it suggests that past and present co-exist at the same instant, as do different sentences in one time slice of a book. On the other hand if the book is a record of the universe, the metaphor reiterates the fact that *we* have traces of the past but not the future. There is also the idea that we can change the future but not the past: what the Moving Finger has written is unalterable but it has free choice as to what it will write.

Without our getting into questions about free will it is sufficient at present to point out that if the Moving Finger writes *p* tomorrow and not *not-p* then the writing of *p* is its future, and the event described by *p* is a future event. Suppose that I try to alter the future by doing *A* rather than *B*. Then my doing *A* just *was* the future. It no more makes sense to talk of altering the future than it does to talk of altering the past. I can either alter or not alter a thing, such as a manuscript: this is to make one later time slice of the manuscript dissimilar to earlier time slices. Similarly I may alter my character: it is to make my later behaviour different from the earlier behaviour. But I cannot alter the future: whatever change I make or do not make in the manuscript is in the future part of that manuscript, and whatever pattern of behaviour I do or do not exemplify is part of my future. There are no alternative futures just as there are no alternative pasts. Anyway the idea of alternative futures is surely one of a multiplicity of futures, not of an unreal future. What the Moving Finger has written it has written, but equally what it will write it will write. We do not know what it is going to write, and perhaps the owner of the Moving Finger himself does not know, but to say that this implies the unreality of the future is, as I have already remarked, to confuse ontology and epistemology.

Dissatisfaction with the space-time view has arisen because to some philosophers it does not explain such things as our relief that pain should be over (Prior 1959), and our dread only of anticipated pain, not of remembered pain (Romney 1977–8, pp. 249–50). My colleague Michael Tooley has also suggested to me the following interesting case. You may have amnesia and someone tells you that there are two possibilities: (a) you have had twenty years of pain and will have one year of pleasure; (b) you have had twenty years of pleasure and will have one year of pain. Would you not prefer (a) to (b)? All these considerations raise a lot of issues, but I see no reason why our differing attitudes to present and past pleasures and pains should not be explicable by evolutionary and biological considerations and by reference to the asymmetry of the causal grain of the universe: there are good reasons why our preferences and choices should be forward looking. It is too drastic to erect a whole metaphysics or these facts about our attitudes, especially when those who do so tend to fall into incoherence, since they seem in the very fact of presenting their case to be quantifying over future events as well as present and past ones.

REFERENCES

Godfrey-Smith, William 1977: Beginning and Ceasing to Exist. *Philosophical Studies*, 32, 393–402.
—— 1978: The Generality of Predictions. *American Philosophical Quarterly*, 15, 15–25.
Prior, Arthur 1959: Thank Goodness That's Over. *Philosophy*, 34, 12–17.
Putnam, Hilary 1967: Time and Physical Geometry. *Journal of Philosophy*, 64, 240–7.
Romney, Gillian 1877–8: Temporal Points of View. *Proceedings of the Aristotelian Society*, 78, 237–52.
Ryle, Gilbert 1954: *Dilemmas*. London: Cambridge University Press.

PART 3
Metaphysics and Philosophy of Science

9

Ryle in Relation to Modern Science

Modern science presents a view of the universe which is very different from that which was available to previous generations. Man is now thought of much more as simply part of nature, rather than as set over nature. Even statistically there has been a great change in emphasis. Some years ago it seemed quite likely that the origin of the solar system was due to a highly improbable celestial accident and that it was not unreasonable to suppose that our own planet was the only place of intelligent life in the universe. There are at present still a number of competing theories of the origin of the solar system, none of them completely satisfactory, but opinion seems to have moved towards thinking it much more plausible that planetary systems and intelligent life should be a feature of innumerable stars even in our galaxy alone. We get an even greater sense of the relative unimportance of the human race in the universe as a whole when we consider the huge number of galaxies in the observable part of the universe. It is even quite a salutary corrective for human arrogance to look at a photograph of (say) the great nebula in Andromeda and reflect on the huge number of stars which appear as a misty cloud. When we go from the very large to the very small we also find that science has changed our views about man's place in the scheme of things. Biology has become increasingly biochemical, and it is hard to recapture the mood in which even so modernistic a prelate as E.W. Barnes, the Bishop of Birmingham, could write (in a book published in 1933, p. 420): 'The mystery of life is unsolved, probably insoluble.' Recent developments, such as the discovery of the structure of DNA and the synthesis of certain macromolecules, are spectacular cases of the general background to an increasingly mechanistic view of man. In particular, it looks as though the main difficulty in understanding the functions of the human brain lies in the difficulty of discovering its organization, and does not lie in the adequacy for this purpose of the known laws of physics and chemistry. The chief evidence in the other direction would seem to come from the comparative lack of success of endeavours to produce artificial intelligence, which have given rise to Chomsky's judgement (1968, p. 12) that we should not be surprised if we find that known physical laws are inadequate to explain the functioning of the brain. But on the whole the indications do not seem to me to support the view that there is anything mysterious about life or mind.

I would suggest, therefore, that it is science, not metaphysics, which has been mainly efficacious in conditioning our present austere and unromantic view of man and his place in the universe, though in some respects the work of philosophers, such as Gilbert Ryle (1949) in *The Concept of Mind*, does useful mopping-up work. However, even in Ryle there can perhaps be found a residue of traditional ideas about the place of man in the world. If we read Ryle we feel that we are in a cosy sort of world of rowing, golf and cricket, card games and cooking, drill movements, tables, chairs and gardens. As Stuart Hampshire (1950) remarks in the last paragraph of his critical notice of *The Concept of Mind*, there is a suggestion of 'a sharply . . . definite view of the world: a world of solid and manageable objects, without hidden recesses, each visibly functioning in its own appropriate pattern'. When we read Ryle neither vast astronomical spaces nor the strange world of the atomic nucleus is likely to be near the forefront of our consciousness. Now Ryle might justifiably say, 'Well, why should it be?' and indeed for most of the time he is not concerned with issues in which his cosy examples do not do the job. But sometimes he does seem to me unjustifiably to play down the way in which the world view suggested by modern science does conflict with our cosy common sense view of the world, and in *Dilemmas* (Ryle 1954, p. 81) he even suggests that any conflicts between science and traditional religion are merely the products of conceptual confusion.

Now I can see Ryle wincing a bit here, because he is (often rightly) suspicious of terms like 'world view', and 'Science' (with a capital 'S'). In fact in *Dilemmas* (Ryle 1954, pp. 71–4) he does a bit of deflation of what he calls 'two over-inflated ideas', the idea of *Science* and the idea of *world*. Let me attempt to carry out a bit of re-inflation.

Ryle says that 'There is no such animal as Science.' There are scores of sciences, he says, and most of them are 'such that acquaintanceship with them or, what is even more captivating, hearsay knowledge about them has not the slightest tendency to make us contrast their world with the everyday world' (Ryle 1954, p. 71). It is indeed true that there are scores of sciences, but we must not overlook the extent to which this is due to arbitrary departmentalism. Thus the study of DNA in plants or bacteria is much like the study of DNA in animals, and more like it than is the study of animal ecology. This example shows the philosophical unimportance of the division 'microbiology–botany–zoology.' No doubt with advancing knowledge new sciences develop, but it is also true that old ones coalesce. There is a move towards unity and simplicity just as much as there is a move towards diversity and proliferation of detail.[1] I would therefore suggest that there is quite a lot of truth in saying that there *is* such an animal as '*Science*'. Incidentally I would not think it illuminating to employ the cluster concept 'science' quite as widely as Ryle does, when after saying that there are scores of sciences he proceeds to illustrate his point with the example of philology. For philosophical purposes I think that it is far more illuminating to classify philology as a *history*. I would also concede to Ryle that there is a non-arbitrary and philosophically important diversity between sciences, in as much as some of them, namely physics and chemistry, are concerned with the discovery of laws of nature, whereas others, like most of the biological ones, are mainly concerned with the application of known laws of nature (physical and chemical ones) to the explanation of generalizations of natural history. (Roughly, in the way in which electronics is physics plus wiring diagrams, biology is physics and chemistry plus natural history.)

Now for 'world'. Ryle's deflection of this idea begins by drawing attention to the use of the word 'world' according to which there might be a periodical entitled *The Poultry World* (Ryle 1954, p. 73). He points out that here the word 'world' could be paraphrased by 'field' or 'sphere of interest' or 'province'. In this sense to speak of the world of physics would just be to speak of the physicist's sphere of interest. Here 'world' does not mean '*the* world' or 'the cosmos', any more than it does in 'the poultry world' or 'the entertainment world'. Ryle says: 'In the articles and books that [physicists] write for their colleagues and pupils the word "world" seldom occurs, and the grand word "cosmos", I hope, never occurs.' Actually the most common synonym is 'universe' and this word occurs very commonly (as might be expected) in cosmology. At its most fundamental physics seems to merge with cosmology, and in cosmo-logical contexts 'world' or 'universe' tends to be used quite unsolemnly. There is, it is true, a tendency (perhaps for unnecessary positivist preconceptions) for cosmologists to mean by 'universe' the observable part of the universe: that is, they may not include as part of 'the universe' galaxies whose velocity of recession is greater than that of light or events which (on the assumption of a 'big bang' theory of cosmic evolution) occurred before the big bang. However, it is dangerous to set *a priori* limits to knowledge, and hypotheses about the world before the big bang (for example, hypotheses about an oscillating universe) and hypotheses about the nature of space extending beyond the observable part of the universe are indirectly testable, or at least may be to some extent supportable by considerations of simplicity or plausibility (Swinburne 1968, chapter 12). In any case, whether a cosmologist uses 'universe' in the wider or narrower sense, he is talking about all or part of 'the world' in the sense in which the metaphysician uses this shudder quoted word.

II

Let me consider a particular way in which science in the past has been thought to suggest consequences for our general metaphysical view of the world, and Ryle's method of dealing with the ideas in question.

In the nineteenth century the philosophical view which seemed most natural to many sciences was a materialistic one. Scientists tended to think of mechanics as the basic science to which all other sciences should ultimately be reduced. They thought of mechanics (and therefore of the universe) as rigidly deterministic: the idea was that if an infinite intelligence were to know the whole state of the universe at a certain moment it would be able to calculate the state of the universe at any time before or after that moment. E. Du Bois-Reymond put it with what now seems quaint nineteenth-century imagery: 'As the astronomer predicts the day on which, after many years, a comet again appears on the vault of heaven from the depths of space, so this "mind" would read in its equations the day when the Greek Cross will glitter from the mosque of Sophia or when England will burn its last lump of coal' (Lange 1925, bk. ii, p. 308). This is the form in which what Ryle has called 'The Bogy of Mechanism' (Ryle 1949, p. 76ff) reared its ugly head, and I think that it is here convenient to discuss mechanism in these nineteenth-century terms. It is true that mechanics is no longer thought of as the fundamental science to which all others, such as the theory of eletricity and magnetism, will ultimately be reduced. Moreover, modern physics is indeterministic, so that even an infinite intelligence could not make the sort of predictions envisaged by Du Bois-Reymond (or by Laplace 1951, p. 4). However, Ryle rightly rejects any attempt to provide a loophole for free will by means of quantum-mechanical indeterminism. As he says: 'The modern interpretation of natural laws as statements not of necessities but of very, very long odds is sometimes acclaimed as providing a desiderated element of non-rigorousness in Nature. . . . This silly view assumes that an action could not merit favourable or unfavourable criticism, unless it were an exception to scientific generalisations' (Ryle, 1949, p. 80).

Let us therefore discuss the bogy of mechanism in nineteenth-century terms. Most of what we have to say will easily be adaptable to modern indeterministic physics, by making the appropriate qualifications. This will enable me to make my discussion more simple, and will avoid irrelevant difficulties.

In what way is mechanism a bogy? I think that there are two reasonably respectable reasons for thinking that the truth of a mechanistic world view would imply emotionally unpalatable consequences. Most importantly, I think that a mechanistic metaphysics implies a threat to those who set their hearts on a life after death. Belief in a life after death is *perhaps* consistent with a mechanistic outlook, provided that one allows certain very unplausible factual assumptions (resurrection of the body, and so on), though there are of course well-known difficulties over personal identity here. But it is surely more plausible to believe in life after death if we regard the soul more on the model of a Cartesian spiritual substance than on the model of some sort of complex of digital or analogue computers. The other possible source of worry about the bogy of mechanism is the thought that if our brains are mere mechanisms, devoid of souls or vital principles, then relatively intelligent people like ourselves will perhaps be superseded by electronic devices, just as the unskilled laborer has been superseded by earth-moving machinery, and the process worker has been done out of a job by automation in factories. (But surely this is also good, if it makes us relatively clever chaps more sympathetic with the Luddite fears of the workers.) There may even lurk in the background of our minds fantasies of electronic Newtons and Beethovens, with a consequent threat to human dignity. (I strongly suspect that much resentment at the threat which a materialistic philosophy makes to traditional religion comes from the fact that materialism is felt as a threat to human vanity.) Already we are beginning to pass from the relatively respectable reasons for seeing mechanism as a bogy, namely the threat to hopes of immortality and the threat posed by extensions of automation, to dark fears perhaps best probed by a psychiatrist. In other ways, however, a mechanistic world view is very far from being a bogy. It appeals to those who treasure theoretical simplicity, classicism rather than romanticism.

How does Ryle deal with the bogy of mechanism? In particular, how would his considerations appear to someone like Du Bois-Reymond? Ryle points out that not all questions are physical questions, and that the laws of nature 'do not ordain everything that happens' (Ryle 1941, p. 76). He then remarks 'Indeed they do not ordain anything that happens. Laws of nature are not fiats.' Well, I don't know much about Du Bois-Reymond, but I would expect him to have wanted to say not that laws of nature are fiats, but simply that everything that happens would seem to be determined by (a) a set of initial conditions and (b) a set of laws of nature. As an answer to most mechanistic philosophers surely the remark that laws of nature are not fiats is an *ignoratio elenchi*. (Du Bois-Reymond's own way out from his worries seems to have been a quite different one from Ryle's. He argued that physics could never explain *consciousness*, and thence to a Kantian type of metaphysics. This solution would presumably appeal to Ryle as little as it does to me.) However, Ryle might have meant something else by the remark that laws of nature do not ordain what happens. This is that even in a completely deterministic universe it is not possible to deduce what happens from the laws of nature alone. Also needed is a specification of initial or 'boundary' conditions. (Thus given 'Everything is such that if it is F then it is G' we can deduce 'Something is G' only if we have the additional existential premiss 'Something is F.') I am not sure whether this is Ryle's point, because if it is then his immediate remark that laws of nature are not fiats seems irrelevant. However, if it is Ryle's point here, then it is of course a good and sound one, but it does nothing to exorcise the bogy of mechanism. Du Bois-Reymond would of course have agreed with it. The point never was that the laws of nature might determine everything that happens: his point was that *together with suitable initial conditions* they might determine everything that happens.

The difficulty of deciding just what Ryle's point is supposed to be here is increased when we look at an illustration which he gives of it (Ryle 1949, p. 77). He points out that in a game of chess the rules govern every move but they do not determine the moves. However, what ice would this illustration cut as far as someone like Du Bois-Reymond is concerned? He would agree that the laws of nature do not determine even the motions of the planets. What determines the motions of the planets is laws plus boundary conditions. Moreover these boundary conditions have to relate either to the whole universe or at least to a sufficiently large part of the universe which can be regarded as a closed system for the period of the prediction in question. The chess analogy is weak because there is not even the possibility of determinism. The configuration of the pieces on the board together with the rules do *not* determine (even probabilistically) the actual moves. In fact, were this not so there would be no real game. Du Bois-Reymond might have been worried that the moves in the game might be determined by the configuration of pieces on the board, together with a great number of other facts, such as the molecular structures of the players' brains (perhaps contingently identifiable with their intelligence, knowledge, intentions, etc.).[2]

A similar objection could be made to Ryle's other analogies. Thus consider his comparison of laws of nature with the rules of grammar, which did not confine Gibbon to 'a fatal groove' (Ryle 1949, p. 79). Just because there are no philological initial conditions which together with the rules of grammar determine what Gibbon will write, the analogy becomes a totally misleading one. Similarly Ryle makes use of the analogy of billiards and remarks that 'a scientific forecaster, who was ignorant of the rules and tactics of the game and of the skill and plans of the players, could predict, perhaps, from the beginning of a single stroke, the positions in which the balls will come to rest. . . .' (Ryle 1949, p. 80). This is not helpful precisely because the balls and the billiard table constitute an open system, not a closed one, and because surely the particles about which a Du Bois-Reymond is most concerned are not those which constitute the balls and the table but those which exist in the spaces between the players' ears.

We can connect this with Ryle's discussion in *Dilemmas* (1954, chapter 5) about alleged incompatibilities between the world of science and the world of everyday life. Physics, he tells us, is *ex officio* about such things as fundamental particles, and has no place in it for either a description or a misdescription of such things as chairs and tables. He compares the situation with that in a college, where every transaction is reflected in the college accounts. If books are bought then a suitable entry is made in the accounts. But though, in a sense, the accounts cover everything that goes on in the college, they neither describe nor misdescribe such things as the literary or scholarly qualities of the books. Once more, the analogy fails to do its job. There are things left indeterminate by the accounts (for example, the exact shape of a bought book), whereas according to a Laplacean determinist everything that happens *does* follow from the laws of nature plus a suitable set of initial conditions. (I hope that we have already agreed that as far as the discussion of the bogy of mechanism is concerned, the issue of quantum-mechanical indeterminism is a bit of a red herring.) Of course the concept of a chair or table is tied to the purposes for which it is used: thus a chair is something normally used for sitting on. This considera-tion, however, does not cut any metaphysical ice either, since the mechanist is presumably willing to identify intentions or purposes (contingently) with brain states, or at any rate to propose some general account of them which would be consonant with mechanism. Once again, of course, Ryle's point here might be that the laws of nature do not determine what happens. This would not be contested by even a Laplacean determinist, whose thesis would be that the laws of nature *together with suitable boundary conditions* determine everything that happens. I am more inclined to think, however, that Ryle's point is the slightly different one that a concept like that of 'chair' or that of 'table' is one which connects with the concepts of intention and purpose, as do concepts like 'carpenter'.

Even if this is so, it seems to me that Ryle is being rather misleading. He says: 'A bit of the theory of ultimate particles has no place in it for a description or misdescription of chairs and tables, and a description of chairs and tables has no place in it for a description of ultimate particles. A statement that is true *or* false of the one is *neither* true *nor* false of the other. It cannot therefore be a rival of the other' (Ryle 1954, p. 79). First, a pedantic quibble. It is unclear to me what 'true of the one' and 'true of the other' mean here, since it is predicates that are 'true of' or 'false of', whereas statements are true or false *simpliciter*. However, we may plausibly interpret Ryle as saying here that a description of a table or chair cannot mention ultimate particles. I think that he has overreached the mark here, even though we can concede that concepts like 'chair' and 'table' are partly anthropological ones. Consider the explanation of why an X-ray photograph of a chair is darkened rather slightly but is heavily darkened at the images of the nails in it. This would have to include the statements that the wood of the chair consists of certain sorts of atoms and that the nails in it consist of other sorts of atoms. Or again, consider an explanation of why the chair becomes electrically charged when it is rubbed with a rough cloth.

Here, when I say that the chair *consists* of atoms, I am following Feyerabend in denying that a useful distinction can be made between 'observation language' and 'theoretical language'. As Feyerabend (1961, pp. 82–3) has put it: a theory can be its own observation language. However, Ryle in sharply distinguishing between talk about chairs and theoretical talk about ultimate particles, might have at the back of his mind a quite different philosophy of scientific theories, of the sort which is often called 'instrumentalism'. According to this sort of view there are sharply different classes of expressions, *observation* words and *theoretical* words. Ryle would probably object to talking of 'observation language' and 'theoretical language' in that a scientist uses one language (say, English or Russian), but if one is permitted to use the word 'language' in the slightly technical sense in which it occurs in logic (e.g. 'meta-language') we may put the instrumentalist theory as follows: a theory is not in itself a meaningful description of the world, but it is a useful device whereby on the basis of certain statements of the observation language we can deduce certain other statements of the observation language. In fact instrumentalism is what is very naturally suggested by Ryle's account of laws of nature as 'inference licences'. Let us now look at this side of Ryle's work.

III

Ryle says: 'At least part of the point of trying to establish laws is to find out how to infer from particular matters of fact to other particular matters of fact, how to explain particular matters of fact by reference to other matters of fact, and how to prevent or bring about particular states of affairs' (Ryle 1949, p. 121). The 'at least part of' disarms criticism, but it is not at all clear what *else* Ryle thinks is the point of trying to establish laws.

Now it is true that according to any philosophical account of laws of nature they can function as inference licences. Suppose that we have two premisses A and B from which we can deduce a conclusion C in accordance with the rules of formal logic. Then the production of B licences a person who already is in possession of A to assert C. This will be the case whether or not B is a universally quantified statement (perhaps a law statement) or whether it is a statement of particular fact. It follows that in *this* sense *any* statement can function as an inference licence. It must therefore be in some stronger sense than this that Ryle wishes to characterise law statements as inference licences. This is presumably that laws are supposed to licence inferences in the way in which rules of inference do, and not in the way in which extra premisses do. But once again we run into difficulties, because *any* premiss, whether a law or not, could be replaced by a corresponding rule of inference. Even a particular or existential premiss could be construed as a rule of inference. Thus H. Gavin Alexander (1958, pp. 310–11) remarks that instead of the statement 'Flossie is a cow' as a suppressed premiss in the inference 'All cows are ruminants; therefore Flossie is a ruminant' we could introduce the material rule: 'From a premiss of the form "(x) (x is a cow $\supset F$ x)" deduce "F (Flossie).'

The above example shows that statements of the form 'F (Flossie)' cannot *always* function as inference licences, because even if 'Flossie is a cow' is elucidated as an inference licence, it is here used to infer to 'Flossie is a ruminant'. That is, not only the licence but the conclusion of the licenced inference is of the form 'F (Flossie)'. It is true that we also deduce laws from laws, so that perhaps it could be argued that this shows that law statements cannot always be construed as rules. However, it would be more plausible to say that this is a case of deducing rules from rules, whereas if we always construed *all* statements, even particular ones, as rules, it would be hard to see what the point of the whole business would be.

'Flossie is a cow' and 'Flossie is a ruminant' could both be observation statements. Someone who is trained to tell cows from other animals can be caused by an objective situation which contained Flossie to respond immediately and without conscious thought with 'Flossie is a cow'. If he can see Flossie's teeth and is well trained in the difference between ruminant and non-ruminant teeth he can equally respond with 'Flossie is a ruminant'. Hence despite the fact that 'Flossie is a ruminant' has, according to Ryle, a law-like or dispositional character, it can be an observation statement, in the sense of Carnap's pragmatic criterion for observation statements (Carnap 1936, 1937; Feyerabend 1958). An observation statement is a report on some particular chunk of the world which causes the relevant utterance of the statement, and hence it must contain names or descriptions or be preceded by existential quantifiers. Thus 'Fa,' '$(\exists x)Fx$', '$(\exists x)\ (\exists y)\ .Fx.Fy.x \neq y$' are some possible forms of observation statements. Thus 'Flossie is a cow', 'The cow is a ruminant', 'Two people have been hurt' could all be observation statements. Something of the form '$(x)\ (Fx \supset Gx)$' could not be an observation statement, because of the universal quantifier at its left-hand side. (It is true that some universally quantified statements could perhaps be observation statements if they contained predicates, such as 'is a lion in this room now', which contain references to small chunks of space-time. However, this does not matter in the present context, since statements containing such predicates would not be laws of nature.) Thus if it is the purpose of inference licences to get us from observation statements to other observation statements, then it is easy to come to think of law statements as being somehow *essentially* inference licences, because (not being observation statements) they cannot function as start or terminus of such a licenced inference.

Ryle follows Ramsey in calling laws 'variable hypotheticals' (Ryle 1949, p. 120). Ramsey held that these are not judgements but 'are rules for judging "If I meet a Φ, I shall regard it as a Ψ"' (Ramsey 1978, p. 137).[3] According to him this 'general enunciation' expresses a 'habit of singular belief' (Ramsey 1978, p. 136). Ramsey seems to have thought, for reasons which he sets out in some detail but which nevertheless are still not very clear to me, that the only alternative to this view would be to regard laws as conjunctions, and such conjunctions would have to be infinite and so could not be written out. Laws therefore cannot be conjunctions, for, as Ramsey said, 'what we can't say we can't say, and we can't whistle it either' (Ramsey 1978, p. 134).

There would seem here to be a reliance on the rather dubious notion of meaning as *expressing* a belief (analogous to the dubious notion of emotive meaning in ethics), but if we eschew this notion what is the advantage of construing a variable hypothetical as of the form 'If I meet a Φ I shall [ought to?] regard it as a Ψ'? This is of the form '$(x)\ (\Phi x\ .\ I$ meet x . $\supset$ I shall regard x as a Ψ),' and so we have presumably replaced an infinite conjunction of statements by an infinite conjunction of imperatives. Possibly this is why later in his paper Ramsey expresses the variable hypothetical not as a universally quantified statement but as an open sentence, 'If Φx then Ψx'. Perhaps Ramsey was under the influence of Wittgenstein's *Tractatus*, where sentences are regarded as pictures of facts. One trouble about this is that observation statements might well have the form '$(\exists x)Fx$,' and these could not be pictures or truth functions of pictures any more than universally quantified statements could be. We can thus envisage a language for science (a Quinean canonical language) of which *no* sentences were proper statement-making sentences according to Ramsey's criteria. It should also be noted that undecidability and unsolvability-results of modern logic, which have accrued since Ramsey's time, point up an additional infelicity in regarding laws of nature as rules of inference. Surely we should demand that there should be an *effective* way of telling whether or not a sentence was a rule of our system. Yet with any reasonably strong scientific theory there is no *effective* way of deciding whether or not a theorem follows from the axioms. Hence if laws of nature be taken as rules of inference there is no effective way of telling whether something is a rule of inference.

I have been construing Ryle's talk of laws as 'inference licences' as following Ramsey's account of laws largely because of Ryle's use of Ramsey's term 'variable hypothetical' (Ryle 1949, p. 120). It is worth noting that as *ordinarily* construed these law statements are neither variable nor hypothetical. Thus '$(x) Fx \supset Gx$' is not of the form '$A \supset B$,' since the scope of the quantifier extends beyond the '$\supset$'. What is variable or 'open' and hypothetical is not '$(x) Fx \supset Gx$' *but* '$Fx \supset Gx$'. Should we therefore, in spite of Ryle's remark about 'any' and 'every', be dealing with '$Fx \supset Gx$'? What is the rule of inference here? Perhaps it could be rephrased: 'If you find anything of which "Fx" is true expect "Gx" to be true of it.' But what on earth is the point of ascending to the metalanguage here? (Especially as we still need a universal quantifier in the formulation of the rule.)

Perhaps, then, the term 'inference licence' is a mere metaphor which should not be taken very seriously. After all, Ryle does say that law statements are true or false (Ryle 1949, p. 121) though he qualifies this by saying that 'they do not assert truths or falsehoods of the same type as those asserted by the statements of fact to which they apply or are supposed to apply. They have different jobs.' Well, perhaps they do have different jobs, but this does not imply that they are inference licences in any sense other than that in which any statement (perhaps a statement of a particular fact) might (as a suppressed premiss) licence an enthymeme. Earlier on the same page Ryle says: 'We have to learn to use statements of particular matters of fact, before we can learn to use the law-statements which do or might apply to them.' He concludes that law statements belong to 'a different and more sophisticated level of discourse' from the statements of fact which satisfy them. But equally we have to learn how to make non-disjunctive statements before we learn to make disjunctive ones, and yet there does not seem to be much temptation to say that disjunctive statements belong to a different level of discourse from non-disjunctive ones. An even more doubtful remark of Ryle's is that 'knowing or even understanding the law does involve knowing that there could be particular matters of fact satisfying the protasis and therefore also satisfying the apodosis of the law' (Ryle 1949, p. 121). Those philosophers who argue that science can be done entirely in an extensional language will presumably hold that a person might understand law statements, say of the form '(x) (*F*x ⊃ *G*x)', without having to understand the modal word 'could'.

I am inclined to think, therefore, that Ryle has not succeeded in giving any reason for thinking of laws of nature as inference licences, except perhaps in the innocuous sense in which a suppressed premiss of an enthymeme may licence a deduction.

In his 'Predicting and Inferring' Ryle (1962) talks of laws and theories as 'recipes' for generating inferences from observation statements to observation statements. Clearly 'recipe' is a variant on the term 'inference licence'. Ryle here uses it to make a point about the problem of induction. The success of inferences which are in accordance with the laws *shows* the goodness of the laws in the same way in which the succesful making of soufflés in accordance with a recipe *shows* the goodness of the recipe. Therefore there does not have to be 'a special sort of argument, to be called an "inductive argument", *from* the successes and failures of the inferences *to* the truth of the theory' (Ryle 1962, p. 170).[4]

I do not think that Ryle has here succeeded in dissolving the philosophical problem of induction. Indeed, I do not think that he has even done much to help the down-to-earth worry of a scientist who knows that a theory has been successful within a restricted range of circumstances, but wonders whether observations in new circumstances may show the theory to be false after all. Newtonian mechanics provides (within the limits of observational error) as good predictions and retrodictions as does special relativity, provided that we are dealing with bodies at small velocities; high velocities show the theory to be false. Indeed, after accepting special relativity, we can see that the theory is even false about small velocities, though the errors in the theory are too small to show up experimentally. It is true that the last sentence makes no sense to an out-and-out instrumentalist philosopher of science, and if Ryle were to hold that within the domain of small velocities Newtonian theory is as good as special relativity, because it works as well in providing correct experimental inferences, then this would suggest (what I suspect) an instrumentalist tenor to his philosophy of science.

Still less does Ryle's manoeuvre deal with the not so down-to-earth worry about the philosophical problem of induction. For this applies to recipes as much as to laws: how do we know that a recipe which works in certain circumstances today will work in even exactly similar circumstances tomorrow? The successes of the recipe (or of a law) certainly show that it works today, but how do we know that even the best tested recipe or law will work toorrow?

Ryle's attempted dissolution of the problem of induction here partly rests on an interesting suggestion of his, that there is no such thing as inductive inference. (In one of his Gavin David Young lectures at the University of Adelaide in 1956 he argued interestingly that 'deductive inference' and 'inductive thinking' make sense, but not 'deductive thinking' or 'inductive inference'.) But even if (as could plausibly be maintained) scientists never (or hardly ever) explicitly argue 'This theory has survived a great number of varied tests, *and so* it is probably true,' nevertheless they do suppose that it is rational to believe well tested theories. The question of the rationality of this belief is still the philosophical problem of induction, even though it has been formulated with reference to the rationality of a belief and not with reference to the validity of an inference. It has long been agreed that inductive procedures cannot be deductively justified (validated) but it is perhaps still an open question whether they might be pragmatically justified (vindicated) in some way. It is interesting that though Ryle follows Ramsey in his account of laws as 'variable hypotheticals', he does not follow up Ramsey's attempt at a pragmatic justification of induction (Ramsey 1978, pp. 98–100). Perhaps such an attempt is (despite the contemporary efforts of people like Wesley Salmon) doomed to failure, but a too quick dissolution of the problem can prevent us from at least investigating this possibility.

IV

I have suggested that Ryle's attitude to science, as something metaphysically neutral, and his treatment of laws of nature, perhaps presuppose an instrumentalist point of view, even though he never makes this explicit. I shall now suggest that a similar conclusion can be got from a consideration of his views on the science of psychology. In *The Concept of Mind*, chapter 10, Ryle argues that psychology is not concerned with explanations of our mental competences or of usual behaviour, but it is typically concerned with explanations of our incompetences and our more peculiar actions. 'The question why the farmer will not sell his pigs at certain prices is not a psychological but an economic question; but the question why he will not sell his pigs at any price to a customer with a certain look in his eyes might be a psychological question. . . . We cannot, from our own knowledge, tell why a straight line cutting through certain crosshatchings looks bent. . . . Yet we feel that the wrong sort of promise is being made when we are offered corresponding psychological explanations of our correct estimations of shape, size, illumination and speed' (Ryle 1949, p. 326). We may agree that we would seldom desire an explanation of a particular exercise of a competence, but nevertheless this could be given via psychological explanation of the general fact that humans possess such competences. Such an explanation would be a causal one via hypotheses about the central nervous system. These may be put in functional (see Fodor 1965) rather than neurological terms. But then an explanation of the working of a radio may be fairly abstract, perhaps because of lack of detailed knowledge: it may talk of, say, 'a frequency changer', rather than about the specific circuitry of the item in question. Just as in electronics we find explanations of the correct functioning of pieces of apparatus, and not merely of their misfunctioning, so in psychology there are explanations of human and animal competences and normalities. As against Ryle's claim to the contrary, this can be checked by looking at psychological journals (Smart 1959; Mandelbaum 1958).

Ryle's idea that (as far as normal behaviour is concerned) psychology does not go deeper than our ordinary common-sense explanations is evidently connected with the view that if it did give causal explanations these would be para-mechanical ones, based on the Cartesian 'two worlds' myth (Ryle 1949, pp. 324–5). It looks as though he cannot see a third possibility beyond either behaviourism or Cartesian dualism. He seems strangely reluctant to allow the identification of 'mental' causes with structures or processes in the central nervous system, whether these are described neurophysiologically or functionally (Medlin 1967). Neglect of this possibility indeed clouds his whole concept of a mental disposition. Thus vanity can naturally be taken as the structure which explains typically vain behaviour. No adequate translation into hypotheticals about behaviour can be produced. Similarly for physical dispositions. We cannot *translate* 'This glass is brittle' by 'If a stone hits it then it breaks', because conditions can exist in which the stone hits the glass without breaking it. We can, however, identify brittleness with an inner structure which *explains* typically brittle behaviour of the glass. This strategy of identifying dispositions with physical structures is as efficacious as Ryle's in disposing of 'ghosts' and it avoids obvious difficulties in Ryle's account (Putnam 1957; Levi and Morgenbesser 1964).

Suppose that something mysterious happened to our window pane, so that we couldn't see through it. Well, then, that would be something for which we should want an explanation, whereas most of the time we do not demand an explanation of why we can see through a (normal) window pane. (We usually can, and so we have the answer 'Because it is transparent'.) However, if we always were satisfied with such simple explanations there would be no real science. It is often the most familiar phenomena (for example the transparency of glass) that require the deepest explanations. A lot of children's 'Why?' questions can be answered only on the basis of something difficult like solid-state physics. Similarly, in psychology, some familiar things, such as normal vision, require quite deep hypotheses about neural circuitry. Yet in his discussion of psychology Ryle seems as though he is satisfied to stop at the rather trite level of common-sense explanation of *normal* behaviour, much as though 'Because it is transparent' were an adequate explanation of the light-transmitting properties of glass.

This attitude once more suggests an instrumentalist philosophy of science. If the common-sense explanations provide as good predictions as the deeper scientific ones, then what need is there of the latter? Of course, even on an instrumentalist philosophy of science the deeper explanations can be defended because of the way in which they do lead to new predictions in unusual cases, and because of the simplicity and unity which they bring to theory. So even an instrumentalist will want to go deeper than the phenomenological generalizations of common-sense. Nevertheless he or she has not *as much* motivation as the scientific realist whose ideal is not just ability to predict or retrodict, but *understanding*.

V

In this essay I have been trying to extract from the many hints which Ryle drops in various places some sort of coherent attitude to science, which boils down to two inter-related tendencies: (a) an inclination to believe that science is metaphysically neutral, and that it is no threat to ordinary commonsense ways of thinking about the world; (b) an instrumentalist attitude to laws and theories. These are at best tendencies only, and perhaps I have been unfair in foisting ideas on to Ryle which he might wish to repudiate. With typical modesty he has disclaimed competence to arbitrate in boundary disputes between sciences, and he says, 'I have long since learned to doubt the native sagacity of philosophers when discussing technicalities which they have not learned to handle on the job, as in earlier days I learned to doubt the judgment of those towing-path critics who had never done any rowing' (Ryle 1954,

p. 12). I fear that he may well discern a fair amount of hot air in the present essay. Nevertheless, even if only by way of hints and metaphors, Ryle has been widely influential in matters of interest in the philosophy of science, and it seemed worth while to try to bring some of Ryle's implicit views into the open. By fastening on to these matters my area of disagreement with Ryle appears greater than it in fact is. At one time Ryle's ideas were the dominating ones in my own thinking. However, my attempt to extract from his writings an explicit and coherent attitude to science may have been doomed to failure, simply because what I sought to find was perhaps never there in the first place, but at least it has seemed a useful exercise to have a go at it.

NOTES

1 On this point see the very instructive remarks by P.B. Medawar (1967, p. 114ff).
2 I do not wish here to argue for such a contingent identification, but see for example D.M. Armstrong (1968).
3 Something may possibly have gone wrong with Ramsey's syntax here. Perhaps a colon should have been inserted after 'judging'.
4 Criticisms of Ryle were made by Peter Achinstein (1960–1) (with a reply by Ryle) and by H.V. Stopes-Roe (1960–1).

REFERENCES

Achinstein, Peter 1980–1: From Success to Truth. *Analysis*, 21, 6–9.
Alexander, H. Gavin 1958: General Statements as Rules of Inference. In H. Feigl, M. Scriven and G. Maxwell (eds), *Minnesota Studies in the Philosophy of Science*, Minneapolis: University of Minnesota Press, 309–29.
Armstrong, D.M. 1968: *A Materialist Theory of the Mind*. London: Routledge and Kegan Paul.
Barnes, E.W. 1933: *Scientific Theory and Religion*. London: Cambridge University Press.
Carnap, Rudolf 1936: Testability and Meaning. *Philosophy of Science*, 3, 419–71.
—— 1937: Testability and Meaning. *Philosophy of Science*, 4, 1–40.
Chomsky, Noam 1968: *Language and Mind*. New York: Harcourt and Brace.
Feyerabend, P.K. 1958: Explanation, Reduction and Empiricism. In H. Feigl, M. Scriven and G. Maxwell (eds), *Minnesota Studies in the Philosophy of Science*, vol. 2, 28–97.
—— 1961: Comments on Sellars' The Language of Theories. In H. Feigl and G. Maxwell (eds), *Current Issues in the Philosophy of Science*, New York: Holt, Rinehart and Winston.
Fodor, J.A. 1965: Explanation in Psychology. In Max Black (ed.), *Philosophy in America*, Ithaca, New York: Cornell University Press, 161–79.

Hampshire, Stuart 1950: Critical Notice of Gilbert Ryle's *The Concept of Mind*. *Mind*, 59, 237–55.

Lange, F.A. 1925: *The History of Materialism*, 3rd edn. Translated by E.C. Thomas. London: Kegan Paul.

Laplace, P.S. de 1951: *A Philosophical Essay on Probabilities*. Translated from the 6th French edn by F.W. Truscott and F.L. Emory. New York: Dover.

Levi, Isaac and Morgenbesser, Sidney 1964: Belief and Disposition. *American Philosophical Quarterly*, 1, 221–32.

Mandelbaum, Maurice 1958: Professor Ryle and Psychology. *Philosophical Review*, 67, 522–30.

Medawar, P.B. 1967: *The Art of the Soluble*. London: Methuen.

Medlin, B.H. 1967: Ryle and the Mechanical Hypothesis. In C.F. Presley (ed.), *The Identity Theory of Mind*, St Lucia, Queensland: University of Queensland Press, 94–150.

Putnam, Hilary 1957: Psychological Concepts, Explication, and Ordinary Language. *Journal of Philosophy*, 54, 94–100.

Ramsey, F.P. 1978: Truth and Probability: General Propositions and Causality. In D.H. Mellor (ed.), *Foundations*, London: Cambridge University Press, 58–100, 133–51.

Ryle, Gilbert 1949: *The Concept of Mind*. London: Hutchinson.

—— 1954: *Dilemmas*. London: Cambridge University Press.

—— 1960–1: Comment on Mr Achinstein's Paper. *Analysis*, 21, 9–11.

—— 1962: Predicting and Inferring. In S. Körner (ed.), *Observation and Interpretation in the Philosophy of Physics*, New York: Dover, 165–70.

Smart, J.J.C. 1959: Ryle on Mechanism and Psychology. *Philosophical Quarterly*, 9, 349–55.

Stopes-Roe, H.V. 1960–61: Recipes and Induction: Ryle *v.* Achinstein. *Analysis*, 21, 115–20.

Swinburne, R.G. 1968: *Space and Time*. London: Macmillan.

10

Under the Form of Eternity

It is a rare privilege and honour for any philosopher to give a lecture at a great scientific institute.[1] Compared with the scientist a philosopher can appear to be a rather parasitic sort of animal, like the radio commentator at a cricket match as opposed to the cricketers out on the field. (There is no doubt which of these a cricket enthusiast would rather be.) Though the scientist is certainly at the place where the main action is, I hope that this lecture may leave you with the impression that it would be wrong to draw too sharp a line between the ways of thought of the scientist and those of the philosopher. However, it is true that philosophers disagree with one another more than scientists do, and so what I shall have to say must be taken as somewhat speculative and controversial.

My title for this lecture is of course a translation of Spinoza's expression *sub specie aeternitatis*. According to Spinoza one of the fruits of philosophy is that it enables us to see the world 'under the form of eternity' and I want to follow him in this, though I do not mean quite the same by these words as Spinoza did. The differences come from the fact that Spinoza was a rationalist philosopher of the seventeenth century, and he thought that we could attain metaphysical knowledge of the universe by purely *a priori* reasoning. Here Spinoza was quite wrong, though it would also be wrong to fly to the opposite extreme of Baconian empiricism. We must test theories by observation, and we must also temper our acceptance of putative reports of observation by considering their plausibility in the light of our theoretical background knowledge. Credulity in accepting so-called observation reports and a failure to consider how they fit into background knowledge is a source of much contemporary superstition and of too ready an acceptance of the claims of psychical research and the like. We need a compromise between pure rationalism and pure empiricism. At the other end of the spectrum from the observational, the apparently *a priori* science of pure mathematics is probably not quite as *a priori* as it may seem to be. The outstanding American philosopher W.V. Quine (of whom I shall have more to say in this lecture) has argued that our reason for believing in the existence of numbers and sets is not of a different kind from our reason for believing in physical entities such as electrons and neutrinos. In physics we find assertions of mathematical sort as well as assertions of a purely physical sort and indeed as well as assertions of a mixed sort, such as that the length in centimetres of a certain pendulum is identical with a certain real number. We test the combination of all these sorts of statement holistically by the hypothetico-deductive method. Hence we have reason to believe as much mathematics as is needed for physics. (Ironically, this probably does not include the more 'theological' regions of set theory, to the understanding of which Quine has himself made important contributions.) Quine's way of looking at mathematics combines a realistic theory about mathematics with an assimilation of mathematics to the hypothetico-deductive method of science. There is therefore no need to suppose that we have a peculiar (and biologically inexplicable) faculty of mathematical intuition.

While I therefore reject Spinoza's theory of knowledge as *a priori*, I do want to go along with part of what he means by seeing the world 'under the form of eternity'. I want to see the world in a universal sort of way. As far as possible I want to avoid any particular perspective in space-time, and I also wish to see the universe divested of conceptions which have a specifically human interest. If we can succeed (to some extent at least) in doing this we can later go back and put our particular spatio-temporal perspective and our specifically human conceptual framework into their correct cosmic places.

In this paper I am of course talking to biologists, and let me say right away that the remarkable developments in biology in the last few decades have greatly helped me to see the world 'under the form of eternity'. Biology forces us to see man as part of nature, not as something apart from nature. This is in spite of the fact that biology is itself a much less cosmically oriented science than is physics or chemistry. Biologists today, not least in the Walter and Eliza Hall Institute, apply the laws of physics and chemistry in order to understand certain structures and processes which occur in certain sorts of terrestrial organisms. On the descriptive level we find much that has the logical character of mere natural history. We find generalizations which may contain technical terms like 'chromosome' or 'ribosome', and which may refer to entities observable only in sophisticated ways, as by means of the electron microscope. These generalizations nevertheless have the character of natural history in so far as they are hedged about with all sorts of qualifications, so that exceptions to them can be tolerated in a way which is not possible in the case of genuine laws of nature. Moreover even if there were statements of descriptive cytology which applied universally in the case of terrestrial organisms, it would be only too probable that exceptions to them would exist in extra-terrestrial living systems.

The situation is of course complicated by the intrusion of chemical theory into the natural history. Suppose that one day exobiologists are able to demonstrate (in some unforeseeable way!) that chromosome-like structures occur in living cells in a planet of some remote star, and that these entities tend to split and separate as in mitosis and meiosis. Suppose further that chemical analysis shows that these exotic structures contain no nucleic acids. Exobiologists might wonder what in that strange region did the work of our terrestrial 'double helixes' and might wonder whether it existed in these chromosome-like structures. Obviously as things are now biologists do not need to worry about these strange possibilities of exobiology. They are more like my son puzzling out the workings of the pumps on the tankers of our local fire brigade, with no concern or need for concern about how the pumps on the tankers of Icelandic fire brigades work.

Partly for this reason I used to compare the central core of biology with engineering, saying that just as electronics was physics applied to wiring diagrams, the central core of biology was physics and chemistry applied to natural history, so that there were not any specifically biological laws and theories any more than there were specifically electronic laws and theories. For this I have been subjected to much probably well merited castigation from philosophers of biology (see Hull 1974; Ruse 1973). I think that I would now concede that there are some principles of biology which can not be regarded as mere generalizations of terrestrial natural history and which can not be reduced to laws of physics and chemistry. This is not because there is anything non-mechanistic about biological entities, but is partly because much biological explanation is like the electronic engineer's explanation by reference to 'block diagrams'. The electronic engineer may on occasion talk simply in terms of 'frequency changers', 'audio amplifiers', and so on, without much attention to the detailed circuitry, and similarly there are some purely biological terms, such as 'gene' (before molecular biology), and there are laws of genetics. Admittedly these laws are only approximately correct, and they require various qualifications, but to some extent this is true of many of the laws of physics. (What happens inside a black hole, for example?) I was setting an impossibly high standard for a statement to qualify as a law, and then showing (easily enough) that biological principles do not measure up to this standard. I would now rather say that there is a difference in degree rather than of kind between physics and biology, but that it is an important difference nevertheless. Specifically biological principles do not loom very large in much of biology. They often have very little content and lead to interesting predictions only when eked out by less law-like propositions of a less general sort and of purely terrestrial import.

This does not mean that the comparison between biology and electronics is not a useful one. Electronics, like biology, contains expressions for entities which are defined functionally (such as 'frequency changer'). The question of whether or in what sense these expressions can be 'reduced' to physical ones is not an easy one, but yet it is evident that any electronic device is a purely physical thing. In electronics, no less than in biology, we do not find any great predominance of special laws or principles (other than those of physics), though as one critic has remarked (Kleiner 1975, p. 526), there are laws in electronics, such as the principle that metal shields prevent radio reception. I think that if an electronic engineer thought it worthwhile to do so he or she could plausibly assert that short wave radio receivers with many stages of amplification usually contain at least one intermediate frequency stage, and he or she might expect this generalization, vague and statistical as it is, to apply to the technologies of even remote planets, and so to have some claim to being regarded as a law. Though I would now concede that there are special laws and theories in biology, they do not loom much larger than they do in electronics. To a very large extent biologists are concerned with applying their knowledge of physical sciences to an understanding of how various sorts of terrestrial organisms (or their parts) work, and it does not matter that the description of these organisms and their parts, however sophisticated it is, has the character of natural history rather than of scientific law. In particular, speculations of exobiology do not matter to most working biologists, especially in such subjects as cytology.

Nevertheless, as I suggested earlier, despite its terrestrial parochialism, biology does help us to see the world 'under the form of eternity'. With its very mechanistic approach modern biology forces us to see man as part of nature, rather than as a peculiar and possibly spiritual being somehow set over against nature. For this reason biologists tend to be on the whole metaphysically hard-headed people, who do not commonly fall for a certain sort of idealism which has often appealed to physicists. Many physicists have been tempted to see the world much as Bishop Berkeley did, and to hold that the aim of science is merely to describe and predict the course of our sense experiences. Such a physicist will be tempted to think that the description of an animal's brain is a description of the course of our sense experiences. A biologist will probably regard this idea as a very odd one: after all he is unlikely to forget that the sense experiences of a man or a rabbit are things that go on inside the man or the rabbit. We get things the wrong way round if we let ourselves be misled by the ingenious but fallacious arguments of Berkeley and like minded philosophers. Berkeley's philosophy comes from a too introverted approach to the theory of knowledge. In contrast to this many contemporary philosophers, notably W.V. Quine, have adopted an extroverted and biological approach to the theory of knowledge. Acquiring knowledge is something which animals do and there ought to be a scientific theory of it. The old introspective or phenomenological theory of knowledge can perhaps be seen as a convenient myth, which will be cashed eventually in terms appropriate to the modern theory of information processing and to physiologically oriented psychology. Moreover Quine has suggested that we can give an evolutionary explanation of the ways in which we classify things together as natural kinds (Quine 1969, chapter 5). It is obviously advantageous for the tiger to be able to recognize his prey, even though the characteristics which form the basis of this recognition may not be of any scientific interest. We come to have a lot of useful and partly innate cognitive mechanisms. The success of high level science is harder to explain in this way, though the actual *operation* of the hypothetico-deductive method may become explicable as a result of a pincer movement between theories of artificial intelligence on the one side and hypotheses of physiological psychology on the other side.

Thus philosophy and biology come together to reject the philosophical tradition according to which we get at the external world on the basis of a bedrock of inner experience. There is no bedrock and no need of bedrock. Quine likes to refer to Otto Neurath's analogy of the sailors who rebuild their ship at sea while still afloat on it (Neurath 1932–3). At a given time any plank of the ship can be replaced but all can not be. We can question anything though we cannot question everything. It is pleasing to see that the zoologist J.Z. Young uses the relevant quotation from Neurath as a motto at the beginning of his *Introduction to the Study of Man*, together with a sentence of Quine's.

The old introspectively based epistemology went along rather naturally with a view that mental events were different in kind from physical events. I think that we should reject this dualistic metaphysics and should see man as a complicated physical mechanism. Because of the mechanistic trend of modern biology the materialistic theory of mind is congenial to biologists, though a few, notably Sir John Eccles (1970), have defended the old dualism of mind and body. Provided that we can rebut the technical objections which philosophers have brought up against materialism, as I think we can, the mechanistic philosophy can be supported on grounds of theoretical simplicity. It is hard to see how an immaterial mind could have arisen from a process of evolution by natural selection. The dualist would have to explain the evolution of mind by supposing that there are laws of nature whereby if a complex physical organization of type Φ occurs then an additional (non-physical) entity of type ψ occurs. Laws of this type would not fit happily into existing science. The usual thing in science is that a very complex entity ought to be explicable in terms of its simpler parts and their arrangements, but this would not be possible in the case of laws of the Φ–ψ type.

Still it may be contended that we just are aware of our inner experiences and we are aware that they have properties different from those which a merely physical event or process could have. Now that spring is here you may smell the fragrance of new mown grass and what you experience does not at first sight (or at first smell?) seem to be a physical process in the brain. Still, the professor of physics may not seem at first sight to be the dean of the faculty of science, and yet this may nevertheless be what he or she in fact is. The sensation of smell from new mown grass is described in common language precisely in those terms, that is, in terms of its cause, and the common-sense description of it is *compatible* with its being a physiological process in the brain. After all, such physiological processes are caused by new mown grass. Certainly it is tempting to think that it is experienced as something non-physiological, but as D.M. Armstrong (1968–9) has remarked, this may be analogous to the illusion of the headless woman. By means of clever lighting and other devices a conjuror causes the audience to fail to perceive a woman's head, and the audience gets the illusion that it has succeeded in perceiving that the woman has no head. Similarly because we are not aware of the specifically physiological characteristics of our experiences we are tempted to suppose that we are aware of them as being non-physiological. In my opinion (and Armstrong's) this temptation should be resisted, though in order for this to be done responsibly it is necessary that we should consider and should refute many subtle philosophical arguments which the dualist will bring up. Naturally it is not possible to do this within the confines of the present lecture.

The poet or the traveller describes the brilliant colours of trees and mountains; the physicist speaks of wavelengths of light. To see the world 'under the form of eternity' we must follow the physicist here. This is because though there really are colours in the physical world, they are of interest only to human beings. Our colour discriminations depend not only on the things which we discriminate but also on the peculiar physiology of the human eye and nervous system. Robert Boyle, in his book *The Origin of Forms and Qualities*, which was first published in 1666, compared colours and other so-called 'secondary qualities' (smell, taste, etc.), to the power or 'disposition' of a key to open a lock. If we take a slight liberty and identify this power or disposition with the shape of the key, we must nevertheless note that the shape of the key would not *be* the power in question if it did not correspond to the shape of the lock. There is usually something rather idiosyncratic about the shape of a key. Without the idiosyncracy life would be too easy for burglars. Similarly though I think that redness is a physical property (say of a tomato) it is a very idiosyncratic one, and it is also a very disjunctive one (like the property of being a book *or* a pen *or* a table *or* a chair). There are infinitely many different combinations of wavelengths of light which will cause the same discriminatory reaction in a normal human being. It is as if there was a vast number of differently shaped keys which fitted one and the same lock. It is this idiosyncracy and disjunctiveness of colour which explains why colour concepts play no part in physical theory. It is a more complicated case of the situation which we have with keys and locks: the operation of a key on a lock can be explained by the laws of geometry and mechanics, but we do not need laws which mention the idiosyncratic shapes of particular sorts of locks.

To see the world under the form of eternity we must therefore eschew talk of colours (and for similar reasons also of sounds, tastes and smells). The cosmic insignificance of such talk can be seen if we consider how inappropriate it would be for the purpose of communicating with an inhabitant of a planet of some distant star, who would presumably have very different sense organs and nervous system from ours. If the view at which I have been hinting is correct we should not be leaving anything out if we used an austere physicalist language. Similarly, a man who described the shape of a key geometrically, instead of by reference to its lock opening powers, would not be leaving anything out in his description of the key itself. If he wished to say something about the relation of the key to the lock he could go on to give a geometrical description of the lock also. Analogously there would be no reason why we should not include in our transmission of news to the distant planet a description of the physical constitution of human sense organs.

We could not expect the inhabitants of distant planets to have our colour vocabulary, but their language might well have another metaphysically misleading feature of our ordinary language. I am thinking here of tenses and expressions like 'past', 'present', 'future', and 'now'. Suppose that we were to exchange signals with an inhabitant of a planet of Alpha Centauri (supposing for the sake of argument that this star does have a suitable planet). We would of course have to wait eight years for an answer. We might find the Alpha Centaurian disposed to use tenses and similar expressions. Of course we should need some new linguistic conventions because of the relativity of simultaneity to a frame of reference. Perhaps we could take it that when the Alpha

Centaurian refers to a distant event as occurring 'now' he means 'now' relative to his rest system, and when we say 'now' we mean 'now' relative to our rest system. With such a convention tensed discourse could go interstellar, though its general usefulness could then be questioned.

However, my main metaphysical objection to tenses and words like 'now', 'past', 'present', and 'future' has nothing to do with the theory of relativity. Such expressions are useful in ordinary life because they fix the time of an event which is mentioned in a given utterance by reference to the time of that utterance itself. They constitute a species of what are called 'indexical expressions'. This useful feature makes them liable to mislead us metaphysically. If we fail properly to realise the semantic point which I have just noted we can easily get a wrong idea that pastness, presentness and futurity are intrinsic properties of events, so that events change during time, losing the property of futurity, gaining that of presentness, and then losing this in favour of pastness. We may connect this up with a picture of time as like a river and of events as like floating objects which get swept down the river (from the future into the past). Alternatively we can think of events as like objects on the bank of the river and of ourselves as being swept down the river past them towards the big waterfall which is our death. Either picture is equally incoherent. Neither we nor events move through time. Motion is rate of change of position with respect to time, and there is something obviously wrong with a notion of rate of change of time with respect to time itself. Thinking in terms of space-time we see ourselves as long worm-like objects and our relative motions are just our relative inclinations. There is clearly no place in the picture for movement through space-time.

Though I have therefore no doubt that our intuitive feeling that we move through time or that time flows past us is an illusory one, it is not easy to explain the illusion. It is likely that it has something to do with the fact that we have memories of the past and not of the future. This asymmetry is a special case of a more general asymmetry, which is that the universe contains traces (footprints, recordings, fossils, etc.) of earlier events and not of future ones. We can of course predict the future (as in astronomy) just as we can retrodict the past, but the sort of knowledge which we get from traces is rather different. It depends in a certain way on probabilistic considerations. We believe that an indentation on a sandy beach was caused by the foot of a pedestrian because this is much less improbable than that it arose by chance from the effects of wind and water. But why can there not be analogous probabilistic argument about the future?

It is not plausible to blame this asymmetry on the laws of nature. Until recently it was believed that the fundamental laws of nature (quantum mechanics and electromagnetism) were time symmetric, and it is still thought that they are very nearly so, so that the asymmetry shows up only with rather recondite phenomena. (Moreover symmetry still holds exactly if we reverse not only time but charge and parity as well.) The usual way of explaining the gross temporal asymmetry which we observe around us is by reference to boundary conditions, and the explanation should go through even on the assumption of complete temporal symmetry in the fundamental laws. Such a temporally asymmetric law as the second law of thermodynamics is of course not a fundamental law and is only approximately true and its approximate truth can be deduced from temporarily symmetric laws together with suitable boundary conditions. These matters have been investigated by physicists in a tradition which goes back to Boltzmann and also by philosophers such as Hans Reichenbach and Adolf Grünbaum. The matter has not been cleared up to everyone's satisfaction, but I think that Reichenbach and Grünbaum are on the right track in characterising traces as 'branch systems', that is as sub-systems which are partially isolated from their surroundings and which have a lower entropy than would be expected from a comparison with these surroundings. Thus in a footprint what was originally a volume of sand becomes a region of which one part contains no molecules of the sand at all and another part contains molecules much more compressed together than elsewhere on the beach.

Those who do not see the world 'under the form of eternity' and who do not see human consciousness as a physical process and part of nature, may make conjectures about what a time-reversed world would look like. They may describe a world in which light rays converge from outer space into a sink, instead of spreading out from a source, in which a javelin is kicked out of the soil by countless surprisingly cooperative molecules of the earth so that it sails in a parabola to be caught in an athlete's hand, in which footprints disapear in the wake of pedestrians walking backwards, and in which milk separates itself from tea and rises upwards into a milk jug. The mistake which I find in this idea is that if the world were reversed in time, so also would be the process in our brain and the formation of memory traces, so that our ideas of past and future would be reversed too, and the world would appear exactly as it does now.

It is perhaps worth mentioning that besides the asymmetry of traces and the like there are two other notable cosmic asymmetries with respect to time. First there is the asymmetry exemplified by the fact that spherical electromagnetic waves go out from sources and do not contract to sinks, though both processes are equally compatible with Maxwell's equations. Secondly there is the asymmetry of the expansion of the universe. These two asymmetries also provide us with a time direction, and there arises the question as to whether they are connected with one another and with the first asymmetry (that of increase of entropy and the formation of branch systems). This is a matter of controversy, but it seems likely that the first asymmetry is the one which is relevant when we try to explain the felt temporal asymmetry in our experience.

Let me revert to the quasi-Spinozistic theme of the beginning of this lecture. Spinoza thought that if we see the world 'under the form of eternity' this somehow frees us from the bondage of desire, because we see both our desires and the things which happen to us dispassionately as part of the causal order of nature. The converse of this might be that we should free ourselves from desire in order to see the world 'under the form of eternity'. I do not want to say this at all, but I do want to consider something which could easily be confused with it. This is that in order to see the world 'under the form of eternity' we must free ourselves from the *concept* of desire. We will still have desires but we will not think of them in those terms.

There is something a bit anthropocentric in our talk of desires and of other so-called 'propositional attitudes', such as beliefs, hopes and fears. Let me say why these things are called 'propositional attitudes'. Suppose that I pat a unicorn on the head, then there must be in the universe a particular unicorn which is patted on the head by me. If on the other hand I desire a unicorn or fear a unicorn or hope for a unicorn or believe in unicorns there need be no unicorn which is desired, feared, hoped for, or believed in. Considerations of this sort show that desiring a unicorn, etc., is not being in a relation to a unicorn. If we think of desiring, believing, fearing and hoping as relations we must think of them as relations between persons and propositions or sentences or something of the sort. Hence these attitudes are called 'propositional attitudes'. By 'a proposition' philosophers mean (roughly) something which is expressed by synonymous sentences, but to the extent that the notion of synonymy is indeterminate so also is the notion of a proposition. If we avoid the notion of a proposition by taking the propositional attitudes to be relations between persons and sentences in some language, there is still some arbitrariness as to what English sentences should be taken as one term of the relation. There is also some unclarity about how to demarcate a language such as English, in view of the multiplicity of idiolects. Is it a clear question whether your present belief is that the cat is drinking some water or is it that your cat is drinking some H_2O, or are there two beliefs here mediated by a further belief that water is H_2O? Is someone's belief that there is a unicorn next door the same belief as his or her belief that there is a one-horned equine quadruped next door? Quine (1960, chapter 6) and Donald Davidson (1974) in different ways (and using more subtle and difficult considerations than those which I have just hinted at) have argued that the language of the propositional attitudes is too indeterminate to be of use for a really scientific psychology, which would have to make use of a radically different set of concepts (such as those of neurophysiology). The language of the propositional attitudes is what Quine calls 'second grade': it is convenient for ordinary life but not sharp enough to be the vehicle of really scientific explanation. If this is so, to see the world 'under the form of eternity' we must avoid our common-sense psychological language and get down to such things as neurophysiology and information theory, so that our discourse will contain words like 'synapse' and 'binary digit' but not 'belief' or 'desire', which have an indeterminateness which comes from the implicit reference to language.

In this lecture I have considered various things which are relevant to an attempt to see the world 'under the form of eternity', in a sense of these words partly similar to that of Spinoza. We try to understand the universe by means of laws which apply everywhere and everywhen, and if we have to be more parochial and deal with the merely terrestrial, as biologists mostly do, we try to do so in ways which explain the particular and the terrestrial in terms of its structure together with laws of cosmic scope. We avoid colour words and words for tastes, smells and sounds, because this vocabulary is too closely bound up with the peculiar circumstances of the human sense organs and nervous system to be of cosmic interest. We also avoid tenses and other indexical expressions, which mislead us if we temporarily forget the way in which they tie what is said to the occasions of their utterance. Finally, we avoid the 'second grade' discourse of the propositional attitudes. All this helps us to see the world in a way which is not too anthropocentric or too dependent on a particular perspective in space-time.

Of course the language in which we do all this is not the language of the poet or the historian or even of the social psychologist. We are not always concerned with metaphysical insight, and for other purposes a less austere discourse is unavoidable. What delights the metaphysician need not delight the historian, and in any case the metaphysician will not wish to use the term 'second grade discourse' in any pejorative sense when he knows very well that it is the language of Gibbon's *Decline and Fall of the Roman Empire*. Certainly we do not, and should not, and can not want to see the world 'under the form of eternity' all the time. In particular we need to use the language of the propositional attitudes in order to think about ethics, which is largely concerned with happiness, the notion of which is closely connected with that of satisfaction of desire. Even so, in ethics we should not be too anthropocentric. I think that we should be concerned with the welfare of all sentient beings, animals as well as men, and Alpha Centaurians (should we come across them) as well as terrestrial beings, to the extent that they can suffer pain and be capable of happiness.

As scientists the members of the Walter and Eliza Hall Institute come to see the world more under the form of eternity than does the man in the street or the poet or the historian. However, you must also come down to a more anthropocentric level, not only in clinical medicine where the language of the propositional attitudes is needed in the conversation of physician and patient, but also because you are particularly involved in humane concern for the health and relief from suffering of a particular species of terrestrial being. None of us wants to see the world 'under the form of eternity' all of the time. But I should like to have persuaded you that we should endeavour to do so at least in some of our philosophical moments.

NOTE

1   This paper was given as the seventh Walter and Eliza Hall Institute Lecture.

REFERENCES

Armstrong, D.M. 1968–9: The Headless Woman and the Defence of Materialism. *Analysis*, 29, 48–9.

Davidson, Donald 1974: Psychology as Philosophy. In S.C. Brown (ed.), *Philosophy of Psychology*, London: Macmillan.

Eccles, J.C. 1970: *Facing Reality*. Berlin: Springer-Verlag.

Hull, David 1974: *Philosophy of Biological Science*. Englewood Cliffs, New Jersey: Prentice-Hall.

Kleiner, Scott A. 1975: The Philosophy of Biology. *Southern Journal of Philosophy*, 13, 523–42.

Neurath, Otto 1932–3: Protokollsätz. *Erkenntnis*, 3, 204–14. An English translation of this will be found in A.J. Ayer (ed.), *Logical Positivism* (1959), New York: The Free Press.

Quine, W.V. 1960: *Word and Object*. Cambridge, Massachusetts: MIT Press.

—— 1969: *Ontological Relativity and Other Essays*. New York: Columbia University Press.

Ruse, Michael 1973: *Philosophy of Biology*. London: Hutchinson.

11

Difficulties for Realism in the Philosophy of Science

In this paper I wish to discuss some difficulties for realism in the philosophy of science.[1] I do this as one who has been concerned to defend realism about the sub-atomic entities of physics (and indeed other unobservables too, such as space-time points). What is such a realism? It is the theory that takes 'There are electrons,' for example, at face value, and neither tries to translate it away into statements about our sense experiences or about macroscopic material things, nor treats it merely as part of a useful instrument for deduction of observable facts. The arguments against translatability[2] or reduction of the former sorts are too well known to need recapitulation here, and so I shall therefore take the opponent of realism to be some sort of instrumentalist. The crudest form of instrumentalist takes talk about electrons to be simply a meaningless instrument of calculation, rather like the beads on an abacus.

The realist's most general argument against instrumentalism is that he can explain the success of microphysics in predicting facts on the macro-level. The instrumentalist just has to accept this success as brute fact. Why should things happen on the macro-level just *as if* there were electrons, neutrinos, and so on, if there really is no micro-level and if discourse that appears to be about unobservable micro-entities is not to be taken at face value? The scientific realist holds that his or her opponent is left with something like a cosmic miracle. That theories work, or that certain generalizations on the observational level hold true, is something for which his instrumentalist opponent can give no explanation.

Now if this is the realist's argument, the instrumentalist can raise the following objection. To explain the facts on the macro-level by reference to supposed facts on the micro-level is to treat the former as non-accidental relative to the latter. But will the latter facts not be just as much cosmic coincidences themselves? That all electrons are attracted by protons is no less a merely contingent constant conjunction than is some universal and projectible generalization on the macro-level. The law about electrons and protons is expressible in the purely extensional notation of predicate logic and there is no place for a full-blooded notion of natural necessity. The scientific realist can be made to look like John Locke's 'Indian', who said that the earth was supported by an elephant, which was supported by a tortoise, which was supported by . . . (see Locke's *Essay Concerning Human Understanding*, bk. II, chapter 13, section 19). In his *Dialogues on Natural Religion*, section 4, David Hume evidently alludes to this passage in Locke. The comparison with natural theology can be carried further, since van Fraassen, in a delightfully witty article (van Fraassen 1974), has compared the sort of scientific realist argument that I have been considering with Aquinas' Third Way.

Van Fraassen follows Hick (1973)[3] in re-interpreting the Third Way. That some particular fact is as it is may be explained by saying that the world is thus or so. But that the world is thus or so is equally a contingent fact. A theologian may contemplate this mass of contingency and may even be led to ask why there is a world rather than nothing. Similarly the scientific realist looks at the facts on the observational level, and asks why they are as they are. The answer 'It is just a matter of fact' does not satisfy him. The theologian is not satisfied with an accidental world, and the scientific realist is not satisfied with an accidental observation level. Aquinas, in his Third Way, concluded to a first cause, God, who was in some sense necessary. Admittedly Aquinas' notion of necessity was not that of a *logically* necessary being, as was the case with Leibniz and Samuel Clarke, but it was that of a being who by his own nature is not subject to decay or dissolution (see Flew 1976, p. 55; Brown 1964). Nevertheless the notion of *necessary* non-decay and non-dissolution is hardly more intelligible than that of logically necessary existence, at least if the necessity is thought of as logical necessity, and if the theologian's notion is not that of logical necessity he has not succeeded in explaining clearly what other sort of notion of necessity it is supposed to be. If existence can never be necessary the existence of God would be no less a 'brute fact' than the existence of the universe itself, and so we might as well accept the existence of the universe as ultimate, without trying to go one step further back, with a loss of ontological economy, to the existence of God. Similarly it may be urged against the scientific realist that he is merely replacing one cosmic coincidence by another, with a similar loss in ontological economy.

How as a scientific realist, can I reply to this challenge? Aquinas' argument depends on a notion of necessary existence which I find unintelligible. As a scientific realist I must not fall back on a similarly unintelligible notion of physical necessity. I think that Hume was right in saying that we can have no such (objective) notion of necessity. My reply to the challenge is that there are accidental generalities and accidental generalities. (Compare the view that all men are equal but some are more equal to others.[4]) There are good cosmic coincidences and bad ones, and the bad ones need to be explained by the good ones. That is, by postulating unobservable particles, and so on, and by stating a relatively small number of laws pertaining to these, a scientist can explain the untidy and multifarious facts about the macro-level in a relatively simple and unified manner. In the words of Perrin (1920, p. vii), we 'explain the complications of the visible in terms of invisible simplicity'. Not only will the laws on the micro-level be fewer than those on the macro-level, but they will not have to be hedged about by qualifications or *ceteris paribus* conditions, at least to anything like as great an extent.

Here I am using simplicity as a criterion of metaphysical believability: it is not a matter of mere convenience or of saving labour of thought. Of course, we have to accept the macroscopic facts anyway, but if they are seen to follow from simpler principles, then they become less puzzling. Somehow we think that simple theories are *antecedently* more likely to be true than are complex and messy theories. I do not know how to justify this assumption (the assumption 'Expect nature to be simple') any more than I can justify the Humean principle 'Expect the future to be like the past'. The assumption is one that scientists themselves feel to be a natural one.[5]

If I have to rely thus on general appeal to the above mentioned sort of simplicity, I am of course open to an objection from the side of the instrumentalist that I have assessed simplicity wrongly. The instrumentalist may say that his theory is simpler, because he posits fewer sorts of entities than the realist does.

It would be an advantage, therefore, if the realist could give up his reliance on mere appeal to simplicity (or other aesthetic qualities) and could show that his argument is one of a sort that scientists unquestionably use when arguing to previously unknown facts about the macro-realm, and that it would be unreasonable for them to reject such an argument when it is used in order to assert the real existence of micro-entities. The sort of argument I have in mind is that which has been called 'argument to the best explanation'. But in what way is the realist's explanation the 'best' one? As I have noted, the instrumentalist might be unimpressed by the realist's appeal to simplicity. This could be either because he is not interested in simplicity as such or because he has a different idea of what makes a theory simple. He does not wish to go beyond the regularities, such as they are, which he finds on the macro-level, though he is happy to use merely instrumentally understood theories as a way of connecting these regularities and of predicting new ones.

Dissatisfied, perhaps, with the vagueness of appeal to 'the best explanation', Wesley Salmon has argued that good explanation typically postulates a *causal mechanism*. In Salmon (1978) he adds to his previous account of explanation in terms of a set of 'statistically relevant factors' and 'pertinent probability values' a requirement of 'causal explanations of the relevance relations'. Subsumption under statistical regularities is important, he says, but that 'if the regularity invoked is not a causal regularity, then a causal explanation of the regularity must be made part of the explanation of the event' (Salmon 1978, p. 699). Salmon gives an interesting discussion in its own right of certain forms of statistical and causal explanation; in particular he supplements Reichenbach's notion of a 'causal fork' by means of the notion of an 'interactive fork', thus bringing statistical ideas to bear on the analysis of causality. We postulate a common cause of different events when we find a conjunction of phenomena which would be antecedently improbable, but which are much less improbable (though the probability can be less than 1/2 and even quite small) relative to the hypothesis of a common cause. According to Salmon, this postulation of a common cause is an essential feature of scientific explanation. This may be doubted. Consider, for example, explanations in the theory of relativity which are not causal but geometrical, or explanations in quantum mechanics, such as by reference to the Pauli exclusion principle, which are quite notoriously hard to reconcile with causality.

Still, Salmon could contend that explanation by reference to a causal mechanism is a common enough feature of scientific explanation, and that the instrumentalist is being simply arbitrary when in certain cases he refuses to accept the real existence of unobservable particles. He points out the sort of astonishing coincidence that seems to be explicable only by the real existence of an underlying causal mechanism. Consider first the experimental determination of Avogadro's number with the help of considerations of the kinetic theory of gases and of the theory of the Brownian motion of particles suspended in a gas. Consider secondly the determination of Avogadro's number by measurement of the amount of silver deposited on the cathode during electrolysis of a solution of a salt of silver, and with knowledge of the amount of electric charge required to deposit a single silver ion, which comes from Millikan's and J.J. Thomson's experimental determinations of the charge of an electron. Here we have two very different ways of determining Avogadro's number. The two very different sets of experiment yield the same number within the limits of experimental error. If we do not think realistically about the gas as made up of molecules, of the silver ions lacking one electron each, and so on, why should we expect this antecedently unlikely equality?[6]

Surely, says Salmon, this coincidence can be explained only by the principle of the common cause: there must be a common causal mechanism. Perhaps Salmon is using 'common cause' a bit widely here, because there is no single event in question here as a 'common cause' and to talk of a common *sort* of mechanism here is perhaps stretching things a bit. Moreover, Avogadro's number is not an event and so cannot have a cause. But whether or not Salmon's example connects up very readily with his account of explanation as causal, the example is certainly a very striking one, and shows the sort of consideration that many of us find quite persuasive for realism. The antecedent probability of the numerical coincidence from the two sets of experiments is low, but becomes high relative to the hypothesis of electrons, molecules, ions, etc. The instrumentalist does not have a good explanation of this coincidence because he is precluded from regarding his theoretical sentences as *true*. Admittedly if a sentence $\ulcorner p \urcorner$ is a good computational device a working scientist will probably be willing also to say that $\ulcorner p \urcorner$ is true, and to assent to the Tarskian paradigm ' $\ulcorner p \urcorner$ is true if and only if p'. Now this is all right for mere substitutional quantification over 'p', provided that certain constraints to avoid antinomies are met. But to get the Tarski theory of truth we need objectual quantification over individuals and the notion of 'satisfaction'. We need things like '(y) "x is an electron" is satisfied by y if and only if y is an electron', quantifying over a universe that contains electrons. For the semantics to be genuinely explanatory 'is satisfied by' has to be an extensional context, like 'kicked' and unlike 'is a fictional description of'. For Tom to kick the football both Tom and the football must exist.

It is true, however, that the instrumentalist *could* make use of Tarski's notion of *truth in a model*. We cannot say that a sentence $\ulcorner p \urcorner$ is true in a certain model M if and only if p, unless of course M just is the *universe*, with the right mappings between the predicates of the language in question and sets of things (or sets of sequences of things) in the universe. If the instrumentalist's theory is a consistent set of sentences, as he hopes it is, then it has a mathematical model, indeed a model in the domain of the natural numbers. But this model-theoretic fact does not entitle the instrumentalist to say that he is talking about numbers when he *seems* to be talking about electrons and protons. We must not confuse truth in a model with truth *simpliciter*. Moreover even if we did allow the instrumentalist to say that he was talking about numbers and not about electrons and protons, we could accuse him of straining at a physical gnat and swallowing at a Platonistic camel. I myself want to swallow both the gnat and the camel, for reasons that are due to Quine: in physics we find sentences quantifying over numbers and sets no less than over electrons and protons. I do feel uneasy about the camel, but can unfortunately see no way of avoiding the hypothesis of Platonistic entities. Indeed in the final paragraph of this paper I shall make some compromise with the model-theoretic sort of instrumentalism, so that in the context of microphysics I shall indeed myself strain at the gnat and swallow the camel. But if I strain at the gnat I shall want to keep *some* hold on realism in a more indirect way.

To say that realism is the right account of theoretical physics is therefore much the same as to say that the sentences of theoretical physics are true in the objectual Tarski sense. (True, not just true in a model.) So another threat to realism might come from neo-verificationist theories of truth, such as have been proposed by Michael Dummett. Dummett extends an intuitionist way of looking at mathematics to language generally. I must say that I find intuitionism philosophically obscure. Even though the intuitionist may not exactly confuse use and mention when he equates $\ulcorner p \urcorner$ with ' $\ulcorner p \urcorner$ is provable', nevertheless the equation of the sense of an object language sentence with that of a metalanguage sentence seems very odd. Nor am I attracted to any form of verificationism generally. However, I am not familiar with Dummett's recent theories about all this and would not be able to do justice to them: I shall therefore merely note them as a possible threat to realism.

I now come to another sort of threat to realism, which arises from the fact of scientific revolutions. I have connected realism to truth, but what confidence have we that any scientific theory is true? The Newtonian theory of gravitation, so it may be said, was overturned by Einstein's general theory of relativity, while the Newtonian laws of force and the laws of classical electro-magnetism were replaced by quantum theory. And so on. Making an induction from the revolutions in the past to the probability of revolutions in the future, we may be tempted to say that existing physical theories are almost certainly false. Yet they are quite successful. So it looks as if the realist's argument, the argument from success to truth, must be rejected. The next move is therefore to see whether we can replace the argument from success to truth by an argument from success to *approximate* truth. We might not be able to conclude that there is any object that exactly satisfies the predicate 'is an electron', for example, but we might be able to reassure ourselves that there must be some object that *approximately* satisfies it. That a theory of approximation to truth, or of 'verisimilitude', was required for the defence of realism was clearly stated some years ago by Sir Karl Popper (see Popper 1963, p. 235; 1972, pp. 47–61, 101–3 and 331–5). Popper's qualitative definitions of verisimilitude have been criticized by David Miller, Pavel Tichý, and others, including Popper himself.[7] In particular see Miller (1974) and Tichý (1974). For a defence of realism it would be good, in particular, if we could say in what way theories might approximate ontologically to the truth (and hence to one another). Can a theory about particles be *ontologically* an approximation to a theory about fields, for example?

At least, it may be said, there is a sense in which the laws of an old theory approximate to the laws of a new theory. According to Putnam (1965) to say that a law or theory is approximately true is to say that a certain logical consequence of it is true *simpliciter*. For example, a correct theory might contain an inverse 2.001 law and a theory that approximated to it might contain an inverse square law. However, what we should like would be a theory of verisimilitude according to which we could say that the new theory, even if not true, is *nearer* the truth than the old theory. Miller (1975) has argued that unless the laws of theory *B* are exactly true, then even if some laws of *B* are more nearly correct than those of *A* there will be other laws of *B* which are less correct than corresponding laws of *A*. This parallels the criticism of Popper's qualitative theory of verisimilitude in Miller (1974), where it is argued that on Popper's theory *B* can be nearer the truth than *A* only if *B* is true *simpliciter*. Perhaps for a merely metaphysical defence of realism we might wish to rely on an account of verisimilitude in terms of mere nearness to an unknown quite-correct theory, but such a notion will be found by anti-realists to be quite vague, or even obscure, if it does not allow us to say, for example, that special relativity is nearer the truth than Newtonian mechanics. We might have wildly differing estimates of the population of China, with no idea which were more correct, but at least we could say what it was for one to be nearer the truth than another. This sort of assurance is lacking in the case of verisimilitude of theories.

Theories that succeed one another in the manner of a Kuhnian revolution can differ from one another ontologically and not just in respect of laws, as when, for example, a field theory replaces a particle theory. For simplicity I shall illustrate the point not by any real scientific theories but by means of an imaginary example. Consider two theories each of which has a sort of pre-Socratic simplicity. Imagine first a cosmology according to which everything is made up of variously shaped solid massy particles, like Democritus' atoms, and let this be replaced by a cosmology according to which instead of particles in a void we have a plenum with variously shaped holes in it. Suppose that these holes move about and rebound from one another much in the way in which the original massy atoms were supposed to do. It is clear that these holes could still be referred to by the same word 'particle'. The adherent of the new theory would of course reject certain sentences of the old theory in which the word 'particle' occurred, for example sentences to the effect that particles were continuously filled with matter, but many sentences in the old theory, such that certain sorts of particles move in ellipses, might still occur in the new theory. Thus a lot of sentences common to the two theories could still contain the word 'particle', and for acceptance of these sentences it would not matter whether particles were thought of as massy lumps in a void or as empty spaces in a plenum. In a sense the two theories would be 'approximately about' the same things. (Nor, of course, would it matter if the new theorists coined a neologism to replace the old word 'particle'.) This sort of case is not too worrying, because there is a one–one correlation between the fundamental entities of the two theories (or at least there would be if the putatively correlated entities existed). A worry is that there may not be such a one–one correlation between the fundamental entities of different theories. Hence the sense in which the ontological statements of successive theories approximate to truth is still very obscure.

Some of the sentences that the rival theorists will use will be observation sentences, which can be characterized, following Quine (1974, pp. 39–41), as those sentences which would be assented to (or dissented from) by all members of a linguistic community who were in the appropriate perceptual situations. Thus a true observation sentence might be to the effect that the needle of a certain ostensively defined device pointed to the numeral '1.5'. Those who knew that the device was a properly functioning ammeter would also of course assent to the statement that the electric current through the device was 1.5 ampères. On the other hand, many members of the linguistic community would not understand the expression 'ampère' or 'ammeter' and so the sentence 'The current through the device is 1.5 ampères' would not count as an observation sentence, though it could be made to do so if we restricted the linguistic community to scientifically trained persons who knew that the ammeter was correctly calibrated and so on. Now if we think of observation sentences in this way we can see that even revolutionary changes in physics will be unlikely to affect observation sentences. Even if a revolutionary theory led us to say quite novel things about electrons and electric currents it would not lead us to give up our assent to sentences such as that the current through a circuit was 1.5 ampères.

Nor indeed need such a revolutionary change of our theory about electrons lead us to change our assent or dissent to many sentences about electrons themselves (i.e. containing the word 'electron'), such as that, for example, electrons and protons have opposite electric charge. Whatever revolutions there are in the theory of the nucleus, and whatever hypotheses may be developed to explain the present complicated taxonomy of elementary particles, we can be sure that water will still be H_2O and that a hydrogen atom will still contain one proton and one electron. We must not allow the fact of scientific revolutions to blind us to the solid mass of ascertained and never-to-be overturned theory in physics. 'Hydrogen' and 'electron' are not likely to go the way of 'phlogiston'. I conclude therefore that provided a good theory of verisimilitude can be worked out (and this is a big 'if') realism has probably nothing to fear from the fact of scientific revolutions.

Approximation to truth may be thought of in terms of reference to 'ideal entities'. But it is easier to talk in terms of 'ideal entities' than it is to know what one is talking about. Are the 'real entities' of current theory, such as electrons and protons, no more than 'idealizations', like the continuous fluids of hydrodynamics, the isolated dynamical systems of classical mechanics, or the isolated harmonic oscillator whereby students are introduced to quantum mechanics? There is something confusing in saying that physics talks about idealizations, since idealizations do not exist in the real world, and so are not there for the theory to be about, in a referentially transparent sense of 'about'. There is an intensional sense of 'about', in which we say that Dickens wrote a book about Mr Pickwick or that Mallory wrote one about the knights of the Round Table, but I think we should analyse this as purporting, pretending, or something of the sort, to 'talk about' in the extensional sense; i.e. not in terms of actually operating an intensional semantics but in terms of purporting (etc.) to operate an extensional one. (In a sense I want to say that there can be no intensional semantics.)

Now the problem of ideal objects in science is more difficult to deal with than is that of outright fiction. Neither Dickens nor Mallory were providing explanations, and their stories have no use in prediction. The explanatory and predictive efficacy of 'ideal theories' needs to be explained. One possible explanation may come from the predicates of the ideal theory being aproximately satisfied by real objects (or sequences of them) and not from their being exactly satisfied by ideal objects (or sequences of them).

In conclusion, however, I want to canvas a possible explanation of the explanatory and predictive value of physics which is a compromise between an out-and-out realism and instrumentalism. I do not think that this compromise should have been used prior to the development of quantum mechanics, and perhaps it can be put aside in the future if quantum mechanics is replaced by some more satisfactory theory. Many of us do, however, sense a special difficulty in giving a completely realistic philosophy of quantum mechanics.

Earlier in this paper I argued that realism was plausible, because it gave the best explanation of the predictive success of physics and because only if there is a realistic theory can we avoid supposing an implausible cosmic coincidence on the observable level. But plausibilities must be weighed relatively to one another, and there are things about quantum mechanics that make a plausible realistic interpretation hard to achieve. Consider the sort of situation envisaged in Einstein, Podolsky and Rosen (1935), in which there are two interacting systems S_1 and S_2, which then separate. By doing appropriate experiments on S_1 it is possible to determine properties of S_2. Einstein, Podolsky and Rosen used this as an argument for realism, because alternative experiments on a system S_1 could make it possible to determine at will either the position or the momentum of S_2, or perhaps one or other of some other pair of conjugate properties. Since S_1 and S_2 could by this time be distant and not interacting, this suggests that S_2 had these two conjugate properties all along, contrary to the uncertainty principle. Subsequent investigation showed that such a realistic interpretation was not possible, and indeed the argument now goes against realism. It appears that an experiment on S_1 does actually change the properties of S_2 even though the two are distant from one another.[8] This seems to smack either of subjectivism or of action at a distance, and both alternatives are unpalatable. (Of the two, however, I would choose action at a distance, if I had to choose.)

If we think that a realist interpretation of quantum mechanics is not possible, must we go back to a thoroughgoing instrumentalism or some other form of anti-realism?[9] A realist interpretation of quantum mechanics lacks plausibility, but so on the other hand, as I have urged earlier in the paper, does an anti-realist metaphysics of science. I think that perhaps we can get a compromise which implies an ultimate metaphysical realism but which allows an instrumentalist view of present-day microphysics. Let us recall the fact that the instrumentalist might deny straight-out truth to theoretical sentences but can talk of their truth in a model. A consistent set of sentences must have a mathematical model. Now at the stage of classical physics we shall have come to postulate a domain of mathematical entities no less than of physical particles, since (as Quine has urged) physics is tested holistically and contains mathematics as an integral part of it. We can surely retain this ontology of mathematical entities when we pass to microphysics, and so we can believe realistically in a domain of mathematical entities that provides a model for the sentences of microphysics. Let us regard these sentences of microphysics as purely instrumental, but nevertheless we may suppose that the success of this instrumentalist theory may perhaps be explained by the idea that in some appropriate sense the model of the instrumentalist theory is an approximation to some mathematical model of some unknown but true realist theory. This sort of instrumentalism would therefore be realist in principle. Not only would it be realist about mathematical objects (which is not important in the present connection) but it would point to an unknown realist theory in the background. I do not know whether this sort of compromise between realism and anti-realism could be worked out. In particular, I do not know whether this sort of model-theoretic situation could obtain without the supposedly 'instrumentalist' theory approximating to the realist theory in the background, i.e. possessing verisimilitude, and so bringing us back to an earlier attempt at defending realism.

NOTES

1 This paper was written while I was a Fellow of the Center for Advanced Study in the Behavioral Sciences, Stanford, California. I should like to thank various friends who have commented on an earlier draft of this paper: Nancy Cartwright, David Cole, John Etchemendy, Antony Flew, Bas van Fraassen, Susan Haack, Ian Hacking, Bruce Kuklick, Ruth Barcan Marcus, Wesley Salmon, Robert Stalnaker and Mark Wilson. After completing the first draft of this paper I was fortunate to be able to read a typescript of Bas van Fraassen's (1980) book *The Scientific Image*, in which van Fraassen defends a novel and sophisticated form of anti-realism. Properly to discuss van Fraassen's book would require a separate paper. Even before reading his book I had come some way nearer his position: see my tentative suggestions about quantum mechanics in the final paragraph of my paper. However, I still want there to be a realistically interpretable (though perhaps unknown) theory somewhere in the background.

2 Apart from more traditional attempts at showing translatability, I also rule out metalinguistic detours, as in Craig's method (Craig 1956). Even assuming that physics could be effectively axiomatized so as to allow for an application of Craigian transcription – for some scepticism on this score see Leeds (1975) – the manner in which the transcribed theory is obtained can be understood only by meta-linguistic discourse about an ostensibly realist theory. If we did not take the ostensibly realist theory at face value the success of the transcribed theory would be a mystery.

3 Hick himself refers (p. 21) to various contemporary Thomist philosophers.

4 As in George Orwell's *Animal Farm*.

5 For some purposes a justification of the criterion of simplicity may be possible. See Sober (1975). Nevertheless Sober's justification of simplicity makes use of this criterion itself. Though he holds that simpler theories are in a certain sense more likely to be true (1975, p. 168) he nevertheless holds that 'support and simplicity are irreducibly different goals in hypothesis choice'. Sober holds also (p. 175) that as a methodology realism scores over anti-realism as being more simple.

6 Jean Perrin used such coincidences from at least a dozen different ways of determining Avogadro's number as a clinching argument for the reality of

atoms and molecules (Perrin 1920, pp. 206–7). See also Nye (1972, p. 171). I am indebted to Wesley Salmon for referring me to these two books.

7 Chris Mortensen has exploited the possibility that if a theory has a base in relevant logics or alternatively in modal logic, then it might be possible to avoid Miller's objections to a theory of verisimilitude along Popper's lines. There is some initial reason to think that it could (see Mortensen 1978), but later results suggest that Popperian verisimilitude has serious problems in even very weak logics (Mortensen 1983 and personal communication).

8 The evidence has been surveyed and assessed in Clauser and Shimony (1978).

9 Such as van Fraassen's model-theoretic approach (1980).

REFERENCES

Brown, Patterson 1964: St Thomas on Necessary Being. *Philosophical Review*, 73, 76–90.

Clauser, John F. and Shimony, Abner 1978: Bell's Theorem: Experimental Tests and Implications. *Reports on Progress in Physics*, 41, 1881–927.

Craig, William 1956: Replacement of Auxiliary Expressions. *Philosophical Review*, 65, 38–55.

Einstein, A., Podolsky, B. and Rosen, N. 1935: Can Quantum-mechanical Description of Reality be Complete? *Physical Review*, 47, 777–80.

Flew, Antony 1976: *The Presumption of Atheism*. London: Pemberton.

Hick, J.H. 1973: *Philosophy of Religion*. Englewood Cliffs, New Jersey: Prentice-Hall.

Leeds, Stephen 1975: A Note on Craigian Instrumentalism. *Journal of Philosophy*, 72, 177–84.

Miller, David 1974: Popper's Qualitative Theory of Verisimilitude. *British Journal for the Philosophy of Science*, 25, 166–77.

Miller, David 1975: The Accuracy of Predictions. *Synthese*, 30, 159–91.

—— 1976: Versimilitude Redeflated. *British Journal for the Philosophy of Science*. 27, 363–81.

Mortensen, Chris 1978: A Theorem on Verisimilitude. *Bulletin of the Section of Logic*, 7, 34–43.

—— 1983: Relevance and Verisimilitude. 55, 353–64.

Nye, Mary Jo 1972: *Molecular Reality*. London: Macdonald.

Perrin, Jean 1920: *Atoms*. London: Constable.

Popper, K.R. 1963: *Conjectures and Refutations*. London: Routledge and Kegan Paul.

—— 1972: *Objective Knowledge*. Oxford: Clarendon Press.

Putnam, Hilary 1965: How Not to Talk about Meaning. *Boston Studies in the Philosophy of Science*, 2, 205–22. Reprinted in 1975: *Philosophical Papers*, vol. 2, London: Cambridge University Press, 117–31.

Quine, W.V. 1974: *The Roots of Reference*. La Salle, Illinois: Open Court.

Salmon, Wesley C. 1978: Why Ask, 'Why?' An Inquiry Concerning Scientific Explanation. *Proceedings and Addresses of the American Philosophical Association*, 51, 683–705.

Sober, Elliot 1975: *Simplicity*. Oxford: Clarendon Press.

Tichý, Pavel 1974: On Popper's Definitions of Verisimilitude. *British Journal for the Philosophy of Science*, 25, 155–60.

van Fraassen, B.C. 1974: Theoretical Entities: The Five Ways. *Philosophia*, 4, 95–109.

—— 1980: *The Scientific Image*. Oxford: Clarendon Press.

12

Sellars on Process

I

Are words like 'before' and 'after' fundamentally temporal *predicates*, true of ordered pairs of events, processes and the like, or are they fundamentally (non-truthfunctional) sentential connectives? According to surface grammar, of course, it would appear that they can be both, since we have sentences like 'The battle was before the earthquake' and also sentences like 'Socrates drank the hemlock before he died'. But which is fundamental? Which most nearly shows the logical form?[1] Most philosophers and scientists have assumed that the former alternative is correct. Wilfrid Sellars opts for the latter alternative in his second Carus lecture 'Naturalism and Process' (Sellars 1981, hereafter referred to as CL2) and in his much earlier 'Time and the World Order' (Sellars 1962, hereafter referred to as TWO), though he concedes that in some ideal future 'scientific image' the former alternative may be appropriate. In what follows I shall be concerned with Sellars's views on 'the manifest image' unless I indicate otherwise.[2] Another important philosopher who has elucidated temporal discourse in terms of 'before', 'after', etc., as sentential connectives, is P.T. Geach (1965).

Contrary to Sellars I do not see the same unbridgeable gulf between our ordinary 'manifest image' talk and that of some ideal 'scientific image'. For example I would hold that a physicalist account of Sellars's well-known pink ice cube is possible (Sellars 1981, sections 17–35). More germane to the present purpose, I do not see a wide gulf between our ordinary talk of objects, such as tables, men, cats, stones, clouds, and stars, as substances – the permanent in change – and Minkowski type talk of these things as four-dimensional space-time solids. I want to say that just as a man is so many centimetres tall, broad and thick, so he is (say) seventy years long in time.[3] (Furthermore the special theory of relativity shows how by settling on some value, say unity, for the velocity of light, we can express the man's height, breadth, thickness and endurance in time in the same units.) What then are events and processes? Before giving my answer to this question I shall adumbrate some 'ordinary language' considerations.

We talk of processes changing or becoming something or other (as a battle can become fiercer). It would be odd, however, to talk of such a change or becoming itself changing or becoming something or other. Many years ago I tried to make an analogy between the 'event-process' distinction and Gilbert Ryle's 'task-achievement' distinction (Smart 1949). One can run hard and for a long time, but one can hardly win hard and for a long time. The traffic light can change from red to green, but can the changing from red to green change? It seems that often 'event' works rather like 'result'. This ties in with etymology, where 'event' = 'outcome'. In Sir Walter Scott's *Ivanhoe* we get a perhaps somewhat archaic use of the word in this sense. Thus in chapter 16 we have 'the event of the tournament' and 'he was justified by the event', and even more clearly, chapter 39, 'I am . . . friend or foe, Rebecca, as the event of this interview shall make me'. Now 'result' has a propositional feel about it ('What was the result?' 'I passed.') Such uses of 'event' tie in with Sellars's views.

It is tempting to say that the reason we might not be able to talk of events changing is that they are (or are associated with) mere instantaneous time-slices of four-dimensional objects. To say that a thing changes is to say that earlier and later time-slices of it are different, but a single time-slice cannot be different from itself. Are events, then, if they are not propositional, perhaps instantaneous time-slices? Consider the beginning of a war. Was there an *instant* at which the war began? (Indeed, in view of quantum-mechanical indeterminacy, is there a definite instant at which anything begins?) Also we talk of a battle sometimes as if it were an event ('The battle happened in 1915') and sometimes as if it were a process ('The battle grew fiercer'). I am now therefore inclined to suspect that the difference between events and processes is a contextual one, not an ontological one (not a category difference). We speak of a process as an event when we are not much concerned with its inner temporal structure, and as a process when we are so concerned. Events need not be instantaneous. (Nor, I think, despite the archaic use mentioned in the last paragraph, need they be propositional. But I shall give reasons for thinking this later.) The fact that the oddity of talking of events changing may be contextual rather than categorical is indeed brought out by the fact, pointed out by F.I. Dretske in his valuable paper, 'Can Events Move?' (Dretske 1967), that we *do* sometimes talk of a picnic moving indoors, and things of that sort, and it seems artificial to say that 'picnic' is ambiguous, so that it here functions as a process word, not an event word, as when we say that the picnic occurred on a certain date.

If events and processes are not to be distinguished ontologically, nor need states. States of an object can be regarded as unchanging processes, i.e., temporal stages whose time-slices are similar to one another. Could we follow W.V. Quine and say, furthermore, that events and processes need not be distinguished from objects, as conceived four-dimensionally? Physical objects, events and processes, alike consist, as Quine put it, of 'the content, however heterogeneous, of some portion of space-time, however discontinuous and gerrymandered' (Quine 1960, p. 171). This view runs up against semantic difficulties, but I want to play with it for a moment or two.

Consider a battle. We might consider this as a space-time object consisting of the mereological sum of all the space-time objects (temporal stages of men, machines, projectiles, etc.) that make it up. Thus we would identify processes with temporal stages of space-time objects. Sometimes such objects cannot be specified separately from their stages. Thus thunder and lightning are processes, but we can say 'It thunders' and 'It lightnings'. We can supply noun phrases for the 'It' by simply saying 'The thunder thunders' and 'The lightning lightnings'.[4] Indeed we could treat a chair as a process that lasts all the time the chair lasts, and say 'The chair chairs'. According to this view the difference between substances and processes is an artefact of language and of contextual interests. Ontologically they are the same.

We now come up against a difficulty for this attractively simple view. Consider Davidson's example of a metal ball that is (a) heating up and (b) rotating (Davidson 1980, p. 178). There is an inclination to say that we have *two* processes here. But if we suppose that the heating up begins and ends just when the rotating does, then on the Quinean view I have canvassed we must identify event (a) and event (b) with the same temporal stage of the ball. Hence the events must be the same. On reflection, however, this is not so paradoxical as our first intuitions may suggest. Possibly these intuitions may depend on confusing event types with event tokens, i.e., classes of events with particular concrete events. The particular heating up is in fact a rotating, even though the class of heatings up of the ball may be different from the class of rotatings of the ball. The identity of the rotation with the heating up may be made plausible if we consider the matter from the point of view of the kinetic theory of heat. (I think the point could be made also from the point of view of caloric theory, or of pre-scientific common sense, though perhaps less persuasively.) The heating up is an increasingly violent vibratory motion of the molecules of the ball. But the motion is not only vibratory but is also a revolving about an axis. Similarly the rotation is a mainly revolving motion of the molecules, with vibrations superimposed on it. So the heating up and the rotation are the same. When we are considering the situation from the point of view of the kinetic theory of heat we think of it as a case of the ball getting warmer, and when we are thinking of the situation from the point of view of solving a problem in the mechanics of a rigid body we think of it as a rotation. Forgetting the contextual differences we may come to think that we are concerned with two events, not one.

However, there does seem to be a difficulty for this view. It arises from adverbs. The ball may heat up steadily and rotate jerkily. So the heating up is steady and the rotation jerky. It looks as though in ordinary non-canonical language we need an ontology of events distinct from the temporal stages of substances. The difficulty would not, however, arise for *science*, if this can be expressed in Quinean canonical notation. 'Heating up' would not be an event expression but would be comparable to 'length' and eliminible in favour of the predicate 'heats up in . . . calories per second' just as 'length' is eliminible in favour of 'has a length in centimetres of'. Similarly we need not refer to rotations but get by with the predicate 'rotates at . . . radians per second' (Quine 1960, section 50). However, for ordinary language, we do seem to need an ontology that postulates events as a separate category of objects.

One possibility would be to construe events as ordered pairs of temporal stages of objects on the one hand and predicates or properties on the other. This would be to go over to a theory with affinities to those of Jaegwon Kim (1969) and R.M. Martin (1969). According to Kim an event is the exemplification of a property by a substance at a time. (Martin construes an event in somewhat similar fashion, but attempts to elucidate properties nominalistically.) If we do it with properties we have problems about the respectability of these entities, though I am aware that Sellars claims to give a nominalist account of these.[5] If we do it with predicates we run up against the difficulty that synonymous predicates will distinguish events as different which should not be different. Moreover whether we do it with predicates or with properties we will distinguish events that should not be so distinguished, for example (as Donald Davidson has argued in 'The Individuation of Events' in Davidson 1980) Brutus' stabbing Caesar and Brutus' killing Caesar. Perhaps events should be regarded as an ontological category irreducible to any others as is perhaps Davidson's view. But whether reducible or irreducible these theories hold that events exist and are something other than temporal stages of substances.[6]

II

In the previous section I have discussed Quine's account of events and processes as not ontologically different from substances. If this were correct it would follow trivially that events exist. Other theories give a non-trivial account of events. I have mentioned Kim's and Martin's and alluded to Davidson's. Davidson's theory is attractive because of the lucidity of its underlying semantics, which is essentially Tarski's. Davidson's semantic theory tries to give a recursive semantics for a certain class of adverbs by supposing that the logical form of sentences containing adverbs is best given by transforming them into sentences quantifying over events and such that the adverbs get replaced by predicates of events. Davidson also applies this sort of idea to other sorts of sentences, such as causal ones. Now it is possible that a different approach to the semantics of ordinary language might be possible, which would not quantify over events, but which would yield a truth theory of the appropriately recursive sort. (That is, which will show how the truth conditions of any of the infinitely many sentences of a language depend recursively on the satisfaction conditions for a finite number of constituents.) But as Davidson remarks, it is extraordinary how smoothly things work if one is allowed to quantify over events (Davidson 1980, p. 166).

Sellars's theory might be called a 'no event' theory. He says (CL2, section 29), that 'there are no events *in addition* to changing things and persons'. Of course if the Quinean suggestion that events are temporal stages of objects were acceptable there would be no disagreement with the above quotation from Sellars, but the real difference comes out in the next paragraph (CL2, section 30, where Sellars asserts that '*There are no temporal relations*.' Sellars rejects the four-dimensional view of substances and he eschews temporal relations (use of words like 'before', 'after' as predicates) in favour of using such words as sentential connectives. Or rather, if such words occur as grammatical predicates, as in 'Socrates' drinking the hemlock was before his death', the sentences in which they occur give surface structure only, and the deep structure is better given by 'Socrates drank the hemlock before he died'. Despite the difficulties raised by Davidson against eschewing quantification over events, Sellars's view has some initial plausibility. After all it seems highly plausible that children learn sentences of the form 'A did X before B did Y' before they learn expressions of the form 'A's doing of X'. Sentences such as 'Socrates ran before he dined' and 'Nero fiddled while Rome burned' sound much less strained than 'Socrates' running occurred before his dinner', 'Nero's fiddling was simultaneous with Rome's burning', and so on.

Similarly (CL2, section 15) 'Socrates ran' is more natural than 'A running by Socrates took place', just as 'Snow is white' is more natural than ' "Snow is white" is exemplified by snow'. Sellars argues that expressions like 'occurs' and 'took place' are 'alethic predicates', that is metalinguistic predicates defined in terms of 'true of'. Sellars elucidates 'true of' by means of substitutional quantification, but we can ignore this issue of substitutional quantification for the moment. Just as 'Being white is exemplified by snow' is a way of saying ' "is white" is exemplified by snow', so according to Sellars 'A running by Socrates at t took place' is a roundabout way of saying ' "runs" was true of Socrates at t'. (Sellars operates with a conception of tensed truth.)

According to this account event talk is metalinguistic talk, which itself is parasitic on the more fundamental assertions in the object language that do not mention events. The metalinguistic talk mentions predicates like 'runs', not nouns like 'runnings', and the more fundamental object language talk uses such predicates, and once more does not have noun phrases for events. In this object language talk 'before', for example, occurs as a sentential connective, not as a relational predicate.

One must of course not confuse a sentence with a name, and so one must not fall into the confusion of thinking that sentences like 'Socrates ran' refer to events. On the surface 'Socrates ran' is about Socrates, not about an event of Socrates running. Of course Davidson has given arguments, such as from the implication of sentences like 'Socrates ran' by sentences like 'Socrates ran quickly', that the deep structure of 'Socrates ran' is that of a sentence containing the noun phrase 'Socrates' running'. Nevertheless according to Sellars's theory it is 'Socrates' running was quick' that needs transforming away into 'Socrates ran'. According to Sellars, if 'Socrates ran' is about Socrates, not about an event of Socrates' running, neither is 'A running by Socrates occurred' about an event. Sellars' account of event talk as metalinguistic and of 'occurs' as an alethic predicate leads him to deny an ontology of events, while not wishing to deny that in a sense there are events, i.e., that sentences such as 'Socates ran' are true.

In section I of this paper I noted that Sellars's views tie in with the perhaps archaic use of 'event' as like that of 'outcome' or 'result'. There is a naturalness also in treating 'Socrates ran' as more fundamental than 'There was a running by Socrates'. There seem, however, to be powerful Davidsonian arguments (from semantics) on the other side, the apparent naturalness of Sellars's views notwithstanding. The appeal of Sellars's theory may diminish if we note that if 'before' and the like are sentential connectives they are non-truthfunctional ones. Thus if I say 'Wittgenstein wrote the *Tractatus* before Gödel proved the incompleteness of arithmetic', I say something true. But if I substitute for 'Gödel proved the incompleteness of arithmetic' the true sentence 'Russell wrote the *Principles of Mathematics*', I get something false. But if such sentences are non-truthfunctional what is their semantics?[7] Davidson's strategy, of course, would be to show that they are not really non-truthfunctional at all, that the apparent non-truthfunctionality comes from misconstruing their surface structure, in particular from misconstruing 'before' as a connective. What alternative strategy does Sellars propose? What are his semantics for sentences containing 'before'? How does he deal with adverbs? One would like Sellars to say more about this, though he does refer to the interesting and well-written dissertation by Jack Norman (1974). However, one might be dissatisfied with fhe Fregean semantics used by Norman, since it makes use of intensions, and might wonder whether it is not open to objections raised by Davidson in his 'Theories of Meaning and Learnable Languages' (Davidson 1984, pp. 3–15) to Church's theory of sense and denotation. Also in an earlier paper Sellars speaks enthusiastically about Romane Clark's theory of predicate modifiers. (This is mentioned in Jack Norman's thesis.) Sellars says that Clark's analysis 'provides the key to the problem of the identity of events. . . .' (Sellars 1974, p. 212). Clark's theory is very attractive in many ways, though I am unclear about the ontic commitments of his semantics. Clark says at the end of the paper (Clark 1970) to which Sellars refers that 'It is that language which the theory formalizes, and not our semantical discourse about it, which houses our ontology.' This seems too easy a disclaimer: if we take semantics seriously we must surely count it as part of total science, and hence its ontic commitments as part of those of total science. I should be interested in Sellars's views on these matters.

Even if such a semantics can satisfactorily be given, and if Sellars can elucidate event talk as parasitic on talk with 'before', 'after', etc., as sentential connectives, how much does this prove metaphysically? It is on the face of it indeed plausible that we initially learn words like 'before', 'after', etc., by hearing them used in sentences in which they function syntactically as sentential connectives, and if this indeed turned out to be the semantically fundamental use it would not be too surprising. (This would be so even with sentences like 'Lightning before thunder', since here 'Lightning' and 'Thunder' function as one word sentences, equivalent to 'It lightnings' and 'It thunders' or my preferred formulation 'The lightning lightnings' and 'The thunder thunders'.) Nevertheless the fact that we may initially use 'before', 'after', etc., as sentential connectives does not show that we can not come to use them independently as relational predicates of events. Consider as a parallel Quine's account in *The Roots of Reference* of how a child might first learn quantification as substitutional, and then by an analogy between relative clauses and general terms leap (perhaps by a beneficial confusion of thought) to using variables and quantification as objectual (Quine 1973, p. 104).

The issue is complicated by Sellars's distinction between the manifest image and the scientific image. It is further complicated by Sellars's insistence on the primacy of tensed language in the manifest image. I shall say something about this latter complication first.

III

In CL2, section 27, Sellars refers to his argument in TWO where he claims that tense, in a broad sense including not only temporal inflections of verbs but also indicator words such as 'now', is an irreducible feature of temporal discourse (Sellars 1969). However, when when he says 'indicator words such as "now" ' does he mean specifically *temporal* indicator words such as 'now' or any indicator words whatever, including 'this'? It seems to me that if one has the word 'this' one can say all that one normally wants to say with tenses, using only tenseless verbs.[8] Thus instead of saying 'Jones will come' one can say 'Jones *comes* later than this utterance', and so on (where the italics signify the tenseless present). There are of course complications with the difference betwen perfect and imperfect, and other complex tenses, but perhaps they can be accommodated. What can not be accommodated are such meta-physically misleading sentences as 'The battle was future, is present, and will be past'. That these can not be accommodated seems to me to be a virtue, not a vice.

Sellars might object to the phrase 'this utterance' in the above elimination of tenses, because it seems to take an ontology of events (utterances) as fundamental. Instead of 'Smith *comes* later than this utterance' we could say 'Smith *comes* later than I *utter* this', and if one wishes to eliminate the indexical 'I' also one could say 'Smith *comes* later than the person who *utters* this *utters* this'. Sellars might still worry about the reference of 'this', which seems to be an *event*, that is, a particular utterance. At any rate the problem would not arise with 'Smith *writes* this', where 'this' can refer to a physical object, say a chalk mark on a blackboard.

Assuming, then, that one who disbelieves in an ontology of events can still think of some suitable referent for 'this' in the context 'utters this', Sellars's insistence on the necessity for tenses seems a very dubious one. Apart from the minor worries that I have expressed at the end of the last paragraph, this insistence seems to me to be independent of his account of expressions like 'before' as sentential connectives and of his denial of an ontology of events. But perhaps Sellars is understanding tense in a still wider sense, so that any indexical language counts as tensed. (Though this interpretation seems to be inconsistent with his denial of spatial tenses in TWO, p. 558.) If any indexical language were to count as tensed, then for some purposes (but not, I think, scientific or metaphysical ones) tensed language would be indispensable. The indispensability (in some contexts) of indexicals has been well argued by John Perry (1979) in his well-known paper on the problem of the essential indexical. For example Perry gives the example of a person lost in the wilderness who knows he is in one of two different localities, which he is unable to distinguish by any perceptually relevant descriptive expressions. The one he calls 'here' is one or other of them, and which it is may be highly relevant to the problem of the best way of getting himself home. In such a case the indexical sentence 'Such and such a place is here' is not only not translatable into a non-indexical one (which is always the case) but furthermore there is no non-indexical sentence that will meet the person's needs. Again, a professor who has to get to a meeting at noon may move off at 11.50: he needs to know that 11.50 is *now*. However, I think that all cases of the essential indexical are of practical relevance only and do not arise in theoretical science or metaphysics. So I do not see that tenses, or even indexicals in general, are needed to state any ontological fact about the world that could not be stated in non-indexical language.

IV

Consider the question, discussed by Sellars in TWO, whether tenses are needed in discourse about Minkowski space-time. More importantly for our present purposes (for I have suggested that the two questions are largely independent of one another) do we need to refer to events in the physics of Minkowski space-time? Does acceptance of Minkowski involve acceptance of an event ontology and of 'earlier', 'later', etc. as relational predicates of events? Sellars does not say much about this in his Carus lectures. There is more about his views about space-time and events in scientific theory in 'Time and the World Order'.

In TWO Sellars gives an account of relativistic space-time physics whereby it is an adjunct to the ordinary discourse of spatial objects enduring in a separate non-spatial time which he holds to be characteristic of the manifest image. According to Sellars, what relativity teaches us is not that space and time taken separately are unreal with a unitary space-time the only reality, but is that 'the metricizing of a set of events into a three-dimensional spatial array and the metricizing of spatially related events into a one-dimensional temporal array *are not independent operations'* (TWO, p. 571). And I take it that here he still holds that talk of events is not ontologically serious talk, but is to be elucidated in terms of statements about things changing. The Minkowski world, on Sellars's view, seems to be just a mathematical device to enable calculations to be made in the manifest world of separable space and time. If I have interpreted Sellars correctly, his attitude contrasts markedly with that of Minkowski in his famous statement that 'Henceforth space by itself, and time by itself, are doomed to fade away into mere shadows, and only a kind of union of the two will preserve an independent reality' (Minkowski 1952, see first paragraph). Nevertheless I think that Sellars holds that Minkowski's statement would be correct in relation to the scientific image, but he seems to hold that this is something for the far future, not for relativity physics as it is used today (Sellars 1962, p. 593). At present, he says, we have for this conception only 'a partially covered promissory note'. Only in this not yet realized scientific world view does he think that we would have a genuine ontology of events and of 'earlier' and 'later' as relational predicates of events.

Earlier in this paper I manifested some indecisiveness and unclarity about the notion of an event, and of course we have to contend with Sellars's arguments that event talk is merely a notational variant on more fundamental discourse that does not refer to such entities. So it seems that either it is unclear what events are or else Sellars is right in his 'no event' theory. This might be taken as a difficulty for special relativity if this is taken as an ontologically serious modification of the manifest image. It has sometimes been thought that the topology of space-time has to be eludicated in terms of causal relations between events.

Sellars's solution, as I understand it, is to be quasi-instrumentalist about Minkowski space-time. I wish to avoid the worry about whether there are events by denying the legitimacy of a causal theory of space-time.[9] Even if events exist, there are not events everywhere, and the construction of space-time in terms of causal relations requires contrary-to-fact conditionals. It seems odd that so transparent a business as space-time geometry should be held to depend on such tricky matters as counterfactuals and their attendent modal notions. We should avoid all this trouble by simply postulating space-time and its geometry. Space-time is a genuinely explanatory entity just as electrons are. The geometry of space-time figures holistically in all physical explanations, but the point I wish to make can be made most vividly by means of a kinematical example. Consider the Langevin twin who travels by a space ship to a distant star and then returns. On his return he is younger than his stay-at-home brother. The explanation of this is purely geometrical. If *AB*,

BC and *AC* are all time-like (each within some light cone), the geometry of Minkowski space-time is such that in the triangle *ABC* we have *AB* + *BC* < *AC*. In general relativity the explanatory power of space-time is even more striking, where gravitation is explained by means of geodesics in a space-time of variable curvature.

For space-time to be genuinely explanatory it must exist. And if it exists then genuine space-time entities must exist. Sellars in TWO seems to me to treat space-time as a purely mathematical and instrumental adjunct to the manifest image (as merely a means of facilitating deductions of manifest image propositions from other manifest image propositions). As I remarked earlier in this paper I do not myself think that there is the great gulf that Sellars sees between the scientific and the manifest image, and it is not clear to me that saying that a substance changes at time *t* is to say anything different from saying that parts of a four-dimensional thing later than *t* are different from parts of it earlier than *t*.[10]

I shall now argue that the question of whether or not there are events is of no interest for the philosophy of physics. Can we identify events and processes with temporal slices or stages of space-time processes? If the answer is 'Yes' then events are related by the space-time relations that uncontroversially relate these slices or stages. We have seen semantic objections to this. However, if the theory of predicate modifiers, commended by Sellars, is acceptable, then it could be used to revive the Quinean identification of events and processes with temporal slices or stages, without going all the way to Sellars's 'no event' theory. If the answer is 'No', or if events do not exist at all, then there is still no problem for science. In that case science does not need to talk of events and processes: slices and stages of space-time objects (or related things) do the job perfectly well. Suppose for example that one wants to talk about the space-time interval between (a) the collision and mutual annihilation of an electron and a positron and (b) the collision of an electron and a neutron. Here we appear to talk of events but we can do all that physics requires by talking of certain discontinuities in the direction of the world line of the electron in (a) (treating the positron in Feynman's way as a 'bent back' part of the electron) and in the direction of the world line of the electron in (b). We do not need to worry about whether these entities are events, because whatever they are, they are what physics needs to talk about.[11]

NOTES

1   Here I am using 'logical form' in something like Davidson's sense. See for example Donald Davidson 'The Logical Form of Action Sentences' (in

Davidson 1980). However, if 'before' is a non-truthfunctional sentence connective, we will be not all the way to logical form until we have got down to something extensional.

2　On Sellars's distinction between the manifest image and the scientific image see Wilfrid Sellars (1963), chapter 1.

3　P.T. Geach in his 'Some Problems about Time' objects to such locutions as talking of temporal stages of philosophers having beliefs or temporal stages of cats eating mice. But it seems to me that his opponent could simply deny that these locutions are illegitimate, while conceding that they perhaps lack literary elegance.

4　This suggests my answer to Sellars when he discusses 'absolute processes'.

5　In correspondence W.V. Quine has pointed out that I can easily avoid worry about the philosophical respectability of properties by construing events not as ordered pairs of temporal stages and properties but as ordered pairs of temporal stages and classes. In the example of the heating up and rotating ball, the heating up event can be distinguished from the rotating event because the class of things that heat up differs from the class of things that rotate.

6　Acceptance of a Kim-like theory of events need not be incompatible with physicalism. Let a be a substance, P a physical property, and Q a property belonging to common sense psychology. Then the physical event might be (a, P, t) and the 'mental' event (a, Q, t). However, if Q were a 'topic neutral' property (see chapter 15 of this volume 'Sensations and Brain Processes', then (a, Q, t) would still count as physical. Still it would be awkward not to be able to identify a sensation with a brain process, or a flash of lightning with an electric discharge, as would not be prohibited by a Davidsonian theory of events.

7　Dr Aubrey Townsend has pointed out to me that though non-truthfunctional such sentences are referentially transparent: substitution of coextensive predicates is possible *salva veritate*. Townsend thinks of this combination of non-truthfunctionality and referential transparency as making more difficulty for Sellars's view.

8　I regard this observation as of metaphysical interest but as not important for semantics. The semantics for 'this' should be given by the method suggested by Donald Davidson in his 'Truth and Meaning' (Davidson 1984, pp. 17–36) and this method can be applied to all indicator expressions without any partiality to 'this'.

9　'Causal Theories of Time', chapter 5 of this volume. See also Lacey (1968).

10　If I am right there is no separate entity S outside the rectangles of diagrams VII–IX on pp. 576–77 of TWO.

11　I have read earlier drafts of this paper to staff seminars at the two philosophy departments at the Australian National University and at the philosophy department of Monash University. I am grateful to all who attended these seminars for very helpful comments in discussion, and I should particularly like to thank Dr Aubrey Townsend of Monash University who made detailed comments on the typescript of an earlier draft.

REFERENCES

Clark, Romane 1970: Concerning the Logic of Predicate Modifiers. *Noûs*, 4, 311–35.

Davidson, Donald 1980: *Essays on Actions and Events*. Oxford: Clarendon Press.

—— 1984: *Inquiries into Truth and Interpretation*. Oxford: Clarendon Press.

Dretske, F.I. 1967: Can Events Move? *Mind*, 76, 479–2.

Geach, P.T. 1965: Some Problems about Time. *Proceedings of the British Academy*, 51, 321–36. Reprinted 1972 in *Logic Matters*, Oxford: Basil Blackwell.

Kim, Jaegwon 1969: Events and Their Descriptions: Some Considerations. In Nicholas Rescher (ed.), *Essays in Honor of Carl G. Hempel*, Dordrecht, Holland: D. Reidel.

Lacey, Hugh M. 1968: The Causal Theory of Time: A Critique of Grünbaum's Version. *Philosophy of Science*, 35, 332–54.

Martin, R.M. 1969: *Belief, Existence and Meaning*. New York: New York University Press, chapter 9.

Minkowski, H. 1952: Space and Time. In W. Perrett and G.B. Jeffery (trans.), *The Principle of Relativity*, New York: Dover.

Norman, Jack 1974: *Events and Semantic Theories*. Pittsburgh: University of Pittsburgh.

Perry, John 1979: The Problem of the Essential Indexical. *Noûs*, 13, 3–21.

Quine, W.V. 1960: *Word and Object*. Cambridge, Massachusetts: MIT Press.

—— 1973: *The Roots of Reference*. La Salle, Illinois: Open Court.

Sellars, Wilfrid 1962: Time and the World Order. In Herbert Feigl and Grover Maxwell (eds), *Scientific Explanation, Space and Time*, Minnesota Studies in the Philosophy of Science, vol. III, Minneapolis: University of Minnesota Press.

—— 1963: *Science, Perception and Reality*. London: Routledge and Kegan Paul.

—— 1969: Metaphysics and the Concept of a Person. In Karel Lambert, *The Logical Way of Doing Things*, New Haven: Yale University Press. Reprinted 1974 in Wilfred Sellars, *Essays in Philosophy and History*, Dordrecht, Holland: D. Reidel.

—— 1974: *Essays in Philosophy and History*. Dordrecht, Holland: D. Reidel.

—— 1981: The Carus Lectures for 1977–78. *The Monist*, 64, no. 1.

Smart, J.J.C. 1949: The River of Time. *Mind*, 58, 483–94. Reprinted 1956 with slight revisions in A.G.N. Flew (ed.), *Essays in Conceptual Analysis*, London: Macmillan.

13

Laws of Nature and Cosmic Coincidences

In the past I have argued for the reality of the 'theoretical entities' of physics as follows. I have argued that the multifarious irregularities at the observational level can be explained by simple regularities at the theoretical level: it is too much to believe that the universe is just *as if* there were electrons, protons, etc. I have said that to believe this '*as if*' story would be to believe in a vast 'cosmic coincidence' at the observational level. Appeal to simplicity of explanation suggests that we should believe full-bloodedly in the reality of the theoretical entities or (to cope with possible theory change in the future) something rather like them. (That is, the predicate '. . . is an electron' must be true of real entities, or at any rate approximately true of them.) My position contrasts with that of Bas van Fraassen (1980), who has the idea that theories need not be true but need only be realisable in some model that ensures their empirical adequacy. Van Fraassen does not actually *deny* the reality of theoretical entities, but holds that his theory, which says that what is important in scientific theories is not truth but empirical adequacy, is truer to the actual procedures of scientists. He also holds that his view has an advantage in probability, as the disjunction of (a) 'Electrons are real and the theory of them is empirically adequate', and (b) 'Electrons are not real but the theory of them is empirically adequate', cannot have less probability than the first disjunct (a) on its own.

I shall attempt to answer this last probabilistic consideration later, but let me pose the main problem I wish to discuss in this paper by saying something else that I am strongly inclined to hold true. When I think of laws of nature I am strongly inclined to think of them as extensional propositions, so that the difference between a law of nature and a mere accidental generalization (e.g. that all the screws in my tool box in the garage are made of brass) is that a law of nature is a cosmically extensive accidental generalization. The main problem in this paper is whether I can think of laws of nature as 'accidental' or as describing 'cosmic coincidences' while at the same time I use the unbelievability of cosmic coincidences as a premiss in my argument for realism. My answer will have to be that just as (so it has been said, George Orwell, *Animal Farm*) all men are equal but some are more equal than others, so there are cosmic coincidences and cosmic coincidences – a good sort and a bad sort. It is only the bad sort that I reject. My argument depends on giving a non-negligible *a priori* probability to the proposition that the universe is simple, i.e. described by simple fundamental laws. These fundamental laws describe the good sort of cosmic coincidence.

Let $p =$ the observational facts are as if there are electrons, etc.
$q =$ the universe is simple
$r =$ there really are electrons, etc.

We can agree with van Fraassen that $P(p) > P(pr)$, as of course we have to! But I want to say $P(pr/q) > P(p\bar{r}/q)$. Here I use concatenation to indicate conjunction and the bar to indicate negation.

Let us put $P(r/pq)$ near to 1, and also let us assert q. I do not know how to justify this assertion of q, just as I do not know how to justify induction, and here I acknowledge a weak point in my position. But given this premiss I can make some progress and do something to defend myself against certain objections by van Fraassen, to be discussed below. Therefore I assert pqr. Contrary to van Fraassen I deny $p\bar{q}\bar{r}$. (Most anti-realists hold $p\bar{q}\bar{r}$, though van Fraassen in effect holds simply $p\bar{q}$, that is $p\bar{q}.r \lor \bar{r}$, thus being merely agnostic about r. In this paper I am concerned to contrast my position pqr, with one like van Fraassen's (either $p\bar{q}$ or $p\bar{q}\bar{r}$). However, David Lewis has pointed out to me that $pq\bar{r}$ and $p\bar{q}r$ might also be considered.)

Thus $pq\bar{r}$ says that there are simple laws about the observable which are as if they are about electrons, etc., but that the true theories might be quite different from the theories we believe, so that the latter are not even approximately true. I reject this on the ground that it is unlikely that two radically different theories might explain all the phenomena. Science has gone too far for this. As a local example of this sort of thing, consider the way in which certain phenomena of quantum mechanics could be explained equally by wave mechanics and by matrix mechanics, which were almost able to be seen as mathematical transcriptions of one another, but further observational knowledge made it necessary to devise a unified theory into which the old wave mechanics and matrix mechanics were simply absorbed. It seems implausible that we shall ever deny that there are electrons or protons, and that quantum mechanics is at least a close approximation to the truth, even though we may come to believe new and strange facts about electrons and protons. Similarly, we did not give up belief in atoms (despite etymology) when the atom was found to be complex and even splittable.

As for *pɋr*, this is roughly the theory of Nancy Cartwright (1983), that there are electrons and so on but that they do not obey simple laws. I say 'roughly' here because Cartwright is concerned with the fundamental-phenomenological distinction, in the sense in which the *physicist* uses 'phenomenological', not with the philosopher's 'theoretical-observational' distinction. She holds that the laws of physics are true only in ideal models, simplified ideal systems that do not really exist, and in order to apply physics to the real world a lot of tact and 'cooking' of calculations becomes necessary. Cartwright's position is a very powerful one, and I am not confident of giving a convincing answer to her. We do know that *some* simple laws apply to real systems: for example all electrons and protons have equal or opposite charges. Moreover the fact that simple laws can be used in the case of simple isolated systems does suggest to me that the difficulty with real systems is due merely to complexity of boundary conditions. Thus if relativistic considerations could be ignored we could say that Schrödinger's equation is true of the entire universe, though the function for the potential would be indescribably complicated.

The term 'cosmic coincidence' is of course a little misleading. To say that unless realism about theoretical entities were true the phenomena on the observational level would constitute a cosmic coincidence is to say that these phenomena have no explanation in terms of simple laws about real entities. Normally, of course, we do not think of coincidences as inexplicable.[2] We would think it a coincidence that all members of Tillicoultry Academy soccer team are red haired, but not a coincidence that the committee of the red haired persons' association are red haired. The latter has a very simple explanation. Nevertheless the former has an explanation too. McTavish is red haired and is the best outside right, Campbell is red haired and the best inside right, Smith is red haired and the best centre forward, and so on. Ultimate laws of nature would in a sense be inexplicable, though I would want to call them in a way explicable in that they form an essential part of a coherent and adequate web of belief (to use Quine's and Ullian's phrase, Quine and Ullian 1978). By calling a law of nature a cosmic coincidence (though of the good sort) I am saying no more than what could be put more technically by saying that it is extensional. Cosmic coincidences of the bad sort are those that have no simple explanation. Van Fraassen, of course, would say that even on his view the observational phenomena *can* have simple explanations, in terms of empirically adequate theories. But then I want an explanation, which I think realism gives, why theories *are* empirically adequate. I must record, however, that van Fraassen is aware of this problem, and does propose his own sort of explanation of the empirical adequacy of theories, which is in terms of a Darwinian sort of natural selection of theories in the struggle for survival in the face of observation and experiment (van Fraassen 1980, pp. 39–40).

In a final chapter ('Gentle Polemics') to his book *The Scientific Image*[3] van Fraassen, with tongue well in cheek, pretends to be converted to scientific realism. He compares my arguments for scientific realism with St Thomas Aquinas' Five Ways, arguments for the existence of God. With tongue even more firmly in cheek, and after suggesting that the arguments for scientific realism are formally similar to Aquinas' arguments, van Fraassen pretends to find the arguments for scientific realism quite convincing, though he says that the theological arguments are unsound. This chapter of van Fraassen's book is an admirably witty and ingenious *tour de force*. I shall not here attempt to summarize van Fraassen's chapter in any detail, but I will indicate the main difficulty that van Fraassen here poses for the scientific realist. The theist seeks to account for the existence and characteristics of the universe by postulating something outside, namely God, as the cause of the universe. This is liable to prompt the intelligent child's question 'Who made God?'. If God does not require something outside for his existence, why does the universe? Moreover if God is the creator of the universe it would seem that he must possess all the ultimate and irreducible complexity of the universe itself. (Some complexity in the effect can arise without complexity in the cause, as when ever more complex organisms evolve by natural selection. But here I am talking about the complexity of ultimate hypotheses of physics and cosmology.) Thus the hypothesis of God plus universe is at least as complex as that of an uncaused universe itself. In the same sort of way, van Fraassen is asking in his tongue in cheek way, why cannot we rest with the mere empirical adequacy of our theories? Why do we need to suppose that the empirical adequacy of a theory needs to be explained by reference to a realm of postulated entities (electrons, space-time points, or whatever)?

My answer to this is as follows. If we postulate God in addition to the created universe we increase the complexity of our hypothesis. We have all the complexity of the universe itself, and we have in addition the at least equal complexity of God. (The designer of an artefact must be at least as complex as the designed artefact.) Van Fraassen in effect asks why the philosopher of science cannot rest content with empirically adequate theories, just as the atheist rests content with the existence of the universe, which he holds to require no further explanation. I answer that postulating non-observable entities does increase the ontic complexity of the theory, but it more than compensates for it by reducing the complexity of our system of ultimately explanatory laws, since the complex empirical regularities (or perhaps I should say non-regularities) depend on relatively simple theoretical laws. (If the theist can show the atheist that postulating God actually reduces the complexity of one's total world view, then the atheist should become a theist.)

It will be recalled that when confronted with the challenge that on the extensionalist view laws of nature are just themselves statements of 'cosmic coincidences' or are 'accidental' I replied that all laws are accidental but that some are more accidental than others. That is, simple brute facts on a cosmic scale are more believable than complex and idiosyncratic ones. There is of course a question of whether this demand for simplicity can be justified, and also of whether this demand is part of the notorious problem of justifying induction or whether it is something in addition. I shall not try to go into this matter now: indeed I am not at all clear as to what should be said here. When I reject belief in ultimately complex brute fact in favour of belief in cosmically simple brute fact, I want also to distinguish cosmic complexity from randomness, which has its own sort of simplicity.

Roughly, my view is that laws of nature state cosmic uniformities. They are universally quantified but must in general be multiply instantiated in order to count as laws. Otherwise any non-instantiated generalization would be a true law. For example, '$(x)(Ax \supset Bx)$' and '$(x)(Ax \supset \sim Bx)$' are both true if there are no As. However, we might give '$(x)(Ax \supset Bx)$' the status of a law even if there are no As if it is deducible from some multiply instantiated law. Newton's first law of motion is like this. Probably there are no bodies not acted on by some force or other, but this is not the only reason for saying that Newton's first law is true. It is also deducible from (or model-theoretically implied by) a statement that *is* multiply instantiated, namely Newton's second law.[4] More generally, functional laws always imply laws relating to particular but never instantiated values of the variables in the more general laws. Such particular laws are trivially true, but nevertheless more interestingly true also in that they are deducible from the more general laws which *are* instantiated.

Consider the law that electrons and protons mutually attract one another. This is of the form $(x)(y)(Ex . Py . \supset Axy)$. Some philosophers hold that the law needs a stronger connective than '$\supset$' because if it is a law it must support counterfactuals. I am willing to concede that a law must *in some way* support a counterfactual, though counterfactual sentences are none too clear. Is it true that if David Armstrong had been an electron and David Stove had been a proton the two Davids would have attracted one another?[5] Goodness knows what would happen if David Armstrong were an electron. The mind boggles! Perhaps the whole material universe would have disappeared into a black hole! Still, as I said, I am willing to concede that laws of nature support counterfactuals. They differ from 'All the screws in my tool box are made of brass' which does not support the proposition that if some screw which I had found lying in the road had been in my tool box it would have been of brass. The matter is somewhat technical and the fine details are not too necessary for the purpose of this paper but we can say roughly that the counterfactual 'If it had been the case that p it would have been the case that q' is supported by a law statement if '$p \supset q$' is deducible from a body of theory whose laws are stated with '$\supset$' and which contains the law statement, and if '$p \supset q$' would not have been a deducible without the law statement, and if this deduction does not make use of any statement which implies the falsity of the antecedent of the counterfactual.

Mere accidental generalizations, such as 'All the screws in my tool box are brass', typically contain an indexical expression (such as 'my') or refer to particular regions of space-time. However, it would be possible, no doubt, to think of a description of my tool box that used perfectly general predicates, so that it singled out my tool box. Nevertheless a generalization that was stated in these perfectly general terms would still count as merely accidental – there is no purely formal criterion for distinguishing laws from accidental generalizations. This is as it should be, because in my view laws are accidental, though cosmically accidental. This too resists formal characterisation, since even 'All the screws in my tool box are brass' says of everything in the universe including the remotest galaxy that it is either not in my tool box or brass.

One way in which those who like strong conditionals have nevertheless retained extensionality is by quantifying over possible worlds. Thus they would say that there is a possible world in which an elephant holds the chair of moral philosophy at St Andrews (or rather a counterpart of St Andrews). This world will be different from ours, and the philosophical elephant will hold that *his* world, not ours, is the *actual* world. Thus David Lewis has claimed that the word 'actual' is an indexical one: it refers to the world in which the user of it happens to be.

Those of us who do not follow David Lewis in his realism about possible worlds, whether because they object to the bloated ontology, or for other reasons, may interpret possible worlds as sets in the actual world, but if they do this they come back to a model theoretic version of the metalinguistic account of strong conditionals (in terms of the deducibility of '$\supset$' statements) at which I hinted a little earlier in this paper. I have no great objection to this.

Ultimately, then, I want to say that laws of nature just describe cosmic accidents in the one and only actual world. (Hume was right.) But not any universal '⊃' statement counts as a law of nature. It must form part of a well integrated body of theory, or be deducible from such statements or be such that we think it will one day be deducible from simple theory. Thus even before modern physics explained Ohm's Law, the law was given the honorific status. So I now return to the central question of this paper. It seems that I do believe in cosmic accidents after all. Am I not therefore inconsistent in using the unlikelihood of cosmic coincidence as an argument for scientific realism?[6]

It is a matter of simplicity of explanation. I assume that ultimate explanatory uniformities are simple. We explain the multifarious minor regularities and apparent irregularities in the world by reference to a few (or relatively few) universal regularities. My view may be contrasted with D.M. Armstrong's theory, according to which laws of nature state relations beween universals. He claims certain advantages for his theory but it seems to me that the Humean type of view can give us all we need.[7] Armstrong does not need to give the admittedly rather strained interpretation of uninstantiated and single-case laws that I have had to give in terms of deducibility from a set of well integrated statements of uniformity. Armstrong also can deal with the objection that people spoke of laws long before there were well integrated theories. Armstrong attributes this point to David Stove, who has also emphasized the difficulty for the regularity view with respect to uninstantiated laws, which could never formally contradict one another. I would say that the last point merely states that Quine (1976) has called 'a veridical paradox'. As for the point about belief in the past about unintegrated laws, perhaps in the past the concept of a law of nature was in part theological, and this explains why unintegrated laws were thought of as more than mere regularities. Armstrong can make a clear distinction between uniformities of necessitation and mere accidental generalizations, and he can say that on his view a law explains why if an object has two different properties one may necessitate the other. I would balance these advantages against some difficulties or implausibities that we may find in Armstrong's theory of universals. The merits of Armstrong's theory of universals are considerable, and how much we should claim associated demerits would take quite a different paper to discuss.[8]

One important merit that Armstrong claims for his theory must, however, be briefly discussed now. Armstrong claims that what universals (properties) belong to an object is a contingent matter, to be found out by science, and that the postulated relations between properties that constitute laws of nature are contingent too. Nevertheless Armstrong believes that though his theory does not solve the problem of induction it helps with it. If the 'lawfulness' of a situation is a matter of relations between universals, then the unobserved must resemble the observed. This is because if these same properties crop up in other situations they must nevertheless be related to each other in the same way. However, as Armstrong surely recognizes, there is still the *main* problem of induction. It would require an inductive argument to discover that Armstrong's properties have a certain relation, no less than it would to argue that a sequence of events forms part of a universal cosmic pattern. Why should induction to cosmic patterns ('cosmic geography' one might almost say) be more problematic than induction to associated properties and their relations?[9] At least the regularity theorist is not faced (unless he otherwise rejects nominalism about properties) with mysteries about what exactly properties are and how they are related to the particulars that have them.

Of course I do not myself have a good answer to Hume's sceptical problem of induction, though I would like to mention some good work towards this end by John Clendinnen (1982). Even pre-theoretically, as Quine has pointed out, our innate tendencies to make certain sensory discriminations rather than others perform something of the function of a theoretical background. Our knowledge develops by modifying our theories so as to fit them in to one another and to new sensory evidence in the simplest possible way. Sometimes, of course, we may have to reject the apparent deliverances of our senses. Thus I reject the reports of paranormal phenomena because I am aware of how hard it would be to reconcile them with the general scientific picture of the world, and I am aware of the well-known tendency of humans to credulity, mendacity and wishful thinking. Also I have met good conjurors. So something like the coherence theory of knowledge of the nineteenth-century idealists is right, though we should not make their mistake of in effect confusing the concept of knowledge (or warranted assertibility) with that of truth. In developing our theories we have at least two guiding rules. One is to expect regularities to continue, at least if our background knowledge does not give positive reason for doubting that they will. But another one is to search for simplicity. Now a sceptic about projection of regularities will also no doubt be sceptical about simplicity as a criterion of warranted assertibility, and perhaps the converse holds too. We do of course run up against Hume's sceptical problem of induction, but we are in no worse case than the believer in strong conditionals or laws as relations between universals, who runs up against the sceptical problem in a slightly different guise. (For example the difficulty of knowing whether the future will be like the past comes up in a different form about knowing whether there is really a suitable relation between universals.)

Now if one allows simplicity as a criterion of warranted assertibility one wants the simplest empirically adequate theory of the world. The postulation of 'theoretical entities' and of cosmic uniformities (however, in a sense 'accidental') seems to me to produce a simpler metaphysical picture than does the non-realist's array of observational generalizations or even non-generalizations. That the non-realist has an 'empirically adequate theory' does not seem to me to help metaphysically, if this theory is not realistically construed.

My conclusion then is as follows. There are good cosmic coincidences and bad ones, and it is the bad (*ad hoc* or *as if* ones) that I reject as constituting good explanatory laws of nature. And for good explanation I want something more than van Fraassen's mere empirical adequacy of mere model-theoretic structures. It is the rejection of the bad sort of cosmic coincidence that is the basis of my argument for scientific realism, and I contend that the argument can stand even if all laws are regarded as 'cosmic coincidences', so long as the ultimately explanatory ones are of the good sort and contribute to the simplicity of total theory.

NOTES

1   Some of the points in this paper were made in my paper 'Cosmic Coincidence' read to the Russellian Society (Sydney University), which appeared in the *Proceedings of the Russellian Society* (Smart 1977). However, in the present paper I am also concerned explicitly to continue some friendly polemics with Bas van Fraassen (1980, chapter 7).

2   See van Fraassen (1980, p. 25). Van Fraassen refers to Aristotle, *Physics II*, especially 196a 1–20 and 196b 20–197a 12.

3   Except for minor changes chapter 7 of van Fraassen's book is the same as van Fraassen's 'Theoretical Entities: The Five Ways' (1974).

4   Some writers deny that Newton's first law is merely a special case of the second law. They see it as necessary for asserting the existence of an inertial frame. However, in celestial mechanics it is possible to define (and discover) a class of inertial systems by means of the third law, making pairwise hypotheses about masses and mutual accelerations, so as to fit observed apparent motions. See Macaulay (1896–7). There is more of a problem with the mechanics of special relativity, since in this case there is nothing like the third law except in the case of collisions, and (happily for us all) celestial bodies rarely collide. In practice one would approximate to an inertial system by using Newtonian considerations.

5   D.M. Armstrong considers such a difficulty on p. 47 of *What is a Law of Nature?* (1983). He nevertheless has a very different theory of counterfactuals from the one I rely on in this paper.

6   Of course this sort of view about physical necessity has been congenial to extensionalists and is by no means original. Quine has elucidated a harmless

notion of necessity in terms of what can be deduced from contextually agreed background assumptions. Integration with theory was stressed by N.R. Campbell (1957, p. 53). This is a reprint of Campbell's *Physics: The Elements.* Compare also R.B. Braithwaite (1953, p. 300ff). These last two references are given by Imre Lakatos (1978, p. 123). Lakatos does not approve of this manoeuvre. Though like Braithwaite I have used the word 'honorific' I think it could mislead, because whether a sentence is embedded in a set of other sentences (a theory) is a matter not merely of 'honorific' but of ontological import.

7 See Armstrong (1983). Armstrong has engaged in useful polemics against my paper (Smart 1977), see Armstrong (1979). This is now superseded by part I of Armstrong's *What is a Law of Nature?*

8 Views about laws of nature largely similar to those of Armstrong have been independently proposed by Dretske (1977) and Tooley (1977). Interesting defences of the regularity view may be found in essays by D.H. Mellor and Mary Hesse, in Mellor (1980).

9 Here my view is, verbal differences apart, much the same as one suggested by Peter Forrest and reported in Armstrong (1983, p. 5).

10 I should like to thank various friends for comments (not all of which I have heeded) on an earlier draft of this paper, especially D.H. Mellor who replied to my paper when I read it at the Moral Sciences Club at Cambridge, and Bas van Fraassen, David Lewis, John Clendinnen, and D.M. Armstrong (all in correspondence).

REFERENCES

Armstrong, D.M. 1983: *What is a Law of Nature?* London: Cambridge University Press.

Braithwaite, R.B. 1953: *Scientific Explanation.* London: Cambridge University Press.

Campbell, N.R. 1957: *Foundations of Science.* New York: Dover.

Cartwright, Nancy 1983: *How the Laws of Nature Lie.* London: Cambridge University Press.

Clendinnen, F. John 1982: Rational Expectation and Simplicity. In R. McLaughlin (ed.), *What? Where? When? Why?* Dordrecht, Holland: D. Reidel.

Dretske, F.I. 1977: Laws of Nature. *Philosophy of Science,* 44, 248–68.

Lakatos, Imre 1978: *Mathematics, Science and Epistemology: Philosophical Papers,* vol. 2. London: Cambridge University Press.

Macaulay, W.H. 1896–7: Newton's Theory of Kinetics. *Bulletin of the American Mathematical Society,* 3, 363–71.

Mellor, D.H. (ed.) 1980: *Science, Belief and Behaviour, Essays in Honour of R.B. Braithwaite.* London: Cambridge University Press.

Quine, W.V. 1976: *The Ways of Paradox and Other Essays,* enlarged edition. Cambridge, Massachusetts: MIT Press.

—— and Ullian, J.S. 1978: *The Web of Belief,* 2nd edn. New York: Random House.

Smart, J.J.C. 1977: Cosmic Coincidence. *Proceedings of the Russellian Society, Sydney University*, 2, 23–30.

Tooley, Michael 1977: The Nature of Laws. *Canadian Journal of Philosophy*, 7, 667–98.

van Fraassen, Bas 1974: Theoretical Entities: The Five Ways. *Philosophia*, 4, 95–109.

—— 1980: *The Scientific Image*. Oxford: Clarendon Press.

14
Realism v. Idealism

It is characteristic of realists to separate ontology from epistemology and of idealists to mix the two things up. By 'idealists' here I am mainly referring to the British neo-Hegelians ('objective idealists') but the charge of mixing up ontology and epistemology can be made against at least one 'subjective idealist', namely Bishop Berkeley, as his well-known dictum '*esse* is *percipi*' testifies. The objective idealists rejected the correspondence theory of truth and on the whole accepted a coherence theory. The qualification is needed here, because H.H. Joachim, in his *The Nature of Truth* (1906), found the coherence theory unable to deal with the problem of error. However, coherence all the same seemed to him to provide the best account he could think of. The idealists' notion of coherence included that of comprehensiveness, which allows for empirical control. (The notion differed from that of mere consistency in another way, as it involved the doctrine of internal relations. However, I shall ignore this latter obscure doctrine.) Now coherence provides a good account of warranted assertibility, but it is a poor definition of truth. This confusion between epistemology and ontology is starkly evident in H.H. Joachim's use of the horrible phrase 'knowledge-or-truth' in his posthumously published lectures (1948). I might mention by the way that these turgidly written lectures compare badly with Joachim's earlier and elegantly written *The Nature of Truth*, which I have just mentioned, and which in my youth I found highly instructive (and I still so regard it).

Recently this sort of confusion of ontology with epistemology has broken out again in the very influential writings of Michael Dummett and of younger philosophers who have been influenced by him, in that the mathematical philosophy of intuitionism has been generalized, so as to base the notion of truth on that of warranted assertibility in general, not just on that of rigorous proof. This account of truth seems to me to show a slide into idealism and a loosening intellectual grip on the real world. I shall try to explain why I think this later in the paper, but in brief it is that the epistemological approach restricts the real to the field of the cognitive abilities of rational beings, and we have no reason to suppose that reality must be so restricted. There is another strain in contemporary anti-realism, which comes from Hilary Putnam (1983, see 'Models and Reality' and 'Reference and Truth'), and which is due to worries about indeterminacy of reference. Putnam distinguishes empirical realism from metaphysical realism, and rejects the latter as unintelligible. His distinction is reminiscent of the Kantian and Bradleyan distinction between the phenomenal and the noumenal. In connection with Bradley this distinction is a major theme of C.A. Campbell's *Scepticism and Construction* (1931). So two strains of contemporary anti-realism may be coming together in a slide towards something not too unlike nineteenth and early twentieth century British idealism.

Michael Devitt (1984) has taken the view, in his recent book, that the issue between realism and idealism has nothing to do with the notion of truth, and that idealism can be stated quite simply as the view that the universe is mental or mind-dependent. Of course up to a point I agree with Devitt. For example the question of the reality of so-called 'theoretical entities' in physics can be discussed independently of the issues about truth and reference raised by Dummett and Putnam. Here we are on what the neo-Hegelian or 'objective' idealists would have called the phenomenal level. Contrariwise, it need not be inconsistent for a neo-Hegelian to hold that electrons are as real as tomatoes, or even more real. (It would possibly be inconsistent for a Berkeleyan or 'subjective' idealist to hold this.)

I remember a very interesting seminar that G.A. Paul gave in Oxford when I was a graduate student, on the nature of metaphysics. The answer that Paul eventually gave, after sympathetically considering and rejecting many suggestions from members of the class (he liked to keep us guessing!) was that the metaphysician re-defined the word 'real'. I remember how struck I was on returning to my college and opening Berkeley's *Principles of Human Knowledge* and seeing the words '*esse* is *percipi*'! (However, I would not now follow Paul in his definition of metaphysics.) Paul compared F.H. Bradley with the early A.J. Ayer. For Ayer (in a sense) things got less real as they became more theoretical – they were more and more elaborate logical constructions out of sense data. According to Paul, for Bradley things got more real as one got away from sense experience into theory. As an interpretation of Bradley I now believe that this will not do. Bradley thought that it was a vicious abstraction to separate thought from feeling, as in the scientist's description of the colours of a sunset, and so he often regarded science rather operationistically, as a useful fiction. Nevertheless it is easy to see how neo-Hegelian idealism in general could be seen in Paul's way. Certainly theorizing is one side of experience, and it is natural to think of theorizing as transcending individuality. Bradley characterized truth as 'satisfying the intellect'. I do not take this as implying 'satisfying the *individual* intellect'. Intellectual activity is a social phenomenon. Nevertheless, though Bradley's thought is rather elusive here, in his essay 'On Some Aspects of Truth' (Bradley 1914), he seems to be thinking of theories as satisfying the *individual* intellect. A scientific theory can exist and be accepted by scientists without being fully within the experience of any single mind. Thus we can imagine a physicist taking over a mathematical theory which he or she does not fully understand from a mathematician who only partially understands the applications that will be made of it by the physicist. Theories, as systems of ideas, are indeed becoming more and more difficult to be grasped by any single scientist. As systems of ideas, they are inter-personal entities. (As a realist I think of theories as neither personal nor inter-personal. I think of them as systems of sentences or perhaps propositions. However, in what I am saying at the moment I am trying to keep close to the idealist point of view.)

As theories become even more coherent and comprehensive they are supposed by idealists (but perhaps not by Bradley) to approach closer to absolute reality. Notice that there is some suggestion here that idealists have confused our theories or thoughts with what these theories or thoughts refer to. It is the psychologistic equivalent of a 'use-mention' fallacy, in which a name is confused with what it names. I think that if this suggestion is right the confusion must be something like a sub-acute infection, since it is too obvious a confusion to be accepted if made explicitly. Bradley himself often argues against the assimilation of ideas and their objects. See his *Principles of Logic* (Bradley, 1922, vol. I, bk. 1, chapter 1, and his criticism of the theory of the association of ideas in bk. II, part 2, chapter 1). Of course he is not on the deeper metaphysical level here, as he is in *Appearance and Reality* (Bradley 1930), but even here see chapter 15.[1] As Guy Stock has reminded me in this connection, for Bradley thought is symbolic and discursive, whereas reality is individual. Nevertheless in Bradley's metaphysics, as opposed to his logic, the discursive cannot be fully real, and in so far as it is real, Bradley surely holds that it is not distinct from reality, i.e. the Absolute. However, if Bradley does thus in the end fail to distinguish theories from what they are about, this is perhaps a consequence of his metaphysics only, and not a motivation for it. Confusion of theories and the world they are about is a persistent temptation: it is at least suggested by the title of even so hard-headed a philosopher as Nelson Goodman's recent book *Ways of Worldmaking* (Goodman 1978).[2]

In idealism the confusion (if it exists) may be kept hidden from view because of the use of psychologistic language. Theory is supposed to articulate what in less sophisticated experience is apprehended as 'a vague whole of immediate feeling', to use G.R.G. Mure's words in his *Idealist Epilogue* (Mure 1978, p. 8). Mure says 'The intuitive moment is the immediate grasp of the experienced content' (Mure 1978, p. 8) and '. . . attention selects within a vague whole of immediate feeling' (Mure 1978, p. 13). With this selection comes articulation and synthesis and we are on the way to physics and other sciences. It is easy to see how this sort of talk can lead temptingly to idealism. Thus Mure talked (characteristically of neo-Hegelian idealists) of an experienced content. But it can be confusing to say that we experience contents. A drunkard may have an experience as of seeing a pink rat. We must not say, however, that a pink rat is part of the content of the drunkard's experience. There is no pink rat and so no pink rat to be part of the content of the experience. An idealist might reply that the pink rat has some sort of minimal reality, since it forms part of a system of ideas, even though a not very coherent or comprehensive one. Once more I detect the same sort of analogue of a use-mention fallacy. It is the idea of a pink rat that forms part of a not very coherent or comprehensive system of ideas, and the idea of a pink rat is not a pink rat.

I have indicated that I suspect this fallacy of operating, in a hidden way, in G.R.G. Mure's system. I may be wrong, of course. I am more uncertain about Bradley. As I have remarked, in Bradley there are plenty of passages in which he distinguishes ideas from a reality beyond them. (Even so, at least in *Appearance and Reality*, where he is more metaphysical than in *The Principles of Logic*, though reality is 'beyond' ideas, these ideas are not *distinct* from a reality beyond them, since the ideas are rather a confused *aspect* of such a reality.) But there are other passages which do strongly suggest the confusion I have in mind. Thus in *Essays on Truth and Reality* Bradley (1914, pp. 425–6) says 'that ideal construction in which for us the entire past consists' and later he refers to past and future as 'constructions' which though 'ideal' are also 'real'. He even says 'I have . . . an idea of Caesar's immediate experience and my idea is true, and, so far as it goes, it is real, and actually, so far, it *is* Caesar's own direct awareness of himself.' These and other passages suggest that Bradley was prone to the fallacy that I have mentioned, despite other passages that could be cited in which he very much implies the contrary.

One should not accuse contemporary anti-realists of such an obvious analogue of the use-mention fallacy, but I do not contend that this fallacy is the only route from an epistemological concept of truth to idealism, or something like idealism. What is in common to idealism and to modern anti-realism is the assimilation of truth to warranted assertibility. Coherence provides the clue to a good theory of warranted assertibility. It should be remembered that the idealists included comprehensiveness in the notion of coherence. We can easily have consistent theories that are obviously false – so that the theories cover only a limited part of our experience. They do not make our total experience coherent. For our 'web of belief' (to use W.V. Quine's and J.S. Ullian's phrase, Quine and Ullian 1978) to be totally coherent it needs to be a web that takes in (and in some cases may modify) our observation beliefs, and that is capable of taking in future observations that we have or may decide to acquire by means of possibly highly ingenious experimentation. One of our beliefs (or sentences) is warrantedly assertible if it fits easily into our web of belief. That is, Quine's theory of knowledge is not very different from that of the idealists. One would have to subtract the idealists' insistence on 'internal relations', but in other respects their epistemology was a great advance on the empiricists' attempt to construct our knowledge on a basis of indubitable sense experience, mainly because of the idealists' holistic approach to inductive justification. The dynamics of the web of belief presumably need elucidation by means of considerations of subjective probability. Nicholas Rescher (1973) has written on the coherence theory in this vein.

It has been common to distinguish the question of the *definition* of truth from that of the *criterion* of truth. I want to say that coherence is no good as a definition of truth, but it does well as an account of warranted assertibility. (I think that the word 'criterion' is too strongly suggestive of essential and inviolable connection for me to want to say that warranted assertibility is even a criterion of truth.)

While thus defending a coherence theory of warranted assertibility, I oppose it as a theory of truth. Recently, as I remarked earlier, a form of anti-realism has become popular in which this sort of assimilation of truth to warranted assertibility is a central theme. In this paper I shall not be specially concerned with any particular anti-realist but will discuss what I conceive to be the general spirit of anti-realism. What applies to Dummett may not apply to Crispin Wright or to Neil Tennant for example. Anti-realism is a generalization of the so-called intuitionist position in the philosophy of mathematics in which, roughly speaking, truth of a sentence is elucidated as possession of a proof of it. This entails the rejection of the principle of bivalence, since there may be mathematical sentences of which we know neither a proof nor a disproof. Of course in the extension of this idea to language in general the notion of proof has to be weakened to that of warranted assertibility, since scientific or historical statements are not susceptible of proof or disproof in the mathematical sense. I shall distinguish various ways in which this sort of philosophical theory may be developed.

1   It may be held that a proposition p is true if and only if p can be established now.
2   It may be held that p is true if and only if p could be established by some more developed science in the future.
3   It may be held that p is true if and only if it could be established by some ideal or perfect science.

Even though this third form takes us further from intuitionist ways of thought, it is the most interesting because it is clear that there must be propositions that we are warranted in asserting now but which, against all present probability, will be overturned by further evidence or by novel ways of thought. The history of our epistemic activities surely gives good inductive grounds for thinking this. However, an anti-realist who adopts this third form may come up against the problem of whether there could be an ideal or perfect science. (Indeed if a perfect science had to be effectively axiomatized, Gödel's theorem would imply that it could not contain all truths.) Hilary Putnam (1983, pp. 84–5) has suggested that we think of truth as justification in epistemically ideal conditions, to which we may in many cases approximate, though we may never reach them.[3]

Unless he or she is willing to adopt a theory of truth as time-dependent, the anti-realist will be forced into a doctrine of degrees of truth. Once more a comparison with absolute idealism may be of interest. F.H. Bradley held that there were degrees of truth, since he held that truth was coherence (which includes comprehensiveness) and coherence comes in degrees. Let me make an aside here, one nostalgic of my undergraduate days in Glasgow, because it brings in the views of my old professor, C.A. Campbell. Campbell argued that in Bradley's thought there was a tension between his doctrine of degrees of truth and his metaphysics. In Bradley's Note A to the second edition of *Appearance and Reality*, a Note on which Campbell put much stress, Bradley argued that any proposition must be incoherent. Campbell therefore held that Bradley should have said that any proposition (or 'judgement' as the idealists psychologistically put it) must lie infinitely far from the truth and that there can be no degrees of truth. Bradley's Note A does of course seem to be a tissue of confusions, but perhaps he is not *quite* as simple minded as a reading of this Note out of the context of what he says elsewhere would indicate. Stewart Candlish (1984) has argued that Bradley well understood the difference between predication and identity, which seems to be confused in the Note, but that he rejected predication as unsatisfying to the intellect.[4] In Campbell's interesting book *Scepticism and Construction* (Campbell 1931) Campbell out-Bradleys Bradley, and in a way he gives a more coherent version of Bradley's absolute idealism than Bradley does himself. If this line of thought is right, Bradley should have said that theories cannot possess degrees of truth, just as natural numbers cannot possess degrees of infinity. Ten to the power ten to the power ten is no nearer $aleph_o$ (the smallest infinite cardinal number) than two or seven are.

According to the theories of less sceptical idealists than Bradley it is more plausible that ever more coherent and comprehensive theories approach absolute truth. Avoiding the tendency to fallacies analogous to the use-mention one, according to which absolutely coherent and comprehensive experience would come to be *identified* with absolute reality as a whole, we might interpret idealists (and indeed the latter-day Putnam) as holding a view similar to that of C.S. Peirce, according to which truth would be identified with warranted assertibility in the limit. That is, a proposition would be true if it occurred in an ideal theory, and for a theory to be ideal is the same as for it to be maximally coherent and comprehensive.

This is where the nineteenth century idealists, C.S. Peirce, and modern anti-realists seem to me to be tarred by the same brush. It is important to keep the notion of truth sharply distinct from that of warranted assertibility, even warranted assertibility in the limit. In the case of warranted assertibility *not* in the limit the distinction can be made easily enough. One can have excellent reasons for believing a proposition, and later one can have even better reasons for disbelieving the proposition. We also have good inductive grounds for believing that some of the propositions that we believe to be warrantedly assertible are false, even though we never come to have reason to think any particular one of them false. $\sim p_1 \lor \sim p_1 \ldots \lor \sim p_n$ can have high warranted assertibility, even though all of p_1, p_2, $\ldots$, p_n also have high warranted assertibility. (The so-called paradox of the preface.) Innocent people do get convicted by reasonable juries, scientists and historians do make mistakes, and if one resists the intuitionist's or the anti-realist's unusual way of talking we can surely say that undetected falsehoods are often warrantedly assertible according to the best theories. That is, we have good inductive reasons for thinking that many reasonable hypotheses that have never turned out to be false, and never will turn out to be false, nevertheless are false.

The idealist or anti-realist will presumably say that turning out to be false is simply not fitting into a more coherent and comprehensive system of propositions (or judgements). He or she might say that when a previously warranted assertion turns out to be false this is just warranted assertion of its negation within a wider system.

There seem to be true propositions that no one was, is, or will be warranted in asserting. That Winston Churchill sneezed twice more on a certain date in 1941 than did Franklin Roosevelt may well be true, but it is unlikely that either of them, or anyone else for that matter, would ever have been warranted in asserting it. Nor is it likely that future historical or scientific research could ever ascertain the truth or falsity of this proposition about the sneezes.[5] It looks here as though we have a case of truth not only outrunning warranted assertibility but also outrunning warranted assertibility 'in the limit'. Similarly Hartry Field (1982, pp. 556–7) has posed the case of the dinosaurs: we can establish for some large number n that there were no more than n dinosaurs at a certain precise time in the age of dinosaurs. That is we can establish the disjunction of the propositions 'There were n_i dinosaurs' for $i = 0,1,2,$ . . . n, without being able to establish 'There were n_i dinosaurs' for any i. Does the sentence 'There were exactly n_i dinosaurs' have no meaning? Surely this would be a paradoxical thing to say. Surely for some i 'There were exactly n_i dinosaurs' is not only meaningful but *true*! Of course the anti-realist (modelling his anti-realism on intuitionism in mathematics) will presumably deny this, but such a denial looks a heroic and implausible move on the anti-realist's part. The recourse to an ideal or perfect science does not help at all. Surely it is implausible that even an ideal science of the future, if there could be such, could ascertain the exact number of dinosaurs at a particular time. Nor could it settle the question of Churchill's sneezes. Examples could be multiplied *ad nauseam*.

C.S. Peirce rejected the view that truth could outrun warranted assertibility even 'in the limit'. He held that it was not possible to put limits on what science might be able to assert in the future. As against that, I want to say that we *do* know enough (largely from science) to know that it would never be possible to decide the question of Churchill's sneezes or of the exact number of the dinosaurs at a certain moment in pre-historic times. Peirce was not really interested in truth. In his essay 'The Essentials of Pragmatism' he says: 'Your problems would be greatly simplified if instead of saying that you want to know the "Truth", you were simply to say that you want to attain a state of belief unassailable by doubt' (Peirce 1950, p. 257).[6]

As a realist I certainly want to agree that I desire to attain a state of belief unassailable by doubt, and not just by indoctrination or brain washing but by the sorts of rational methods of which Peirce approved. But this is because I think that belief unassailable by doubt, if achieved by these methods, is likely to be true belief, in an independently understandable sense of 'true'. If all Peirce is doing is to re-define 'true' so that it means something like 'rationally indubitable', he is perhaps saying something with which no realist need disagree, but then (because of the theft for epistemological duty of the semantic word 'true') it will have no bearing on what the realist wants to say about truth.

What is this independent realist sense of 'true'? I want to say that it is the sense of 'true' explicated by Tarski. Modern anti-realists want to say that we can understand a sentence only if it is in some sense possible to establish it or to refute it. As a realist, and following Davidson, I understand meaning in terms of truth conditions. Now we can know the Tarski-type truth conditions of a sentence (in terms of a finitely axiomatized truth theory) without knowing how to verify or falsify it. Tarski-type truth outruns provability, even within mathematics, as Gödel's theorem shows. However, when I point to Tarski's theory of truth in order to indicate a notion of truth which differs from any notion of provability or warranted assertibility, I need to proceed with caution. When the sentential connectives and quantifiers are interpreted intuition-istically all the Tarski recursions still go through and T-sentences of the form $\ulcorner \ulcorner p \urcorner$ is true if and only if $p \urcorner$ are provable.[7] (The 'if and only if' here has to be understood as the intuitionist one.) The difference comes from the proof of bivalence ($\ulcorner p \urcorner$ is true or $\ulcorner p \urcorner$ is false) where Tarski needs excluded middle (p or not-p) in the meta-language. Apart from this, the Tarski truth theory does not distinguish truth from provability. Acceptance of excluded middle is thus important for the realist so as to fix his or her notion of truth as different from the intuitionist or anti-realist one. The intuitionist or anti-realist does not allow excluded middle, and not having it in his or her meta-language he or she does not have bivalence in the object language. But the question is: What is the anti-realist's motivation for not allowing 'p or not-p'? It comes from a notion that to be true is *a fortiori* to be meaningful, that to be meaningful is to be understandable, and that understanding has to come from verifiability or warranted assertibility of what is understood (or of its negation). I shall argue shortly that this is too narrow a notion of understanding.

The idea that warrantedly assertible theories must 'in the limit' approach truth can be developed in various ways. There is warranted assertibility on the part of a single individual on the one hand and warranted assertibility on the part of a group of individuals on the other hand. Consider a group of individuals who collaborate to produce a theory T. In practice each of the experts will usually familiarize himself or herself in a non-expert or not quite expert way with the work of other experts. We can also envisage situations in which this is not possible and in which the experts just have to trust one another for various conclusions that are used in establishing and testing T. Something like this is indeed true of our ordinary inexpert grasp of many of the findings of modern science. We do have to take a lot on the authority of specialists. The warranted assertibility of science in general becomes a collective thing. Even a good scientist is a layman in specialities well removed from his or her own one.

The question of whether this collective warranted assertibility can be reduced to individual warranted assertibility is one that I shall not try to decide here.[8] Even if we suppose that warranted assertibility belongs only to groups of individuals and is not reducible to single person warranted assertibility, we must remember that such groups cannot be arbitrary sets of individual scientists. They must be groups of intercommunicating persons. If a number of different persons have warranted beliefs about different bits of the cosmic jigsaw their beliefs do not come together so as to form a single theory unless these persons communicate with one another. This consideration becomes important if we consider several interpretations of 'in the limit'.

1   'In the limit' might refer to some perfected state of knowledge on the part of some actual group of rational beings. One trouble about this is that there is no assurance that such a group (or its state of knowledge) will ever exist. Moreover, however perfect was the state of knowledge of some actual group of rational beings there will be very many true propositions that would be left out of such a perfected science. Consider the example of Winston Churchill's sneezes or Hartry Field's example of the number of the dinosaurs.

2   'In the limit' might refer to a mere aggregate (without synthesis) of perfected theories (so far as they *can* be perfected) that are held by non-intercommunicating groups of rational beings, for example humans and the inhabitants of a planet of a star in some other galaxy. Similar objections apply as in the case of the first interpretation.

3   'In the limit' might refer to actual and possible perfected science of actual and possible rational beings. This interpretation runs up against the objection that (unless one agrees here with David Lewis) there are no possible but not actual beings.

However, there are other ways in which one may understand talk of possibility. In general possibility can be elucidated as (model theoretic) consistency with certain contextually understood background assumptions. There are difficult technical problems about what can go into the contextually understood background assumptions. Thus it is physically possible for David Armstrong to drive his car from Sydney to Canberra on a certain date in less than four hours. Here the background assumptions will typically include not only the laws of nature but boundary conditions that determine the physical state of his car, the availability of petrol, the road distance from Sydney to Canberra, the smoothness of the roads, and so on. However, we must not include too much in the boundary conditions: for example we must not include the physical state of his brain that underlies (or rather, is) his desire to stay at home in Sydney on that occasion. Indeed if determinism were true and we included all the boundary conditions in our set of contextually agreed background assumptions, we would have to say that there was only one possible course of events. So subtle considerations are needed in order to describe how we could tinker with background assumptions without leading to inconsistency (Reichenbach 1954).

An extreme sort of possibility is logical possibility. In this case the set of contextually agreed background assumptions is the null set. Now, returning to interpretation (3) of 'in the limit', I suppose that there is no logical inconsistency in supposing that there should be a (possibly) non-countable infinity of supernatural beings who always have existed and always will exist, and who observe by supernatural means every atom, quark, or ripple of probability wave in the entire universe, and who communicate with one another instantaneously (with respect to some preferred frame of reference) by supernatural means. Such a group of beings would be able to decide the question about Churchill's sneezes or that of whether a neutrino was emitted from some particular atom in the depths of space, but this would not be because the warranted assertibility of some existential proposition conferred existence on Churchill's sneezes or on the neutrino. Of course on this supernaturalist hypothesis warranted assertibility that p and warranted assertibility that not-p would exhaust the possibilities, and so the bivalence of sentential truth value in classical logic would be mirrored by bivalence of warrantedness (or otherwise). But even on this supernaturalist hypothesis the realist could distinguish his or her position by pointing to the following asymmetry: the bivalence of warranted assertibility in this fantastic hypothetical case would be explained by the bivalence of truth values and not the other way round.

Let us now consider interpretation (3) as modified in a different way, namely by taking the contextually understood background assumptions (when we talk of possibility) to be the laws of physics as they occur in an ideal science, together with certain rather indefinitely specified boundary conditions. Then the examples such as that of Winston Churchill's sneezes and that of the neutrino in the depths of space, suggest that truth can outrun warranted assertibility, even in the limit of a physically ideal science. An anti-realist, such as Dummett, might say that I am begging the question, but equally I feel that such an anti-realist is begging the question against the realist. Dummett has his reasons of course. One of these seems to be that truth is what we *aim* at, but we cannot aim at what is impossible to get – something that even in the limit outruns physical possibility. As a realist I would reply that we aim at truth when we can get it, but that often we aim at getting members of a class of things some of which are nevertheless out of our reach. An analogy with utilitarianism in ethics may be in order. What the utilitarian would like to do would be to maximize total happiness (of all sentient beings). However, we do not know for certain many of the effects of our actions and so we have to rely on probability. So what the utilitarian will set himself to do will be to maximize not utility but *expected* utility. Similarly in science we will look to the warranted assertibility of our theories, but our ultimate aim will be truth, just as the utilitarian's real desire, if he could get it, would be for utility itself, not mere expected utility.

The trouble, as the realist sees it, is that warranted assertibility is an epistemological notion and the question of real existence must not be confused with an epistemological one. There may of course be an epistemological question about our warrant for holding true a proposition asserting real existence, but the proposition thus held true will in general not be an epistemological one.

As a realist, then, I hold that truth might outrun warranted assertibility even in the limit. It might also do more than *outrun* warranted assertibility: it might *conflict* with it, though I shall argue that there is a sort of paradox in supposing that most of our core scientific beliefs should be *wildly* far from the mark. So there are two questions that may be at issue between the realist and the idealist or anti-realist.

1 Can truth *outrun* warranted assertibility even in the limit?
2 Can truth significantly *conflict* with warranted assertibility even in the limit?

I have already suggested various examples that show that truth could outrun warranted assertibility, even in the limit. However, these are examples of rather particular and localized facts. Even Hartry Field's example of the exact number of the dinosaurs is at most of terrestrial rather than cosmic importance. I shall therefore invite you to consider an example of how truth could outrun warranted assertibility in a cosmically (and hence, I should say, metaphysically) significant way. Consider the 'could' in 'the universe could be as follows . . .' where 'as follows' is succeeded by a description of something we are not warranted in believing. I shall take this 'could' to refer to physical possibility, and as implying consistency with the laws of nature as localized to the already known universe, as well as consistency with the more obvious cosmological features of the observable universe. I shall assume that present-day science has got somewhere near the truth about all this. That is, I shall take it that the central core of present-day science has got somewhere near the truth. The historical phenomenon of theory change should not blind us to the great body of scientific beliefs that will probably never be overturned, e.g. that water contains atoms of hydrogen (or one of its isotopes) and of oxygen, that the transparency of glass is partly due to its non-crystalline structure, that light is an electro-magnetic phenomenon, that the gravitational field not too near too massive a body goes approximately as an inverse square law, that stars belong to galaxies, that some chalks were once the matter of the shells of marine animals, and so on and so on.

Let us call this body of propositions that almost certainly will never be overturned 'the central core of science'. So the 'can' in 'Can truth outrun warranted assertibility in the limit?' should be taken as consistency with this central core of accredited scientific fact. In this connection I refer to a most interesting paper by Gerald Feinberg (1966). In this paper Feinberg argues that Thales' problem about the constitution and observable behaviour of ordinary bulk matter has now been finally solved. To explain the doings of this 'ordinary matter' no more knowledge is needed beyond what can be gained from present-day physics. We need only the laws relating to the proton, neutron, electron, photon and neutrino and the forces between these particles. There is no need to take account of the transitory particles being discovered as a result of high energy collisions in huge accelerators. (Transitory particles are needed to explain the ordinary forces, but to solve Thales' problem these forces can be taken as phenomenological.) Nor are new discoveries in cosmology directly relevant to understanding the physics of ordinary bulk matter. So the 'can' in 'Can truth outrun warranted assertibility?' should be taken as a matter of consistency with this central core of finally understood scientific fact. From the standpoint of this core of scientific fact can we consistently imagine that there might be important but unascertainable truths, unascertainable even in the limit?

In the light of these considerations I invite you to consider an example that I used in an article in *Analysis* (Smart 1982) in order to produce heuristic considerations against a largely semantic argument that Hilary Putnam (1983, 'Models and Reality') had used against metaphysical realism. I believe that Putnam's semantic arguments can be refuted, though it would take another paper to justify this. (However, see Hacking 1983, pp. 105–7; Devitt 1983, pp. 188–91; Lewis 1983.) As I do not accept Putnam's arguments I do not myself distinguish ordinary realism from metaphysical realism: indeed I hold that metaphysics should be continuous with natural science. Now for the example.

Suppose that what we think of as our four-dimensional space-time universe is a cross-section of a larger five-dimensional universe, with another four-dimensional sub-universe as another cross-section. Let us suppose also that the laws of nature as pertaining to the total five-dimensional universe are such that there can be no causal connections between the two four-dimensional sub-universes. We can think of the total universe as containing not only these sub-universes but also points of the containing hyperspace. Now consider an ideal science adopted by rational beings in our sub-universe. We can suppose these rational beings to be as well informed as you may like about our sub-universe and to have a perfectly rational well-tested theory which fits these particular facts. But they can know nothing about the other sub-universe. Indeed, because they are rational they would apply Ockham's Razor and *deny* the existence of the other sub-universe (and of the containing hyperspace) if the hypothesis of such a thing ever occurred to them.[9]

The other sub-universe might also have intelligent beings in it or it might not. We in our sub-universe would surely feel aggrieved at the thought that intelligent beings in the other sub-universe might regard the proposition that we exist as having no truth value! I say this for vividness. My example is designed also to show that another epistemically inaccessible sub-universe without intelligent beings in it might exist. 'Might' here is consistency with the laws of nature we have reason to believe apply in our sub-universe. It could be that the other sub-universe has different laws applying to it. Thus our science might be false in that the laws we believe would not hold unrestrictedly over the whole five-dimensional total universe. Even so our science would not be wildly or radically false – our law sentences would be true (or approximately true) if the quantifiers 'all' and 'some' were restricted to range over entities in our sub-universe. Nevertheless truth would outrun warranted assertibility even in the ideal of warranted assertibility by an intercommunicating group of maximally well informed and intelligent beings in our sub-universe. (Intelligent beings in the other sub-universe would not help because there could be no intercommunication between the two sub-universes.)

Perhaps some of those who I am addressing do not believe in the possibility of absolute space-time, let alone my supposed absolute hyperspace. To them I would say that the example of the two sub-universes could be modified so that they were not supposed to be embedded in a single hyperspace. But for those who do not mind postulating points of absolute space my example is perhaps a bit more easily imaginable. (I am inclined to think that general relativity requires absolute space-time – not space on its own of course – and so why should we not suppose an absolute hyperspace too?)

I expect anti-realists to say that all I have given in my example is an appealing *picture* and that the case I have described is not intelligible, or at least that its main sentences could have no truth value. They might say that intelligibility or possession of a truth value (known or unknown) must come from our web of belief (to use Quine's phrase) and our web of belief *ex hypothesi* could not extend to the other sub-universe. In reply I say that such subjects as set theory, topology and analysis are part of our web of belief since they are needed in science (this is a familiar Quinean point), and though they get their life from our web of belief we are able to form understandable conjectures that go beyond our web of belief or any physically justifiable extension of it. Our web of belief contains mathematical concepts and it is these concepts that enable me to extend our description of the accessible universe (or sub-universe) to yield my example.

Since it was first published I have indeed had some qualms about my example. One explanation that has been proposed for the apparently unlikely accident that certain of the fundamental constants are just right, to many decimal points, to produce a universe with stars, galaxies, etc., is that there are many universes, many of them chaotic, and we happen to be in the right one.[10] So perhaps we have reason to believe in many universes (or more correctly, sub-universes) not connected to ours, and so the assertion of their existence *might* occur in an ideal scientific theory. In my example, of course, there is only *one* other sub-universe, and it is hard to see how we could ever have reason to assert this. On the other hand if the hypothesis of infinity (or a very large number) of sub-universes were accepted there would be reason to reject my example. Still, since the hypothesis of very many sub-universes is not part of core science, even those who accepted the hypothesis could still argue that it might be false. I could still say that the hypothesis of the one universe causally disconnected to ours might be true, even though we could have no reason to assert it.

My example is designed to suggest that (contrary to the anti-realist's view) truth about the universe *might* outrun warranted assertibility. And why should it not? Why should reality be limited by our ability to form warranted beliefs about it? Of course I do not believe that my example of the inaccessible sub-universe *is* true. Part of my use of the example against Putnam is that all methodological constraints (especially Ockham's Razor) should lead us to deny that it *was* true. So if it were true the universe would trick us. I believe that the universe probably does trick us in various ways. I say this because of my empirical beliefs about scientific methodology and about the human cognitive apparatus. However, there would be a pragmatic paradox in my believing that it is physically possible that the *main core* of my scientific beliefs might be wrong. This is because it is this core of scientific beliefs that gives me my notion of what is physically possible. The pragmatic paradox is like that which would occur were I to say 'p and I believe that not-p'. Yet of course it could well *be* that p and I believe that not-p. Let us consider the case of Descartes and his supposition of a deceiving demon. Let us indeed suppose that Descartes' fantasy were true. (We of course skirt pragmatic paradox here.) I would say that Descartes would be rational in disbelieving the fantasy. The story of the demon and his activities is in a sense more complex and less plausible than the usual one. (This is even more obvious in the case of the well-known science fiction somewhat equivalent fantasy of the brain in the vat, stimulated to think that it had a body, etc., by a mad scientist of the future.) The demon could know that Descartes was wrong in believing in the external world, etc., but Descartes himself could not rationally believe this. Nevertheless the fantasy would be seen by the demon to be not only meaningful but true!

In the same sort of way I believe that the universe might trick us in ways that the anti-realist does not believe possible, or even meaningful. On the other hand, on pain of pragmatic paradox, I can not believe that it tricks us all that much about our *central* scientific beliefs. And sometimes the universe does not trick us but leaves us invincibly ignorant (cf. the example of Churchill's sneezes or of a neutrino being emitted in some unknown particular interaction of particles).

Donald Davidson has argued in a transcendental manner that one's core beliefs must be true. His argument is different from mine because it proceeds from the notion of radical interpretation of a language. He still holds to something like a correspondence view of truth in his somewhat misleadingly titled paper 'A Coherence Theory of Truth and Knowledge' (Davidson 1983, p. 425). Philip Pettit has suggested to me that the concept of truth cannot be a totally non-epistemological one (as I hold it is) because in Davidsonian radical interpretation we need to make hypotheses about speaker's beliefs and desires when constructing a truth theory for the language. In reply I would say that we do indeed need to make such hypotheses when deciding that a word should be translated as 'banana', say, but this does not make the concept of a banana an epistemological one. Nor, similarly, should these considerations make the concept of truth an epistemological one.

The anti-realist can not accept the idea of an ideal theory being false. The anti-realist's theory seems to me to imply that the universe is not only limited but that it has a lot of fuzzy holes in it too. (Churchill neither did nor did not sneeze on a certain day!) And this does suggest that anti-realism is just the old idealism, since it is our experience or our system of ideas that can have fuzzy gaps in it: the universe itself is surely determinate and complete.[11]

NOTES

1   I am indebted to Thomas Baldwin for these references.
2   Goodman makes an attempt to wriggle out of the idealistic morass in his paper 'On Starmaking' (1980) which is in reply to papers by Carl G. Hempel (1980) and Israel Scheffler (1980) respectively.
3   For Putnam's views about reference, see his papers 'Models and Reality' and 'Reference and Truth', reprinted in Putnam (1983).
4   See the very impressive paper by Stewart Candlish (1984). See especially p. 255 and see also Manser and Stock's introduction to the same volume, especially pp. 21–2.
5   Charles Pigden has drawn my attention to a similar case 'It snowed on Manhattan Island on the first of January in the year 1 AD', in Bertrand Russell (1940, p. 277).
6   Roger Trigg in his *Reality at Risk* (1980, p. 17ff) has also taken issue with this remark by Peirce.
7   I have been made to see this by Neil Tennant, in conversation. See Tennant (1981; 1986, especially section 4 'Truth Theory and Logical Operators'). Hilary Putnam has frequently argued that Tarski's theory of truth is metaphysically neutral. For a good statement see Hilary Putnam (1983, p. 83.)
8   C.A.J. Coady's work on testimony is of interest in this connection. See Coady (1973, 1975, 1981).
9   Russell in his *Inquiry into Meaning and Truth* (1940, pp. 278–88) has also discussed the meaningfulness of the sentence 'There is a cosmos which has no spatio-temporal relation to the one in which we live'. (See also note 5.)
10 For a survey of this problem and a different solution see John Leslie (1983).
11 In 1983 I read an early draft of this paper at a number of universities in Britain. I wish to thank numerous friends there for helpful comments in discussion and, in particular, Thomas Baldwin (University of York), David Holdcroft (University of Leeds), Peter Smith (University College of Wales, Aberystwyth), Guy Stock (University of Aberdeen), Neil Tennant (University of Stirling), and Crispin Wright (University of St Andrews). For comments at a later stage I am grateful to Philip Pettit, Charles Pigden and Richard Sylvan (Australian National University). A later draft of this paper was read at the annual conference of the Australasian Association of Philosophy in 1984.

REFERENCES

Bradley, F.H. 1914: *Essays on Truth and Reality*. Oxford: Clarendon Press.
—— 1922: *Principles of Logic*, 2nd edn. Oxford: Clarendon Press.
—— 1930: *Appearance and Reality*, 2nd edn. Oxford: Clarendon Press.
Campbell, C.A. 1931: *Scepticism and Construction*. London: Allen and Unwin.
Candlish, Stewart 1984: Scepticism, Ideal Experiment and Priorities in Bradley's

Metaphysics. In Anthony Manser and Guy Stock (eds), *The Philosophy of F.H. Bradley*, Oxford: Clarendon Press, chapter 13.

Coady, C.A.J. 1973: Testimony and Observation. *American Philosophical Quarterly*, 10, 149–55.

—— 1975: Collingwood and Historical Testimony. *Philosophy*, 50, 409–24.

—— 1981: Mathematical Knowledge and Reliable Authority. *Mind*, 90, 542–56.

Davidson, Donald 1983: A Coherence Theory of Truth and Knowledge. In Dieter Henrich (ed.), *Kant oder Hegel?*, Stuttgart: Klett-Cotta.

Devitt, Michael 1984: *Realism and Truth*. Princeton, New Jersey: Princeton University Press.

Feinberg, Gerald 1966: Physics and the Thales Problem. *Journal of Philosophy*, 66, 5–13.

Field, Hartry 1982: Realism and Relativism. *Journal of Philosophy*, 79, 553–67.

Goodman, Nelson 1978: *Ways of Worldmaking*. Indianapolis: Hackett Press.

—— 1980: On Starmaking. *Synthese*, 45, 211–15.

Hacking, Ian 1983: *Representing and Intervening*. London: Cambridge University Press.

Hempel, Carl G. 1980: Comments on Goodman's *Ways of Worldmaking*. *Synthese*, 45, 193–9.

Joachim, H.H. 1906: *The Nature of Truth*. Oxford: Clarendon Press.

—— 1948: *Logical Studies*. Oxford: Clarendon Press.

Leslie, John 1983: Cosmology, Probability and the Need to Explain Life. In Nicholas Rescher (ed.), *Scientific Explanation and Understanding*, CPS Publications in Philosophy of Science, University of Pittsburgh, Latham, Maryland: University Press of America.

Lewis, David 1984: Putnam's Paradox. *Australasian Journal of Philosophy*, 62, 221–36.

Mure, G.R.G. 1978: *Idealist Epilogue*. Oxford: Clarendon Press.

Peirce, C.S. 1950: The Essentials of Pragmatism. In Justus Buchler (ed.), *The Philosophy of Peirce, Selected Writings*, London: Routledge and Kegan Paul.

Putnam, Hilary 1983: *Realism and Reason, Philosophical Papers, vol. 3*. London: Cambridge University Press.

Quine, W.V. and Ullian, J.S. 1978: *The Web of Belief*, 2nd edn. New York: Random House.

Reichenbach, H. 1954: *Nomological Statements and Admissible Operations*. Amsterdam, Holland: North Holland.

Rescher, Nicholas 1973: *The Coherance Theory of Truth*. Oxford: Clarendon Press.

Russell, Bertrand 1940: *Inquiry into Meaning and Truth*. London: George Allen and Unwin.

Scheffler, Israel 1980: The Wonderful Worlds of Goodman. *Synthese*, 45, 201–9.

Smart, J.J.C. 1982: Metaphysical Realism. *Analysis*, 42, 1–3.

Tennant, Neil 1981: From Logic to Philosophies. *British Journal for the Philosophy of Science*, 32, 287–301.

—— 1986: Holism, Molecularity and Truth. In B. Taylor (ed.), *Festschrift for Michael Dummett*, The Hague: Martinus Nijhoff.

Trigg, Roger 1980: *Reality at Risk*. Brighton: Harvester.

PART 4
Philosophy of Mind

15

Sensations and Brain Processes

This paper[1] takes its departure from arguments to be found in U.T. Place's 'Is Consciousness a Brain Process?' (Place 1956). I have had the benefit of discussing Place's thesis in a good many universities in the United States and Australia, and I hope that the present paper answers objections to his thesis which Place has not considered and that it presents his thesis in a more nearly unobjectionable form. This paper is meant also to supplement the paper 'The "Mental" and the "Physical" ', by H. Feigl (1958), which in part argues for a similar thesis to Place's.

Suppose that I report that I have at this moment a roundish, blurry-edged after-image which is yellowish towards its edge and is orange towards its centre. What is it that I am reporting? One answer to this question might be that I am not reporting anything, that when I say that it looks to me as though there is a roundish yellow-orange patch of light on the wall I am expressing some sort of *temptation*, the temptation to say that there *is* a roundish yellow-orange patch on the wall (though I may know that there is not such a patch on the wall). This is perhaps Wittgenstein's view in the *Philosophical Investigations* (see sections 367, 370). Similarly, when I 'report' a pain, I am not really reporting anything (or, if you like, I am reporting in a queer sense of 'reporting'), but am doing a sophisticated sort of wince. (See section 244: 'The verbal expression of pain replaces crying and does not describe it.' Nor does it describe anything else?)[2] I prefer most of the time to discuss an after-image rather than a pain, because the word 'pain' brings in something which is irrelevant to my purpose: the notion of 'distress'. I think that 'he is in pain' entails 'he is in distress', that is, that he is in a certain agitation-condition (Ryle 1949, p. 93). Similarly, to say 'I am in pain' may be to do more than 'replace pain behaviour': it may be partly to report something, though this something is quite non-mysterious, being an agitation-condition, and so susceptible of behaviouristic analysis. The suggestion I wish if possible to avoid is a different one, namely that 'I am in pain' is a genuine report, and that what it reports is an irreducibly psychical something. And similarly the suggestion I wish to resist is also that to say 'I have a yellowish-orange after-image' is to report something irreducibly psychical.

Why do I wish to resist this suggestion? Mainly because of Ockham's razor. It seems to me that science is increasingly giving us a viewpoint whereby organisms are able to be seen as physicochemical mechanisms (see Oppenheim & Putnam 1958): it seems that even the behaviour of man himself will one day be explicable in mechanistic terms. There does seem to be, so far as science is concerned, nothing in the world but increasingly complex arrangements of physical constituents. All except for one place: in consciousness. That is, for a full description of what is going on in a man you would have to mention not only the physical processes in his tissues, glands, nervous system, and so forth, but also his states of consciousness: his visual, auditory, and tactual sensations, his aches and pains. That these should be *correlated* with brain processes does not help, for to say that they are *correlated* is to say that they are something 'over and above'. You cannot correlate something with itself. You correlate footprints with burglars, but not Bill Sikes the burglar with Bill Sikes the burglar. So sensations, states of consciousness, do seem to be the one sort of thing left outside the physicalist picture, and for various reasons I just cannot believe that this can be so. That everything should be explicable in terms of physics (together of course with descriptions of the ways in which the parts are put together – roughly, biology is to physics as radio-engineering is to electro-magnetism) except the occurrence of sensations seems to me to be frankly unbelievable. Such sensations would be 'nomological danglers', to use Feigl's expression (Feigl 1958, p. 428).[3] It is not often realized how odd would be the laws whereby these nomological danglers would dangle. It is sometimes asked, 'Why can't there be psychophysical laws which are of a novel sort, just as the laws of electricity and magnetism were novelties from the standpoint of Newtonian mechanics?' Certainly we are pretty sure in the future to come across new ultimate laws of a novel type, but I expect them to relate simple constituents: for example, whatever ultimate particles are then in vogue. I cannot believe that ultimate laws of nature could relate simple constituents to configurations consisting of perhaps billions of neurons (and goodness knows how many billion billions of ultimate particles) all put together for all the world as though their main purpose in life was to be a negative feedback mechanism of a complicated sort. Such ultimate laws would be like nothing so far known in science. They have a queer 'smell' to them. I am just unable to believe in the nomological danglers themselves, or in the laws whereby they would dangle. If any philosophical arguments seemed to compel us to believe in such things, I would suspect a catch in the argument. In any case it is the object of this paper to show that there are no philosophical arguments which compel us to be dualists.

The above is largely a confession of faith, but it explains why I find Wittgenstein's position (as I construe it) so congenial. For on this view there are, in a sense, no sensations. A man is a vast arrangement of physical particles, but there are not, over and above this, sensations or states of consciousness. There are just behavioural facts about this vast mechanism, such as that it expresses a temptation (behaviour disposition) to say 'there is a yellowish-red patch on the wall' or that it goes through a sophisticated sort of wince, that is, says 'I am in pain'. Admittedly Wittgenstein says that though the sensation 'is not a something', it is nevertheless 'not a nothing either' (section 304), but this need only mean that the word 'ache' has a use. An ache is a thing, but only in the innocuous sense in which the plain man, in the first paragraph of Frege's *Foundations of Arithmetic*, answers the question 'What is the number one?' by 'a thing'. It should be noted that when I assert that to say 'I have a yellowish-orange after-image' is to express a temptation to assert the physical-object statement 'There is a yellowish-orange patch on the wall', I mean that saying 'I have a yellowish-orange after-image' is (partly) the exercise of the disposition[4] which is the temptation. It is not to *report* that I have the temptation, any more than is 'I love you' normally a report that I love someone. Saying 'I love you' is just part of the behaviour which is the exercise of the disposition of loving someone.

Though for the reasons given above, I am very receptive to the above 'expressive' account of sensation statements, I do not feel that it will quite do the trick. Maybe this is because I have not thought it out sufficiently, but it does seem to me as though, when a person says 'I have an after-image', he *is* making a genuine report, and that when he says 'I have a pain', he *is* doing more than 'replace pain-behaviour', and that 'this more' is not just to say that he is in distress. I am not so sure, however, that to admit this is to admit that there are non-physical correlates of brain processes. Why should not sensations just be brain processes of a certain sort? There are, of course, well-known (as well as lesser-known) philosophical objections to the view that reports of sensations are reports of brain-processes, but I shall try to argue that these arguments are by no means as cogent as is commonly thought to be the case.

Let me first try to state more accurately the thesis that sensations are brain-processes. It is not the thesis that, for example, 'after-image' or 'ache' means the same as 'brain process of sort X' (where 'X' is replaced by a description of a certain sort of brain process). It is that, in so far as 'after-image' or 'ache' is a report of a process, it is a report of a process that *happens to be* a brain process. It follows that the thesis does not claim that sensation statements can be *translated* into statements about brain processes (Place 1956, p. 102; Feigl 1958, p. 390 near top). Nor does it claim that the logic of a sensation statement is the same as that of a brain-process statement. All it claims is that in so far as a sensation statement is a report of something, that something is in fact a brain process. Sensations are nothing over and above brain processes. Nations are nothing 'over and above' citizens, but this does not prevent the logic of nation statements being very different from the logic of citizen statements, nor does it ensure the translatability of nation statements into citizen statements. (I do not, however, wish to assert that the relation of sensation statements to brain-process statements is very like that of nation statements to citizen statements. Nations do not just *happen to be* nothing over and above citizens, for example. I bring in the 'nations' example merely to make a negative point: that the fact that the logic of A-statements is different from that of B-statements does not ensure that As are anything over and above Bs.)

When I say that a sensation is a brain process or that lightning is an electric discharge, I am using 'is' in the sense of strict identity. (Just as in the – in this case necessary – proposition '7 is identical with the smallest prime number greater than 5'.) When I say that a sensation is a brain process or that lightning is an electric discharge I do not mean just that the sensation is somehow spatially or temporally continuous with the brain process or that the lightning is just spatially or temporally continuous with the discharge. When on the other hand I say that the successful general is the same person as the small boy who stole the apples I mean only that the successful general I see before me is a time slice (Woodger 1939, p. 38)[5] of the same four-dimensional object of which the small boy stealing apples is an earlier time slice. However, the four-dimensional object which has the general-I-see-before-me for its late time slice is identical in the strict sense with the four-dimensional object which has the small-boy-stealing-apples for an early time slice. I distinguish these two senses of 'is identical with' because I wish to make it clear that the brain-process doctrine asserts identity in the *strict* sense.

I shall now discuss various possible objections to the view that the processes reported in sensation statements are in fact processes in the brain. Most of us have met some of these objections in our first year as philosophy students. All the more reason to take a good look at them. Others of the objections will be more recondite and subtle.

Objection 1. Any illiterate peasant can talk perfectly well about his after-images, or how things look or feel to him, or about his aches and pains, and yet he may know nothing whatever about neurophysiology. A man may, like Aristotle, believe that the brain is an organ for cooling the body without any impairment of his ability to make true statements about his sensations. Hence the things we are talking about when we describe our sensations cannot be processes in the brain.

Reply. You might as well say that a nation of slugabeds, who never saw the Morning Star or knew of its existence, or who had never thought of the expression 'the Morning Star', but who used the expression 'the Evening Star' perfectly well, could not use this expression to refer to the same entity as we refer to (and describe as) 'the Morning Star' (Feigl 1958, p. 439).

You may object that the Morning Star is in a sense not the very same thing as the Evening Star, but only something spatiotemporally continuous with it. That is, you may say that the Morning Star is not the Evening Star in the strict sense of 'identity' that I distinguished earlier.

There is, however, a more plausible example. Consider lightning (Place 1956, p. 106; Feigl 1958, p. 438). Modern physical science tells us that lightning is a certain kind of electrical discharge due to ionization of clouds of water vapour in the atmosphere. This, it is now believed, is what the true nature of lightning is. Note that there are not two things: a flash of lightning and an electrical discharge. There is one thing, a flash of lightning, which is described scientifically as an electrical discharge to the earth from a cloud of ionized water molecules. The case is not at all like that of explaining a footprint by reference to a burglar. We say that what lightning really is, what its true nature as revealed by science is, is an electrical discharge. (It is not the true nature of a footprint to be a burglar.)

To forestall irrelevant objections, I should like to make it clear that by 'lightning' I mean the publicly observable object, lightning, not a visual sense-datum of lightning. I say that the publicly observable physical object lightning is in fact the electrical discharge, not just a correlate of it. The sense-datum, or rather the having of the sense-datum, the 'look' of lightning, may well in my view be a correlate of the electrical discharge. For in my view it is a brain state *caused* by the lightning. But we should no more confuse sensations of lightning with lightning than we confuse sensations of a table with the table.

In short, the reply to Objection 1 is that there can be contingent statements of the form 'A is identical with B', and a person may well know that something is an A without knowing that it is a B. An illiterate peasant might well be able to talk about his sensations without knowing about his brain processes, just as he can talk about lightning though he knows nothing of electricity.

Objection 2. It is only a contingent fact (if it is a fact) that when we have a certain kind of sensation there is a certain kind of process in our brain. Indeed it is possible, though perhaps in the highest degree unlikely, that our present physiological theories will be as out of date as the ancient theory connecting mental processes with goings on in the heart. It follows that when we report a sensation we are not reporting a brain-process.

Reply. The objection certainly proves that when we say 'I have an after-image' we cannot *mean* something of the form 'I have such and such a brain-process'. But this does not show that what we report (having an after-image) is not *in fact* a brain process. 'I see lighting' does not *mean* 'I see an electrical discharge'. Indeed, it is logically possible (though highly unlikely) that the electrical discharge account of lightning might one day be given up. Again, 'I see the Evening Star' does not *mean* the same as 'I see the Morning Star', and yet 'The Evening Star and the Morning Star are one and the same thing' is a contingent proposition. Possibly Objection 2 derives some of its apparent strength from a 'Fido' – Fido theory of meaning. If the meaning of an expression were what the expression named, then of course it *would* follow from the fact that 'sensation' and 'brain-process' have different meanings that they cannot name one and the same thing.

Objection 3.[6] Even if Objections 1 and 2 do not prove that sensations are something over and above brain-processes, they do prove that the qualities of sensations are something over and above the qualities of brain-processes. That is, it may be possible to get out of asserting the existence of irreducibly psychic processes, but not out of asserting the existence of irreducibly psychic *properties*. For suppose we identify the Morning Star with the Evening Star. Then there must be some properties which logically imply that of being the Morning Star, and quite distinct properties which entail that of being the Evening Star. Again, there must be some properties (for example, that of being a yellow flash) which are logically distinct from those in the physicalist story.

Indeed, it might be thought that the objection succeeds at one jump. For consider the propert of 'being a yellow flash'. It might seem that this property lies inevitably outside the physicalist framework within which I am trying to work (either by 'yellow' being an objective emergent property of physical objects, or else by being a power to produce yellow sense-data, where 'yellow', in this second instantiation of the word, refers to a purely phenomenal or introspectible quality). I must therefore digress for a moment and indicate how I deal with secondary qualities. I shall concentrate on colour.

First of all, let me introduce the concept of a normal percipient. One person is more a normal percipient than another if he can make colour discriminations that the other cannot. For example, if A can pick a lettuce leaf out of a heap of cabbage leaves, whereas B cannot though he can pick a lettuce leaf out of a heap of beetroot leaves, then A is more normal than B. (I am assuming that A and B are not given time to distinguish the leaves by their slight difference in shape, and so forth.) From the concept of 'more normal than' it is easy to see how we can introduce the concept of 'normal'. Of course, Eskimos may make the finest discriminations at the blue end of the spectrum, Hottentots at the red end. In this case the concept of a normal percipient is a slightly idealized one, rather like that of 'the mean sun' in astronomical chronology. There is no need to go into such subtleties now. I say that 'This is red' means something roughly like 'A normal percipient would not easily pick this out of a clump of geranium petals though he would pick it out of a clump of lettuce leaves.' Of course it does not exactly mean this: a person might know the meaning of 'red' without knowing anything about geraniums, or even about normal percipients. But the point is that a person can be *trained* to say 'This is red' of objects which would not easily be picked out of geranium petals by a normal percipient, and so on. (Note that even a colour-blind person can reasonably assert that something is red, though of course he needs to use another human being, not just himself, as his 'colour meter'.) This account of secondary qualities explains their unimportance in physics. For obviously the discriminations and lack of discriminations made by a very complex neurophysiological mechanism are hardly likely to correspond to simple and non-arbitrary distinctions in nature.

I therefore elucidate colours as powers, in Locke's sense, to evoke certain sorts of discriminatory responses in human beings. They are also, of course, powers to cause sensations in human beings (an account still nearer Locke's). But these sensations, I am arguing, are identifiable with brain processes.

Now how do I get over the objection that a sensation can be identified with a brain process only if it has some phenomenal property, not possessed by brain processes, whereby one-half of the identification may be, so to speak, pinned down?

Reply. My suggestion is as follows. When a person says, 'I see a yellowish-orange after-image', he is saying something like this: '*There is something going on which is like what is going on when* I have my eyes open, am awake, and there is an orange illuminated in good light in front of me, that is, when I really see an orange.' (And there is no reason why a person should not say the same thing when he is having a veridical sense-datum, so long as we construe 'like' in the last sentence in such a sense that something can be like itself.) Notice that the italicized words, namely 'there is something going on which is like what is going on when,' are all quasilogical or topic-neutral words. This explains why the ancient Greek peasant's reports about his sensations can be neutral between dualistic metaphysics or my materialistic metaphysics. It explains how sensations can be brain-processes and yet how a man who reports them need know nothing about brain-processes. For he reports them only very abstractly as 'something going on which is like what is going on when. . . .' Similarly, a person may say 'someone is in the room,' thus reporting truly that the doctor is in the room, even though he has never heard of doctors. (There are not two people in the room: 'someone' *and* the doctor.) This account of sensation statements also explains the singular elusiveness of 'raw feels' – why no one seems to be able to pin any properties on them (Farrell 1950). Raw feels, in my view, are colourless for the very same reason that *something* is colourless. This does not mean that sensations do not have plenty of properties, for if they are brain-processes they certainly have lots of neurological properties. It only means that in speaking of them as being like or unlike one another we need not know or mention these properties.

This, then, is how I would reply to Objection 3. The strength of my reply depends on the possibility of our being able to report that one thing is like another without being able to state the respect in which it is like. I do not see why this should not be so. If we think cybernetically about the nervous system we can envisage it as able to respond to certain likenesses of its internal processes without being able to do more. It would be easier to build a machine which would tell us, say on a punched tape, whether or not two objects were similar, than it would be to build a machine which would report wherein the similarities consisted.

Objection 4. The after-image is not in physical space. The brain-process is. So the after-image is not a brain-process.

Reply. This is an *ignoratio elenchi*. I am not arguing that the after-image is a brain-process, but that the experience of having an after-image is a brain-process. It is the *experience* which is reported in the introspective report. Similarly, if it is objected that the after-image is yellowy-orange, my reply is that it is the experience of seeing yellowy-orange that is being described, and this experience is not a yellowy-orange something. So to say that a brain-process cannot be yellowy-orange is not to say that a brain-process cannot in fact be the experience of having a yellowy-orange after-image. There is, in a sense, no such thing as an after-image or a sense-datum, though there is such a thing as the experience of having an image, and this experience is described indirectly in material object language, not in phenomenal language, for there is no such thing.[7] We describe the experience by saying, in effect, that it is like the experience we have when, for example, we really see a yellowy-orange patch on the wall. Trees and wallpaper can be green, but not the experience of seeing or imagining a tree or wallpaper. (Or if they are described as green or yellow this can only be in a derived sense.)

Objection 5. It would make sense to say of a molecular movement in the brian that it is swift, straight or circular, but it makes no sense to say this of the experience of seeing something yellow.

Reply. So far we have not given sense to talk of experiences as swift or slow, straight or circular. But I am not claiming that 'experience' and 'brain-process' mean the same or even that they have the same logic. 'Somebody' and 'the doctor' do not have the same logic, but this does not lead us to suppose that talking about somebody telephoning is talking about someone over and above, say, the doctor. The ordinary man when he reports an experience is reporting that something is going on, but he leaves it open as to what sort of thing is going on, whether in a material solid medium or perhaps in some sort of gaseous medium, or even perhaps in some sort of non-spatial medium (if this makes sense). All that I am saying is that 'experience' and 'brain-process' may in fact refer to the same thing, and if so we may easily adopt a convention (which is not a change in our present rules for the use of experience words but an addition to them) whereby it would make sense to talk of an experience in terms appropriate to physical processes.

Objection 6. Sensations are private, brain processes are *public*. If I sincerely say, 'I see a yellowish-orange after-image,' and I am not making a verbal mistake, then I cannot be wrong. But I can be wrong about a brain-process. The scientist looking into my brain might be having an illusion. Moreover, it makes sense to say that two or more people are observing the same brain-process but not that two or more people are reporting the same inner experience.

Reply. This shows that the language of introspective reports has a different logic from the language of material processes. It is obvious that until the brain-process theory is much improved and widely accepted there will be no *criteria* for saying 'Smith has an experience of such-and-such a sort' *except* Smith's introspective reports. So we have adopted a rule of language that (normally) what Smith says goes.

Objection 7. I can imagine myself turned to stone and yet having images, aches, pains, and so on.

Reply. I can imagine that the electrical theory of lightning is false, that lightning is some sort of purely optical phenomenon. I can imagine that lightning is not an electrical discharge. I can imagine that the Evening Star is not the Morning Star. But it is. All the objection shows is that 'experience' and 'brain-process' do not have the same meaning. It does not show that an experience is not in fact a brain process.

This objection is perhaps much the same as one which can be summed up by the slogan: 'What can be composed of nothing cannot be composed of anything'.[8] The argument goes as follows: on the brain-process thesis the identity between the brain-process and the experience is a contingent one. So it is logically possible that there should be no brain-process, and no process of any other sort either (no heart process, no kidney process, no liver process). There would be the experience but no 'corresponding' physiological process with which we might be able to identify it empirically.

I suspect that the objector is thinking of the experience as a ghostly entity. So it is composed of something, not of nothing, after all. On his view it is composed of ghost stuff, and on mine it is composed of brain stuff. Perhaps the counter-reply will be[9] that the experience is simple and uncompounded, and so it is not composed of anything after all. This seems to be a quibble, for, if it were taken seriously, the remark 'What can be composed of nothing cannot be composed of anything' could be recast as an *a priori* argument against Democritus and atomism and for Descartes and infinite divisibility. And it seems odd that a question of this sort could be settled *a priori*. We must therefore construe the word 'composed' in a very weak sense, which would allow us to say that even an indivisible atom is composed of something (namely, itself). The dualist cannot really say that an experience can be composed of nothing. For he holds that experiences are something over and above material processes, that is, that they are a sort of ghost stuff. (Or perhaps ripples in an underlying ghost stuff.) I say that the dualist's hypothesis is a perfectly intelligible one. But I say that experiences are not to be identified with ghost stuff but with brain stuff. This is another hypothesis, and in my view a very plausible one. The present argument cannot knock it down *a priori*.

Objection 8. The 'beetle in the box' objection (see Wittgenstein, *Philosophical Investigations*, section 293). How could descriptions of experiences, if these are genuine reports, get a foothold in language? For any rule of language must have public criteria for its correct application.

Reply. The change from describing how things are to describing how we feel is just a change from uninhibitedly saying 'this is so' to saying 'this looks so'. That is, when the naïve person might be tempted to say, 'There is a patch of light on the wall which moves whenever I move my eyes' or 'A pin is being stuck into me', we have learned how to resist this temptation and say 'It *looks as though* there is a patch of light on the wallpaper' or 'It *feels as though* someone were sticking a pin into me.' The introspective account tells us about the individual's state of consciousness in the same way as does 'I see a patch of light' or 'I feel a pin being stuck into me': it differs from the corresponding perception statement in so far as it withdraws any claim about what is actually going on in the external world. From the point of view of the psychologist, the change from talking about the environment to talking about one's perceptual sensations is simply a matter of disinhibiting certain reactions. These are reactions which one normally suppresses because one has learned that in the prevailing circumstances they are unlikely to provide a good indication of the state of the environment.[10] To say that something looks green to me is simply to say that my experience is like the experience I get when I see something that really is green. In my reply to Objection 3, I pointed out the extreme openness or generality of statements which report experiences. This explains why there is no language of private qualities. (Just as 'someone', unlike 'the doctor', is a colourless word.)[11]

If it is asked what is the difference between those brain processes which, in my view, are experiences and those brain processes which are not, I can only reply that it is at present unknown. I have been tempted to conjecture that the difference may in part be that between perception and reception (in D.M. MacKay's terminology) and that the type of brain process which is an experience might be identifiable with MacKay's active 'matching response' (MacKay 1956). This, however, cannot be the whole story, because sometimes I can perceive something unconsciously, as when I take a handkerchief out of a drawer without being aware that I am doing so. But at the very least, we can classify the brain processes which are experiences as those brain processes which are, or might have been, causal conditions of those pieces of verbal behaviour which we call reports of immediate experience.

I have now considered a number of objections to the brain-process thesis. I wish now to conclude with some remarks on the logical status of the thesis itself. U.T. Place (1956) seems to hold that it is a straight-out scientific hypothesis.[12] If so, he is partly right and partly wrong. If the issue is between (say) a brain-process thesis and a heart thesis, or a liver thesis, or a kidney thesis, then the issue is a purely empirical one, and the verdict is overwhelmingly in favour of the brain. The right sorts of things don't go on in the heart, liver, or kidney, nor do these organs possess the right sort of complexity of structure. On the other hand, if the issue is between a brain-or-liver-or-kidney thesis (that is, some form of materialism) on the one hand and epiphenomenalism on the other hand, then the issue is not an empirical one. For there is no conceivable experiment which could decide between materialism and epiphenomenalism. This latter issue is not like the average straight-out empirical issue in science, but like the issue between the nineteenth-century English naturalist Philip Gosse[13] and the orthodox geologists and palaeontologists of his day. According to Gosse, the earth was created about 4000 BC exactly as described in *Genesis*, with twisted rock strata, 'evidence' of erosion, and so forth, and all sorts of fossils, all in their appropriate strata, just as if the usual evolutionist story had been true. Clearly this theory is in a sense irrefutable: no evidence can possibly tell against it. Let us ignore the theological setting in which Philip Gosse's hypothesis had been placed, thus ruling out objections of a theological kind, such as 'what a queer God who would go to such elaborate lengths to deceive us.' Let us suppose that it is held that the universe just *began* in 4004 BC with the initial conditions just everywhere as they were in 4004 BC, and in particular that our own planet began with sediment in the rivers, eroded cliffs, fossils in the rocks, and so on. No scientist would ever entertain this as a serious hypothesis, consistent though it is with all possible evidence. The hypothesis offends against the principles of parsimony and simplicity. There would be far too many brute and inexplicable facts. Why are pterodactyl bones just as they are? No explanation in terms of the evolution of pterodactyls from earlier forms of life would any longer be possible. We would have millions of facts about the world as it was in 4004 BC that just have to be *accepted*.

The issue between the brain-process theory and epiphenomenalism seems to be of the above sort. (Assuming that a behaviouristic reduction of introspective reports is not possible.) If it be agreed that there are no cogent philosophical arguments which force us into accepting dualism, and if the brain process theory and dualism are equally consistent with the facts, then the principles of parsimony and simplicity seem to me to decide overwhelmingly in favour of the brain-process theory. As I pointed out earlier, dualism involves a large number of irreducible psycho-physical laws (whereby the 'nomological danglers' dangle) of a queer sort, that just have to be taken on trust, and are just as difficult to swallow as the irreducible facts about the palaeontology of the earth with which we are faced on Philip Gosse's theory.

1   This is the very slightly revised version which appeared in V.C. Chappell (ed.), *The Philosophy of Mind* (1962) of a paper which was first published in the *Philosophical Review*, 68 (1959), pp. 141–56. Since that date there have been criticisms of my paper by J.T. Stevenson, *Philosophical Review*, 69 (1960), pp. 505–10, to which I have replied in *Philosophical Review*, 70 (1961), pp. 406–7, and by G. Pitcher and by W.D. Joske, *Australasian Journal of Philosophy*, 38 (1960), pp. 150–60, to which I have replied in the same volume of that journal, pp. 252–4.

2   Some philosophers of my acquaintance, who have the advantage over me in having known Wittgenstein, would say that this interpretation of him is too behaviouristic. However, it seems to me a very natural interpretation of his printed words, and whether or not it is Wittgenstein's real view it is certainly an interesting and important one. I wish to consider it here as a possible rival both to the 'brain-process' thesis and to straight-out old-fashioned dualism.

3   Feigl uses the expression 'nomological danglers' for the laws whereby the entities dangle: I have used the expression to refer to the dangling entities themselves.

4   Wittgenstein did not like the word 'disposition'. I am using it to put in a nutshell (and perhaps inaccurately) the view which I am attributing to Wittgenstein. I should like to repeat that I do not wish to claim that my interpretation of Wittgenstein is correct. Some of those who knew him do not interpret him in this way. It is merely a view which I find myself extracting from his printed words and which I think is important and worth discussing for its own sake.

5   I here permit myself to speak loosely. For warnings against possible ways of going wrong with this sort of talk, see my note 'Spatialising Time' (1955).

6   I think this objection was first put to me by Professor Max Black. I think it is the most subtle of any of those I have considered, and the one which I am least confident of having satisfactorily met.

7   Dr J.R. Smythies claims that a sense-datum language could be taught independently of the material object language ('A Note on the Fallacy of the "Phenomenological Fallacy"', 1957). I am not so sure of this: there must be some public criteria for a person having got a rule wrong before we can teach him the rule. I suppose someone might *accidentally* learn colour words by Dr Smythies' procedure. I am not, of course, denying that we can learn a sense-datum language in the sense that we can learn to report our experience. Nor would Place deny it.

8   I owe this objection to Dr C.B. Martin. I gather that he no longer wishes to maintain this objection, at any rate in its present form.

9   Martin did not make this reply, but one of his students did.

10 I owe this point to Place, in correspondence.

11 The 'beetle in the box' objection is, *if it is sound*, an objection to *any* view, and in particular the Cartesian one, that introspective reports are genuine

reports. So it is no objection to a weaker thesis that I would be concerned to uphold, namely, that if introspective reports of 'experiences' are genuinely reports, then the things they are reports of are in fact brain processes.

12 For a further discussion of this, in reply to the original version of the present paper, see Place's note 'Materialism as a Scientific Hypothesis' (1960).

13 See the entertaining account of Gosse's book *Omphalos* by Martin Gardner in *Fads and Fallacies in the Name of Science* (1957).

REFERENCES

Farrell, B.A. 1950: Experience. *Mind*, 59, 170–98.

Feigl, H. 1958: The 'Mental' and the 'Physical'. *Minnesota Studies in the Philosophy of Science*, 2, 370–497.

Gardner, Martin 1957: *Fads and Fallacies in the Name of Science*, 2nd edn. New York: Dover, 124–7.

MacKay, D.M. 1956: Towards an Information-Flow Model of Human Behaviour. *British Journal of Psychology*, 47, 30–43.

Oppenheim, Paul and Putnam, Hilary 1958: Unity of Science as a Working Hypothesis. *Minnesota Studies in the Philosophy of Science*, 2, 3–36.

Place, U.T. 1956: Is Consciousness a Brain Process? *British Journal of Psychology*, 47, 44–50. Reprinted 1962 in V.C. Chappell (ed.), *The Philosophy of Mind*, Englewood Cliffs, New Jersey: Prentice-Hall, 101–9. (Page references are to the reprinted version.)

—— 1960: Materialism, as a Scientific Hypothesis. *Philosophical Review*, 69, 101–4.

Ryle, Gilbert 1949: *The Concept of Mind*. London: Hutchinson.

Smart, J.J.C. 1955: Spatialising Time. *Mind*, 64, 239–41.

Smythies, J.R. 1957: A Note on the Fallacy of the 'Phenomenological Fallacy'. *British Journal of Psychology*, 48, 141–4.

Woodger, J.H. 1939: Theory Construction. *International Encyclopedia of Unified Science*, 2, no. 5, 38.

16

Materialism

First of all let me try to explain what I mean by 'materialism'. I shall then go on to defend the doctrine.[1] By 'materialism' I mean the theory that there is nothing in the world over and above those entities which are postulated by physics (or, of course, those entities which will be postulated by future and more adequate physical theories). Thus I do not hold materialism to be wedded to the billiard-ball physics of the nineteenth century. The less visualizable particles of modern physics count as matter. Note that energy counts as matter for my purposes: indeed in modern physics energy and matter are not sharply distinguishable. Nor do I hold that materialism implies determinism. If physics is indeterministic on the micro-level, so must be the materialist's theory. I regard materialism as compatible with a wide range of conceptions of the nature of matter and energy. For example, if matter and energy consist of regions of special curvature of absolute space-time, with 'worm holes' and what not (Wheeler 1962), this is still compatible with materialism: we can still argue that in the last resort the world is made up entirely of the ultimate entities of physics, namely space-time points.

It will be seen that my conception of materialism is wider than that of Bertrand Russell in his Introduction to Lange's *History of Materialism* (Lange 1925). But my definition will in some respects be narrower than those of some who have called themselves 'materialists'. I wish to lay down that it is incompatible with materialism that there should be any irreducibly 'emergent' laws or properties, say in biology or psychology. According to the view I propose to defend, there are no irreducible laws or properties in biology, any more than there are in electronics. Given the 'natural history' of a superheterodyne (its wiring diagram), a physicist is able to explain, using only laws of physics, its mode of behaviour and its properties (for example, the property of being able to receive such and such a radio station which broadcasts on 25 megacycles). Just as electronics gives the physical explanation of the workings of superheterodynes, etc., so biology gives (or approximates to giving) physical and chemical explanations of the workings of organisms or parts of organisms. The biologist needs natural history just as the engineer needs wiring diagrams, but neither needs non-physical laws (see Smart 1959).[2]

It will now become clear why I define materialism in the way I have done above. I am concerned to deny that in the world there are non-physical entities and non-physical laws. In particular I wish to deny the doctrine of psychophysical dualism.[3] (I also want to deny any theory of 'emergent properties', since irreducibly non-physical properties are just about as repugnant to me as are irreducibly non-physical entities.)

Popular theologians sometimes argue against materialism by saying that 'you can't put love in a test tube'. Well you can't put a gravitational field in a test tube (except in some rather strained sense of these words), but there is nothing incompatible with materialism, as I have defined it, in the notion of a gravitational field.

Similarly, even though love may elude test tubes, it does not elude materialistic metaphysics, since it can be analysed as a pattern of bodily behaviour or, perhaps better, as the internal state of the human organism that accounts for this behaviour. (A dualist who analyses love as an internal state will perhaps say that it is a soul state, whereas the materialist will say that it is a brain state. It seems to me that much of our ordinary language about the mental is neither dualistic nor materialistic but is neutral between the two. Thus, to say that a locution is not materialistic is not to say that it is immaterialistic.)

But what about consciousness? Can we interpret the having of an after-image or of a painful sensation as something material, namely, a brain state or brain process? We seem to be immediately aware of pains and after-images, and we seem to be immediately aware of them as something different from a neurophysiological state or process. For example, the after-image may be green speckled with red, whereas the neurophysiologist looking into our brains would be unlikely to see something green speckled with red. However, if we object to materialism in this way we are victims of a confusion which U.T. Place (1956) has called 'the phenomenological fallacy'. To say that an image or sense datum is green is not to say that the conscious experience of having the image or sense datum is green. It is to say that it is the sort of experience we have when in normal conditions we look at a green apple, for example. Apples and unripe bananas can be green, but not the experiences of seeing them. An image or a sense datum can be green in a derivative sense, but this need not cause any worry, because, on the view

I am defending, images and sense data are not constituents of the world, though the processes of having an image or a sense datum are actual processes in the world. The experience of having a green sense datum is not itself green; it is a process occurring in grey matter. The world contains plumbers, but does not contain the average plumber; it also contains the having of a sense datum, but does not contain the sense datum.

It may be objected that, in admitting that apples and unripe bananas can be green, I have admitted colours as emergent properties, not reducible within a physicalist scheme of thought. For a reply to this objection I must, for lack of space, refer to my article 'Colours' (1961).[4] Here colours are elucidated in terms of the discriminatory reactions of normal percipients, and the notion of a normal colour percipient is defined without recourse to the notion of colour. Colour classifications are elucidated as classifications in terms of the highly idiosyncratic discriminatory reactions of a complex neurophysiological mechanism. It is no wonder that these classifications do not correspond to anything simple in physics. (There is no one–one correlation between colour and wave length, since infinitely many different mixtures of wave lengths correspond to the same colour, i.e., produce the same discriminatory reaction in a normal percipient.)

When we report that a lemon is yellow we are reacting to the lemon. But when we report that the lemon looks yellow we are reacting to our own internal state. When I say 'it looks to me that there is a yellow lemon' I am saying, roughly, that what is going on in me is like what goes on in me when there really is a yellow lemon in front of me, my eyes are open, the light is daylight, and so on. That is, our talk of immediate experience is derivative from our talk about the external world. Furthermore, since our talk of immediate experience is in terms of a typical stimulus situation (and in the case of some words for aches and pains and the like it may, as we shall see, be in terms of some typical *response* situation) we can see that our talk of immediate experience is itself neutral between materialism and dualism. It reports our internal goings on as like or unlike what internally goes on in typical situations, but the dualist would construe these goings on as goings on in an immaterial substance, whereas the materialist would construe these goings on as taking place inside our skulls.

Our talk about immediate experiences is derivative from our language of physical objects. This is so even with much of our language of bodily sensations and aches and pains. A stabbing pain is the sort of going on which is like what goes on when a pin is stuck into you. (Trivially, you also have a stabbing pain when a pin is in fact stuck into you, for in this essay I am using 'like' in a sense in which a thing is like itself. That I am using 'like' in this sense can be seen by reflecting on what the analysis of the last paragraph would imply in the case of having a veridical sense datum of a yellow lemon.) However, some of our sensation words do not seem to work like 'stabbing pain'. Consider 'ache'. Perhaps here the reference to a typical stimulus situation should be replaced by a reference to a typical response situation. Instead of 'what is going on in me is like what goes on in me when a yellow lemon is before me' we could have some such thing as 'what is going on in me is like what goes on in me when I groan, yelp, etc.' In any case it is not inconsistent with the present view to suppose that, when children have got the idea of referring to their own internal goings on as like or unlike what goes on in some typical situation, they can then in some cases go on simply to classify them as like or unlike one another. (All the aches are more like one another than any of them are to any of the itches, for example.) In other words, they may be able to report some of their internal goings on as like or unlike one another, and thus to report these goings on, even when their language is not tied closely to stimulus or response situations. Notice that I am still denying that we introspect any nonphysical property such as *achiness*. To say that a process is an ache is simply to classify it with other processes that are felt to be like it, and this class of processes constitutes the aches.

An important objection is now sure to be made. It will be said that anything is like anything else in *some* respect or other. So how can our sensation reports be classifications in terms of likenesses and unlikenesses alone? And if you say that they are likenesses or unlikenesses in virtue of properties that are or are not held in common, will these properties not have to be properties (e.g., *achiness*) that are beyond the conceptual resources of a physicalist theory?

Looked at in the abstract this argument appears impressive, but it becomes less persuasive when we think out, in terms of bits of cybernetic hardware, what it is to recognize likenesses and unlikenesses. Thus, consider a machine for recognizing likenesses and unlikenesses between members of a set of round discs, square discs, and triangular discs. It would probably be easier to construct a machine that just told us (on a tape, say) 'like' or 'unlike' than it would be to construct a machine that told us wherein the likenesses consisted, whether in roundness, squareness, or triangularity. Moreover, we may agree that everything is like everything else and still say that some things are much liker than others. Consider the notion of following a rule, which plays so important a part in Wittgenstein's philosophy (Wittgenstein 1953, section 185ff). Suppose that one man continues the sequence 0, 1, 2, 3, . . . up to 1000 and then continues 1001, 1002, 1003, 1004, ... Here we certainly feel like saying that he goes on doing the same thing after 1000 as he did before 1000. Now suppose that a second man goes 0, 1, 2, 3, . . . 1000, 1002, 1004, . . . , and a third man goes 0, 1, 2, 3, . . . 1000, 1001, 1002, 1003, 1005, 1007, 1011, 1013, ... According to Wittgenstein's account, it would seem that the second and third men also could say that they were doing the same thing after 1000 as they did up to 1000. Indeed there are rules to cover these cases too, for example, 'add one up to 1000 and then add twos until 2000, threes until 3000, and so on' and 'add ones up to 1001 and then go up by prime numbers'. These rules are more complicated than the original one; moreover, like even the first rule, they could be divergently interpreted. We can concede Wittgenstein all this. Nevertheless, it does not follow that there is no sense in which some sequences are objectively more like one another than are others. It will not do to say that the continuations of the sequence 0, 1, 2, 3, . . . that go 1002, 1004, 1006, . . . or 1001, 1002, 1003, 1005, 1006, 1011, 1013, . . . are as like what goes before 1000 as is the continuation 1001, 1002, 1003, ... This can be seen if we reflect that a machine built to churn out the symbols of the sequence 0, 1, 2, 3, . . . 1001, 1002, 1003, 1004, . . . could be a simpler machine (i.e., could contain fewer parts) than one built to churn out either of the other two sequences. This indicates that absolute likeness and unlikeness is something objective, even though it is also a matter of degree.

I conclude, therefore, that it is by no means empty to say that some of our internal processes are like or unlike one another, even though we do not indicate in what respect they are like. This makes our reports of immediate experience quite open or 'topic neutral', to use a phrase of Ryle's. They do not commit us either to materialism or to dualism, but they are quite *compatible* with the hypothesis which I wish to assert: that the internal goings on in question are brain processes.[5]

It may be said: but on your view you can have no criterion of correctness when you report a sensation simply as *like* one you had before (cf. Wittgenstein 1953, section 258). But must I have such a criterion? On my view my internal mechanism is just built so that I react in the way I do. And I may *in fact* react correctly, though I have no criterion for saying that my reaction is correct. That is, when I report my internal processes as alike, it may always, or at least mostly, be the case that they *are* alike. Indeed, on the basis of common-sense psychology, scientific psychology, or perhaps (in the future) electroencephalography, we may gain indirect evidence that our reactions are correct in reporting likenesses of internal processes. A slot machine that puts out a bar of chocolate only when a shilling (or a coin indistinguishable in size and shape from a shilling) is inserted into it certainly has no criterion for the size and shape. But its reactions are veridical: it will not give you a bar of chocolate if you put a sixpence into it.

It is important to realize that, if the view that I wish to defend is correct, conscious experiences must be processes involving millions of neurons, and so their important likenesses and unlikenesses to one another may well be statistical in nature. As P.K. Feyerabend (1981, pp. 164–5) has pointed out, this shows how a sensation (or a brain process) can possess such properties as of being clear or confused (well-defined or ill-defined), as well as why a sensation seems to be a simple entity in a way in which the details of a brain process are not simple. Brain processes can well have statistical properties that cannot even meaningfully be asserted of individual neurons, still less of individual molecules or atoms. Feyerabend compares this case with that of the density of a fluid, the notion of which can be meaningfully applied only to a large statistically homogeneous ensemble of particles and which has no application in the case of a single particle or small group of particles. Notice also that the materialist hypothesis does not imply that there is anything like consciousness in a single atom, or even in a single neuron for that matter. A conscious experience is a very complex process involving vast numbers of neurons. It is a process, not a stuff. The materialist does not need to accept Vogt's crude and preposterous idea that the brain secretes thought much as the liver secretes bile (Lange 1925, vol. 2, p. 312). We can certainly agree with Wittgenstein thus far: that thought is not a *stuff*. Indeed this side of Wittgenstein's thought is particularly attractive: his elucidation of mental concepts in terms of bodily behaviour would, if it were adequate, be perfectly compatible with the sort of physicalist world view which, for reasons of scientific plausibility, it seems to me necessary to defend. (I differ from Wittgenstein since I wish to elucidate thought as inner process and to keep my hypothesis compatible with a physicalist viewpoint by identifying such inner processes with brain processes.) The trouble with Wittgenstein is that he is too operationalistic.[6]

This can perhaps be brought out by considering something Wittgenstein says in section 293 of his *Philosophical Investigations*. He there argues against the tendency to construe 'the grammar of the expression of sensation on the model of "object and name"'. He says that if we try to do so 'the object drops out of consideration as irrelevant'. I imagine that he would argue equally strongly against the model (more relevant to the present issue) of *process* and name. I am not sure how seriously we are to take the word 'name' here. Surely all we need are predicates, e.g., '. . . is a pain'. (Wittgenstein is considering the case of someone who says 'here is a pain' or 'this is a pain'.) Indeed, in a Quinean language there would be no names at all. Suppose, therefore, that we construe the word 'name' rather more widely, so that we can say, for example, that 'electron' is a name of electrons. (More properly we should say that '. . . is an electron' is a predicate true of anything which is an electron.) Now let us apply Wittgenstein's argument of 'the beetle in the box' to electrons (Wittgenstein 1953, section 293). A person can see only the beetle in his own box (just as, on the view Wittgenstein is attacking, my pain is something of which only I can be acquainted), but the case with electrons is even worse, since no one at all can literally see an electron. We know of electrons only through their observable effects on macroscopic bodies. Thus Wittgenstein's reasons for saying that pains are not objects would be even stronger reasons for saying that electrons are not objects either (see Hervey 1957, p. 67).

I have no doubt that Wittgenstein would have been unmoved by this last consideration. For I think he would have been likely to say that electrons are grammatical fictions and that electrons must be understood in terms of galvanometers, etc., just as pains are to be understood in terms of groans, etc. In reply to the question, 'Are you not really a behaviourist in disguise? Aren't you at bottom really saying that everything except human behaviour is a fiction?' he replies: 'If I do speak of a fiction it is of a *grammatical* fiction' (section 307). Certainly, if a philosopher says that pains are grammatical fictions, he is not denying that there are pains. Nevertheless he is denying that pains are anything (to use John Wisdom's useful expression) 'over and above' pain behaviour. Such a philosopher is not a crude behaviourist who denies that there are pains, but surely he can well be said to be a behaviourist of a more sophisticated sort. Why should he be shy of admitting it? Now the very same reasons which lead Wittgenstein to go behaviourist about pains would surely lead him to go instrumentalist (in an analogously sophisticated way) about electrons.

This is not the place to contest instrumentalism about the theoretical entities of physics. But I wish to put forward one consideration which will be followed by an analogous one in the case of sensations. Can we conceive of a universe consisting only of a swarm of electrons, protons, neutrons, etc., that have never and never will come together as constituents of macroscopic objects? It would seem that we can, even though the supposition might be inconsistent with certain cosmological theories, and it might become inconsistent with physics itself, if physics one day becomes united with cosmology in a unified theory. On this supposition, then, there could be electrons, protons, etc., but no macroscopic objects.[7] On the other hand, there could not be the average plumber without plumbers, or nations without nationals. (In arguing thus I am indebted to C.B. Martin.) It is therefore not clear in what sense electrons and protons could be said to be grammatical fictions. Now let us ask analogously in what sense Wittgenstein could allow that pain experiences are grammatical fictions. It is not evident that there is any clear sense.

Consider this example.[8] In some future state of physiological technology we might be able to keep a human brain alive *in vitro*. Leaving the question of the morality of such an experiment to one side, let us suppose that the experiment is done. By suitable electrodes inserted into appropriate parts of this brain we get it to have the illusion of perceiving things and also to have pains, and feelings of moving its nonexistent limbs, and so on. (This brain might even be able to think verbally, for it might have learned a language before it was put *in vitro*, or else, by suitable signals from our electrodes, we might even give it the illusion of learning a language in the normal way.) Here we have the analogue to the case of the world of electrons, etc., but with no macroscopic objects. In the present case we have mental experiences, but no behaviour. This brings out vividly that what is important in psychology is what goes on in the central nervous system, not what goes on in the face, larynx and limbs. It can of course be agreed that what goes on in the face, larynx and limbs provides observational data whereby the psychologist can postulate what goes on in the central nervous system. If experiences are postulated on the basis of behaviour, instead of being grammatical fictions out of behaviour, then we can deal with the case of the brain *in vitro*. For whereas grammatical fictions are nothing over and above what they are fictions out of, entities such as are postulated in an hypothesis could still exist even if there had been no possible evidence for them. There could be electrons even if there were no macroscopic bodies, and there could be processes in the central nervous system even if there were no attached body and, hence, no bodily behaviour. Of course I do not wish to deny that in the case of the brain *in vitro* we could have evidence other than that of bodily behaviour: electroencephalographic evidence, for example.[9]

It is true that Wittgenstein is arguing against someone who says that he knows what pain is only from his own case. I am not such a person. I want to say that sensations are postulated processes in other people and *also* processes which, when they occur in ourselves, we can report as like or unlike one another. If we cannot look at the beetle in another person's box, that does not matter; no one can look into any box at all when in the simile the beetle is taken to be not a pain but an electron. We have very good indirect evidence for asserting that all electrons are like one another and unlike, say, protons.

I have suggested that, in spite of his own disclaimer, Wittgenstein is in fact a sort of behaviourist. I have also suggested that such a behaviourism is no more tenable than is an analogous instrumentalism about the theoretical entities of physics. Nevertheless. Wittgenstein's philosophy of mind, if it could be accepted, would be very attractive. For, like the analysis that I am advocating, it would be compatible with materialism;

it would not land us with emergent properties or non-physical entities. But even a disguised or Wittgensteinian behaviourism falls down because, as I have argued, it cannot account for the overriding importance of the central nervous system: the example of the brain *in vitro* shows that what is essential to a pain is what goes on in the brain, not what goes on in the arms or legs or larynx or mouth. Furthermore, it is hard to accept the view that so-called 'reports' of inner experience are to be construed as surrogates for behaviour, as if a report of a pain were a wince-substitute. To say that these behaviour surrogates are properly called 'reports' in ordinary language does little to mitigate the paradoxical nature of theory.

It may be asked why I should demand of a tenable philosophy of mind that it should be compatible with materialism, in the sense in which I have defined it. One reason is as follows. How could a non-physical property or entity suddenly arise in the course of animal evolution? A change in a gene is a change in a complex molecule which causes a change in the biochemistry of the cell. This may lead to changes in the shape or organization of the developing embryo. But what sort of chemical process could lead to the springing into existence of something non-physical? No enzyme can catalyse the production of a spook! Perhaps it will be said that the non-physical comes into existence as a by-product: that whenever there is a certain complex physical structure, then, by an irreducible extraphysical law, there is also a non-physical entity. Such laws would be quite outside normal scientific conceptions and quite inexplicable: they would be, in Herbert Feigl's phrase, 'nomological danglers' (Feigl 1938). To say the very least, we can vastly simplify our cosmological outlook if we can defend a materialistic philosophy of mind.

In defending materialism I have tried to argue that a materialist and yet non-behaviourist account of sensations is perfectly consistent with our ordinary language of sensation reports. (Though I have had space to consider only a selection of the arguments commonly put forward against materialism; for example, I have not considered the argument from the alleged incorrigibility of reports of inner experience. Elsewhere (Smart 1962) I have argued that, even if such incorrigibility were a fact, it would provide as much of a puzzle to the dualist as it does to the materialist.)

Nevertheless there is also in ordinary language a dualistic overtone: to some extent it enshrines the plain man's metaphysics, which is a dualism of body and soul. We cannot therefore hope (even if we wished) to reconcile *all* of ordinary language with a materialist metaphysics. Or, to put it otherwise, it is hard to decide just where to draw the line between non-metaphysical ordinary language and the plain man's metaphysics. Nevertheless, I think that the attempt to reconcile the hard core of

212 — *Philosophy of Mind*

ordinary language with materialism is worth while. For one thing, some features of ordinary language will probably remain constant for a very long time. This is because much of our perception of macroscopic objects depends on innate mechanisms, not on mechanisms that have developed through learning processes. For example, consider our perception of objects as three-dimensional. Again, we shall probably continue indefinitely to need a colour language, anthropocentric though it is. The colour classifications we make depend on the peculiarities of the human visual apparatus, and, so long as we retain our present physiological characteristics, we shall retain our present colour language. With these reservations, however, I am also attracted to P.K. Feyerabend's contention that in defending materialism we do not need to show its consistency with ordinary language, any more than in defending the general theory of relativity we need to show its consistency with Newtonian theory.[10] (Newtonian theory and general relativity are indeed inconsistent with one another: for example, the advance of the perihelion of Mercury is inconsistent with Newtonian theory, but follows from general relativity.) Feyerabend is perhaps therefore right in arguing that the scientific concept of pain does not need to be (and indeed should not be) even extensionally equivalent to the concept of pain in ordinary language. (The concept of a planetary orbit in general relativity does not quite coincide extensionally with that in Newtonian theory, since the orbit of Mercury fits the former but not the latter.) Perhaps, therefore, even if it should be shown that materialism is incompatible with the core of our ordinary language, it could still be defended on the basis of Feyerabend's position. Nevertheless, just as J.K. Galbraith in his book *The Affluent Society* prefers where possible to argue against what he calls 'the conventional wisdom' on its own ground, so I think that it is worth while trying to meet some of my philosophical friends as far as possible on their own ground, which is the analysis of ordinary language. Indeed it seems probable that the ordinary language of perception and of inner experience has more to recommend it than has the conventional wisdom of the last generation of economists: we are not confronted with a rapidly changing universe or with a rapidly changing human physiology in the way in which the economist is faced with a rapidly changing human environment.

NOTES

1 This was the first paper in a symposium with Norman Malcolm on 'Materialism' at the sixtieth annual meeting of the American Philosophical Association, Eastern Division, 27 December 1963. A more recent statement

of Malcolm's objections to materialism can be found in the second part of Armstrong and Malcolm (1984). I wish to thank Dr C.B. Martin and Mr M.C. Bradley, who have commented on an earlier version of this paper. I have made some slight changes, but space prevents me from taking up some of their fundamental objections.

2 For a modification of this view of biology see the essay 'Under the Form of Eternity' in the present volume. What I say in the present essay still seems to fit pretty well the central biochemical and biophysical part of biology of which I was primarily thinking.

3 In recent years essentially dualistic theories have been propounded in rather sophisticated forms, for example, by P.F. Strawson (1959). That Strawson's view is essentially dualistic can be seen from the fact that he admits that disembodied existence is logically compatible with it.

4 But see the essay 'On Some Criticisms of a Physicalist Theory of Colours' in the present volume in which I modify this account of colours. This does not affect the essential point made here, however.

5 Jerome Shaffer, in his interesting article 'Mental Events and the Brain' (1963) thinks (pp. 163–4) that it is implausible that what we notice in inner experience are brain processes. If my view is correct, we do notice brain processes, though only in a 'topic-neutral' way: we do not notice *that* they are brain processes. I do not find this implausible – not as implausible as non-physical entities or properties, anyway.

6 In coming to this conclusion I have been very much influenced by my colleague C.B. Martin. See also H. Putnam 'Dreaming and "Depth Grammar" ' (1962).

7 An analogous argument, based on a gaseous universe, is used by B.A.O. Williams (1961, pp. 321–2).

8 I gather that D.M. Armstrong has also been using this example to make the same point.

9 H. Reichenbach in his *Experience and Prediction* (1938), in one of the best defences of physicalism in the literature, has put forward a similar account of experiences as postulated things; see sections 19 and 26.

10 And Wilfrid Sellars has argued that what he calls 'the scientific image' should be sharply separated off from 'the manifest image', and would probably say that in the present paper I am wrongly importing elements of the manifest image into the scientific image.

REFERENCES

Armstrong, D.M. and Malcolm, Norman 1984: *Consciousness and Causality: A Debate on the Nature of Mind*. Oxford: Blackwell.

Feigl, Herbert 1958: The 'Mental' and the 'Physical'. *Minnesota Studies in the Philosophy of Science*, 2, 370–497.

Feyerabend, P.K. 1981: Materialism and the Mind Body Problem. *Realism, Rationalism and Scientific Method, Philosophical Papers*, 1, 160–75.

Hervey, Helen 1957: The Private Language Problem. *Philosophical Quarterly*, 7, 63–79.

Lange, F.A. 1925: *The History of Materialism*, 3rd edn. Translated by E.C. Thomas, with an introduction by Bertrand Russell, New York: Harcourt Brace.

Place, U.T. 1956: Is Consciousness a Brain Process? *British Journal of Psychology*, 47, 44–50.

Putnam, Hilary 1962: Dreaming and 'Depth Grammar'. In R.J. Butler (ed.), *Analytical Philosophy*, Oxford: Blackwell.

Reichenbach, H. 1938: *Experience and Prediction*. Chicago: University of Chicago Press.

Shaffer, Jerome 1963: Mental Events and the Brain. *Journal of Philosophy*, 60, 160–6.

Smart, J.J.C. 1959: Can Biology Be an Exact Science? *Synthese*, 11, 359–68.

—— 1961: Colours. *Philosophy*, 36, 128–42.

—— 1962: Brain Processes and Incorrigibility. *Australasian Journal of Philosophy*, 40, 68–70.

Strawson, P.F. 1959: *Individuals*. London: Methuen.

Wheeler, J.A. 1962: Curved Empty Space-Time as the Building Material of the Physical World: An Assessment. In E. Nagel, P. Suppes and A. Tarski (eds), *Logic, Methodology and Philosophy of Science*, Stanford: Stanford University Press.

Wittgenstein, L. 1953: *Philosophical Investigations*. Translated by G.E.M. Anscombe, Oxford: Blackwell.

Williams, B.A.O. 1961: Mr Strawson on Individuals. *Philosophy*, 36, 309–32.

17

Further Thoughts on the Identity Theory

The so-called 'identity theory' may be characterized roughly as the theory that the mind is the brain, or more concretely that mental events, states and processes are brain events, states and processes. This is put forward as a contingent identification: it is not held to be part of (or at least the main part of) the meaning of 'mental entity' that it entails 'brain entity'. Otherwise the theory would have little plausibility, because quite clearly a materialist can talk quite happily about his aches, pains, itches, desires, emotions, perceptions, images, thoughts, and so on, with someone who does not know anything at all about brains, or who perhaps, like Aristotle, thinks that it is an organ for cooling the blood.[1] However, if we wish to stick to what Richard Rorty (1965) has called the 'translation form' of the identity theory, we must hold that although our ordinary talk about mental entities does not entail that they are brain entities, it must be shown to be *compatible* with the view that they are brain entities. In other words the identity theorist needs to show that our ordinary common sense talk about the mental is *neutral* as between materialist and non-materialist theories of the mind. For since, as we have seen, it does not imply materialism, it either implies immaterialism or it is neutral. If it implies immaterialism then either the identity theorist has to give up his or her theory (which he is probably reluctant to do, because of considerations of scientific plausibility and Ockham's razor) or else he has to retreat to what Richard Rorty has called 'the disappearance form' of the identity theory. I regard this as a retreat because it seems on the face of it implausible to relegate talk of our aches, pains, and the like to the realm of talk of witches and poltergeists, and also because it seems too easy a way out of the debate with my antagonists.[2] In particular, where the identity theory seems to clash with what to our opponents are obvious empirical (and phenomenal) facts, the wholesale imputation of error about these facts to our opponents is a bit implausible. Is a person really in metaphysical error when he reports a toothache or the having of an after-image?

II

I think, then, that in defending the identity theory we have to lean towards a translation form of the theory. But I do not think that we should do so too wholeheartedly. I think we have to make compromises with the 'disappearance' form of the theory. The situation is not so simple as to enable us to make a straight out choice between one form of the theory and the other. I shall give a number of reasons for saying this.

In the first place, the notion of 'translation' is itself not one hundred per cent clear. In defending the identity theory I gave what I called a 'topic neutral' translation of certain sensation statements.[3] Now let S be a sensation statement and T its topic-neutral translation. (If the proposed form of the identity theory is correct, of course, then S will itself be topic neutral, but T is in a form which makes this topic neutrality obvious.) Then $S \equiv T$ will be analytic. Otherwise we should not say that one is a translation of the other. However, $S \equiv T$ will not be logically true, in the sense of being an instantiation of a quantificationally valid schema. The notions of translation, synonymy, and analyticity are interconnected, and any obscurities about one of them are reflected in the others. That such obscurities exist has seemed all too evident since Quine drew attention to them. I conclude that the programme of producing a 'translation form' of the identity theory suffers from the unclarity of the very notion of translation itself. The 'disappearance form' of the theory is better off in this respect.

Nevertheless we do often, whether clearly or not, regard some sentences as translations of others. A case which is pretty clear is that 'Smith is an unmarried adult male' is a correct translation of 'Smith is a bachelor'.[4] So perhaps the translation form of the identity theory has to be weakened to the following: in so far as the notion of translation makes sense here, the topic neutral formula provides a translation schema. To the extent that the notion of translation does not makes sense, the translation form of the identity theory goes over into the disappearance form. Instead of trying to get an opponent of the identity theory to agree with us that a sentence S can be translated into an obviously topic neutral equivalent T we get him or her to admit that T would serve his purposes as well as S. In such a form there does not seem to be much difference between the translation and disappearance versions of the identity theory: instead of an obligation to show translatibility the identity theorist has an obligation to show that the formula T is as attractive to an opponent as the formula S was. It is not the easy form of the disappearance version, in which the identity theorist gaily wipes off all our ordinary mentalistic idioms as infected with outworn theories.

Let me now pass on to the second respect in which I need to qualify my adherence to a translation form of the identity theory by making concessions towards the disappearance form. I espoused the translation form because it seemed necessary to allow for the fact that we, whether materialists or dualists, can talk happily together in terms of ordinary common sense discourse. Now since it seems obvious that materialism is not implied by common-sense mentalistic discourse (though the stock arguments against materialism do not prove much, they do seem to prove this much) and so *either* common-sense talk must imply the falsity of materialism *or* it must be metaphysically neutral. It is this second alternative which the defender of the translation form of the theory must try to show to be the case. The defender of the disappearance form takes a different tack: he embraces the first alternative, and rejects common sense.

The present qualification which I think needs to be made to the translation form of the theory is that though the hard core of common-sense mentalistic idioms is topic neutral, it may well be that some of common-sense talk does imply the falsity of materialism. But this does not matter so long as a hard core of neutrality remains. The hard core of neutrality will be sufficient to explain the fact that a materialist could swap chat about aches, pains, thoughts, and desires with someone like Socrates or Descartes, the *Phaedo* and the *Meditations* notwithstanding. Nevertheless it is probable that our ordinary common-sense mentalistic idioms are to some extent infected with non-materialistic metaphysical overtones. The influence of Socrates and Descartes, not to mention sundry priests, preachers, and the like is to be found in many of the mentalistic idioms and beliefs of the man in the pub, the street, or the paddy field. These idioms imply certain beliefs which are inconsistent with physicalism. In so far as the most general beliefs, within a certain field of discourse, serve to some extent to define implicitly the key terms of that field of discourse, we can not be sure that the man in the street's mentalistic discourse is quite topic neutral. One sort of man in the street is a Roman Catholic man in the street, and may it not be part of the average Catholic's concept of mind that the mind is non-material? Or is this just a contingent belief that the average Catholic has *about* the mind? If we cannot make a clear distinction between these two alternatives then we can not say quite wholeheartedly that the average Catholic's mentalistic discourse is susceptible to a topic neutral analysis.

Because to *some extent* ordinary mentalistic idioms may be contaminated with a common-sense immaterialistic metaphysics, the 'topic neutral' pattern of analysis of these may not entirely do justice to them. Nevertheless it may come pretty near to doing justice to them, and this nearness will explain the fact that materialists and non-materialists can perfectly well swap talk about their aches, pains, etc. The translation form of the identity theory comes pretty near to being the correct form, but there is no harm in the materialist appealing to the disappearance form if there are some immaterialist accretions to our mentalistic idioms. Metaphysics is not merely the occupation of an esoteric group of philosophers. The ordinary man wonders about such things as whether survival of death is possible, and the savage wonders where he goes in his dreams. It is not surprising that metaphysical ideas might colour all of his thinking.

A third reason why a translation form of the identity theory may be no more than an approximation to the truth has to do with time. The world picture of modern science is a four-dimensional one. We must think not of space and time separately but of space-time. Instead of thinking of the furniture of the world as made up of enduring substances, the permanent in change, we must think of it as made up of four-dimensional, spatiotemporal entities. Instead of saying that a substance S changes from being P to being Q we must talk instead of a four-dimensional spatiotemporal solid having a P-ish time slice at an earlier time and a Q-ish time slice at a later time.

It looks as though our ordinary language is wedded to a pre-relativistic view of the world: words like 'now' and the tenses of verbs imply a conception of absolute simultaneity, whereas in the theory of relativity simultaneity is a triadic relation between two events and a frame of reference. Hence our ordinary common-sense discourse does not appear to be compatible with a language suitable for modern physics. A philosopher who is a physicalist will wish to erect the language of total science on a four-dimensional framework. Hence if our ordinary language of substance and change is not translatable into a four-dimensional space-time language, then a translation form of the identity theory will not be possible for one who wishes to take total science as that which delineates reality for us.

When I say that a sensation is a brain process I want to say that a sensation is some sort of four-dimensional entity. As a first shot (and I shall return to this matter later in this paper) I want to think of a brain process as represented by a four-dimensional cat's cradle of world lines – the world lines of the particles which make up the process. For example suppose, contrary to fact, that the brain process is just a process in which two particles participate, one oscillating to and fro in a straight line while the other remains at rest nearby, then the process is as in figure 17.1.

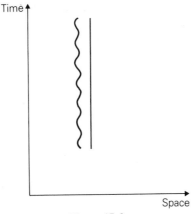

Figure 17.1

Any actual brain process, involving perhaps thousands of millions of neurons, and each neuron consisting of an immense number of protons, electrons, neutrons, etc., would be represented by a colossally complex and intertwined skein of world lines of particles. (I say 'represented by' here because the process itself consists of the aggregate of particles themselves, thought of four-dimensionally, and these, though worm like, are not geometrical lines.) Unfortunately, however, the matter is more complicated, because a particle might be vibrating both at 50 cycles per second and at 500 cycles per second. Scientists commonly think of these as two separate processes ('components' of a resultant process). It is not clear to me how to express this in the Quinean canonical notation which I want my theory to be expressible in, though I expect that it could be. (See the remarks towards the end of section V of this paper.)

Now if (or in so far as) talk of substances, processes, and events can not be translated into talk of four-dimensional solids, thing-stages, boundaries between temporally adjoining thing-stages, and the like, then ordinary common-sense talk can not be neutral with respect to a physicalist form of materialism. Sensations might be identified with brain processes, where 'brain process' is a concept of the common-sense conceptual scheme of the permanent in change (what elsewhere I have called the Strawsono-Aristotelian Conceptual Scheme).[5] This, then, is another respect in which my form of physicalism may have to take a bow or two towards the disappearance form of the identity theory. But once more, it tries to keep as near as possible to the translation form. To say that our mentalistic talk fails to be topic neutral with reference to a physicalistic language based on the four-dimensional world view of modern physics simply because of the difference between the Strawsono-Aristotelian and the 'Minkowskian' conceptual schemes is not to say anything damaging to materialism. The same inability to translate would go through with ordinary discourse about stones and stars!

III

I now wish to consider a matter which according to some philosophers shows that a translation form of the identity theory is quite ruled out. It has been argued that mentalistic talk is Intentional in Brentano's sense, which, so far as I can understand it, implies that it is intensional, with referentially opaque contexts. Hence, so it is argued, ordinary mentalistic discourse is not translatable into the extensional language of total science, such as is envisaged by a physicalist like me.

I would suggest that Intentional language can not be as intensional and referentially opaque as it looks. Because of Donald Davidson's (1965, 1967, 1968) considerations about learnable languages it must be possible so to construe it that it admits of Tarski-type truth definitions, which it certainly could not be if it were really as intensional as it looks. Davidson (1968) has made considerable strides towards giving such an account, and his argument based on the learnability of languages suggests very strongly that complete success should be possible. In which case the argument from the Intentionality of psychological idioms can not prove anything very much. It is clear that Davidson's argument from the learnability of languages (and the possibility of Tarski-type truth definitions) must be faced by the dualist too. If our language of belief and attitude were really as intensional as it looks at first sight then a dualist would have as good reason to abhor it as a materialist has. If it is not susceptible of a Tarski-type truth definition then neither the materialist nor the dualist understands what he is saying. Besides which, of course, we often ascribe Intentional properties to purely physical systems.[6]

However, Davidson's account makes use of the notion of synonymy, or rather 'same saying' and therefore we have also to fall back on Quine's notion of 'the double standard'. According to this, the idioms of propositional attitude are part of a second-grade notation, which we must reject when 'limning the true and ultimate structure of reality' (Quine 1960, p. 221). This is not because of intensionality, since this may be dealt with on the lines referred to in the last paragraph. It is because of indeterminacy of translation, the indefiniteness of the notion of 'same saying' which is needed for the individuation of psychological attitudes.

This indeterminacy prevents us having scientific laws expressible in the terminology of 'attitude'. It is not that there are any 'psychic' laws or entities. In so far as we take this line, the translation form of the identity theory is eroded in the direction of the disappearance form. But the translation form might work very well nevertheless, for dealing with reports of the havings of sense data, images, pains, tickles, and the like, which do not seem to be intentional in the same way as beliefs, desires, etc., are.[7] And it is these manifestations of 'consciousness', rather than the propositional attitudes, which have always seemed to me (and to U.T. Place) to pose the main problem for the materialist, anyway.[8]

IV

However, there are other problems for the physicalist which may be connected with those of intensionality in a different way from those discussed in the last section. Materialists like me are wont to say things like 'Sensations are brain processes', 'Beliefs and desires are brain states', 'Experiences are brain processes and they have no emergent, non-physical, properties'. Now in a purely extensional language for science, of the sort in which, following Quine (1966, 'The Scope and Language of Science'), I hope and believe total science to be expressible, we should not have to talk about 'properties'. It would be a pity if my physicalist metaphysics could not be expressed in a physicalist language! Certainly I feel rather horrified when I recollect the way in which, in defending the identity theory, I have availed myself of such (at least prima facie) intensional looking concepts as those of 'property' and 'state'. Let us consider these notions. We had better also have a quick look at the related notions of 'process' and 'event'.

The objection to properties is not that they are abstract entities, because sets are abstract entities, and I am impressed by Quine's arguments for the thesis that physics has to postulate sets much as it postulates electrons.[9] The trouble with properties is that the notion of a property is an obscure one. Consider two ways in which it has been attempted to elucidate the notion of a property. These are (a) by reference to the notion of *meaning* and (b) by reference to the notion of *possible worlds*.

Take (a) first. The principle of individuation of properties is that of synonymy of predicates. F-hood is the same property as G-hood if and only if the predicate 'is an F' is synonymous with the predicate 'is a G'. This sort of talk is infected with the obscurity, to which Quine has drawn attention, of the notion of synonymy. But even if the notion of synonymy were clear, it would probably have to be elucidated in partly psychological terms, so that there would be something bad about making the latter notion a key part of the object language of science and metaphysics, which for the most part treats non-psychological and non-linguistic matters.

Now take (b), the elucidation of the concept of a property in terms of that of a possible world. The property of being an F might be said to be the same as that of being a G if in every possible world a thing is an F if it (or perhaps its counterpart) is a G. However, to work out the semantics of this we have to postulate a rather bloated universe. It is still also controversial as to whether such a semantics is properly intelligible. I therefore prefer at present not to follow up this approach, though I am nevertheless impressed by the work of David K. Lewis who shows ingeniously that many well-known philosophical problems can be neatly solved if we do allow ourselves to postulate this ontology of possible worlds.

Lewis has pointed out to me in conversation that Quine himself, in his paper 'Propositional Objects' (Quine 1969) has given a clear account, using set theoretical notions, of the concept of a possible world. As Quine says 'This explication of possible worlds is predicated on the view that every possible world has homogeneous matter, Euclidean space, and a time dimension independent of frame of reference' (Quine 1969, p. 152). Nevertheless, as Quine remarks, it could probably be complicated so as to be compatible with current physics (in which his simplifying assumptions are denied). Even so, it would not provide a suitable notion of 'property' to replace that which the physicalist incautiously uses in the defence of physicalism, at least against a dualist who held that the world was not made up entirely of physical particles or other spatiotemporal entities.[10]

The notion of a property or of particular properties, as I have remarked, does not occur in the language of total science as envisaged in a Quinean way. Sometimes, of course, a scientist may appear to be referring to a property as when he talks of electrical resistance, saying for example that a wire a has an electrical resistance of 100 ohms. Following Quine (1960, pp. 244–5), we can construe 'a has a resistance of 100 ohms' by using the binary predicate 'has a resistance in ohms of' and say 'the resistance in ohms of $a = 100$' or 'resistance in ohms $(a, 100)$'. Here '100' names not a resistance but a real number. In this sort of way reference to properties can be eliminated from the business parts of scientific discourse.

However, the notion of 'property' or 'state' does seem to occur in a different way in less businesslike parts of science. Thus a scientist may say 'We see that the property of temperature is really just mean kinetic energy', and so on. Here I think that the scientist is talking *about* his theories, rather than *within* them, and that locutions of this sort might be given some sort of metalinguistic interpretation. The scientist is saying something like this: that the sentences about phenomena which are deducible from the subtheory containing 'has a temperature T' are also deducible from a wider theory together with the statement 'has a mean kinetic energy E' (or else that near-approximations to them are deducible from a different theory which is formally inconsistent with the subtheory in question). Such an analysis is far from clear: it needs a clear account of 'theory', which reduces in part to giving a clear account of 'law of nature'. A law of nature is a universal generalization but no philosophical criteria are available *a priori* for deciding which universal generalizations count as laws and which as accidental generalizations. I am inclined to say roughly that a universal generalization is to be regarded as a law if competent scientists confer a certain sort of honorific status on it, or if we are hopeful that competent scientists will do so in future (Smart 1968, p. 64). We do have certain necessary conditions, however, such as that it is part of a true theory, it is deducible from a true theory, or we have a hunch that one day it will be deducible from a true theory. However, since we can not understand 'theory' without understanding 'law', this can not without circularity be part of the definition of 'law'. To mark off laws of nature is not a task which can be achieved by philosophers in their studies (Putnam 1969, p. 253).

It is possible that words like 'property' and 'state' as they ordinarily occur, refer to entities postulated in common-sense language, different from concrete objects or any physically distinguishable part of them. Thus a state of a gas would not be identifiable with the gas itself or any temporal part of the gas – 'gas-stage', as Quine might say. Nor would talk about the state of an object be explicable metalinguistically in terms of predicates applicable to concrete objects. Properties or states would just be irreducible entities of common-sense ontology. I think that David Armstrong is happy to accommodate such entities in his physicalist universe, but I hanker after a stricter physicalism, whose ontology contains nothing over and above the ultimate entities of physics, including sets. But to state the identity theory without talking about properties in this irreducible sense is not easy.

Perhaps we could identify a property, in something like the extensional sense hinted at above, with a temporal part of something. Thus the untidy state of a boy's bedroom might just *be* the room as a four-dimensional entity over the period of untidiness in question. But then besides the untidy state of the room there is the smelly state of the room. If the smelly state is also a temporal stage of the room then the untidy state is identical with the smelly state. A similar problem arises with the concept of a process. If a process is a temporal stage of a thing,

Philosophy of Mind

perhaps a cat's cradle of world lines of elementary particles (or rather of the particles themselves, but to talk loosely of 'world lines' makes for vividness), then a heating up process of an iron ball is the same thing as a simultaneous rotatory process of the iron ball. That similar problems arise for processes as arise for states is not surprising if we reflect that, from the point of view being discussed at present, a state is just a null process – one of zero change.

We might think of states and processes as individuated by their causes and effects, as Donald Davidson (1969) thinks of events. Thus the untidy state of the boy's room is a different state from the smelly state, because the former was caused by a pillow fight and the latter by the cat getting in, and the former causes his homework to be lost, while the latter causes his mother to apply disinfectant. Similarly the heating process of the iron ball is caused by proximity to a gas fire, while the rotatory process is caused by a mechanical force.

The notion of 'cause' does not occur in the type of physicalist language I want, though it might be elucidated metalinguistically with reference to such a language. Nevertheless the entities which are individuated by reference to causes and effects could of course in fact be entities which could also be individuated in purely physical terms. Thus the smelly state of the room might be identified with the spatially scattered four-dimensional solid consisting of those smell producing chemicals in the room. The untidy state might be identified with the formless spatially scattered heap of pillows, blankets, books, leaking ink pots, and so on. In the case of the iron ball the heating up process might be identified with the random components of the motions[11] of the molecules and the rotatory process with the non-random components. With its set theoretic resources, a physicalist language should be capable of talking of components of motion, I have not investigated how this should be done in the canonical form of quantification theory, but it should be possible. If not there is a grave problem for anyone who hopes to express physics in canonical notation.

The latter qualifications aside, let us say that brain states are four-dimensional parts of brain stages which vary little from time slice to time slice. Brain processes will be parts of brain stages which differ markedly from time slice to time slice. I put in the words 'parts of' because we should identify the brain state which is a belief with a perhaps spatially scattered part of a total brain stage. For example, at any rate if it is a belief about mathematics, the olfactory area of the brain will not come into it. It will be that part of the brain which, to fall back on our second-grade language, is the cause of belief behaviour, and caused by belief stimuli. Similarly, I would not say that the brain process which was a pain was more than a (possibly spatially scattered part) of a whole brain stage.

To elucidate the remark that there are no 'emergent' properties, that nomological danglers relating properties are as bad as nomological danglers relating entities, we must go back to the other sense of 'property', discussed earlier in this section, which is defined in terms of synonymy.[12] We are saying that there must be no predicates that are not definable in a physicalist language. ('Neutral' predicates of course would be all right: they would belong both to physicalist and non-physicalist language.)

V

In this paper I have discussed various difficulties for the identity theory which arise from intentionality (and consequent intensionality) and of the use of intensional looking notions like 'property'. I might add that the fact that it relies heavily on the concept 'property' makes me uneasy about what otherwise seems to me to be far the best, most sophisticated, and most convincing form of the translation theory, namely that which has been given recently by David K. Lewis (1970, 1972). I have not solved all my problems, and have even had to fall back on Quine's distinction between first-grade and second-grade notation. I have tried to explore how far these difficulties force us to modify the 'translation' form of the identity theory by seeking help on occasion from the disappearance form, or a least by making some tentative bows towards the latter. That I have not tidied up my loose ends or solved all my problems may be because they are insoluble, but it may be merely that I am not clever enough to solve them.[13] At any rate I am reluctant to move too easily from a translation form of the identity theory to the disappearance form, which has, to use words which Russell used in another connection, the advantages of theft over honest toil!

NOTES

1 M.J. Deutscher has pointed out to me that the mere fact that the materialist can talk about our sensations, etc., to non-materialists does not by itself prove the necessity for a neutral analysis of such talk. A phenomenalist can talk to a realist about tables. Perhaps we might say that the phenomenalist and the realist have the same concept of a table, even though they give different accounts of the concept. However, the case does seem to me to be different when what we are intending to do is to offer not an analysis but a contingent identification, as in the case of brain and mind.

2 I was indeed at one time rather too easily tempted to take this 'easy' way. See my 'Comments' (1967), especially the last two pages. When I wrote this

I had recently returned from an exciting but exhausting year in USA and I was feeling mentally tired!

3   In my article 'Sensations and Brain Processes' in the present volume, I qualified this by some silly remarks about 'sensation statements' having 'a different logic' from brain process statements. In later publications I dropped this sort of talk, which was due to lingering neo-Wittgensteinian influences on my thought. This business of 'different logics' now seems to me to be pretty well unintelligible.

4   Perhaps this case is a 'pretty clear one' for the reasons given by Hilary Putnam (1962).

5   See my paper 'Space-Time and Individuals' in this volume. Compare also the way in which Wilfrid Sellars contrasts 'the manifest image' with 'the scientific image' not only in the way in which it differs with respect to mentalistic discourse but also in the way in which it differs with respect to temporal discourse. See Sellars (1963).

6   D.C. Dennett has argued that in doing so we take out certain loans on mentalistic discourse, talking of 'messages' in neurons and the like, but he holds that if we can find physical mechanisms that will process such 'messages' appropriately the loans can be paid back. See D.C. Dennett (1971, especially near the bottom of p. 99).

7   For an argument that the inability of fit attributions of attitude into serious scientific discourse can be reconciled with a purely physicalist ontology, see Donald Davidson (1970).

8   See my paper 'Sensations and Brain Processes' in this volume and Place's earlier paper 'Is Consciousness a Brain Process? (Place 1962).

9   The terminology 'abstract entity' is misleading, since our knowledge of abstract entities would appear to arise through the hypothetico-deductive method. They are not known through a process of 'abstraction' as in eighteenth-century epistemology. So perhaps they might better be characterized by some other terminology. (Perhaps as 'timeless entities'.) I owe this insight to D.M. Armstrong (1978, p. 15 and chapter 4).

10 Lewis has remarked to me in correspondence that Quine's construction of possible worlds does not have built in to it a full-blooded physicalism. According to Lewis, the possible worlds need not obey any reasonable physical laws: for example, they could have 'emergent' or 'holistic' laws. I have some doubts about this, since if a possible world is a configuration of physical particles, can the notion of 'particle' be understood in abstraction from the *physical* laws which they presumably obey?

11 For a better solution see my essay 'Sellars on Process' in the present volume and Quine's comment (reported in note 5 of that essay).

12 For this sense, unfortunately I think, Putnam (1969) revives an old fashioned use of the world 'predicate'. It seems best to retain the word 'predicate' for linguistic expressions.

13 And *a fortiori* not before the *Monist* deadline!

REFERENCES

Armstrong, D.M. 1978: *Nominalism and Realism, Universals and Scientific Realism*, vol. 1. London: Cambridge University Press.
Davidson, Donald 1965: Theories of Meaning and Learnable Languages. In Yehoshua Bar-Hillel (ed.), *Logic, Methodology and Philosophy of Science: Proceedings of an International Conference*, Amsterdam: North Holland, 383–94. Reprinted 1984 in Donald Davidson, *Inquiries into Truth and Interpretation*, Oxford: Clarendon Press, 3–15.
—— 1967: Truth and Meaning. *Synthese*, 17, 304–23. Reprinted 1984 in Donald Davidson, *Inquiries into Truth and Interpretation*, Oxford: Clarendon Press, 17–36.
—— 1968: On Saying That. *Synthese*, 19, 130–46. Reprinted 1984 in Donald Davidson, *Inquiries into Truth and Interpretation*, Oxford: Clarendon Press, 93–108.
—— 1969: The Individuation of Events. In Nicholas Rescher (ed.), *Essays in Honor of Carl G. Hempel*, Dordrecht, Holland: D. Reidel. Reprinted 1980 in Donald Davidson, *Essays on Actions and Events*, Oxford: Oxford University Press, 93–108.
—— 1970: Mental Events. In Lawrence Foster and J.W. Swanson (eds), *Experience and Theory*, Amherst: University of Massachusetts Press. Reprinted 1980 in Donald Davidson, *Essays on Actions and Events*, Oxford: Oxford University Press, 207–25.
Dennett, D.C. 1971: Intentional Systems. *Journal of Philosophy*, 68, 87–106.
Lewis, David 1970: How to Define Theoretical Terms. *Journal of Philosophy*, 67, 427–46. Reprinted 1983 in David Lewis, *Philosophical Papers*, vol. 1, Oxford: Oxford University Press, 78–95.
—— 1972: Psychological and Theoretical Identifications. *Australasian Journal of Philosophy*, 50, 249–58.
Place, U.T. 1962: Is Consciousness a Brain Process? In V.C. Chappell (ed.), *The Philosophy of Mind*, Englewood Cliffs, New Jersey: Prentice-Hall, 101–9.
Putnam, Hilary 1962: The Analytic and the Synthetic. In Herbert Feigl and Grover Maxwell (eds), *Minnesota Studies in the Philosophy of Science*, vol. 3, Minneapolis: University of Minnesota Press. Reprinted 1975 in Hilary Putnam, *Mind, Language and Reality*, *Philosophical Papers*, vol. 2, London: Cambridge University Press.
—— 1969: On Properties. In Nicholas Rescher (ed.), *Essays in Honor of Carl G. Hempel*, Dordrecht, Holland: D. Reidel. Reprinted 1975 in Hilary Putnam, *Mind, Language and Reality*, *Philosophical Papers*, London: Cambridge University Press.
Quine, W.V. 1960: *Word and Object*. Cambridge, Massachusetts: MIT Press.
—— 1966: *The Ways of Paradox and Other Essays*. New York: Random House.
—— 1969: Propositional Objects. In *Ontological Relativity and Other Essays*, New York: Columbia University Press.
Rorty, Richard 1965: Mind–Body Identity, Privacy, and Categories. *Review of Metaphysics*, 19, 24–54.

Sellars, Wilfrid 1963: *Science, Perception and Reality*. London: Routledge and Kegan Paul.

Smart, J.J.C. 1967: Comments. In C.F. Presley (ed.), *The Identity Theory of Mind*, Brisbane: University of Queensland Press, 84–93.

—— 1968: *Between Science and Philosophy*. New York: Random House.

18

On Some Criticisms of a Physicalist Theory of Colours

I want to discuss some criticisms made by M.C. Bradley (1963, 1964) of the account of colours in my book *Philosophy and Scientific Realism* (Smart 1963). I shall put forward a modified account of colours, which was first suggested to me by David K. Lewis, though a rather similar view has been put forward by D.M. Armstrong (1968, pp. 256–60, 272–90). In fact there turn out to be certain differences between Lewis' present view of colours and that which he first suggested to me, and also between Armstrong's and Lewis', as also between Armstrong's and mine (or Lewis' original one). However, these differences seem to me to be of no ontological significance, but are rather differences as to which account of colours best fits our ordinary ways of talking. I suspect that our ordinary colour discourse contains enough obscurity to make the choice between various philosophical analyses to some extent an arbitrary one.

In *Philosophy and Scientific Realism* I elucidate colours as dispositions of physical objects to evoke characteristic patterns of discriminatory colour behaviour by normal human percipients in normal circumstances. (Colour discrimination, it will be remembered, can be elucidated antecedently to the notion of colour, and so there is no circularity here.) Bradley brings up two imaginary cases to show the inadequacy of this view. One was originally C.B. Martin's, and is as follows. All colours can be represented on a colour circle, where the various radii represent the various hues, and hues which are nearly indistinguishable from one another correspond to radii which are near to one another. The various amounts of saturation of a colour are represented by distances along the radii. Thus, points near the centre of the circle represent a high degree of additive mixing of white. (For simplicity of exposition I am here neglecting differences of brightness, and hence that between white, grey and black, but the full story can easily be adapted to the full colour cone, which takes these differences into account. For 'colour circle' read 'any cross-section of the colour cone'.) Now let us envisage a miraculous transformation of things in the world so that the colours of things change into the diametrically opposite colours on the colour circle. Thus if O is the centre of the colour circle and P and P' are points on opposite radii such that O P = O P', a thing whose colour is represented by P will change to the colour which is represented by P', and vice versa. The only things that will not change will be those things (white ones) whose colour is represented by the centre O of the colour circle.

In the envisaged case the physical constitutions of things will change and so will the wavelengths of the light radiated from them. That is, the change is a perfectly objective and scientifically detectable one. It might correctly be remarked that such a miraculous change would be physically inexplicable, and it would almost certainly lead to difficulties for even the existence of human life. Both food and human flesh would have to undergo changes in order for them to have the chemical constitutions required for the new colours. Moreover, we would have to make all sorts of assumptions about boundary conditions in order to keep our story compatible with the laws of physics. For example, we would have to suppose the non-existence of rainbows. (For how could colour interchange occur on a rainbow without there being a change in the laws of physics?) Such objections can probably be set aside as quibbles, because for the purposes of the objection we can even suppose the laws of physics to be different from what they are, so long as they remain the same throughout the story. After all, we are concerned with elucidating common-sense colour concepts, which have mostly grown up before the rise of modern science.[1]

Now in the envisaged case, everybody will want to say (on the basis both of physics and of immediate experience) that there has been a systematic change of the colours of things in the world. Yet the patterns of discriminatory responses will *not* have changed. Normal human percipients will still find it hard to pick geranium petals from a pile of ripe tomatoes, but easy to pick them from a heap of unripe ones, and hard to pick out lettuce leaves from a distant part of the lawn, but easy to pick out delphinium petals which have fallen on to the lawn. Thus the systematic interchange in the constitutions of things will not lead to any change in discriminatory responses of normal human percipients. (This supposes, of course, that the nervous systems of normal human percipients will continue to function as before, even though the constitution of blood, nerve tissue, etc., may have changed. We have already agreed to neglect any objection of this sort as being something of a quibble.) On the basis of immediate experience, and also on the basis of physics, people will say that a systematic interchange of colours will have occurred. And yet there will be no change in the patterns of discriminatory responses which are evoked by things in the world. Consequently there must be something wrong with an account of colours in terms of power to cause certain patterns of discriminatory behaviour.

In my book I tried unavailingly to get out of this difficulty by bringing in colour experiences; in the envisaged case we should notice that our colour experiences had changed. I elucidated the experience of something looking red in terms of 'something going on in me which is like what goes on in me when I am in normal health and in normal light and there is something in front of my eyes which *really is* red.' That is, the experience of red is elucidated in terms of the redness of objects. (Not the other way round, as by John Locke, although my account is like the Lockean one, in so far as it elucidates colours as powers. But to elucidate redness as the power to cause red ideas or sense data, as in Locke, leads to obvious difficulties for a thoroughgoing physicalism.) Bradley shows convincingly that if I modify my account so that redness becomes not just the power to cause a certain pattern of discriminatory responses but the power to cause the experience of 'seeing something red' as well, I am caught in a vicious circularity. Colours are elucidated in part in terms of colour experiences, and these are elucidated in terms of colours, which are elucidated in part in terms of experiences, which are. . . .

I admit that this objection from colour reversal is damaging to my original account of colours. I am therefore disposed to give up my original account in favour of a different one which is, however, equally compatible with physicalism. In correspondence, David Lewis asked me why I did not say that a colour is a physical state of the surface of an object, that state which normally explains certain patterns of discriminatory reactions of normal human percipients. (Fairly obvious modifications would have to be made to deal with the colours of public yet illusory objects, such as the sky or a rainbow.) I replied at the time that I did not like this because the state would be a very disjunctive and idiosyncratic one. In effect, Lewis replied, 'Very disjunctive and idiosyncratic – so what?' And I then thought to myself, 'So what?' Let me explain this.

Consider the following absurd piece of fiction. A man (Smith, say) has a peculiar neurosis. If he sees a tomato, a rainbow, a bulldozer, or an archbishop, he goes red in the face and stands on his head. No other objects produce this odd behaviour. Then doubtless the property corresponding to the open sentence 'tomato x or rainbow x or bulldozer x or archbishop x' would be of some interest to this man and to his psychiatrist. It is a perfectly objective property, but because of its peculiar disjunctiveness (the oddity of the different components of the disjunction occurring within the same disjunction) it is both a disjunctive and an idiosyncratic property. Let us call this disjunctive and idiosyncratic property 'snarkhood'. Now, although snarkhood is a perfectly objective property, it is only Smith's neurosis which makes it of any interest to anyone. Were it not for Smith's neurosis, neither he nor his psychiatrist would have any reason to single it out from the infinity of other highly disjunctive and idiosyncratic properties. Similarly, the disjunction of physical properties which is the physical property of greenness seems to be a very disjunctive and idiosyncratic physical property. We single it out only because of certain highly complex facts about the human eye and nervous system. This is because infinitely many different mixtures of light of various wavelengths and intensities can produce the same discriminatory response. Just as the property of snarkhood is of no interest except to Smith or his psychiatrist, so we need not expect the physical property of greenness to be of any interest to extraterrestrial beings, who would have differently constituted eyes and nervous systems.

A simple formula F might be suggested which would describe all the mixtures of wavelengths which would give rise to the same colour behaviour (and colour experience) in a normal percipient. For this reason Armstrong is tempted to say that if there is no such simple formula there are not really any colours, because it is an aspect of our colour perception that all red things look to have some simple and non-disjunctive property in common. Compare the case in which a disease is described by some complex syndrome, and medical scientists come to divide it into two diseases characterized by different (although possibly overlapping) parts of the syndrome and ascertainably different aetiologies. We would be inclined to say in such a case that the scientists had discovered the existence of two new diseases, and also the non-existence of the original disease. There seems to be a choice here: we could redescribe the old disease as a disjunction of the two new diseases, or else say that the old disease is nonexistent. My own inclination in the case of colours would be to take the analogue of the former choice. That is, if no suitable F exists Armstrong would say that there are not really any colours. I do not think that any ontological issue depends on the difference, even if the simple formula F exists.

It may be worth recalling my reason for thinking that no simple formula exists. Consider an arrangement of three photoelectric cells in a circuit which approximately simulates the human visual system, as elucidated by the three-colour theory of vision (Bouma 1949, pp. 154–6). We should have to choose three cells with appropriately related characteristic curves (current plotted against wavelength of light) such that the shapes of the curves were such-and-such, and their maxima were such-and-such. These specifications would have a quite arbitrary look about them and would be dictated by the nature of the human visual system. In this way the properties of physical objects which explain human visual discriminations are idiosyncratic properties. Presumably they are disjunctive properties because quite different mixtures of light can lead to the same visual response. Moreover, a mixture of light for which the intensity–wavelength curve is single peaked, say at wavelength λ, can produce the same reactions as light with a many-peaked intensity–wavelength curve, and this last curve may even have a trough around λ. Nevertheless, there *may* be a non-disjunctive specification of the physical properties which are colours of objects although it is at least not obvious what this might be. I shall, however, mention an ingenious suggestion which David Lewis has communicated to me in correspondence. Consider a hyperspace of infinitely many dimensions, indeed as many dimensions as there are points in the real number continuum. A particular spectrum could be represented by a point in this hyperspace. Suppose that we give the space a metric, perhaps by taking the interval between two points in the hyperspace to be the mean square difference of intensities (for the two spectra) averaged over all wavelengths. Then, according to Lewis, it is possible that a colour might correspond to (be the power to reflect light corresponding to) a simple shaped volume in this hyperspace. But at any rate it seems clear that if there is a simple formula of the sort for which Armstrong hankers, it cannot be anything very obvious, such as the capacity to reflect light of such-and-such a single wavelength. And if colour should be such a simple property, so much the better. My defence of physicalism, however, will allow that it can be as idiosyncratic and disjunctive as you wish; like snarkhood it will nevertheless be a perfectly *objective* property.

Let me now revert to the earlier 'so what?'. A highly complex, disjunctive or idiosyncratic property would be objectionable at one end of a correlation law (nomological dangler). The assertion, however, that the colour *is* the property, however disjunctive and idiosyncratic it may be, does not lead to this trouble. (If it should turn out to be less disjunctive or idiosyncratic than I fear, so much the better.) If the colour *is* the physical property, then we have no nomological dangler depending from the property.

The property of snarkhood is disjunctive in that it might be defined by means of the disjunction:

Snarks $x =$ df tomato x or rainbow x or bulldozer x or archbishop x.

Nevertheless snarkhood could also be described non-disjunctively as the property which things have if and only if they cause the neurotic behaviour in question. Snarkhood is the property which *causes* or which *explains* the peculiar behaviour; it is the property such that it is a *lawlike* proposition that, if and only if Smith is presented with something possessing the property, then he stands on his head. Such a description of the property makes use of words like 'causes', 'explains', 'is law-like'. (Another possibility, related to the last one, is that we teach 'snarks *x*' ostensively; snarkhood would then in a sense be indefinable, but we would be teaching someone to come out with the word 'snarks' on any of a disjunctively describable set of occasions, whether or not he was aware of the disjunctiveness of the property of snarkhood.)

Notice that the identification of snarkhood with the property which causes the behaviour in question is a contingent one. There is no difficulty about the contingent identification of properties, although it has for some reason been hard for many philosophers (including myself) to come to see this.[2] To use an example which I got from Lewis in correspondence, consider the statement that the property of conductivity is identical with the property measured by the piece of apparatus with such-and-such serial number. This statement is quite clearly a contingent and factual one. We must resist the temptation to suppose that all true statements of identity of properties would have to be necessary. It is clear then, that although colours may be disjunctive and idiosyncratic physical properties, it need not be the case that those who use colour words need know that this is so. For them, colours are described in a purely topic-neutral way (neutral between physicalist and non-physicalist meta-physical theories). They are the properties, whatever they are, which could explain the characteristic patterns of discriminatory responses of normal human percipients. It would be perfectly possible for an Aristotelian type of person to agree with the analysis, but to suppose that the property which explains the pattern of responses is a non-physicalist, emergent, and perhaps non-disjunctive one. We, with our scientific knowledge, will suspect that it is an idiosyncratic and possibly very disjunctive, purely physical property of the surfaces of objects. Not at first knowing or suspecting that the property is an idiosyncratic and possibly very disjunctive one, people might wrongly claim that they know that it is not an idiosyncratic and disjunctive one.

Armstrong (1968b) suggests that mistakes of this sort can arise from a tendency of mind which gives rise to the headless woman illusion. To cause this illusion, a dark cloth is put between the woman's head and the audience, and the background is similarly dark. Armstrong points out that the illusion arises from the tendency to suppose that because we do not perceive the woman to have a head we think that we perceive that she does not have a head, and he holds plausibly that a similar error causes people to think that they have an intuition that experiences are not brain processes. Such an error could occur in thinking about the possible identity of colours and physical states.[3]

Notice now that though greenness is the very property which (in normal circumstances) explains a certain pattern of discriminatory reactions, a different colour could explain the same pattern in the case of the miraculous colour reversal. Two different things can explain the same thing. There is no reason why we should not therefore say that the colours had changed over. No doubt our inner experiences and memories would incline us to take this course because there will be a systematic change in our colour experiences. (I go along with Martin and Bradley in supposing this; it seems to be probable. But since there would also have to be a complete change in our semantic habits we might simply feel dizzy or go mad.) Percipients will notice the change and will say (for example) that tomatoes are blue and that delphiniums are red. They will want to rewrite the *Concise Oxford English Dictionary* and interchange the entries 'shades . . . seen in blood' (see the definition of 'red') and 'coloured like the sky' (see the definition of 'blue'), though they might allow 'red' and 'blue' to be defined as 'the shade *formerly* seen in blood' and 'the colour *formerly* of the sky.' In short, then, the revised account of colours, which defines colours as the physical states of objects which (in our normal world) explain a pattern of discriminatory reactions, allows us consistently to describe the colour reversal case: A and B can be different and yet each can explain the same phenomenon C. The trouble which arose for the account of colours as simply powers to cause patterns of discriminatory reactions does not arise. The colours are the physical states which explain these powers, but other states could explain the very same powers after the miraculous interchange.

I think that the revised account of colours also saves the physicalist from Bradley's objection that it is conceivable that everyone might have the appropriate discriminatory responses so that they would satisfy the behavioural tests for colour vision, and yet everything would look grey to them. I am not completely sure that Bradley's case really is conceivable, because if someone has not at least a tendency not to discriminate (with respect to colour) red things from grey things, can he really see red things as grey? Just as in Martin's example, however, the inability to think through the example in a scientific manner probably does not suffice to discredit the *philosophical* potency of the example, and so I shall waive this point. Now I think that we can accommodate this case to the revised account of colours as follows. Colours are the (perhaps highly disjunctive and idiosyncratic) properties of the surfaces of objects that explain the discriminations with respect to colour of normal human percipients, and also the experiences of these percipients, the looking red, or looking blue, etc., of objects. They would also, however, help to explain the abnormal experiences of the people in Bradley's proposed case.

We might consider that there would be some abnormality in the brains of people who always had inner experiences of seeing grey even though their behaviour showed a complete range of colour discrimination. Then colours (properties of surfaces of objects) would help to explain the normal discriminatory behaviour of these people and would also help to explain the abnormal colour experiences of the people with the abnormal brains. It is interesting to speculate whether and in what sense these people would have a colour language. They might learn colour words purely by reference to discriminatory behaviour and would have no words for colour experiences. They would doubtless be able to describe illusory colour perceptions, in the sense that someone might in slightly abnormal circumstances want to match A with B even though a normal human percipient (behaviouristically speaking) would not want to do so. They would need at least a behaviouristic analogue of 'B looks the colour of A.'

Let us revert to Bradley's case. He strengthens it (so as to avoid the considerations of the last paragraph) by supposing that both the discriminatory colour behaviour and the looking grey of everything were *ex hypothesi* inexplicable. Then could I say, as I have done, that the colours of things are those objective physical properties (perhaps highly disjunctive and idiosyncratic) which explain the patterns of discriminatory behaviour of human beings? If the answer is negative, I do not see how Bradley can suppose that there could be a colour vocabulary at all. Surely a certain degree of explicability is presupposed by any colour vocabulary? How would we teach or learn a purely private language of colour discrimination or of colour experiences? Both colours (which I am arguing to be objective properties of the surfaces of objects) and colour experiences (which in my view are physical processes in human brains) are identified by their typical causes and effects (in the case of the colours themselves, mainly by effects, and in the case of colour experiences, mainly by causes). This does not mean that for the purpose of giving sense to our colour language we need strict causal laws, which would give strict necessary or sufficient conditions for colour behaviour or colour experiences. The difficulties into which philosophical behaviourism has run provide sufficient evidence of the fruitlessness of a search for such strict conditions. Typical causes and effects in typical conditions are all that we need.[4]

I think that the revised account of colours will even enable us to follow Bradley in saying that colour discriminations must be on 'the different observed appearances of things' (Bradley, 1963, p. 393). For (a) we hypothesize colours as the (perhaps highly disjunctive and idiosyncratic) physical states of the surfaces of objects which in fact explain (from the side of the objects) typical colour discriminations, and also (b) we hypothesize colour experiences as those processes which (from the side of the person – in fact, the brain) explain this same discriminatory behaviour. That the causal chain goes not direct from the surface of the object to behaviour but goes via the person (his brain and hence his inner experiences) is perfectly consistent with the physicalist thesis.

A colour sensation, in this view, is what is hypothesized as a typical cause of the typical response of normal colour percipients in typical circumstances. ('Normal' can be defined without circularity.) Such a sensation will also partially serve to explain the non-typical false reports of percipients who suffer from illusion or from intention to deceive. (Illusion leads to false reports about external things, while intention to deceive can also lead to false sensation reports.) I therefore see no difficulty for the amended view in Bradley's remarks (1964, p. 269) about false sensation reports which arise from intention to deceive. Nor shall I touch on Bradley's argument (1964, pp. 272–8) from the alleged incorrigibility of sensation reports, since he no longer subscribes to this argument (Bradley 1969).

I have no doubt that I have been unable to do justice to all of Bradley's criticisms or even to the full subtlety of any of them, but I hope that I have been able to explain why I think that, although my earlier account of colours must be given up, there is nevertheless another physicalist account of colours which avoids these objections.

Ideally, for Quinean reasons, I should like to supplant my talk of colours as properties by a more extensional set theoretic account.[5] Ideally, too, the notion of 'explains' or 'causes' which comes into the account should rest on an extensional account in terms of the syntax (or possibly semantics) of the language of science.[6] It should be noticed, in any case, that this property talk, as well as the use of the concept of explanation ('colours are the physical states of objects which explain certain discriminatory behaviour') is needed only to identify the colours of our ordinary common-sense talk with physicalist properties, that is, as a defence against someone who thinks that a physicalist world view leaves something out. Once this is conceded, we can drop the words 'property' and 'explain' within our statement of world view. But it would be good to do the job set-theoretically, rather than in terms of properties.[7]

NOTES

1 It may be questioned whether the concept of the sort of colour change which we are envisaging can be made structurally consistent. See Paul E. Meehl (1966, pp. 147–8) also Bernard Harrison (1967). I welcome such considerations if they can be made out, but even so I do not want my defence of physicalism to have to depend on them.

2 I myself learned this point from Lewis. N.L. Wilson argued, however, for the possibility of contingently identifying properties in his interesting paper (Wilson 1964).

3 In the paper as originally published I said: 'I do not mean to say that Armstrong approves of this particular application of his idea about the headless woman illusion. He has told me that because all red things look to have something in common he does not think that the apparent simplicity of colours can be explained by a failure to perceive a real disjunctiveness.' However, in very recent correspondence (1986) I have now learned that he has changed his mind about this and does now accept this application of his Headless Woman idea.

4 See Lewis (1966, p. 22).

5 See my paper, 'Further Thoughts on the Identity Theory', chapter 17 of this volume.

6 To elucidate 'explanation' we need to elucidate 'law'. A law is a universally quantified sentence which occurs either as an axiom or a theorem of an important and well-tested theory (or, in an informal theory, somehow 'follows from' it) or is such that we guess that it will one day be incorporated in such a theory. Thus to elucidate 'explanation' we seem to need value words (e.g., 'important'). Value expressions enable us to avow preferences; there is nothing contrary to physicalist metaphysics about them.

7 I wish to thank Professor D.K. Lewis and Professor D.M. Armstrong for commenting on an earlier version of this paper.

REFERENCES

Armstrong, D.M. 1968a: *A Materialist Theory of Mind*. London: Routledge and Kegan Paul.
—— 1968b: The Headless Woman Illusion and the Defence of Materialism. *Analysis*, 29, 48–9.
Bouma, P.J. 1949: *Physical Aspects of Colour*. Eindhoven, Netherlands: Philips Industries.
Bradley, M.C. 1963: Sensations, Brain Processes and Colours. *Australasian Journal of Philosophy*, 41, 385–93.
—— 1964: Critical Notice of *Philosophy and Scientific Realism*. *Australasian Journal of Philosophy*, 42, 262–83.
—— 1969: Two Arguments against the Identity Theory. In R. Brown and

C.D. Rollins (eds), *Contemporary Philosophy in Australia*, London: Allen and Unwin.

Harrison, Bernard 1967: On Describing Colours. *Inquiry*, 10, 38–52.

Lewis, David K. 1966: An Argument for the Identity Theory. *Journal of Philosophy*, 63, 17–25. Reprinted 1983 in David Lewis, *Philosophical Papers*, vol. 1, Oxford: Oxford University Press, 99–107.

Meehl, Paul E. 1966: The Compleat Autocerebroscopist: A Thought-Experiment on Professor Feigl's Mind–Body Identity Thesis. In Paul K. Feyerabend and Grover Maxwell (eds), *Mind, Matter and Method: Essays in Philosophy and Science in Honor of Herbert Feigl*, Minneapolis: University of Minnesota Press, 103–80.

Smart, J.J.C. 1963: *Philosophy and Scientific Realism*. London: Routledge and Kegan Paul.

Wilson, N.L. 1964: The Trouble with Meanings. *Dialogue*, 3, 52–64.

19

The Revival of Materialism

There is nothing in the universe over and above the entities postulated by physics. Of course, these aren't the hard, massy particles of nineteenth-century physics, but I see no point in tying the notion of 'the material' to the physics of our great-grandfathers. For me, the material is just the *physical*, and I feel entitled to believe in all the entities which the physicist needs to assume. As a materialist, I am quite prepared to acknowledge that my vocabulary outruns that of physics, since we talk about such things as rivers, trees, tables, and so on. But I must insist that these rivers, trees, tables, and so on are just suitably structured aggregates of the fundamental entities of physics.

The claims which I have just made may be contested in two opposite ways. First of all, you might say that we have no reason to suppose that contemporary physics is the last word. Electrons and neutrons may go the way of the hard, massy particles of nineteenth-century physics. I am prepared to concede this point. I tie my present notion of materialism to contemporary physics because I know nothing better, but I agree that if theories of the physical world change, so will our views about what it is to be 'material' or 'physical'. Nevertheless, fundamental changes in physics may leave much of science (for example, organic chemistry or the physiology of respiration) fairly undisturbed. Changes in the foundations need not affect the superstructure. The main thrust of materialism is that it denies the existence of ultimate non-physical laws and entities. But now there is the second possible objection: you might object that what I have said is true, but that it is perfectly trivial.

Suppose that, in order to explain the working of the brain, it was necessary to postulate some sort of psyche or vital force. Now, brains are part of the physical universe, and so would not the psyche or vital force have to be postulated by an enlarged and adequate physics? It thus looks as though my account of materialism might allow even a quite ghostly universe to count as material. To prevent this, I must now expand what I have said and proceed in a rather roundabout way. I shall begin by talking about a radio apparatus, such as the one which is enabling you to listen to this talk.

If you look inside such a radio apparatus, you will find various lumpy objects. Whether or not you know any physics, you may be able to classify these lumpy objects as 'capacitors', 'inductors', 'resistors', 'transistors', and so on. You may be able to make this classification simply because you have learned to associate the appropriate words with the various sorts of lumpy object. You may also be able to do much more than this. If you know a little physics, you may be able to explain why a circuit consisting of an inductor and a capacitor in series will oscillate at a certain definite frequency, why a transistor will rectify or amplify signals, and many other things of the same sort. Indeed, you may be able to put all this knowledge together and explain how this particular piece of hardware before you, in a brown box and with shiny knobs on it, will receive radio talks from the BBC. Let us call the ordinary untutored knowledge of capacitors, inductors, resistors, transistors and so on, the 'natural history' of radio. Then the scientific understanding of radio comes as a sort of mixture of physics and natural history.

Compare now the sort of account which biologists give of occurrences in a living cell or assemblage of cells. For example, consider certain minute granules, called 'ribosomes', which are found in the interior of cells. They are too small to be seen by means of an ordinary optical microscope. Nevertheless, the description of ribosomes as granules should be regarded as a piece of natural history, no less than a more ordinary piece of natural history, such as the description of a tiger as a striped animal. The biologist goes beyond natural history when he or she describes the ribosomes in terms of physics and chemistry, as when he or she says that they contain ribonucleic acid, and that they take part in the synthesis of proteins.

Psychology is a part of biology. In the really scientific core of psychology, there is a close tie-up with neurophysiology, and hence with biophysics and biochemistry. Now, the brain's circuitry is too complex for us to know it in detail, and so the psychologist tends to conjecture methods of information-processing in the brain: he or she makes hypotheses about various functional units which may or may not be identical with certain distinct anatomical units. The electronics engineer does something similar when he or she does not want to bother about detailed circuitry, as when he or she talks of a 'frequency changer' or a 'power amplifier'.

So let us now state the materialist thesis as follows. To explain the facts about the universe, including living creatures both human and non-human, there is no obstacle (other than the finiteness of our minds and our inevitable ignorance) to the programme of using a mixture of natural history on the one hand, and physics and chemistry on the other hand. We may concede that, in biology, there are sometimes special forms of explanation, such as the theory of evolution by natural selection, but these are perfectly consistent with a mechanistic biology. The types of explanation which, as a materialist, I must reject are of a different sort. In particular, I must reject the sort of law postulated by psycho-physical dualists. Such a law would relate a very complex neural process, involving perhaps tens of millions of neurons, to the occurrence of a certain sort of conscious experience, say, the having of a visual sensation or an itchy feeling. That such laws should exist seems to be quite implausible when we consider the mechanistic thrust of contemporary biology. Such laws would be the excrescences on the fair face of science.

It was U.T. Place, then a colleague of mine at the University of Adelaide, who first convinced me of the weakness of the usual arguments against materialism. Let us consider a couple of these arguments. Suppose that I have a green-and-purple striped visual image. You might say that there is very likely nothing in the brain which is green-and-purple striped, and so the thing of which I am conscious cannot be a state of the brain. In reply I want to say that having a visual image – or any other sensation or experience – is rather like playing an off-drive in cricket. A visual image is not part of the furniture of the world, any more than an off-drive is a piece of cricket equipment such as a bat or a stump. There are no visual images, but only the havings of them, just as there are no off-drives, but only the playings of them. To have a green-and-purple striped visual image is to have a sort of inner 'going-on' which is like the sort of inner going-on that typically occurs when a normal human percipient has a green-and-purple striped object in front of his eyes in a good light. Similarly, to have a pain in the leg is to have the sort of inner going-on (in the brain, *not* in the leg) which typically occurs when my leg is damaged, and I say 'Ouch!' The local vicar and I can agree on this, even though I claim that the inner going-on is a brain process, and he may claim that the inner going-on is a spiritual process. This consideration points the way to refuting another old argument against materialism.

This argument is as follows. I can talk about my experiences to someone who knows nothing about the brain, perhaps someone who thinks that the soul affects the body through the heart. How, then, can we be talking about brain processes when we swap remarks about visual sensations and images, pains, and so on? My reply is that we both agree on enough things for communication to be possible. We have learned to react to likenesses and unlikenesses between certain of our inner goings-on, and classify them according to their typical causes and their typical behavioural effects. That one person may think that the inner going-on is a spiritual process, and another may think that it is a brain process, does not affect their community of belief that our experiences are the typical causes and effects of certain reactions and stimuli. We need only a fair community of belief for communication to be possible. I might say to you that John Jones plays cricket, and you might reply that he also plays football. We both identify him neutrally as the red-faced man with the long nose, despite the fact that you believe that John Jones is the youngest lecturer in physics, and I believe that he is the chemistry laboratory manager. Just as we can talk about John Jones's sporting activities without agreeing about his job, so I can talk (with the local vicar perhaps) about my aches and pains or visual sensations in a way which is neutral between materialism and a more spiritual view of man.

I have been a bit unfair to opponents of materialism, in that I have discussed only two of their arguments. Especially in Oxford, a raised eyebrow used to be the usual philosophical reaction to materialist theses, but, of late, more subtle objections to materialism have been produced. One of the most recent of these has been put forward by Robert Kirk of the University of Nottingham. It turns on the idea that a materialist cannot describe the difference between a man and a complete physical replica of him which behaved in the same way but was not conscious. Kirk's case *would* provide a sound objection to me if I claimed that reports of inner experiences can be translated into materialist or neutral language. However, in expounding materialism, I have tried to avoid the notion of translation and sameness of meaning, notions which the work of Quine has, indeed, taught us to view with suspicion. (It is only fair to add that Kirk himself believes that his argument is good against any form of materialism, whether or not it is a translation theory.)

This reference to translation leads me to speak of a very interesting new development in the defence of materialism. Just as experience should be identified with brain processes, so also beliefs and desires can plausibly be identified with brain states. Now, there is something special about beliefs and desires. They are relations between persons and propositions, and so they are often called 'propositional attitudes'. Tom's desire for a 15-speed bicycle is not a relation between Tom and a 15-speed bicycle, because he may desire no particular one of the many 15-speed bicycles in the world, or, again, there may not even be any 15-speed bicycles. So Tom's desire is not a relation between him and a bicycle. It is a relation between Tom and the proposition 'Tom possesses a 15-speed bicycle'. Similarly, with belief. Tom's belief that quarks exist is a certain relation between Tom and the proposition 'quarks exist'.

Now, a proposition is what is expressed by two or more sentences which mean the same or can be translated into one another. It follows that if the notions of sameness of meaning and translation are not clear, then the notion of a proposition is not clear either, and is not suitable for scientific purposes. And if the notion of a proposition is not suitable for scientific purposes, then the notions of the propositional attitudes (beliefs and desires) are not suitable for scientific purposes either.

Here I have been following a line of thought which derives from Quine. Another American philosopher, Donald Davidson, has developed this into an ingenious defence of materialism, which has caused considerable excitement in philosophical circles. In fact (to oversimplify a bit), he argues first for a certain indeterminacy of desires and beliefs, and goes on to deduce the indeterminacy of meaning and translation. Now, though he holds that our language of the propositional attitude is not suitable for scientific purposes, Davidson nevertheless wants to say, as most of us do, that our actions are caused by our beliefs and desires. Tight causal laws occur only in the physically-based sciences. It follows that a particular belief or desire must be a particular physical state. There can be identity statements to the effect that a given belief or desire is a certain brain state, but because of the indeterminateness of our language of beliefs and desires, there can be no general identities of the following form: 'for any belief or desire of a sort A, it is identical with a brain state of sort B.' Davidson, therefore, ingeniously deduces a form of materialism from the irreducibility of the mental. It is a clever turning of the tables on traditional philosophical lines of thought.[1]

I think that Davidson's approach should be regarded as a supplement to the sort of approach which I have advocated earlier in this talk. In the first place, Davidson deals only with the propositional attitudes, and we need a different argument for the materiality of sensations and the like. In the second place, Davidson's argument is an argument for only a very weak sort of materialism, compatible with the existence of biological laws which are not reducible to any physics which is at all like present-day physics. So, for a full-blooded materialism of the sort which I wish to advocate, the sorts of considerations which I put forward earlier in this talk are still needed. These considerations suggest that a human being is a very complicated physical mechanism, and nothing more.

NOTE

1 I have discussed Davidson's minimal materialism in my paper 'Davidson's Minimal Materialism' (1985).

REFERENCE

Smart, J.J.C. 1985: Davidson's Minimal Materialism. In Bruce Vermazen and Merrill Hintikka (eds), *Essays on Davidson: Actions and Events*, Oxford: Clarendon Press, 173–82.

20

Physicalism and Emergence

I

In recent Commentaries in *Neuroscience* (Bunge 1977; MacKay 1978; Sperry 1980) much of the argument has related to the notion of *emergence*. (For discussions of this notion see also Berenda 1953; Nagel 1961.) Now, physicalists like myself have been concerned to deny emergence, in a strong sense of this word, but to accept it in a very weak sense of the word. In the case of Sperry's commentary (Sperry 1980), I have had a good deal of difficulty in trying to make up my mind whether emergence is being advocated in the strong sense or whether it is being advocated only in the weak sense, or whether it is sometimes being advocated in the strong sense and sometimes in the weak sense. My main purpose in this Commentary is to try to sort things out a bit.

Let me begin by adumbrating my own position and saying what I mean by describing it as 'physicalist' or 'materialist'. I want to say that a person is nothing but a very complicated physical mechanism (on this point, see also Place 1956, and Armstrong 1968a); that is, the behaviour of the brain is determined solely by the physical laws that apply to the innumerable physical particles that make up the brain. To prevent this statement from degenerating into a triviality, I must rule out the suggestion that psychic forces or entities, or forces that apply only to complex configurations such as brains, might one day be absorbed into physics. For this purpose, I take 'physics' to mean 'present-day physics'. We can envisage revolutionary changes to physics at the level of quarks and the like, and also in cosmology, but the physics of ordinary matter seems to be well understood. We are not in the position of eighteenth-century physicists who could not understand certain macroscopic phenomena that required for their explanation the postulation of as yet unknown electric forces (Feinberg 1966). Thus, as far as discussion of the mind-body problem is concerned, let us identify physics with present-day physics. Contrary to Chomsky, for example, I do not envisage that new ideas in physics will help us to understand better the neurophysiology or behaviour of the brain (Chomsky 1968).

By tying my concept of physicalism to present-day physics, I avoid the charge that it is an empty doctrine. Those who make this charge say that if psychic entities or emergent laws were needed for us to understand the behaviour of brains, then physics would have to be extended so as to include reference to these entities or laws. According to my definition of physicalism, in terms of present-day physics, I can envisage the possibility of physicalism being false, and can then make this strong statement that it is nevertheless true (Smart 1978).

In saying that the behaviour of the brain is determined by the laws of physics (as they relate to the physical particles of which it is composed), and the spatial configuration and motions of these particles at some initial time, I am not committed to the view that neurophysiology can be reduced deductively to physics. I concede that words like 'neuron' are not part of the vocabulary of physics. Nor, even, is 'protein'. To see proteins and neurons as, themselves, physical mechanism, we do not need to be able to carry out a deductive reduction as envisaged by some of the logical empiricists, which would mean describing proteins and neurons entirely in the language of physics and deducing their properties from physical theory. (Here I am indebted to some remarks made by Richard Boyd somewhere.) Such an endeavour is Utopian. What we need is simply some background theory that makes it plausible that the entities in question are determined purely by physical laws (as well as initial conditions, of course).

Richard Boyd also has argued persuasively that in science mechanistic theories have come to be accepted simply because they have been shown to give *possible* explanations. Thus, for natural selection to be accepted, Darwin did not have to prove directly that it *must* have been the reason for the diversity of species. Once he had shown (partly by analogy with artificial selection) that evolution *could* have occurred in this way it was a short step to believing that it *did* occur in this way. Boyd also gives the example of DNA. He explains how J.S. Haldane was (at his own time) rational in supposing that no self-replicating mechanism was possible, but once it was shown how DNA could self-replicate, and how the DNA in a cell could affect the production of enzymes and the way the cell develops, with some sketchy ideas about how such a mechanism might account for the facts of embryology, then a mechanistic story became accepted by scientists as the correct account of what actually happens. That is, in order to establish that the more complex processes are reducible to simpler ones, we do not need to define the expressions in which we speak about the more complex processes in terms of expressions appropriate to the simpler processes. All we need is to make it plausible, that under a suitable (very complex and unknown) description, the more complex entity is a mechanism such as is, in principle, explicable at the more simple level.

II

To apply this to the concerns of this Commentary, I assert that in order to defend the view that the brain is a physical mechanism I do not need to replace words such as 'neuron' by means of practically impossible physical definitions. We have good plausible reasons to see neurons as purely physical mechanisms. The inappropriateness of the search for physical definitions of 'neuron', and the like, also depends on the fact that words like 'neuron' are learned partly ostensively: young physiologists learn how to *recognize* neurons. My physicalism is therefore a non-definitional and non-deductive physicalism. Though I can not define 'brain' in the language of physics, I can still reasonably assert that, metaphysically speaking, a brain is no more than a physical mechanism. 'Bulldozer' is not a word in the language of physics, but it is undeniable that a bulldozer is nothing but a physical mechanism. Of course 'nothing buttery' is often said to be a heinous metaphysical crime, but I see nothing wrong with it: in saying that a complex is nothing but an arrangement of its parts, I do not deny that it can do things that a mere heap or jumble of the parts could not do. (Who on earth would want to deny this? If 'nothing-buttery' had such an absurd consequence it would be a view that no one has ever held.) I might also here mention that when I said 'metaphysically speaking' earlier in this paragraph, I do not sharply distinguish this from 'scientifically speaking', since I regard metaphysics as continuous with science. Science gets metaphysical when it gets very general and controversial and relates itself also to humanistic and other not-typically scientific concerns. A criterion for metaphysical truth is plausibility in the light of total science. Among this total science that provides grist for the metaphysical mill is, of course, the work of Sperry (Sperry 1970a) and other physiologists. The work on patients with the corpus callosum cut, so that the two hemispheres of the brain are able to act independently, contains surprising and interesting results of great importance to philosophers thinking about personal identity (Nagel 1971; Puccetti 1973).

III

Sometimes we speak of mechanisms and parts of mechanisms in terms of *function*. Thus, in radio engineering, we have such terms as 'detector', 'frequency changer', 'audio frequency amplifier', and so on. The use of such functional terms does not, of course, imply that concrete realizations of the sorts of entity referred to by such terms are not physical mechanisms. Similarly, it has been argued (Putnam 1960), that common-sense psychological expressions refer to abstract logical states, like those of a Turing machine. As such, they can be neutral between materialism and dualism (since presumably a spiritual mechanism might be functionally equivalent to a physical one, just as a mechanical adding machine might do the same job as a simple electronic one). Though this implies that the language of psychology is not part of the language of physics, chemistry and neurophysiology, it does not imply that the function is not carried out by purely physical mechanisms. Thus, a human thought may be a brain process even though a psychologically-equivalent robot thought might be an electronic process. Similarly, a frequency changer in one radio apparatus might employ thermionic valves, and a functionally equivalent one in another apparatus might employ transistors. We must not think of the functional entity as anything over and above its embodiment. Any particular frequency changer must have a definite material constitution, including thermionic valves, say. My concrete mental process or state must be neuronal, even though the robot's (roughly isomorphic) process or state must be electronic.

Now, it is all right to talk of a frequency changer causally acting on an intermediate frequency stage, say, (to continue the example from radio). But this is talking at a high level of abstraction, and of course the more concrete story tells more, how the thermionic valves or transistors and other components of circuits act on and interact with one another. Confusion can arise if we separate off in thought the entity described in functional terms from the very same entity, described in concrete terms (or a component of it), as though there were two different entities involved here.

A similarly misleading crossing of levels is suggested by Sperry's talk (e.g., in Sperry 1980) of the system properties (mental properties) of the brain affecting the detailed neuronal activity, as when he says (Sperry 1980, p. 201), 'Interaction is mutually reciprocal between the neural and mental levels in the nested brain hierarchies'. Again, in his analogy of a rolling wheel (Sperry 1969, 1980) he says that the wheel, as it rolls down-hill, 'carries its atoms and molecules through a course in time and space and to a fate determined by the overall system properties of the wheel and regardless of the inclination of the individual atoms and molecules' (Sperry 1980, p. 201). Actually, the motion of the wheel is determined also by the atoms of the ground over which it rolls, and so let us simplify the example by considering a wheel rotating in outer space. Let us also forget twentieth-century physics and suppose that the wheel is made up of a large number of Newtonian particles, perhaps connected by massless rigid rods. I do not think that either of these simplifications essentially affects the purpose of Sperry's example. Now, to say that the motion of the particles is determined by the system as a whole is merely to say that the motion of each particle is determined by the resultant of the forces on it. If this is emergence, then this is a sort of emergence that the most reductionist and mechanistic physicalist will never have dreamed of denying. Sperry has frequently stressed that the motion of a system depends not only on its components but on the spatial configuration and other boundary conditions.

At the envisaged more abstract or functional level, we may talk in terms of information flow. I am, therefore, sympathetic to much of what MacKay says (MacKay 1978). There is a sense in which it is tempting to talk of a computer being determined, not by causes but by an equation. But, as MacKay also contends, to say that the computer's processes are determined by an equation is not to deny that on a more concrete level of discourse we must describe the activity of the computer wholly in terms of electronic causes and effects. However, when we say that the behaviour of the computer is determined by an equation we must of course be on our guard against the misleading suggestion implicit in such crossing of levels. We must not think of the equation as some sort of non-physical or perhaps 'emergent' cause. I want to say, while allowing for the occasional usefulness of speaking in terms of computers being determined by equations, and so on, that what *really* determines the computer is the concrete realization of the equation in modifications of the electronic hardware, and these modifications are caused by the programmer's thinking of the equation, which is a particular brain-process, and so, itself, in principle describable at the more concrete level, though it would then, of course, be describable in a different vocabulary from that of the intensional 'thinking of an equation'.

IV

Physicalists or materialists, such as Place, Armstrong and myself, have identified experiences with brain processes. We are mechanistic about these brain processes, but, of course, we do not deny that in order to describe a brain process in detail we would have not only to describe the physical constituents of the brain, but would have to describe their spatial configurations and interconnections. So, if Sperry is saying anything contrary to mechanistic materialism, he must be taking his assertion of 'emergence' in a stronger sense. I conjecture therefore that we must not take his analogy of the wheel too seriously. I can not help thinking that he may be influenced by something else, which does not arise in the case of the wheel, namely, the phenomenology of consciousness. ('The subjective qualities are recognized to be real and causal in their own right, as subjectively experienced, and to be of very different quality from the neural, molecular and other material components of which they are built' (Sperry 1980, p. 204). Of course, such pronouncements can be understood in more than one way.)

Let us consider a mental image or sense datum of a yellow banana. This seems to pose a difficulty for the physicalist, because the brain process that occurs when we have such an image or sense datum is not a yellow object. Moreover, the banana itself is made up of a discontinuity of physical particles, and yet the perceived colour is continuous. So there seems to be some quality, a subjective quality of the brain, or an objective quality of the banana, which is left out by the physicalist ontology. (On the issue, see Sellars 1963, where he discusses his example of the pink ice cube. I shall not discuss Sellars' position here, since it contains a subtle Kantian twist which would lead us rather far afield.)

We must beware of what U.T. Place has called 'the phenomenological fallacy' (Place 1956). It is easy to suppose that when we have an image or sense datum we are aware of some item in the world which is literally yellow. But to have a yellow sense datum, say, is just to have the sort of inner experience that normally goes with perceiving a yellow object in the world, such as a banana. The experience of 'having a yellow sense datum' is not itself something yellow. I want to deny that the world contains such items as sense data or mental images, with purely phenomenological qualities. What the world contains is the *havings of* images or sense data. We must think of the expression 'have a yellow sense datum' as being a unitary way of referring simply to those inner goings on that in normal circumstances are caused by yellow objects. It is unitary in the way that the idiom 'to kick the bucket' is. When a man dies or 'kicks the bucket', there is no bucket in the case. (I do not want to push the analogy too far, because there is an infinity of expressions of the same form as 'have a yellow sense datum'.)

But is not this merely to postpone the difficulty? If there are no sense data or mental images, apart from the havings of them, then we need not worry about the alleged continuous phenomenal qualities of these non-existent things. But what about the yellowness of a physical object, such as a banana? I want to say here that the yellowness of the banana is a certain (highly disjunctive and idiosyncratic) physical constitution that explains a certain pattern of visual discriminations on the part of a normal human percipient in normal conditions. The banana may be said to be continuously yellow, but this is not in the mathematical sense of 'continuously'. It is continuous only in the sense that a normal human percipient can not discriminate with respect to colour between nearby parts of the banana. (I hold that 'discriminate with respect to colour' can be explicated non-circularly, i.e. antecedently to the concept of colour, and that 'normal human percipient' can be explicated non-circularly too. For my more recent views on colour see Smart 1971 and the essay 'Some Criticisms of a Physicalist Theory of Colours' in the present volume. See also Lewis 1972.)

Here, I am conscious that I am up against strong intuitions that make the argument unpersuasive to some otherwise sympathetic philosophers. They find it hard to accept that these things, sense data and images, that seem to have emergent subjective properties, do not really exist.

Nevertheless, I want to say that what really exists is such a thing as the having of a yellow image, and that this is not itself something yellow. When we describe our inner experience as the having of a yellow image, we are classifying it as similar to what goes on internally when we see a banana; in general, we classify our inner experiences largely by reference to their typical causes and effects. We can also, as in the case of unusual sensations or pains, describe them by their likenesses and unlikenesses to one another. These likenesses and unlikenesses are in respect of properties that are unknown to us, but which I hold to be purely neurophysiological ones. We are able to recognize processes as like and unlike one another without much clue as to wherein these likenesses and unlikenesses consist (see my essay 'Materialism' in the present volume). The having of a yellow triangular sense datum is a brain process that is neither yellow nor triangular. This view, which I have defended on philosophical grounds, of course, fits in well with Sperry's critique of the theory of isomorphism in Sperry (1952, especially pp. 294–5).

In inner experience, we are not acquainted with the physiological nature of the brain process, that is, the having of an image of a yellow triangle, say. We do have the capacity to recognize that the internal going on that we report is in some ways like certain others, such as the having of an image of a yellow square and the having of an image of a purple square. We also recognize the inner going on in question as different from other goings on, such as the having of a pain or of a sense datum of a green leaf. There will of course be neurophysiologically-describable similarities and differences but we know them only as mere similarities and differences, except for certain abstract features, such as getting more or less intense, or being intermittent, as in the case of pains. So we do not much know in what the similarities and differences consist. Nevertheless, they are still, in fact, physical and physiological similarities. D.M. Armstrong has suggested that part of the lure of phenomenological objections to materialism may come from something akin to the illusion of the headless woman (Armstrong 1968b). The stage magician sets up the lighting and other effects so that the audience cannot see the woman's head. From not seeing the head, they get the illusion that they see that there is no head. Similarly, it is easy to go from the undoubted fact that we are unaware of the neurological nature of our inner experiences to the belief that we are aware of special non-neurological qualities of experience.

I conclude, therefore, that the emergence of consciousness is after all the weak sort of emergence, which no mechanist will deny, and which is epitomized by the properties of Sperry's rolling wheel. It is not the strong sort of emergence envisaged for example in Morgan (1927). According to the strong sort of emergence, there are new properties over and above those that are determined by the laws and boundary conditions at the lower level. The idea is that there are now holistically determined forces as well as the ordinary forces that apply at the lower level. Now, as against this, the workings of neurons and their interconnections do seem to be in principle wholly explicable in terms of the ordinary forces that we encounter in physics and chemistry. The brain looks more like a computer than it looks like a detector for novel forces. Thus, it does not seem plausible that the emergence of mind can be emergence in the strong sense.

V

I have read many of Sperry's papers and I am still unclear whether he is an emergentist in the strong sense or only in the weak sense, and so I am still unclear as to whether his position is incompatible with the mechanistic view I want to defend. Despite Sperry (1970b) I still share some of the puzzlement expressed in Bindra (1970).

Trouble about emergence may arise from false antitheses and comparisons. Thus, Freeman (1978), to which Sperry refers in Sperry (1980), quotes from W.H. Thorpe, and then goes on to say (p. 49), that '[a] neurophysiologically and philosophically sophisticated explanation was given in 1969 and 1970 in three papers by R.W. Sperry'. Now I am not sure whether Thorpe's view and Sperry's are alike. I feel more sure that Thorpe is an emergentist in the strong sense than I am that Sperry is. Thorpe says that consciousness 'can accomplish something for which a neuronal mechanism alone, however complex and elaborate, is inadequate' (Thorpe 1965, p. 53). But on the weak interpretation I take it that Sperry is saying that consciousness is a complex neurophysiological process which occurs when a neuronal mechanism is functioning in a certain way, and this is quite compatible with my mechanistic materialism. Moreover, Thorpe says, immediately before the just-quoted remark, that the fact that consciousness occurred as a result of evolution suggests that it is not an accidental by-product. This, of course, would be an argument against epiphenomenalism, but it is not an argument against materialism. As a materialist, I hold that an experience *is* a brain process, and if the capacity for certain sorts of brain processes has arisen in evolution, then so, *ipso facto*, has the capacity for consciousness. Consciousness is no accident, and being a brain process, it is a factor in the causation of actions, and so materialism also contains what is true in interactionism. It is important not to confuse materialism with epiphenomenalism on the one hand or with behaviourism on the other hand. I might add that to say that someone is an emergentist in the weak sense is to say very little. To assert emergentism in the weak sense is merely to emphasize at length what most mechanists take for granted.[1]

NOTE

1 I should like to thank D.K. Lewis and W.D. Joske for valuable comments on a draft of this paper.

REFERENCES

Armstrong, D.M. 1968a: *A Materialist Theory of the Mind*. London: Routledge and Kegan Paul.

—— 1968b: The Headless Woman Illusion and the Defence of Materialism. *Analysis*, 29, 48–9.

Berenda, C.W. 1953: On Emergence and Prediction. *Journal of Philosophy*, 50, 269–74.

Bindra, D. 1970: The Problem of Subjective Experience. *Psychological Review*, 77, 581–4.

Bunge, M. 1977: Emergence and the Mind. *Neuroscience*, 2, 501–9.

Chomsky, N. 1968: Radio Discussion with Stuart Hampshire. *The Listener*, 30 May 1968, 687–91.

Feinberg, G. 1966: Physics and the Thales Problem. *Journal of Philosophy*, 63, 5–17.

Freeman, D. 1978: Towards an Anthropology both Scientific and Humanistic. *Canberra Anthropology*, 1, 44–69.

Lewis, D. 1972: Psychophysical and Theoretical Identifications. *Australasian Journal of Philosophy*, 50, 249–58.

MacKay, D.M. 1978: Selves and Brains. *Neuroscience*, 3, 599–606.

Morgan, C.Ll. 1927: *Emergent Evolution*, 2nd edn. London: Williams and Norgate.

Nagel, E. 1961: *The Structure of Science*. New York: Harcourt Brace.

Nagel, T. 1971: Brain Bisection and Unity of Consciousness. *Synthese*, 22, 396–413.

Place, U.T. 1956: Is Consciousness a Brain Process? *British Journal of Psychology*, 17, 44–50.

Puccetti, R. 1973: Brain Bisection and Personal Identity. *British Journal for the Philosophy of Science*, 24, 339–55.

Putnam, H. 1960: Minds and Machines. In S. Hook (ed.), *Dimensions of Mind*, New York: New York University Press. Reprinted 1975 in Hilary Putnam, *Mind, Language and Reality, Philosophical Papers*, vol. 2, London: Cambridge University Press.

Sellars, W. 1963: *Science, Perception and Reality*. London: Routledge and Kegan Paul.

Smart, J.J.C. 1971: Reports of Immediate Experiences. *Synthese*, 22, 346–59.

—— 1978: The Content of Physicalism. *Philosophical Quarterly*, 28, 339–41.

Sperry, R.W. 1952: Neurology and the Mind–Brain Problem. *American Scientist*, 40, 291–312.

—— 1969: A Modified Concept of Consciousness. *Psychological Review*, 76, 532–6.

—— 1970a: Perception in the Absence of the Neocortical Commissures. In *Perception and its Disorders*, vol. 48, pp. 128–38. Association for Research in Nervous and Mental Disease.

—— 1970b: An Objective Approach to Subjective Experience: Further Explanation of an Hypothesis. *Psychological Review*, 77, 585–90.

—— 1980: Mind–Brain Interaction: Mentalism, Yes; Dualism, No. *Neuroscience*, 5, 195–206.

Thorpe, W.H. 1965: *Science, Man, and Morals*. London: Methuen.

PART 5
Ethics

21

Extreme and Restricted Utilitarianism[1]

I

Utilitarianism is the doctrine that the rightness of actions is to be judged by their consequences. What do we mean by 'actions' here? Do we mean particular actions or do we mean classes of actions? According to which way we interpret the word 'actions' we get two different theories, both of which merit the appellation 'utilitarian'.

1   If by 'actions' we mean particular individual actions we get the sort of doctrine held by Bentham, Sidgwick and Moore. According to this doctrine we test individual actions by their consequences, and general rules, like 'keep promises', are mere rules of thumb which we use only to avoid the necessity of estimating the probable consequences of our actions at every step. The rightness or wrongness of keeping a promise on a particular occasion depends only on the goodness or badness of the consequences of keeping or of breaking the promise on that particular occasion. Of course part of the consequences of breaking the promise, and a part to which we will normally ascribe decisive importance, will be the weakening of faith in the institution of promising. However, if the goodness of the consequences of breaking the rule is *in toto* greater than the goodness of the consequences of keeping it, then we must break the rule, irrespective of whether the goodness of the consequences of *everybody's* obeying the rule is or is not greater than the consequences of *everybody's* breaking it. To put it shortly, rules do not matter, save *per accidens* as rules of thumb and as *de facto* social institutions with which the utilitarian has to

reckon when estimating consequences. I shall call this doctrine
'extreme utilitarianism'.

2   A more modest form of utilitarianism has recently become
fashionable. The doctrine is to be found in Toulmin's book *The
Place of Reason in Ethics* (1950), in Nowell-Smith's *Ethics*
(1954) (though I think Nowell-Smith has qualms), in John
Austin's *Lectures on Jurisprudence* (Lecture II), and even in
J.S. Mill, if Urmson's interpretation of him is correct (1953).
Part of its charm is that it appears to resolve the dispute in
moral philosophy between intuitionists and utilitarians in a way
which is very neat. The above philosophers hold, or seem to
hold, that moral rules are more than rules of thumb. In general
the rightness of an action is *not* to be tested by evaluating its
consequences but only by considering whether or not it falls
under a certain rule. Whether the rule is to be considered an
acceptable moral rule, is, however, to be decided by considering
the consequences of adopting the rule. Broadly, then, actions
are to be tested by rules and rules by consequences. The only
cases in which we must test an individual action directly by its
consequences are (a) when the action comes under two different
rules, one of which enjoins it and one of which forbids it, and
(b) when there is no rule whatever that governs the given case. I
shall call this doctrine 'restricted utilitarianism'.

   It should be noticed that the distinction I am making cuts across, and
is quite different from, the distinction commonly made between
hedonistic and ideal utilitarianism. Bentham was an extreme hedonistic
utilitarian and Moore an extreme ideal utilitarian, and Toulmin (perhaps)
could be classified as a restricted ideal utilitarian. A hedonistic utilitarian
holds that the goodness of the consequences of an action is a function
only of their pleasurableness and an ideal utilitarian, like Moore, holds
that pleasurableness is not even a necessary condition of goodness. Mill
seems, if we are to take his remarks about higher and lower pleasures
seriously, to be neither a pure hedonistic nor a pure ideal utilitarian. He
seems to hold that pleasurableness is a necessary condition for goodness,
but that goodness is a function of other qualities of mind as well. Perhaps
we can call him a quasi-ideal utilitarian. When we say that a state of
mind is good I take it that we are expressing some sort of *rational
preference*. When we say that it is pleasurable I take it that we are saying
that it is enjoyable, and when we say that something is a higher pleasure
I take it that we are saying that it is more truly, or more deeply,
enjoyable. I am doubtful whether 'more deeply enjoyable' does not just
mean 'more enjoyable, even though not more enjoyable on a first look',

and so I am doubtful whether quasi-ideal utilitarianism, and possibly ideal utilitarianism too, would not collapse into hedonistic utilitarianism on a closer scrutiny of the logic of words like 'preference', 'pleasure', 'enjoy', 'deeply enjoy', and so on. However, it is beside the point of the present paper to go into these questions. I am here concerned only with the issue between extreme and restricted utilitarianism and am ready to concede that both forms of utilitarianism can be either hedonistic or non-hedonistic.

The issue between extreme and restricted utilitarianism can be illustrated by considering the remark 'But suppose everyone did the same' (cf. A.K. Stout 1954). Stout distinguishes two forms of the universalization principle, the causal form and the hypothetical form. To say that you ought not to do an action A because it would have bad results if everyone (or many people) did action A may be merely to point out that while the action A would otherwise be the optimific one, nevertheless when you take into account that doing A will probably cause other people to do A too, you can see that A is not, on a broad view, really optimific. If this causal influence could be avoided (as may happen in the case of a secret desert island promise) then we would disregard the universalization principle. This is the causal form of the principle. A person who accepted the universalization principle in its hypothetical form would be one who was concerned only with what would happen *if* everyone did the action A: he would be totally unconcerned with the question of whether in fact everyone would do the action A. That is, he might say that it would be wrong not to vote because it would have bad results if everyone took this attitude, and he would be totally unmoved by arguments purporting to show that my refusing to vote has no effect whatever on other people's propensity to vote. Making use of Stout's distinction, we can say that an extreme utilitarian would apply the universalization principle in the causal form, while a restricted utilitarian would apply it in the hypothetical form.

How are we to decide the issue between extreme and restricted utilitarianism? I wish to repudiate at the outset that milk and water approach which describes itself sometimes as 'investigating what is implicit in the common moral consciousness' and sometimes as 'investigating how people ordinarily talk about morality'. We have only to read newspaper correspondence to realize that the common moral consciousness is in part made up of superstitious elements, of morally bad elements, and of logically confused elements. I address myself to good hearted and benevolent people and so I hope that if we rid ourselves of the logical confusion the superstitious and morally bad elements will largely fall away. For even among good hearted and benevolent people it is possible to find superstitious and morally bad reasons for moral beliefs. These superstitious and morally bad reasons hide behind the protective screen of logical confusion. With people who are not logically confused but who are openly superstitious or morally bad I can of course do nothing. That is, our ultimate pro-attitudes may be different. Nevertheless I propose to rely on *my own* moral consciousness and to appeal to *your* moral consciousness and to forget about what people ordinarily say. 'The obligation to obey a rule', says Nowell-Smith (1954, p. 239), 'does not, *in the opinion of ordinary men*', (my italics), 'rest on the beneficial consequences of obeying it in a particular case'. What does this prove? Surely it is more than likely that ordinary men are confused here. Philosophers should be able to examine the question more rationally.

II

For an extreme utilitarian moral rules are rules of thumb. In practice the extreme utilitarian will mostly guide his conduct by appealing to the rules ('do not lie', 'do not break promises', etc.) of common-sense morality. This is not because there is anything sacrosanct in the rules themselves but because he can argue that probably he will most often act in an extreme utilitarian way if he does not think as a utilitarian. For one thing, actions have frequently to be done in a hurry. Imagine a man seeing a person drowning. He jumps in and rescues him. There is no time to reason the matter out, but usually this will be the course of action which an extreme utilitarian would recommend if he did reason the matter out. If, however, the man drowning had been drowning in a river near Berchtesgaden in 1938, and if he had had the well known black forelock and moustache of Adolf Hitler, an extreme utilitarian would, if he had time, work out the probability of the man's being the villainous dictator, and if the probability were high enough he would, on extreme utilitarian grounds, leave him to drown. The rescuer, however, has not time. He trusts to his instincts and dives in and rescues the man. And this trusting to instincts and to moral rules can be justified on extreme utilitarian grounds. Furthermore, an extreme utilitarian who knew that the drowning man was Hitler would nevertheless praise the rescuer, not condemn him. For by praising the man he is strengthening a courageous and benevolent disposition of mind, and in general this disposition has great positive utility. (Next time, perhaps, it will be Winston Churchill that the man saves!) We must never forget that an extreme utilitarian may praise actions which he knows to be wrong. Saving Hitler was wrong, but it was a member of a class of actions which are generally right, and the motive to do actions of this class is in general an optimific one. In considering questions of praise and blame it is not the expediency of the praised or blamed action that is at issue, but the expediency of the praise. It can be expedient to praise an inexpedient action and inexpedient to praise an expedient one.

Lack of time is not the only reason why an extreme utilitarian may, on extreme utilitarian principles, trust to rules of common-sense morality. He knows that in particular cases where his own interests are involved his calculations are likely to be biased in his own favour. Suppose that he is unhappily married and is deciding whether to get divorced. He will in all probability greatly exaggerate his own unhappiness (and possibly his spouse's) and greatly underestimate the harm done to their children by the break up of the family. He will probably also underestimate the likely harm done by the weakening of the general faith in marriage vows. So probably he will come to the correct extreme utilitarian conclusion if he does not in this instance think as an extreme utilitarian but trusts to common-sense morality.

There are many more and subtle points that could be made in connnection with the relation between extreme utilitarianism and the morality of common sense. All those I have just made and many more will be found in book IV, chapters 3–5 of Sidgwick's *Methods of Ethics* (1974). I think that this book is the best book ever written on ethics, and that these chapters are the best chapters of the book.[2] As they occur so near the end of a very long book they are unduly neglected. I refer the reader, then, to Sidgwick for the classical exposition of the relation between (extreme) utilitarianism and the morality of common sense. One further point raised by Sidgwick in this connection is whether an (extreme) utilitarian ought on (extreme) utilitarian principles to prop-agate (extreme) utilitarianism among the public. As most people are not very philosophical and not good at empirical calculations, it is probable that they will most often act in an extreme utilitarian way if they do not try to think as extreme utilitarians. We have seen how easy it would be to misapply the extreme utilitarian criterion in the case of divorce. Sidgwick seems to think it quite probable that an extreme utilitarian should not propagate his doctrine too widely. However, the great danger to humanity comes nowadays on the plane of public morality – not private morality. There is a greater danger to humanity from the hydrogen bomb than from an increase of the divorce rate, regrettable though that might be, and there seems no doubt that extreme utilitarianism makes for good sense in international relations. When France walked out of the United Nations because she did not wish Morocco discussed, she said that she was within her rights because Morocco and Algiers are part of her metropolitan territory and nothing to do with UN. This was clearly and a legalistic if not superstitious argument. We should not be concerned with the so-called 'rights' of France or any other country but with whether the cause of humanity would best be served by discussing Morocco in UN. (I am not saying that the answer to this is 'Yes'. There are good grounds for supporting that more harm than good would come by such a discussion.) I myself have no hesitation in saying that on extreme utilitarian principles we ought to propagate extreme utilitarianism as widely as possibe. But Sidgwick had respectable reasons for suspecting the opposite.

The extreme utilitarian, then, regards moral rules as rules of thumb and as sociological facts that have to be taken into account when deciding what to do, just as facts of any other sort have to be taken into account. But in themselves they do not justify any action.

III

The restricted utilitarian regards moral rules as more than rules of thumb for short-circuiting calculations of consequences. Generally, he argues, consequences are not relevant at all when we are deciding what to do in a particular case. In general, they are relevant only to deciding what rules are good reasons for acting in a certain way in particular cases. This doctrine is possibly a good account of how the modern unreflective twentieth century Englishman often thinks about morality, but surely it is monstrous as an account of how it is most rational to think about morality. Suppose that there is a rule R and that in 99 per cent of cases the best possible results are obtained by acting in accordance with R. Then clearly R is a useful rule of thumb; if we have not time or are not impartial enough to assess the consequences of an action it is an extremely good bet that the thing to do is to act in accordance with R. But is it not monstrous to suppose that if we *have* worked out the consequences and if we have perfect faith in the impartiality of our calculations, and if we *know* that in this instance to break R will have better results than to keep it, we should nevertheless obey the rule? Is it not to erect R into a sort of idol if we keep it when breaking it will prevent, say, some avoidable misery? Is not this a form of superstitious rule-worship (easily explicable psychologically) and not the rational thought of a philosopher?[3]

The point may be made more clearly if we consider Mill's comparison of moral rules to the tables in the nautical almanack (Mill 1910, pp. 22–3). This comparison of Mill's is adduced by Urmson as evidence that Mill was a restricted utilitarian, but I do not think that it will bear this interpretation at all. (Though I quite agree with Urmson that many other things said by Mill are in harmony with restricted rather than extreme utilitarianism. Probably Mill had never thought very much about the distinction and was arguing for utilitarianism, restricted or extreme, against other and quite non-utilitarian forms of moral argument.) Mill says: 'Nobody argues that the art of navigation is not founded on astronomy, because sailors cannot wait to calculate the Nautical Almanack. Being rational creatures, they go out upon the sea of life with their minds made up on the common questions of right and wrong, as well as on many of the far more difficult questions of wise and foolish. . . . Whatever we adopt as the fundamental principle of morality, we require subordinate principles to apply it by.' Notice that this is, as it stands, only an argument for subordinate principles as rules of thumb. The example of the nautical almanack is misleading because the information given in the almanack is in all cases the same as the information one would get if one made a long and laborious calculation from the original astronomical data on which the almanack is founded. Suppose, however, that astronomy were different. Suppose that the behaviour of the sun, moon and planets was very nearly as it is now, but that on rare occasions there were peculiar irregularities and discontinuities, so that the almanack gave us rules of the form 'in 99 per cent of cases where the observations are such and such you can deduce that your position is so and so'. Furthermore, let us suppose that there were methods which enabled us, by direct and laborious calculation from the original astronomical data, not using the rough and ready tables of the almanack, to get our correct position in 100 per cent of cases. Seafarers might use the almanack because they never had time for the long calculations and they were content with a 99 per cent chance of success in calculating their positions. Would it not be absurd, however, if they *did* make the direct calculation, and finding that it disagreed with the almanack calculation, nevertheless they ignored it and stuck to the almanack conclusion? Of course the case would be altered if there were a high enough probability of making slips in the direct calculation: then we might stick to the almanack result, liable to error though we knew it to be, simply because the direct calculation would be open to error for a different reason, the fallibility of the computer. This would be analogous to the case of the extreme utilitarian who abides by the conventional rule against the dictates of his utilitarian calculations simply because he thinks that his calculations are probably affected by personal bias. But if the navigator were sure of his direct calculations would he not be foolish to abide by his almanack? I conclude, then, that if we change our suppositions about astronomy and the almanack (to which there are no exceptions) to bring the case into line with that of morality (to whose rules there are exceptions), Mill's example loses its appearance of supporting the restricted form of utilitarianism. Let me say once more that I am not here concerned with how ordinary men think about morality but with how they ought to think. We could quite well imagine a race of sailors who acquired a superstitious reverence for their almanack, even though it was only right in 99 per cent of cases, and who indignantly threw overboard any man who mentioned the possibility of a direct calculation. But would this behaviour of the sailors be rational?

Let us consider a much discussed sort of case in which the extreme utilitarian might go against the conventional moral rule. I have promised to a friend, dying on a desert island from which I am subsequently rescued, that I will see that his fortune (over which I have control) is given to a jockey club. However, when I am rescued I decide that it would be better to give the money to a hospital, which can do more good with it. It may be argued that I am wrong to give the money to the hospital. But why?

1   The hospital can do more good with the money than the jockey club can.

2   The present case is unlike most cases of promising in that no one except me knows about the promise. In breaking the promise I am doing so with complete secrecy and am doing nothing to weaken the general faith in promises. That is, a factor, which would normally keep the extreme utilitarian from promise breaking even in otherwise unoptimific cases, does not at present operate.

3   There is no doubt a slight weakening in my own character as an habitual promise keeper, and moreover psychological tensions will be set up in me every time I am asked what the man made me promise him to do. For clearly I shall have to say that he made me promise to give the money to the hospital, and, since I am an habitual truth teller, this will go very much against the grain with me. Indeed I am pretty sure that in practice I myself would keep the promise. But we are not discussing what my moral habits would probably make me do; we are discussing what I ought to do. Moreover, we must not forget that even if it would be most rational of me to give the money to the hospital it would also be most rational of you to punish or condemn me if you did, most improbably, find out the truth (e.g. by finding a note washed ashore in a bottle). Furthermore, I would agree that although it was most rational of me to give the money to the hospital it would be most rational of you to condemn me for it. We revert again to Sidgwick's distinction between the utility of the action and the utility of the praise of it.

Many such issues are discussed by A.K. Stout in the article to which I have already referred. I do not wish to go over the same ground again, especially as I think that Stout's arguments support my own point of view. It will be useful, however, to consider one other example that he gives. Suppose that during hot weather there is an edict that no water must be used for watering gardens. I have a garden and I reason that most people are sure to obey the edict, and that as the amount of water that I use will be by itself negligible no harm will be done if I use the water secretly. So I do use the water, thus producing some lovely flowers which give happiness to various people. Still, you may say, though the action was perhaps optimific, it was unfair and wrong.

There are several matters to consider. Certainly my action should be condemned. We revert once more to Sidgwick's distinction. A right action may be rationally condemned. Furthermore, this sort of offence is normally found out. If I have a wonderful garden when everybody else's is dry and brown there is only one explanation. So if I water my garden I am weakening my respect for law and order, and as this leads to bad results an extreme utilitarian would agree that I was wrong to water the garden. Suppose now that the case is altered and that I can keep the thing secret: there is a secluded part of the garden where I grow flowers which I give away anonymously to a home for old ladies. Are you still so sure that I did the wrong thing by watering my garden? However, this is still a weaker case than that of the hospital and the jockey club. There will be tensions set up within myself: my secret knowledge that I have broken the rule will make it hard for me to exhort others to keep the rule. These psychological ill effects in myself may be not inconsiderable: directly and indirectly they may lead to harm which is at least of the same order as the happiness that the old ladies get from the flowers. You can see that on an extreme utilitarian view there are two sides to the question.

So far I have been considering the duty of an extreme utilitarian in a predominantly non-utilitarian society. The case is altered if we consider the extreme utilitarian who lives in a society every member, or most members, of which can be expected to reason as he does. Should he water his flowers now? (Granting, what is doubtful, that in the case already considered he would have been right to water his flowers.) As a first approximation, the answer is that he should not do so. For since the situation is a completely symmetrical one, what is rational for him is rational for others. Hence, by a *reductio ad absurdum* argument, it would seem that watering his garden would be rational for none. Nevertheless, a more refined analysis shows that the above argument is not quite correct, though it is correct enough for practical purposes. The argument considers each person as confronted with the choice either of watering his garden or of not watering it. However, there is a third possibility, which is that each person should, with the aid of a suitable randomizing device, such as throwing dice, give himself a certain probability of watering his garden. This would be to adopt what in the theory of games is called 'a mixed strategy'. If we could give numerical values to the private benefit of garden watering and to the public harm done by 1, 2, 3, etc., persons using the water in this way, we could work out a value of the probability of watering his garden that each extreme utilitarian should give himself. Let a be the value which each extreme utilitarian gets from watering his garden, and let $f(1)$, $f(2)$, $f(3)$, etc., be the public harm done by exactly 1, 2, 3, etc., persons respectively watering their gardens. Suppose that p is the probability that each person gives himself of watering his garden. Then we can easily calculate, as functions of p, the probabilities that exactly 1, 2, 3, etc., persons will water their gardens. Let these probabilities be $p_1, p_2, \ldots, p_n$. Then the total net probable benefit can be expressed as

$$V = p_1 \left[a - f(1) \right] + p_2 \left[2a - f(2) \right] + \ldots \quad p_n \left[na - f(n) \right]$$

Then if we know the function $f(x)$ we can calculate the value of p for which $(dV/dp) = 0$. This gives the value of p which it would be rational for each extreme utilitarian to adopt. The present argument does not of course depend on a perhaps unjustified assumption that the values in question are measurable, and in a practical case such as that of the garden watering we can doubtless assume that p will be so small that we can take it near enough as equal to zero. However, the argument is of interest for the theoretical underpinning of extreme utilitarianism, since the possibility of a mixed strategy is usually neglected by critics of utilitarianism, who wrongly assume that the only relevant and symmetrical alternatives are of the form 'everybody does X' and 'nobody does X'.

I now pass on to a type of case which may be thought to be the trump card of restricted utilitarianism. Consider the rule of the road. It may be said that since all that matters is that everyone should do the same it is indifferent which rule we have, 'go on the left-hand side' or 'go on the right-hand side'. Hence the only *reason* for going on the left-hand side in British countries is that this is the rule. Here the rule does seem to be a reason, in itself, for acting in a certain way. I wish to argue against this. The rule in itself is not a reason for our actions. We would be perfectly justified in going on the right-hand side if (a) we knew that the rule was to go on the left-hand side, and (b) we were in a country peopled by super-anarchists who always on principle did the opposite of what they were told. This shows that the rule does not give us a reason for acting so much as an indication of the probable actions of others, which helps us to find out what would be our own most rational course of action. If we are in a country not peopled by anarchists, but by non-anarchist extreme utilitarians, we expect, other things being equal, that they will keep rules laid down for them. Knowledge of the rule enables us to predict their behaviour and to harmonize our own actions with theirs. The rule 'keep to the left-hand side', then, is not a logical *reason* for action but an anthropological *datum* for planning actions.

I conclude that in every case if there is a rule R the keeping of which is in general optimific, but such that in a special sort of circumstances the optimific behaviour is to break R, then in these circumstances we should break R. Of course we must consider all the less obvious effects of breaking R, such as reducing people's faith in the moral order, before coming to the conclusion that to break R is right: in fact we shall rarely come to such a conclusion. Moral rules, on the extreme utilitarian view, are rules of thumb only, but they are not bad rules of thumb. But if we *do* come to the conclusion that we should break the rule and if we have weighed in the balance our own fallibility and liability to personal bias, what good reason remains for keeping the rule? I can understand 'it is optimific' as a reason for action, but why should 'it is a member of a class of actions which are usually optimific' or 'it is a member of a class of actions which as a class are more optimific than any alternative general class' be a good reason? You might as well say that a person ought to be picked to play for Australia just because all his brothers have been, or that the Australian team should be composed entirely of the Harvey family because this would be better than composing it entirely of any other family. The extreme utilitarian does not appeal to artificial feelings, but only to our feelings of benevolence, and what better feelings can there be to appeal to? Admittedly we can have a pro-attitude to anything, even to rules, but such artificially begotten pro-attitudes smack of superstition. Let us get down to realities, human happiness and misery, and make these the objects of our pro-attitudes and anti-attitudes.

The restricted utilitarian might say that he is talking only of *morality*, not of such things as rules of the road. I am not sure how far this objection, if valid, would affect my argument, but in any case I would reply that as a philosopher I conceive of ethics as the study of how it would be *most rational* to act. If my opponent wishes to restrict the word 'morality' to a narrower use he can have the word. The fundamental question is the question of rationality of action *in general*. Similarly if the resricted utilitarian were to appeal to ordinary usage and say 'it might be most rational to leave Hitler to drown but it would surely not be *wrong* to rescue him', I should again let him have the words 'right' and 'wrong' and should stick to 'rational' and 'irrational'. We already saw that it would be rational to praise Hitler's rescuer, even though it would have been most rational not to have rescued Hitler. In ordinary language, no doubt, 'right' and 'wrong' have not only the meaning 'most rational to do' and 'not most rational to do' but also have the meaning 'praiseworthy' and 'not praiseworthy'. Usually to the utility of an action corresponds utility of praise of it, but as we saw, this is not always so. Moral language could thus do with tidying up, for example by reserving 'right' for 'most rational' and 'good' as en epithet of praise for the motive from which the action sprang. It would be more becoming in a philosopher to try to iron out illogicalities in moral language and to make suggestions for its reform than to use it as a court of appeal whereby to perpetuate confusions.

One last defence of restricted utilitarianism might be as follows. 'Act optimifically' might be regarded as itself one of the rules of our system (though it would be odd to say that this rule was justified by its optimificality). According to Toulmin (1950, pp. 146–8) if 'keep promises', say, conflicts with another rule we are allowed to argue the case on its merits, as if we were extreme utilitarians. If 'act optimifically' is itself one of our rules then there will always be a conflict of rules whenever to keep a rule is not itself optimific. If this is so, restricted utilitarianism collapses into extreme utilitarianism. And no one could read Toulmin's book or Urmson's article on Mill without thinking that Toulmin and Urmson are of the opinion that they have thought of a doctrine which does *not* collapse into extreme utilitarianism, but which is, on the contrary, an improvement on it.

NOTES

1 Based on a paper read to the Victorian Branch of the Australasian Association of Psychology and Philosophy, October 1955. The present essay is as it was reprinted with amendments in Foot (1967). The original version contained some very bad mistakes.

2 Here I was surely echoing C.D. Broad (1930, p. 143) where Broad says 'Sidgwick's *Methods of Ethics* seems to me to be on the whole the best treatise on moral theory that has ever been written, and to be one of the English philosophical classics'.

3 As I discovered long after the publication of the present paper, similar accusations of rule worship were put as objections to Paley's form of rule utilitarianism. They were put into the mouth of a 'sophistical' utilitarian opponent by the eighteenth and early nineteenth century moralist Thomas Green. Green's intention was to produce a *reductio ad absurdum* of utilitarianism (see Green 1972, p. 201).

REFERENCES

Austin, John 1885: *Lectures on Jurisprudence*, 5th edn, edited by Robert Campbell. London: John Murray.

Broad, C.D. 1930: *Five Types of Ethical Theory*. Kegan Paul, Trench, Trubner.

Foot, Philippa 1967: *Theories of Ethics*. Oxford: Oxford University Press, 171–83.

Green, Thomas 1972: An Examination of the Leading Principle in the New System of Morals. In D.H. Monro, *A Guide to the British Moralists*, London: Fontana, 198–203.

Mill, John Stuart 1910: *Utilitarianism*. London: Everyman.

Nowell-Smith, P.H. 1954: *Ethics*. London: Penguin.

Sidgwick, H. 1907: *Methods of Ethics*. London: Macmillan.

Stout, A.K. 1954: But Suppose Everyone did the Same. *Australasian Journal of Philosophy*, 32, 1–29.

Toulmin, S.E. 1950: *The Place of Reason in Ethics*. London: Cambridge University Press.

Urmson, J.O. 1953: The Interpretation of the Moral Philosophy of J.S. Mill. *Philosophical Quarterly*, 3, 33–9.

22

Benevolence as an Over-Riding Attitude

I wish to make use of a theory of over-riding desires which has been put forward by D.H. Monro (1967, chapter 17) in order to deal with two sorts of difficulties which beset utilitarianism.[1] The first problem arises from the fact that a great deal of human happiness comes from our engagement in activities and projects which are not directly aimed at happiness, whether our own happiness or the happiness of others. Must a utilitarian be in some sense schizophrenic if he engages in such activities and projects (see Stocker 1976)? The second problem arises from the fact that a utilitarian who had a conventional moral upbringing will inevitably feel repugnance against certain acts which might be enjoined on him by his utilitarian principles. If he is a non-cognitivist in meta-ethics he will hold that his utilitarianism is an expression of his feelings, but then do not these feelings of repugnance betray him and show him not to be really a utilitarian after all? I think that the first problem is easier to deal with than the second problem is, but I hope that at least some readers may be convinced on both counts.

As Bernard Williams has pointed out (Smart and Williams 1973, p. 110), the utilitarian has a general project of maximizing the general good, but the general good will come from the satisfaction which people get from carrying out lower order projects in which there is no thought of the general good. As Williams says, 'Unless there were first-order projects, the general utilitarian project would have nothing to work on, and would be vacuous'. Sometimes of course we act from habit, and without taking thought or coming to a decision. Such habitual action does not occur as a result of deliberation of a utilitarian sort; nor does it come as a matter of deliberation of any other sort. What can come about as a result of utilitarian deliberation is a decision to school oneself in a particular habit of unreflective action or to try to inhibit such a habit.

Since I hold that utilitarianism is an ethical theory of how one ought to make decisions when one deliberates, it does not apply directly to spontaneous or merely habitual actions.

Sometimes, however, we do deliberate about certain projects and yet if we did deliberate in a utilitarian way we should get less value from these projects. Similarly the utilitarian must envisage other people, even if they are utilitarians too, deliberating in a non-utilitarian way on many sorts of occasions. Does this lead to an inconsistency, or perhaps what Michael Stocker has called a 'schizophrenia' (Stocker 1976), in utilitarianism itself?

Suppose that a man displays affection to his wife or visits a dear friend, who is perhaps terminally ill in hospital. Certainly Stocker is right in thinking that the wife or the friend would be upset if she or he thought that the display of affection or the visit came about as a result of a calculation of what would maximize the general good. It would not then be a spontaneous expression of love or friendship. We naturally appreciate friendship towards us if we know that it is spontaneous, because it comes without effort and strain on the part of others, and we feel at ease. There are the best of utilitarian reasons for encouraging spontaneity. Our ordinary motives of affection for our friends or for those we love, and to a lesser extent even for those with whom we strike up a casual or transitory relationship, are stronger in the short term than is the utilitarian motive of generalized benevolence, so that there are good utilitarian reasons for discouraging a too calculating bent of mind. This is not rule utilitarianism, however, because if we do calculate and the calculation goes against particular feelings of affection, then we as utilitarians know that we should follow the calculation: whether in an actual case we could in fact bring ourselves to do so is another matter. A utilitarian will indeed make many conscious decisions simply in order to promote whatever things his feelings of love and friendship make him desire. However, love and friendship are rather deep things which I do not like talking about too much in a philosophical context, for fear of trivializing them, and so let me illustrate the point at issue by a more light-hearted example drawn from the hockey field.

Consider a certain occasion on which I scored a goal from a short corner, a feat which even in my even then rather elderly condition could give me considerable pleasure. The rather lowly La Trobe University team for which I was then playing was not well drilled in hand-stopping for corner hits, and so I decided to stop the ball on my stick. I also decided to concentrate my mind entirely on stopping the ball dead (as is required by the rules of hockey as they apply to corner hits) and to allow the actual hitting of the ball at the goal to proceed without thought and according to my in-built hockey habits. Well, with a bit of luck everything went right and the ball did go into the goal as I had planned that it should. But did my planning do anything to maximize the general good? It is true that the goal caused pleasure both to myself and to the other members of my team, but then it also presumably caused annoyance to the members of the opposing team. Certainly when I deliberated about the best way of taking the corner hit I was not deliberating about the general good. No doubt if I had deliberated about how to maximize the general good I should not have been so successful and I should not have enjoyed the game so much.

Consider another case. Suppose that I am asked by the philosophy department of another university (Monash University, for example) to give a paper, preferably on a certain topic. I may decide that the topic is one on which I might like to write a paper, and I accept both the invitation and the suggested topic. I do this because I want to see my friends at that university and to discuss a philosophical topic with them, and I believe that a paper on the suggested topic would please them most. I certainly do not go into difficult utilitarian calculations as to whether this decision (as opposed to some other which I might make) will maximize the good of all sentient beings. And if I did go into such a calculation it would surely do more harm than good, by spoiling the spontaneity and hence the pleasure of my philosophical life and thereby impoverishing my work and hence making it less useful.

I used to justify specific moral rules as 'rules of thumb' of which even an act utilitarian should make use when he has no time to deliberate or when it is best to act spontaneously. Since act utilitarianism is a proposal as to how we should deliberate, when we do deliberate, it does not apply to habitual or spontaneous action, though it does apply to deliberation about whether we should try to school ourselves into (or out of) certain habits and spontaneous tendencies. It now seems to me that this exception of habitual action needs to be extended to certain deliberate actions too, such as occur in the hockey case and the Monash case. Many of an act utilitarian's deliberations will not be utilitarian deliberations. The problem is whether this shows that the supposed utilitarian is not really a utilitarian after all.

I suggest that these cases can be accommodated by D.H. Monro's distinction between over-riding and non-over-riding desires. Monro illustrates the disinction by means of the following example (Monro 1967, p. 212). He goes into a shop in order to buy a pair shoes. His feet are (we are led to suppose) of an unusual shape and it is very hard for him to find a pair of shoes which fit him properly and which will not cause discomfort or harm to his feet later. He has to put up with the tiresome assurances of shop assistants that unsuitable shoes will soon stretch so as to fit him. He has been to several shops already and is getting tired, and though he knows that he ought to go on to other shops until he finds the right pair of shoes, he weakly gives in to the latest shop assistant. Later on he feels his shoes pinching and regrets his decision. Now someone might say that what Monro had wanted most was not to get the right pair of shoes, but was to finish his exhausting and irritating search from shop to shop. The reason for saying this would be that the desire to finish the search was the one which had issued in action. There is, however, as Monro points out, a sense in which getting the right pair of shoes was what he most wanted. The desire to get the right pair of shoes was a more permanent desire, which stands up on reflection, and it may perhaps lead him eventually to school himself out of the more temporary and less reflective desires. In this way we can conceive of a hierarchy of desires. According to this idea, desires higher in the hierarchy strengthen or inhibit desires lower in the hierarchy. Of course there also can be a different sort of conflict between desires, when two relatively temporary and unreflective desires on the same level of the hierarchy oppose one another, but this is not the sort of conflict between desires which is exemplified by Monro's example.

Now I want to say that Monro's idea of a hierarchy of desires explains how a utilitarian may consistently behave as in my examples of planning to score a goal at hockey and of deciding to visit the Monash philosophers. Even so strong an opponent of utilitarianism as Bernard Williams seems to be in agreement that this sort of way out can be taken with very many of our projects. However, he rejects the idea that we can take this way out in the case of all of them, because some of them are connected with deep commitments (Smart and Williams 1973, pp. 113–16). These commitments are seen by the agent as central to his life and the satisfaction of these commitments is seen by him as worth while in some absolute sense: they are not mere satisfactions which can be equated with the satisfactions which he or anyone else might desire from some other project to which he is not committed and around which he has not structured his life. Williams asks how a man can reasonably be asked to dispense with the pursuit of a project to which he is strongly committed, 'just because someone else's projects have so structured the causal scene that this is how the utilitarian sum comes out' (Smart and Williams 1973, p. 116). Such a man is envisaged as not being a utilitarian: he will not be prepared to look at at the sacrifice of a commitment as merely something very disagreeable to him, and of course, as Williams says, if he were prepared to look at it in this way the argument would be pretty well over. But of course a *utilitarian*, if he really *is* a utilitarian and has the one over-riding commitment, namely that to utilitarianism, surely *will* look at it in this way. Perhaps in practice he may put his interest in some cause before the general happiness, but if so in a cool hour and on reflection he will think that this is a piece of backsliding, or even self-indulgence. Moreover it may be right, on utilitarian grounds, to leave some tribe or sect to their tribal or sectarian beliefs and commitments, because the disutility of disorienting them would outweigh the advantages of trying to make them more like utilitarians. The same thing also applies to all sorts of individuals who are wrapped up in scientific, artistic, political or sporting commitments, to name only a few. But of course in a completely utilitarian society it would not be quite like this, because however distressing it might be for an individual to give up his commitment, he would not regard such a commitment (other than that to utilitarianism itself) as an ultimately over-riding one.

Some philosophers may object that the example of the search for well-fitting shoes is misleading because it is not an example of a *moral* decision. In reply to this several points can be made.

1 As a utilitarian I do not draw a line between moral and non-moral decisions in the way in which certain other sorts of moral philosophers do. Since any decision, however small, has either positive, negative or zero effect on the general welfare, it has its place in utilitarian morality.

2 The example was produced in order to show how there can be lower order and higher order desires. The desire to get well-fitting shoes does not have to be an expression of an ultimate moral principle in order for the example to do this elucidatory job.

3 According to Monro we do sometimes describe considerations as 'moral' if they are regarded as over-riding by the community in general, but we may also describe our own attitude as 'moral' if it is our own over-riding attitude. Monro's desire for foot comfort is over-riding relative to his desire to finish shopping. However, it is not *very* high in the 'moral peck order' (Monro 1967, p. 228) and this may explain why it is a bit odd to call it a 'moral' attitude.

The utilitarian's desire to maximize the general good is the highest order attitude, and regulates all other attitudes in the way in which the desire for foot comfort regulates the desire to finish shopping. At least this is so if the utilitarian really is a utilitarian and does not just say that he is one. I am of course using 'regulate' here as a 'try' word not as a 'success' word, because, as the example shows, there can be backsliding.

I hope therefore that many readers, at least, may agree that the first problem which I described at the beginning of this article can be solved by means of a theory of over-riding desires. I now pass on to the more difficult matter of the second problem. Suppose that I, as a utilitarian, find myself in a situation in which I discover that I ought to do something which is revolting according to the standards of the traditional non-utilitarian morality in which I have been brought up. I may have to kill a prisoner in order to save many other prisoners, as in Bernard Williams' case of Jim, the police captain and Pedro (Smart and Williams 1973, p. 98ff.), or worse still I may have to convict an innocent man, as in McCloskey's case of the sheriff (McCloskey 1957, pp. 48–9). It is obvious that I would feel great distress and I might very likely be unable to bring myself to do the act which according to my utilitarian calculations was the one which I ought to do. I will have strong feelings against doing the utilitarian act which will arise as a result of my non-utilitarian moral upbringing. Perhaps these feelings have to be set against my utilitarian feeling of generalized benevolence, my utilitarian desire to maximize the general good, so that some sort of balancing out of these feelings must occur before I choose my course of action. But then if this is so, it would seem that I am not really a utilitarian after all. My non-utilitarian moral feelings would oppose my utilitarian feeling of generalized benevolence rather in the way in which, as Sir David Ross supposed, cognitive intuitions about some *prima facie* duties would have to be balanced against cognitive intuitions about other *prima facie* duties. Is it therefore possible for a person with a normal moral upbringing ever *really* to become a utilitarian? (Short of complete brainwashing at least.)

I tried to deal with this problem in an article 'The Methods of Ethics and the Methods of Science' (Smart 1965). There of course need be no such problem for a utilitarian who has a cognitivist meta-ethics, as Sidgwick had. He could simply say that his moral qualms about doing the utilitarian act were mere feelings, whereas he has a *cognition* of the truth of the utilitarian principle itself. This sort of reply is not open to me, because I wish to advocate utilitarianism, if I can, within the context of a non-cognitivist meta-ethics, according to which it is one's feelings which determine our ethical principles. It would seem to follow that since I have non-utilitarian feelings I must have non-utilitarian principles.

In the afore-mentioned article I suggested that moral philosophers have been misled by a false analogy with science: they have held that just as scientists test their theories by observations, so in morality we should test our general principles by our feelings in particular cases (though cognitivists might call them 'intuitions'). Fortunately most of these tests are by reference to envisaged rather than actual situations. I should like to think that distressing cases like that of Jim and that of the sheriff would hardly ever arise in real life. Against this methodology I suggested that in ethics it is the other way round, so that our particular feelings should be tested by our more general ones. In his study and in a cool hour the utilitarian will feel that his general principle of utility is the only one which matters because the adoption of any other principle will sometimes lead to avoidable misery or to a reduction of total happiness. In particular, if Jim or the sheriff does not do the utilitarian act there will be people killed who would not otherwise be killed. What about the unhappiness of their wives and children? Thus any ethics which conflicts in this way with the utilitarian one can seem to be cruel or inhumane. I suggested therefore that it is possible that there is no one ethical system which can appeal to all sides of our nature and suit all our moods. Perhaps I can contain within myself two or more different and inconsistent ethical systems. Considering the variety of one's moral upbringing this is only too likely.

Perhaps this shows that the utilitarian, and not only the utilitarian but other ethical theorists too, will be likely to lack 'integrity', in something like Bernard Williams' sense, if this implies 'having a harmonious and unified system of attitudes', or to suffer from a sort of 'schizophrenia' which Michael Stocker (1976) has suggested is endemic to modern ethical theories. However, Williams' notion of integrity contains elements other than the idea of inner disharmony. One of Williams' worries about Jim's situation is that Jim has been placed in an intolerable moral position through no fault of his own, and so Jim is concerned to distinguish between his own responsibility and the police captain's responsibility. As a utilitarian I ask merely what this has to do with the price of fish. As a utilitarian I wish to distinguish sharply between questions of rightness on the one hand, and questions of responsibility and of evaluation of motives on the other hand. Stocker's arguments for the schizophrenia of modern ethical theories turn on the tendency of these theories to distinguish these two sorts of things. He argues persuasively that our ordinary moral concepts do not separate them (Stocker 1973–4), but from my point of view this is a deficiency of our common moral thinking, and Sidgwick and others have done a service to ethics by making the distinction. I hope that the theory of morality as an over-riding attitude will show how one can consistently engage in activities which are not morally motivated. These are just hints of my attitude to Stocker's very interesting point of view, the critique of which would demand a separate article.

From the utilitarian point of view Williams' insistence on the preservation of one's integrity can seem to be an egotistical one.[2] Williams' concept of integrity seems to me to be obscure, and it is not my purpose in this paper to argue against Williams and to meet him on his own ground. I suspect that I would have nothing much to add to John Harris' illuminating article 'Williams on Negative Responsibility and Integrity' (Harris 1974). I do not myself feel that it is a fault on the part of utilitarianism that it cannot accommodate the notion of integrity. Why should I as a utilitarian have an obligation to accommodate an obscure notion whose natural home is in a very different type of ethical theory? We have something like the clash of theories which occurs in science: it would not do for a Newtonian to object to the theory of relativity that it cannot accommodate the concept of absolute simultaneity.

Nevertheless I do as a utilitarian feel obliged to solve a problem, the second of those which I have been discussing, which has to do with a concept of integrity which is something *like* Williams', but which is simpler than his, and is one to which I alluded a couple of paragraphs back. The suggestion of my paper of 1965 was that there may be no possible ethical system which could appeal to all sides of my nature. When I contemplate the case of Jim or the sheriff, I find myself giving expression to feelings which arise from my moral upbringing and which conflict with utilitarianism. Thus in some moods I am not a utilitarian, but in other moods, when I think more abstractly, I reflect that any other ethics must prescribe acts which lead to avoidable misery or which fail to allow us to attain so much total happiness. The conclusion may seem to be that in some moods I am a utilitarian and in some moods I am not one. This is unsatisfactory, and I think that Monro's theory of morality as over-riding may enable me to say something better.

Suppose that I were placed in Jim's position. If it were the case that my repugnance was not an over-riding attitude, then the fact that I might not be able to shoot the prisoner would not show that I was not a utilitarian. If I thought that I would be likely to find myself in such cases as that of Jim I might try to inhibit such repugnance, but as I do not think that this *is* likely, thank goodness, I find this repugnance a useful attitude, likely in practice to reinforce rather than inhibit my tendency to do utilitarian acts. However, in the case of Jim or of the sheriff the failure to do the utilitarian act would be a piece of back-sliding. There could be back-sliding in the hockey case and the Monash case too, though of a less distressing sort. I play hockey both because I enjoy it and for the sake of my team, but these motives may need on rare occasions to be inhibited by my over-riding utilitarian attitude. I do not think as a utilitarian while playing hockey or while deciding to read a paper at Monash, but if I am a good utilitarian the utilitarian principle will always be at the back of my mind. Of course it will not be all the time *consciously* in my mind; I do not mean that I will be all the time anxiously vigilant lest I infringe utilitarian principles. Such extreme vigilance would be distracting and counter-productive. However, if in some strange case a utilitarian thought that the general happiness would be promoted by his failing to score a goal, then if he were a good utilitarian (I fear that I myself would probably succumb to temptation!) he would dliberately miss his shot. Similarly if he worked out that going to Monash would do harm or would do less good than something else which he might do, as is perhaps a little less unlikely than the analogous thing in the hockey example, then if he were a good utilitarian he would not go to Monash, unless, as is likely, he succumbed to temptation. Thus his general adherence to the tactics of hockey or of academic etiquette do not make him a rule utilitarian. Suppose that the hockey player lets his team down for utilitarian reasons, perhaps in order to save someone in the opposing team from going mad. (It is hard to think of a convincing example.) Then he loses his integrity as a hockey player, though perhaps this is a sacrifice which he ought to make. A more serious example of sacrifice of integrity comes from Williams' example of George, who considers taking a job in a laboratory for research into chemical and biological warfare. George does so for the sake of his family, and because he knows that if he does not take the job a more efficient scientist will engage in the sinister activities. Perhaps if George takes the job he loses his integrity as a pacific person and as a chemist, but from the point of view of the utilitarian this is just a sacrifice which he must make. Contrary to Williams, therefore, I do not perceive any very great ethical problem in the case of George, though I suspect that I would hate to find myself in George's position almost as much as I would hate to find myself in Jim's.

I hope therefore that Monro's notion of moral attitudes as over-riding ones enables me to deal with the second problem which I distinguished at the beginning of this paper, as well as with the first one. The first problem arose merely from the fact that people enjoy activities, such as playing hockey, precisely because they play with the object of winning, and so on, and not with the notion of maximizing the general good. The second question is more difficult, because as Peter Singer has pointed out to me, the analogy with Monro's example of buying shoes is not so close. If Monro does not give in to his higher order desire for foot comfort he will not afterwards regret his tedious shopping, but if Jim shoots the prisoner will he not afterwards regret doing so? It might be held, therefore, that Jim's desire to avoid shooting the prisoner and his desire to save the other prisoners are simply opposing desires on the same level. What is the behavioural evidence which would enable me to say that Jim's utilitarian desire might be the over-riding one, even though he was in fact motivated by his desire not to shoot the prisoner? For example, Jim will not be likely to inhibit his desire not to shoot an innocent man. After all he is unlikely (let us say) to visit that South American town again and a dislike of shooting people is a desire which on utilitarian grounds it is normally useful to foster, not to inhibit. I think that the evidence for the utilitarian desire being over-riding here would be in the reasons Jim will give himself for not inhibiting the desire not to shoot prisoners. These may be utilitarian reasons. Still, the question is not an easy one, and that is why I am less confident of having satisfactorily solved the second problem than I am of having solved the first one.

It is worth adding that modifications of utilitarianism, for example changing the principle from maximization of happiness to the maximization of some sort of a trade off between happiness and equal distribution (an ethical system which D.H. Monro has told me that he is inclined to accept), would not alter the situation as far as the concerns of this paper are concerned. There would still be hard cases like those of Jim, of George and of the sheriff.

In conclusion, I must put in a not too apologetic apology for the triviality of my own examples, such as the hockey one. I find that anti-utilitarians tend to be very high minded, angry and moralistic when they write against utilitarianism. I think that I used to be just as irritating from my side of the fence (accusations of superstition, rule worship, and so on). So though I have had to consider the distressing examples due to Williams and McCloskey, my own examples have been relatively trivial ones, my hope being that this might help to cool the climate of the discussion. Readers can easily make up more exciting examples if they want to, even though I think that my examples are perfectly adequate to illustrate the conceptual points which I need to make.

NOTES

1 I am grateful to Stanley Benn, D.H. Monro, Peter Singer and Frank Snare for commenting on an earlier draft of this article.
2 See the rather tart footnote on p. 120 of R.M. Hare (1976).

REFERENCES

Hare, R.M. 1976: Ethical Theory and Utilitarianism. In H.D. Lewis (ed.), *Contemporary British Philosophy*, 4th series, 113–31.
Harris, John 1974: Williams on Negative Responsibility and Integrity. *Philosophical Quarterly*, 24, 265–73.
McCloskey, H.J. 1957: An Examination of Restricted Utilitarianism. *Philosophical Review*, 66, 466–85.
Monro, D.H. 1967: *Empiricism and Ethics*. London: Cambridge University Press.
Smart, J.J.C. 1965: The Methods of Ethics and the Methods of Science. *Journal of Philosophy*, 62, 344–9.

—— and Williams, Bernard 1973: *Utilitarianism, For and Against.* London: Cambridge University Press.

Stocker, Michael 1973–4: Act and Agent Evaluations. *Review of Metaphysics*, 27, 42–61.

—— 1976: The Schizophrenia of Modern Ethical Theories. *Journal of Philosophy*, 73, 453–66.

23

Utilitarianism and Generalized Benevolence

In the past I have been concerned to advocate a normative utilitarian theory from the point of view of a non-cognitivist meta-ethics (Smart and Williams 1973). I assumed that Hume was right in thinking that ultimately morality depends on how we *feel* about things. In advocating utilitarianism to a group of people I therefore had to express my feelings and appeal to *their* feelings. I described the feelings to which I wished to appeal as 'generalized benevolence'. I described generalized benevolence as a desire for the happiness, or at any rate in some sense the good, of all mankind, or perhaps of all sentient beings. I now think that the 'perhaps of all sentient beings' should be much more uncompromising. It is a merit of utilitarianism, with its stress on happiness and unhappiness, that lower animals must be considered along with human beings, so that they are not debarred from full or direct consideration because they are not 'rational'. Utilitarians will of course be equally mindful of the higher animals, some of which, such as whales and dolphins, for all we know may be about as rational as we are, and also of course of any creatures which are higher and more rational than we are and which we may conjecture exist in outer space, and, we may hope, in future times here on earth.

Generalized benevolence must be distinguished from altruism. Not only is it a cosmically extensive desire for the good of others, but it also includes a desire for one's own good. However, in so doing it does not give one's own good any favoured position: if I am acting from generalized benevolence I treat my own happiness quite equally with that of Tom, Dick or Harry, or for that matter Moby Dick or even the kangaroo in the paddock. (Bearing in mind of course that Moby Dick may have a capacity for suffering which is equal to mine and the kangaroo in the paddock possibly a rather diminished capacity.) We must inquire later whether I was right in assuming that we *do* have such a sentiment of generalized benevolence, but let us for the moment take it that we do.

We also undoubtedly have a partiality for our *own* happiness: the disposition which Bishop Butler called 'Self-Love'. Besides Self-Love and Benevolence, as Butler emphasized, we also have all sorts of 'particular passions', which are directed to particular objects, or sorts of objects, and are not directed to the happiness or good either of ourselves or others. These particular passions provide the raw material for benevolence and self-love, in so far as the major part of our happiness comes from the satisfaction of the particular passions and from engaging in projects which arise from them, but they also, as in the case of Rashdall's 'average wife-beating ruffian', can lead us away both from our own happiness and from the happiness of other people (Rashdall 1907, vol. 1, p. 13). The utilitarian may well calculate in order to gratify a particular passion. For example, the captain of a football team who is scheming to defeat his opponent, he will not normally worry about whether in so scheming he will maximize the total happiness. (After all the opponents may be more upset at losing than his own team may be happy at winning.) The utilitarian knows that the way to enjoy football is not to engage in utilitarian calculations. His benevolence will act as what D.H. Monro (1967, chapter 17) has called an 'over-riding' attitude, and he will use it to inculcate in himself certain lower order attitudes. This is not inconsistent with act utilitarianism. For example if the footballer did happen to calculate consequences and he came to the conclusion that there would be a net total misery if he *did* defeat his opponents, he might decide to play less wholeheartedly. (Nevertheless self-love might well induce him to behave in a non-utilitarian manner, and so might his ingrained footballing habits!)[1]

My idea was that in asserting the utilitarian principle I would be expressing my own sentiment of generalized benevolence and would be appealing to the sentiment of generalized benevolence in those persons to whom I was addressing myself. I thought that though both I myself and my audience would also be motivated both by self-love and by many sorts of particular passions (to continue using Bishop Butler's terminology), in an inter-personal discussion these would largely cancel out, so that there would be general agreement on the act utilitarian principle. Of course people are not in fact actuated only by self-love and those desires which Butler would call 'particular passions', as well as by benevolence. They are also actuated by the desire to obey certain specific moral rules which had been inculcated in them since childhood. Butler of course ascribed such desires to a faculty superior to both Self-Love and Benevolence, which he called 'Conscience'. From my point of view they should be counted among the particular passions. I rather optimistically thought that philosophical clarification could cause the lure of these particular moral rules to fade away. Of course the act utilitarian would continue to use such rules as rules of thumb. I myself find that I am rather an obsessive rule obeyer, to an extent which probably cannot be justified by my utilitarianism, though my obsessiveness in this regard surely falls short of that of G.E. Moore (1903, p. 162). It seemed to me that if I were talking to benevolent people, they would at once become attracted to utilitarianism provided that (a) they could see that any rules other than the utilitarian one will lead to a less good result than will the rule 'maximizing the probable benefit', and (b) traditional morality was seen to be superstitious 'rule worship', arising perhaps from the origin of morality in magic, religion and other not very rational institutions. Such practices as those of promising and promise keeping seemed to me to smack of arbitrariness and convention. A benevolent person, I thought, would want to keep a promise on a particular occasion only if (as is indeed usually the case) the probable good effects of doing so outweighed those of any alternative action.

In this I am sure that I had Hume's distinction between the natural virtues and the artificial virtues at the back of my mind. (Very much at the *back* of my mind, because Hume's distinction is between those virtues which depend on convention and those which don't, whereas mine is somewhat different, between those which are innate and those which are learned. However, the artificial virtues in Hume's sense must also be those which are artificial in mine.) There seemed to me to be something very artificial about the deontologist's virtues: the rule of promise-keeping certainly seems to be born of human convention (even though perhaps dolphins and certain extra-terrestrial beings could have such conventions too). Thus the virtue of benevolence seemed to me to be 'natural', whereas those connected with justice seemed to be 'artificial'. In this I was certainly wrong. A person who prizes equal distribution of good as well as the maximization of total good is surely concerned with something quite non-conventional. We need conventions to have promising, but we do not need conventions to engage in the practice of equalizing distribution. I came to realize that there are alternatives to utilitarianism which are equally free of convention, of 'rule worship', and of superstition.

In any case if I was preferring benevolence to justice because benevolence was 'natural' and justice was 'artificial', was I not setting up an end ('naturalness') to which the utilitarian end (happiness or whatever) was merely subordinate? And if not was I not committing the naturalistic fallacy in deducing an 'ought' from an 'is'? Furthermore it is not even clear in what sense generalized benevolence is natural.

Perhaps it might be said that generalized benevolence is natural because it is an inherited trait, selected out by the evolutionary process. But this is surely false. There might be selection for a *limited* benevolence, but it is unlikely that there could be selection for *generalized* benevolence. In his book *The Selfish Gene* Richard Dawkins (1976) points out the fallaciousness of ideas of 'group selection'. Selection is of *genes* and Dawkins usefully suggests that we think of an animal as a 'survival machine' for its genes. When a mammal produces offspring half its genes go into the offspring. We can therefore understand how a limited form of altruism can be selected for. Suppose that a man is *consciously* planning to increase his own genes in the gene pool at the expense of other genes. He should be as solicitous of his identical twin as of himself, because the identical twin has the same genes. He should be only half as solicitous of his son because his son contains only half his genes. (Actually this needs modification, because his son might be near the beginning of his reproductive life and the father might be sexually a bit of a has-been.) However, if he has many sons he may propagate more of his genes by being solicitous of them at the expense of his identical twin. Exactly what he should do might be calculated by a game-theoretic argument. (An extreme case arises when from the point of view of propagation of one's own genes there is virtually nothing to lose by self-destructive behaviour. A working bee stings a honey raider, but the worker bee is sterile. The self-destructive behaviour helps to preserve the suicide's own genes by preserving the relatives which possess them and which are able to reproduce.) Now animals which have altruistic behaviour programmed into them genetically do not consciously argue in this sort of way, but they may behave rather as if they did.

It can be seen that the sort of altruism which is selected for need not be species wide, and will more likely extend to those members of the species which have the observable characteristics which go with a high probability of near relatedness. Of course in special cases solicitude may indeed extend to members of other species, when such behaviour indirectly leads to a reproductive advantage. Thus certain large fish may live in close relationship with small 'cleaner fish' that eat parasites which they pick off the bodies of the larger fish. On the average more genes of the larger fish will be propagated if these genes include genes for a mechanism which makes the large fish refrain from eating the small fish, even though on some occasions this would be the best strategy for the larger fish.

These are mere hints at the arguments which show how natural selection may cause animals to evolve with programmes for ostensibly altruistic behaviour, but the arguments are very subtle and I must refer you to Dawkins' book. It certainly is unlikely that in a given species a generalized species-wide altruism can be selected for, still less the universal benevolence that transcends the boundaries of species and that is appealed to by utilitarians like myself. Another difference is, of course, that benevolence goes beyond being a matter of survival and differential reproduction. Thus benevolence might lead us to increase happiness at the expense, somewhat, of survival and reproduction.

Let us agree then that generalized benevolence is not a 'natural' virtue in the sense of being instinctive or genetically programmed. If we have the virtue it is because we have learned it. When I say that benevolence is learned I do not mean that it is necessarily taught us by our elders. Indeed how many of our elders think much of whales and dolphins, let alone sentient creatures in general? I think that we learn it by generalizing on a more directly taught limited benevolence. Suppose that we learn to care for brothers, sisters, friends, etc. We may learn to extend this by such elements in our culture as the parable of the good Samaritan. Then we may think of extending it to lower creatures, as well as to higher ones, such as the putative inhabitants of distant planetary systems. In this we are carrying over to our ethical theories a tendency which we may have acquired in scientific contexts. In science we search for universal laws and by analogy we may refuse to be satisfied with anything less in ethics. In science we may modify our theories by generalizing them. Some of us, when thinking ethically, may analogously generalize our attitude of benevolence: indeed such a progress from tribe or group to country to mankind is a familiar feature of the history of ethical thought, and the generalization beyond the human species is at present getting more acceptance.

This generalizing tendency is therefore a 'natural', that is, a psychologically plausible, tendency of a philosophical or scientific mind. It is not that we can deduce ethical principles from metaphysical or scientific data, but it is rather that there is a tendency to modify the structure of one's feelings in analogy with the structure of one's beliefs about the universe at large. Of course one's genes do in fact partly determine whether one has a philosophic, scientific and generalizing mind, instead of (say) a particularizing and exception making one, but the way in which this result comes about is culturally determined. I might have the same genes but be brought up among a savage tribe, in which case I should be unlikely to tend to generalize my emotions.

The trouble now is that if generalized benevolence is an artificial virtue (in the sense of being culturally determined) then I cannot assume it in those with whom I wish to discuss ethics. It seems to be the other way round: I have to persuade those others to make generalized benevolence their over-riding motive for action. People may have all sorts of other motives, such as the desire to act justly, to keep promises, and so on.

These are culturally determined, but so too, as we have seen, is the utilitarian motive of generalized benevolence.

Still, there does seem to be something particularly 'artificial' about some of our moral feelings, such as the desire to keep promises. They are good feelings to have, because usually they serve the utilitarian end, but they should not be allowed to conflict with the utilitarian end, as happens in ethical systems like that of Sir David Ross. However, in saying this I am assuming the utilitarian position, and so my appeal to the 'artificiality' of particular moral principles does not do much good. The utilitarian principle is itself 'artificial' if 'artificial' means 'being culturally determined'. And if 'artificial' does not mean this, there may be an illegitimate leap from 'is' to 'ought'. Why should we prize naturalness and denigrate artificiality?

I come now to another difficulty in an attempt to found ethics on a sentiment of generalized benevolence. This is that a feeling of generalized benevolence is not a feeling akin to a toothache or an itch. It is a 'feeling' in the sense of 'propositional attitude', and there is indeterminateness in the proposition relevant to the attitude. Or, to put it another way, it is unclear just what we are to understand by 'benevolence'. That is, if we say that we are going to found an ethical system on the sentiment of generalized benevolence, we have got to characterize benevolence. Just as there is no clear distinction between saying what is the meaning of 'whale' and stating facts about whales,[2] so there is no clear distinction between (a) saying (if we wish to say it) that benevolence is the desire to maximize happiness (as opposed to some other form of putative well-being) and (b) making a normative statement that only happiness has intrinsic value.

This sort of ambivalence is reflected in the entries under 'Benevolence' in *The Oxford English Dictionary*. Before going on to these I cannot forbear mentioning a related word 'Benevolist'. This is used to refer to 'a professor of benevolence' and the *OED* gives a phrase from the *Scotsman* of 14 August 1863: 'To be experimented upon . . . by contending sets of sectarians and "benevolists" '. Well, at the risk of being accused of being a benevolist, or even a professor of benevolence, let me proceed with some of the entries under 'Benevolence'. Benevolence is described in the first place as a 'disposition to do good, desire to promote the happiness of others, kindness, generosity, charitable feeling (as a general state or disposition towards mankind at large).' Secondly it is described as 'favourable feeling or disposition, as an emotion manifested towards another; affection; good will (towards a particular person or on a particular occasion).' Thirdly it is described as 'an expression of good will, an act of kindness, a gift or grant of money, a contribution for the support of the poor.' (There is also an account of an apparently quite different sense of the word.) The chief ambivalence here is whether to think of benevolence as the desire to promote happiness or as the desire to do good to others. If one thinks that happiness is the only intrinsic good then the ambivalence disappears. This is probably the case with Bishop Butler. Another ambivalence in Butler is as to whether by 'Benevolence' he means a supreme regulative principle (analogous to Self-Love), that is a desire for the good of all sentient beings as such, or whether 'Benevolence' is just a name for various more particular desires. The latter interpretation is perhaps suggested by his words in Sermon I:

[I]f there be in mankind any disposition to friendship; if there be any such thing as compassion, for compassion is momentary love; if there be any such things as the paternal or filial affections; if there be any affection in human nature, the object and end of which is the good of another; this is itself benevolence, or the love of another. (Butler 1953, p. 35)

However, as C.D. Broad (1930, p. 72) has suggested, Butler is confused here, because Butler could equally well have said that because hunger exists self-love must exist. Broad thinks that Butler is led astray here because his main concern in this passage is to show that benevolence is no more contrary to self-love than are the particular passions. Butler's considered view probably is after all that benevolence is a general principle analogous to self-love. In this respect Butler's concept of benevolence is analogous to my own notion of generalized benevolence, except that my notion is not purely altruistic but treats concern for one's own self as neither more nor less important than is concern for some other person. For me generalized benevolence is the ultimate feeling on which morality is based and thus it also has an analogy with Butler's principle of Conscience, though it differs from Butler's Conscience in not being concerned with particular duties. Butler seems to hold that God is a utilitarian, and has implanted conscience into us so that we will be more likely to act in a utilitarian way than we should if we tried to calculate in a utilitarian way on particular occasions. There is, of course, some analogy here with the act-utilitarian's advocacy of acting from rules of thumb, when either there is no time to calculate, or one thinks one may be too biased or too ignorant or too foolish to calculate properly. (Moreover the utilitarian will praise conscientious action in other people if he or she thinks that they are likely to act in a more nearly utilitarian way than they would if dangerous utilitarian thoughts were put into their heads, so weakening their traditional morality that they might end up without any morality at all, or perhaps with a pernicious one.)

I have noted that by 'benevolence' we may mean either a tendency to further the *happiness* of others, or a tendency to further the good, in some different or more general sense, of others. Ideal utilitarianism would depend on benevolence in the latter sense. So would what I call 'satisfaction utilitarianism', a view recently expounded by R.M. Hare (1976),[3] according to which what is to be maximized is the general satisfaction of desire, so that the satisfaction of a desire for an event to occur after one's death would come into the calculation, even though the satisfaction of the desire would give no 'satisfaction', or enjoyment. (So also would the satisfaction of a deontologist's desire that a promise be kept.) But benevolence could be thought of in a way still further removed from classical utilitarianism. Benevolence might be thought of as the desire so to act that other persons can become a certain sort of person. (The sort of person they would like to be, or perhaps the sort of person that we would like them to be?) I am not attracted to benevolence in this sense, save instrumentally. Of course I might like to make someone become a certain sort of person, but only because this would cause him to produce good results either for himself or for others.

To conclude, the notion of generalized benevolence is not a simple one. There are all sorts of motives which could reasonably be called 'benevolence', and not all of them issue in utilitarian action. Moreover, even if they would do so on their own, they might coexist with other equally 'natural' and general or cosmic motives, such as a liking for equal *distribution* of happiness. Hence I think that I was too optimistic in the past in thinking that people would reject utilitarianism only if they were not benevolent on the one hand, or philosophically confused on the other hand. I think that all one can do is to present the act utilitarian system, refute various specious objections which have been and still are being brought against it, and see whether any of one's audience find it attractive. If some of them do not, I do not now think that it follows that they must be lacking in benevolence.

NOTES

1   On this sort of problem, see my article 'Benevolence as an Over-Riding Attitude' in the present volume.
2   There is no 'fact of the matter' (to use W.V. Quine's phrase) about whether 'All whales are mammals' gives part of the meaning of 'whale' or whether it tells us a fact about whales.
3   I have commented on this in my article 'Hedonistic and Ideal Utilitarianism' (1978).

REFERENCES

Broad, C.D. 1930: *Five Types of Ethical Theory*. London: Routledge and Kegan Paul.

Butler, Joseph 1953: *Fifteen Sermons*, with introduction, analyses and notes by the Very Rev. W.R. Matthews. London: G. Bell and Sons.

Dawkins, Richard 1976: *The Selfish Gene*. Oxford: Oxford University Press.

Hare, R.M. 1976: Ethical Theory and Utilitarianism. In H.D. Lewis (ed.), *Contemporary British Philosophy*, 4th series, London: George Allen & Unwin.

Monro, D.H. 1967: *Empiricism and Ethics*. Cambridge: Cambridge University Press.

Moore, G.E. 1903: *Principia Ethica*. Cambridge: Cambridge University Press.

Rashdall, Hastings 1907: *The Theory of Good and Evil*. Oxford: Oxford University Press.

Smart, J.J.C. 1978: Hedonistic and Ideal Utilitarianism. *Midwest Studies in Philosophy*, 3, 240–51.

—— and Williams, Bernard 1973: *Utilitarianism, For and Against*. Cambridge: Cambridge University Press.

24

Distributive Justice and Utilitarianism

I

In this paper I shall not be concerned with the defence of utilitarianism against other types of ethical theory. Indeed I hold that questions of ultimate ethical principle are not susceptible of proof, though something can be done to render them more acceptable by presenting them in a clear light and by clearing up certain confusions which (for some people) may get in the way of their acceptance. Ultimately the utilitarian appeals to the sentiment of generalized benevolence, and speaks to others who feel this sentiment too and for whom it is an over-riding feeling.[1] (This does not mean that he will always act from this over-riding feeling. There can be backsliding and action may result from more particular feelings, just as an egoist may go against his own interests, and may regret this.) I shall be concerned here merely to investigate certain consequences of utilitarianism, as they relate to questions of distributive justice. The type of utilitarianism with which I am concerned is act utilitarianism, which is in its normative aspects much the same as the type of utilitarianism which was put forward by Henry Sidgwick (1962, especially book IV), though I differ from Sidgwick over questions of moral epistemology and of the semantics of ethical language.

II

The concept of justice as a *fundamental* ethical concept is really quite foreign to utilitarianism. A utilitarian would compromise his utilitarianism if he allowed principles of justice which might conflict with the maximization of happiness (or more generally of goodness, should he be an 'ideal' utilitarian). He is concerned with the maximization of happiness[2] and not with the distribution of it. Nevertheless he may well deduce from his ethical principle that certain ways of distributing the means to happiness (e.g. money, food, housing) are more conducive to the general good than are others. He will be interested in justice in so far as it is a political or legal or quasi-legal concept. He will consider whether the legal institutions and customary sanctions which operate in particular societies are more or less conducive to the utilitarian end than are other possible institutions and customs. Even if the society consisted entirely of utilitarians (and of course no actual societies have thus consisted) it might still be important to have legal and customary sanctions relating to distribution of goods, because utilitarians might be tempted to backslide and favour non-optimific distributions, perhaps because of bias in their own favour. They might be helped to act in a more nearly utilitarian way because of the presence of these customary sanctions.

As a utilitarian, therefore, I do not allow the concept of justice as a fundamental moral concept, but I am nevertheless interested in justice in a subordinate way, as a *means* to the utilitarian end. Thus even though I hold that it does not matter in what way happiness is distributed among different persons, provided that the total amount of happiness is maximized, I do of course hold that it can be of vital importance that the *means* to happiness should be distributed in some ways and not in others. Suppose that I have the choice of two alternative actions as follows: I can either give $500 to each of two needy men, Smith and Campbell, or else give $1000 to Smith and nothing to Campbell. It is of course likely to produce the greatest happiness if I divide the money equally. For this reason utilitarianism can often emerge as a theory with egalitarian consequences. If it does so this is because of the empirical situation, and not because of any moral commitment to egalitarianism as such. Consider, for example, another empirical situation in which the $500 was replaced by a half-dose of a life saving drug, in which case the utilitarian would advocate giving two half doses to Smith or Campbell and none to the other. Indeed if Smith and Campbell each possessed a half dose it would be right to take one of the half doses and give it to the other. (I am assuming that a whole dose would preserve life and that a half dose would not. I am also assuming a simplified situation: in some possible situations, especially in a society of non-utilitarians, the wide social ramifications of taking a half dose from Smith and giving it to Campbell might conceivably outweigh the good results of saving Campbell's life.) However, it is probable that in most situations the equal distribution of the means to happiness will be the right utilitarian action, even though the utilitarian has no ultimate moral commitment to egalitarianism. If a utilitarian is given the choice of two actions, one of which will give 2 units of happiness to Smith and 2 to Campbell, and the other of which will give 1 unit of happiness to Smith and 9 to Campbell, he will choose the latter course.[3] It may also be that I have the choice between two alternative actions, one of which gives −1 unit of happiness to Smith and +9 units to Campbell and the other of which gives +2 to Smith and +2 to Campbell. As a utilitarian I will choose the former course, and here I will be in conflict with John Rawls' theory, whose maximin principle would rule out making Smith worse off.

III

Rawls deduces his ethical principles from the contract which would be made by a group of rational egoists in an 'original position' in which they thought behind a 'veil of ignorance', so that they would not know who they were or even what generation they belonged to (Rawls 1971). Reasoning behind this veil of ignorance, they would apply the maximin principle. John Harsanyi earlier used the notion of a contract in such a position of ignorance, but used not the maximin principle but the principle of maximizing expected utility.[4] Harsanyi's method leads to a form of rule utilitarianism. I see no great merit in this roundabout approach to ethics *via* a contrary to fact supposition, which involves the tricky notion of a social contract and which thus appears already to presuppose a moral position. The approach seems also too Hobbesian: it is anthropologically incorrect to suppose that we are all originally little egoists. I prefer to base ethics on a principle of generalized benevolence, to which some of those with whom I discuss ethics may immediately respond. Possibly it might show something interesting about our common moral notions if it could be proved that they follow from what would be contracted by rational egoists in an 'original position', but as a utilitarian I am more concerned to advocate a normative theory which might replace our common moral notions than I am to explain these notions. Though some form of utilitarianism might be deducible (as by Harsanyi) from a contract or original position theory, I do not think that it either ought to be or need be defended in this sort of way.

Be that as it may, it is clear that utilitarian views about distribution of happiness do differ from Rawls' view. I have made a distinction between justice as a moral concept and justice as a legal or quasi-legal concept. The utilitarian has no room for the former, but he can have strong views about the latter, though *what* these views are will depend on empirical considerations. Thus whether he will prefer a political theory which advocates a completely socialist state, or whether he will prefer one which advocates a minimal state, as Robert Nozick's book (1975) does, or whether again he will advocate something between the two, is something which depends on the facts of economics, sociology, and so on. As someone not expert in these fields I have no desire to dogmatize on these empirical matters. (My own private non-expert opinion is that probably neither extreme leads to maximization of happiness, though I have a liking for rather more socialism than exists in Australia or USA at present.) As a utilitarian my approach to political theory has to be tentative and empirical. Not believing in moral rights as such I can not deduce theories about the best political arrangements by making deductions (as Nozick does) from propositions which purport to be about such basic rights.

Rawls deduces two principles of justice (Rawls 1971, p. 60). The first of these is that 'each person is to have an equal right to the most extensive basic liberty compatible with a similar liberty for others', and the second one is that 'social and economic inequalities are to be arranged so that they are both (a) reasonably expected to be to everyone's advantage, and (b) attached to positions and offices open to all.' Though a utilitarian could (on empirical grounds) be very much in sympathy with both of these principles, he could not accept them as universal rules. Suppose that a society which had no danger of nuclear war could be achieved only by reducing the liberty of one per cent of the world's population. Might it not be right to bring about such a state of affairs if it were in one's power? Indeed might it not be right greatly to reduce the liberty of 100 per cent of the world's population if such a desirable outcome could be achieved? Perhaps the present generation would be pretty miserable and would hanker for their lost liberties. However, we must also think about the countless future generations which might exist and be happy provided that mankind can avoid exterminating itself, and we must also think of all the pain, misery and genetic damage which would be brought about by nuclear war even if this did not lead to the total extermination of mankind.

Suppose that this loss of freedom prevented a war so devastating that the whole process of evolution on this planet would come to an end. At the cost of the loss of freedom, instead of the war and the end of evolution there might occur an evolutionary process which was not only long lived but also beneficial: in millions of years there might be creatures descended from *homo sapiens* which had vastly increased talents and capacity for happiness. At least such considerations show that Rawls' first principle is far from obvious to the utilitarian, though in certain mundane contexts he might accede to it as a useful approximation. Indeed I do not believe that restriction of liberty, in our present society, could have beneficial results in helping to prevent nuclear war, though a case could be made for certain restrictions on the liberty of all present members of society so as to enable the government to prevent nuclear blackmail by gangs of terrorists.

Perhaps in the past considerable restrictions on the personal liberties of a large proportion of citizens may have been justifiable on utilitarian grounds. In view of the glories of Athens and its contributions to civilization it is possible that the Athenian slave society was justifiable. In one part of his paper, 'Nature and Soundness of the Contract and Coherence Arguments,' David Lyons (1975, pp. 148–9) has judiciously discussed the question of whether in certain circumstances a utilitarian would condone slavery. He says that it would be unlikely that a utilitarian could condone slavery as it has existed in modern times. However, he considers the possibility that less objectionable forms of slavery or near slavery have existed. The less objectionable these may have been, the more likely it is that utilitarianism would have condoned them. Lyons (1975, p. 149 near top) remarks that our judgements about the relative advantages of different societies must be very tentative because we do not know enough about human history to say what were the social alternatives at any juncture.

Similar reflections naturally occur in connection with Rawls' second principle. Oligarchic societies, such as that of eighteenth century Britain, may well have been in fact better governed than they would have been if posts of responsibility had been available to all. Certainly to resolve this question we should have to go deeply into empirical investigations of the historical facts. (To prevent misunderstanding, I do think that in our present society utilitarianism would imply adherence to Rawls' second principle as a general rule.)

A utilitarian is concerned with maximizing total happiness (or goodness, if he is an ideal utilitarian). Rawls largely concerns himself with certain 'primary goods', as he calls them. These include 'rights and liberties, powers and opportunities, income and wealth' (Rawls 1971, p. 62). A utilitarian would regard these as mere means to the ultimate good. Nevertheless if he is proposing new laws or changes to social institutions the utilitarian will have to concern himself in practice with the distribution of these 'primary goods' (as Bentham did, see Barry 1973, p. 55). But if as an approximation we neglect this distinction, which may be justifiable to the extent that there is a correlation between happiness and the level of these 'primary goods,' we may say that according to Rawls an action is right only if it is to the benefit of the least advantaged person. A utilitarian will hold that a redistribution of the means to happiness is right if it maximizes the general happiness, even though some persons, even the least advantaged ones, are made worse off. A position which is intermediate between the utilitarian position and

Rawls' position would be one which held that one ought to maximize some sort of trade off between total happiness and distribution of happiness. Such a position would imply that sometimes we should redistribute in such a way as to make some persons, even the least advantaged ones, worse off, but this would happen less often than it would according to the classical utilitarian theory.

IV

Now though I do not believe that ultimate moral principles are capable of proof or disproof, I wonder whether this disagreement about whether we should ever sacrifice some persons' interests for the sake of the total interest may be connected with different views which philosophers have about human personality. Are we concerned simply to produce the greatest net happiness, or is it independently important that we should take account of *whose* happiness a given quantum of happiness should be? The non-utilitarian will hold that the distinction between Smith on the one hand and Campbell on the other hand is different in an ethically important way from the distinction between two different temporal segments of the same man, say Smith throughout his twenties and Smith throughout his forties. (The non-utilitarian generally feels no puzzlement about the rightness of the twenty-five year old Smith sacrificing himself for the sake of the forty-five year old Smith.) I find it hard to see what the morally relevant difference would be. It is true that we do in fact feel a special concern for future temporal segments of ourselves, perhaps because we are most of the time planning for these future temporal segments. However, sometimes we plan for the welfare of temporal segments of other people, and the man who plans martyrdom, for example, is certainly not planning for any future temporal segment of himself (at least if he does not believe in immortality). Since the utilitarian principle is an expression of the sentiment of generalized benevolence, the utilitarian sees no relevant different between the happiness of one person and the happiness of another.

I have suggested that those who see the matter differently may have a strong metaphysical concept of personality. In the context of modern scientific psychology the notion of a person tends to dissolve into a welter of talk in terms of neurophysiology, cybernetics and information theory. Sidgwick may have been similarly sceptical about our ordinary notions of personality. Using an earlier philosophical idiom he remarks (as a *tu quoque* to the Egoist who asks why he should sacrifice his own present happiness for the happiness of another) that one might equally ask why one should sacrifice a present pleasure for a greater one in the future. He

points out that if one accepted Hume's theory of the mind, according to
which the mind is just a cluster of feelings, sensations, and images, one
might ask why one part of the series of feelings which contribute to the
mind should feel concern for another part (Sidgwick 1962, pp. 418–19).

Returning from this speculative excursion, let us simply note that
according to classical utilitarianism it can be right to diminish the
happiness of Smith in order to bring about a more than compensating
increase of the happiness of Campbell. What matters is simply the
maximization of happiness, and distribution of happiness is irrelevant.
Sidgwick himself qualified this uncompromising stand in a minor way
when he introduced a principle of equal distribution which would come
into play when each of two alternative actions would produce the same
amount of total happiness, each greater than that which would be
produced by any other alternative action. Of course there must be an
almost zero probability that two alternative actions would produce *exactly*
the same total happiness, but as Sidgwick points out, it may be quite
common *that as far as we know* the two alternatives would produce equal
total happiness. Sidgwick introduces his principle of equal distribution in
order to break this sort of tie (Sidgwick 1962, pp. 416–17), and he claims
that the principle is implicit in Bentham's somewhat obscure formula
'Everybody to count for one, and nobody for more than one.' Actually, if
Sidgwick's principle is needed only to break ties (but why not toss a
coin?) then it merely postpones the problem. It would lead us to prefer
giving 3 units of happiness to Smith plus 3 to Campbell to giving 2 to
Smith plus 4 to Campbell. We could still have a tie between giving 2
units to Smith and 4 to Campbell, on the one hand, and giving 4 units to
Smith and 2 to Campbell, on the other hand.

It is not clear to me that in proposing this supplementary principle if
distribution Sidgwick is being quite consistent. Suppose that alternative
A maximizes happiness and also that *B* is the alternative action which
comes nearest to *A* in producing happiness, producing only slightly less.
Suppose also that *A* would distribute happiness rather unequally and that
B would distribute happiness quite equally. Nevertheless because *A*
produces more happiness Sidgwick would say that *A* should be done.
Since, given a suitable example, the difference between the amounts of
happiness produced can be supposed as small as one pleases, it appears
that Sidgwick gives equal distribution a vanishingly small value
compared with that which he gives to maximization. In fact, according to
usual mathematical theories such a vanishingly small value could be no
other than zero, and so instead of applying his principle of distribution in
order to break ties Sidgwick could surely just as well have tossed a coin.
The only way for him to avoid this conclusion, I think, would have been
for him to say that the value of equal distribution is non-zero but

infinitesimal.[5] However, it does seem to be an odd ethical position that one should give an *infinitesimal* value to equal distribution. It seems more plausible to reject Sidgwick's supplementary principle altogether (as I am inclined to do) or else to try to work out a theory in which equality of distribution comes into the calculation of consequences in all cases, and not just in order to break ties. According to the second alternative, we should be concerned with maximizing some sort of compromise between total happiness and equal distribution of it. Such a theory might make more concessions to common sense notions of distributive justice than classical utilitarianism does.

One proposal for compromising between maximization of happiness and distribution of it is given by Nicholas Rescher in his book *Distributive Justice* (Rescher 1966, pp. 31–41). (Rescher modifies utilitarianism in other ways too, but I shall not be concerned with these here.) Rescher's proposal is not for a compromise between *total* happiness and distribution but between *average* happiness and distribution, though an analogous account would hold for the case of total happiness. Rescher proposes that we should maximize an *effective average*, which is the average happiness less half the standard deviation from it. Lawrence H. Powers has argued that Rescher's definition of an effective average leads to unacceptable consequences, and has suggested replacing Rescher's definition by a new one, according to which the effective average is the average happiness less half the average deviation (Powers 1970). He gives an example which shows that Rescher's criterion could forbid a change which made everybody better off (a Pareto improvement). Powers claims that his modified criterion does not have bad consequences of this sort. Some philosophers may find this sort of compromise between utilitarianism and egalitarianism more palatable than classical utiltiarianism. However, I shall now return to the consideration of distributive justice as it relates to the classical utilitarian position.

V

In thinking about distributive justice we commonly think about the problem of distributing happiness between members of a set of contemporary individuals. However, this is to oversimplify the situation with which the utilitarian should be concerned. The consequences of his actions stretch indefinitely into the future, and the happiness to be maximized is that of all sentient beings, whatever their positions in space and time.[6] It is in the context of future generations that the question of whether we should maximize *average* happiness or whether we should maximize *total* happiness becomes particularly relevant. Like Sidgwick[7] I am inclined to advocate the latter type of utilitarianism. In thinking about this issue it is useful once more to compare the question of the happiness of different temporal segments of one person with the question of the happiness of a number of distinct persons. If we think that it is better to have 50 happy years of life than it is to have 20 happy years, then we should also think that it is better to have 50 happy people than to have 20 happy people, and this not just because the 50 happy people would raise the average happiness of the total population of the universe more than the 20 happy people would. (Even if the total population of the universe were 50 or 20, as the case may be, the universe with 50 happy people would be better than the universe with 20.) My argument here is of course meant to be persuasive rather than logically compelling. I suppose that a proponent of average utility could consistently reply that 50 happy years of life are intrinsically no better than 20 such years, though we may prefer a man to live the longer life because of extrinsic considerations, for example the sorrow of a widow with small children to bring up and no husband to help her.

As a utilitarian I hold that we should think of future generations no less than we should think of members of our own generation. Distance in time is no more pertinent to utilitarian considerations than is distance in space. Just as we would not conduct a bomb test on a distant island without considering the possibility that the island contained inhabitants, so also we ought to consider the effects of our actions on our remote or unknown descendants or possible descendants. I have heard it argued that the two cases are not parallel: what inhabitants are now on the island does not depend on our present actions, but who our descendants are does depend in part on our present actions. I cannot see myself why this should be a morally relevant difference. Suppose that one action would cause an island to have in the next generation a population of 1000 whereas an alternative action would cause the island to have a population of 2000 and that the question of the larger or smaller population has no significant effect on the rest of the world. Then as a utilitarian I want to prefer causing the larger population to exist, though a proponent of maximizing average utility would be indifferent between the two cases. Some philosophers might say that we have no duties towards merely possible people. If we opt for the population of 1000 then these 1000 will be actual and we will have duties towards them, but the remainder of the possible population of 2000 would not be actual and would not have rights. However, such an argument should not be accepted by a utilitarian, who should not have the notion of 'duty' as a fundamental concept of his system.[8]

Anyway, let us take it that we are concerned here with utilitarianism as a theory of maximizing *total* happiness (not *average* happiness). Let us consider the question of the distribution of happiness and of the means to happiness between different generations. Just as in the case of distribution between contemporaries, utilitarianism is indifferent to various patterns of distribution of total happiness provided that the total is the same. (However, the theory will not be indifferent in this sort of way to questions of the distribution of the *means* to happiness.) We must ask what sacrifices we should make now for the sake of the greater happiness of our descendants. Not so long ago it seemed that the fruits of science and technology were bringing the human species towards a golden age. (Unfortunately we have tended to forget the deleterious effect of modern technology – e.g., factory farms – on animal happiness. See Singer 1975b.) People are nowadays more sceptical about a future golden age: they point to problems of overpopulation, environmental pollution, the danger of nuclear war, possible accidents in genetic engineering, and so on. But let us consider what would be the right policy about savings for future generations, assuming that future generations would be happier than ours. In 'future generations' I would want to include 'future generations of non-humans' too, but I shall neglect this point in comparing utilitarianism with Rawls' theory. It indeed is a defect in the contractual theory that it neglects the sufferings of animals: the veil of ignorance prevents us from knowing who we are, i.e. which human being, but it does not, I think, prevent us from knowing that we are at least human. Now if future generations are going to be happier than our generation, it would seem to follow from Rawls' difference principle that we should make no savings for future generations. If we did we should be disadvantaging the worse off for the benefit of the better off. Rawls escapes this consequence by what seems to be an *ad hoc* modification of his original theory: he modifies the egoistic inclinations of people in his 'original position' by allowing them some altruistic feelings, namely feelings for the welfare of their children and grandchildren.

Utilitarianism might seem to imply an opposite conclusion. Instead of implying zero savings (as Rawls' theory could if it did not have the above mentioned modification) utilitarianism would seem to require what many people would regard as an unacceptably high amount of savings. In a discussion of F.P. Ramsey's pioneering paper 'A Mathematical Theory of Saving' (Ramsey 1928), John C. Harsanyi (1975) has pointed out that on certain plausible assumptions about the relation between increments of wealth to increments of happiness (assumptions about utility functions), Ramsey's argument might well imply that the present generation should save more than half of their national incomes. However, Harsanyi has argued that utility functions applicable to the present generation do not properly relate savings to future felicity. New technological discoveries may well make present capital investments of little use in the future. For this reason, as well as others which I shall not go into here, Harsanyi has argued that optimal saving would be less than might at first have been supposed on the basis of Ramsey's argument.

Nevertheless it may well be that utilitarian considerations imply that savings for future generations should be much greater than many people think. The less we think that a golden age is coming the stronger these reasons will be. Very much expense and effort need to be made, for example, to show that radioactive waste materials do not harm our remote descendants, or failing that, we must forgo the use of nuclear reactors for generating power. Similarly with respect to the rich countries in relation to the Third World, the wasteful technologies, certain fishing areas, and so on, for the benefit of the poorer ones. The fact that such savings or renunciations that are enjoined by utilitarian considerations may well come to far more than would be politically acceptable is no criticism of utilitarianism: it is a reflection of the fact that people are usually more swayed by self-interest than they ought to be. Of course utilitarianism is a theory for individual decision making, and prevailing political attitudes constitute part of the empirical facts about the world with which, like it or not, a utilitarian decision maker will have to contend. Some actions which would be right if they were generally imitated would be merely Quixotic if there were no prospect of such imitation. For example when there was a proposal to raise the salaries of Australian professors, some friends of mine wrote letters to the newspapers saying that it would be better to use this amount of taxpayers money to increase the number of junior faculty members. When this idea did not catch on, there was obviously no point in their refusing (as individuals) the proposed salary increases. (I neglect the fact here that there would have been great administrative difficulties in putting such individual decisions into effect.) Though utilitarianism is *in theory* not egalitarian, because it does not protect the interests of the worst off people in the way that Rawls' theory does, it is possible that there might be situations in which Rawls' constraint of not making the worst off even more badly off would force Rawls into a decision which would lead to a greater difference between rich and poor than would utilitarian theory. This is because removal of the constraint might, at the cost of making a very few of the worst off members of society still worse off, bring about a more general levelling off on the whole. (Here we must of course make allowance for the fact that if we are concerned with the redistribution of the *means* to happiness, taking what people have may produce more unhappiness than not giving it to them in the first place.) To take a rather fanciful example, suggested to me by some remarks of Harsanyi's (1975), suppose that society spent astronomical sums on very badly off mentally defective people, thus making them able to perform some simple tasks which would otherwise be beyond them, and that this vast expenditure for the mentally defective prevented ordinary health care for the ordinary poor but not handicapped people. On the above supposition utilitarianism would suggest a redistribution of resources *from* the mentally defective *to* better health care for the generality of the poor. This would seem to be forbidden by Rawls' difference principle. Whether in any actual situations Rawls' theory or utilitarian theory would lead to the greater egalitarianism in practice depends on many empirical considerations, and I would not like to pronounce on this matter.

VI

General adherence to Robert Nozick's theory (in his *Anarchy, State and Utopia*, 1975) would be compatible with the existence of very great inequality indeed. This is because the whole theory is based quite explicitly on the notion of *rights*: in the very first sentence of the preface of his book we read 'Individuals have rights. . . .' The utilitarian would demur here. A utilitarian legislator might tax the rich in order to give aid to the poor, but a Nozickian legislator would not do so. A utilitarian legislator might impose a heavy tax on inherited wealth, whereas Nozick would allow the relatively fortunate to become even more fortunate, provided that they did not infringe the *rights* of the less fortunate. The utilitarian legislator would hope to increase the total happiness by equalizing things a bit. How far he should go in this direction would depend on empirical considerations. He would not want to equalize things too much if this led to too much weakening of the incentive to work, for example. Of course according to Nozick's system there would be no reason why members of society should not set up a utilitarian utopia, and voluntarily equalize their wealth, and also give wealth to poorer communities outside. However, it is questionable whether such isolated utopias could survive in a modern environment, but if they did survive, the conformity of the behaviour of their members to utilitarian theory, rather than the conformity to Nozick's theory, would be what would commend their societies to me.

VII

In this article I have explained that the notion of justice is not a fundamental notion in utilitarianism, but that utilitarians will characteristically have certain views about such things as the distribution of wealth, savings for the benefit of future generations and for the Third World countries and other practical matters. Utilitarianism differs from John Rawls' theory in that it is ready to contemplate some sacrifice to certain individuals (or classes of individuals) for the sake of the greater good of all, and in particular it may allow certain limitations of personal freedom which would be ruled out by Rawls' theory. *In practice,* however, the general tendency of utilitarianism may well be towards an egalitarian form of society.

NOTES

1   In hoping that utilitarianism can be rendered acceptable to some people by presenting it in a clear light, I do not deny the possibility of the reverse happening. Thus I confess to a bit of a pull the other way when I consider Nozick's example of an 'experience machine' (Nozick 1975, pp. 42–5) though I am at least partially reassured by Peter Singer's remarks towards the end of his review of Nozick (Singer 1975a). Nozick's example of an experience machine is more worrying than the more familiar one of a pleasure inducing machine, because it seems to apply to ideal as well as to hedonistic utilitarianism.

2   In this paper I shall assume a hedonistic utilitarianism, though most of what I have to say will be applicable to ideal utilitarianism too.

3   There are of course difficult problems about the assignment of cardinal utilities to states of mind, but for the purposes of this paper I am assuming that we can intelligibly talk, as utilitarians do, about amounts of happiness.

4   See Harsanyi (1953, 1955). Harsanyi has discussed Rawls' use of the maximin principle and has defended the principle of maximizing expected utility instead, in a paper 'Can the Maximin Principle Serve as a Basis for Morality? A Critique of John Rawls' Theory' (1975). These articles have been reprinted in Harsanyi (1976).

5   Of course during the nineteenth century the notion of an infinitesimal fell into disrepute among mathematicians, for very good reasons, but it has recently been made mathematically respectable by Abraham Robinson (1970). A simple account of Robinson's idea can be found in an article by Martin Davis and Reuben Hersh (1972).

6   There is a question as to whether Jeremy Bentham himself thought in this universalistic way or whether the interests with which he was concerned were restricted in various ways. See David Lyons (1972).

7   For Sidgwick's remarks on the question of average happiness versus total happiness see Sidgwick (1962, pp. 414–16).

8   An interesting discussion of the problem of future generations is to be found in Jan Narveson (1967). Narveson is a utilitarian, though his view differs somewhat from my own form of utilitarianism, and his conclusions about future generations are opposed to mine. On p. 63 Narveson says 'Whenever

one has a duty, it must be possible to say on whose account the duty arises – i.e. whose happiness is in question'. I want to deny this statement: I think that I ought to maximize happiness, and I can work out the best ways of achieving this end without knowing who are the people who will be happy or miserable. This is why I expect that Narveson's notion of 'duty' differs from my notion of 'ought' and that his notion is perhaps even related to the correlative and non-utilitarian notion of a right. But I am not clear about this and I could easily have misunderstood Narveson's notion of 'duty'.

REFERENCES

Barry, Brian 1973: *The Liberal Theory of Justice*. London: Oxford University Press.

Davis, Martin and Hersh, Reuben 1972: Non-Standard Analysis. *Scientific American*, June, 78–86.

Harsanyi, John C. 1953: Cardinal Utility in Welfare Economics and the Theory of Risk-Taking. *Journal of Political Economy*, 61, 434–5.

—— 1955: Cardinal Welfare, Individualistic Ethics and Interpersonal Comparisons of Utility. *Journal of Political Economy*, 63, 309–21.

—— 1975: Can the Maximin Principle Serve as a Basis for Morality? A Critique of John Rawls' Theory. *The American Political Science Review*, 69, 594–606.

—— 1976: *Essays on Ethics, Social Behaviour, and Scientific Explanation*. Dordrecht, Holland: D. Reidel.

Lyons, David 1972: Was Bentham a Utilitarian? *Reason and Reality, Royal Institute of Philosophy Lectures*, vol. 5, 1970–71, 196–221.

—— 1975: Nature and Soundness of the Contract and Coherence Arguments. In Norman Daniels (ed.), *Reading Rawls*, Oxford: Blackwell, 141–67.

Narveson, Jan 1967: Utilitarianism and New Generations. *Mind*, 76, 62–72.

Nozick, Robert 1975: *Anarchy, State and Utopia*. Oxford: Blackwell.

Powers, Lawrence H. 1970: A More Effective Average: A Note on Distributive Justice. *Philosophical Studies*, 21, 74–8.

Ramsey, F.P. 1928: A Mathematical Theory of Saving. *Economic Journal*, 38, 543–59.

Rawls, John 1971: *A Theory of Justice*. Cambridge, Massachusetts: Harvard University Press.

Rescher, Nicholas 1966: *Distributive Justice*. Indianapolis: Bobbs-Merrill.

Robinson, Abraham 1970: *Non-Standard Analysis*. Amsterdam: North-Holland.

Sidgwick, Henry 1962: *Methods of Ethics*, 7th edn. Chicago: University of Chicago Press.

Singer, Peter 1975a: Review of Nozick. *New York Review of Books*, 6 March.

—— 1975b: *Animal Liberation*. New York: Random House.

Index

Achinstein, Peter, 118n
actions, and utilitarianism, 259–60
Acworth, Richard, 21
Adelaide, University of, 2, 30
Alexander, H. Gavin, 111
altruism, 283, 286–7
analytic–synthetic distinction, 2, 32
anthropocentricity, 33, 36n, 129
anti-realism, 141, 169–84
Aquinas, St Thomas, 133
Armstrong, D.M., 3, 45, 118n, 125,
    164, 213n, 223, 229, 233, 234, 253
artificial intelligence, 104
artificial virtues, see virtues
Austin, John, 260
Avogadro's number, 135–6, 142n
Ayer, A.J., 170

Barnes, E.W., 103
Barnett, Dene, 75n
becoming, see time
behaviouristic analysis, 2–3, 30, 116,
    190–1
benevolence
    as an over-riding attitude, 272–81
    generalized benevolence, 283–90
Bentham, Jeremy, 259, 260, 296, 298,
    304n
Berenda, C.W., 22n
Bergson, H., 87

Berkeley, George, 71, 123–4, 169
Berlin, Isaiah, 18–19
Bindra, D., 253
biology, 103–5
    and philosophy, 121–31
Black, Max, 201
Blanshard, Brand, 30
Böhm, D., 12
Bois-Reymond, E. du, 106–9 passim
Boltzmann, Ludwig, 1, 128
Boscovich, R., 17, 41
Bouma, P.J., 232
Boyd, Richard, 247
Boyle, Robert, 125
Bradley, F.H., 6, 170–2 passim
Bradley, M.C., 5, 229, 231, 235–7
    passim
brain processes, 4, 13–15, 43–5, 70–1,
    189–200, 218–21, 224–5, 234–5,
    243, 250–3
Braithwaite, R.B., 167n
Brandt, R.B., 6
Brentano, Franz, 220
Broad, C.D., 80, 81, 84, 289
Brown, Patterson, 133
Buchan, John, 167
Butler, Bishop, 284, 289

Cajori, F., 79
Campbell, C.A., 16, 21, 29, 31, 170, 174

Campbell, N.R., 167n
Candlish, Stewart, 174
Capitan, W.H., 7n
Carnap, R., 112
Cartwright, Nancy, 160
category mistake, 32
causal mechanism, 135–6
causality, and time, 51–9, 155
cause, 224
certainty, and demonstrability, 19–20
change, 66–7, 46
Christensen, Ferrel, 89n
Chomsky, N., 102, 247
Church, Alonzo, 151
Clark, Romane, 151
Clarke, Samuel, 133
Clauser, John F., 143n
Clendinnen, John, 41–2, 165
Coady, C.A.J., 185n
Cochiarella, N.B., 65
coherence, 173–5
coincidence, 135–6
   cosmic coincidence, 158–66
colours, 125, 130, 194–5, 205, 229–37, 252
Condillac, É.B. de, 39
conscience (Butler), 289
contingency, 83–4
Copenhagen interpretation (of quantum mechanics), 25–7 *passim*
counterfactuals, 163
Cousin, D.R., 29
Craig, William, 143n

Darwin, Charles, 11, 247
Davidson, Donald
   and intensional language, 220
   and materialism, 244
   and process, 147–50 *passim*, 224
   and propositional attitudes, 129
   and tenses, 75n, 89n
   and truth-conditions, 177, 184
Davis, Martin, 304n
Dawkins, Richard, 286
demonstrability, and certainty, 19–20
Descartes, R., 15, 184

determinism, 18–19, 21, 31–2, 83, 109, 179, 203
Devitt, Michael, 170
De Witt, Boyce, 81–2
distributive justice, 292–305
dualism, 15, 19, 43–6, 70, 116, 125, 204
Dummett, Michael, 6, 137, 169, 173, 179–80
Dunbar, M.J., 43

Eccles, J.C., 124
Eddington, A.S., 79
Einstein, A., 53, 63, 141
electronics, 122–3
emergence, 16–18, 225, 246–54
epiphenomenalism, 254
Escher, Martin, 85
ethics, 34
events, 145–55, 224
Everett, Hugh, 81–2

Farrell, B.A., 196
fatalism, 67
Feigl, Herbert, 11, 13, 14, 22n, 41, 44, 189, 192, 193, 211
Feinberg, Gerald, 181
Feuer, Lewis S., 47n
Feyerabend, P.K., 12, 26, 72, 73, 110, 112, 208, 212
Field, Hartry, 176, 180
Flew, A.G.N., 133
fly and fly bottle, 20, 31
Fodor, J.A., 116
Forrest, Peter, 167n
four-dimensional world view, 61–74
   passim, 94, 218–19
free will, 15–19, 21, 31–2
Freeman, D., 253
Frege, G., 191
functionalism, 3–4
future, the, 6n, 41, 91–9, 127–8
future generations, 300–3, 304–5n

Galbraith, J.K., 212
Gasking, D.A.T., 22n
Geach, P.T., 64–70, 145, 156n

Gellner, Ernest, 22n
Gibbon, Edward, 109
God, existence of, 133–4, 161–2
Gödel's theorem, 174, 177
Godfrey-Smith, William, 93
Goodman, Nelson, 38, 54, 68, 172, 185n
Gosse, Philip, 200
Graham, Neill, 81
Grünbaum, Adolf, 5, 52, 54–9 passim, 88, 128

Haldane, J.S., 247
Hamilton, William, 39
Hampshire, Stuart, 104
Harsanyi, John, 294, 301–2, 304n
'headless woman' illusion, 45, 125, 234–5, 253
Hersh, R., 304n
Hesse, Mary, 167n
Hick, J.H., 133, 142n
Hilbert space, 59n
Hobart, R.E., 18–19
Hollis, Martin, 33
Holsinger, Kent E., 42, 43
Hopkins, James, 7n
Hull, David, 122
Hume, David, 18, 27, 63, 133, 134, 165, 283, 285, 298
Hurst, C.A., 22n

ideal entities, 140
idealism, 6, 169–84
identity, 81
identity theory (mind–brain), 2–4, 215–25
see also dualism, materialism, physicalism
indeterminacy of translation, 87, 220, 243, 244
indexical expressions, 86–7, 89n, 95, 127, 130, 153
individuals, and space-time, 61–76
induction, 41–2, 111–15, 165
inference licences, 111–15
instrumentalism, 63, 110, 115–17, 132–43 passim, 209

integrity, 278–80
intensionality, 220, 221, 225
intentionality, 220, 225
intuitionism, 137, 169

Joachim, H.H., 169
justice, 292–305

Kant, Immanuel, 88
Katz, Bernard, 71
Kim, Jaegwon, 148
Kirk, Robert, 243
Kleiner, Scott A., 123
Kripke, Saul, 93
Krips, Henry, 88

Lacey, Hugh M., 59n, 156n
Lakatos, I., 47n
Lange, F.A., 106, 208
language games, 30
Laplace, P.S. de, 106
laws of nature, 53, 106–9, 111–15, 158–66, 190–1
Leeds, Stephen, 142n
Leibniz, Gottfried, 133
Leslie, John, 185n
Levett, M.J., 29
Levi, Isaac, 116
Lewin, K., 55
Lewis, David, 159
and colours, 229, 231, 233, 234
and identity theory, 3
and possible worlds, 85, 163, 178, 222
and translation theory, 225
libertarianism, 15–19, 31
life after death, 107
Locke, John, 133, 231
Lyons, David, 296, 304n

Macaulay, W.H., 166n
McCall, Storrs, 5, 81–5, 89n
McCloskey, H.H., 277
McGinn, Colin, 7n
Mach's principle, 56
MacKay, D.M., 199, 250
Malcolm, Norman, 212n

Mandelbaum, Maurice, 116
mark method (Reichenbach), 52
Mortensen, Chris, 143n
Martin, C.B., 2, 3, 201n, 209, 229,
    235
Martin, R.M., 148
materialism, 30–1, 70, 106, 124–5,
    203–12, 217, 240–4, 251–4
mathematics, 20, 121
maximin principle (Rawls), 294, 304n
Maxwell, J.C., 53
mechanism, bogy of, 106–10
Medawar, P.B., 118n
Medlin, B.H., 3, 116
Mehlberg, Henryk, 52, 55, 56, 59
Mellor, D.H., 167n
memory, and time, 66, 87–8, 127
Merrill, D.D., 7n
Mill, J.S., 39, 40, 260, 264–5
Miller, David, 138
Millikan, R.A., 135
mind–brain identity theory, 2–4,
    215–25
    see also dualism, materialism,
    physicalism
Minkowski, H., 61–73 *passim*, 94–5,
    154, 220
Moody, E.A., 43
Moore, G.E., 29, 259, 260, 285
Morgan, C.L., 253
Morgenbesser, S., 116
Munro, D.H., 272, 274–81 *passim*, 284
Mure, G.R.G., 172

Nagel, E., 22n
naming, 93–4
Narveson, Jan, 304–5n
natural kinds, 124
natural selection, 11, 17, 125, 247,
    286–7
necessity, 133–4
Neurath, Otto, 124
Newton, I., 14, 53, 54, 79
nomological danglers, 13–16, 22n, 44,
    190, 211, 225, 233
Norman, Jack, 151
Nowell-Smith, P.H., 18, 260, 262

Nozick, Robert, 295, 303, 304n
Nye, Mary-Jo, 143n

observation statements, 111–15, 139
Ockham, William of, 38, 42–3
Ockham's Razor, 38–46, 183, 190
Ohm's law, 164
Ornstein, Robert E., 88
Orwell, George, 142n, 159
over-riding attitudes, 272–81, 284

particular passions (Butler), 284
Paul, G.A., 30, 170
Peirce, C.S., 175, 176
Perrin, Jean, 134, 142n
Perry, John, 153
personality, 297–8
Pettit, Philip, 184
phenomenalism, 33
phenomenological fallacy, 204
philosophy
    anthropocentricity in, 33, 36n, 129
    ethics, 34
    political philosophy, 34
    and scientific plausibility, 11–22
    its social relevance, 35–6
    standards in, 27–34
physicalism, 38, 43–6, 217, 219, 221–3
    passim
    and colours, 229–37
    and emergence, 246–54
physics, 109, 132–42 *passim*, 221, 224,
    240, 246
Place, U.T., 2–3, 6n, 14, 45, 189, 192,
    193, 199, 204, 241, 242, 251
Podolsky, B., 141
Polya, G., 31
Popper, K.R., 137–8
possibility, 178–9
possible worlds, 85, 162–3, 178–9,
    221–2
Powers, Laurence H., 299
Prior, A.N., 65, 75n, 92, 98
Prisoner's Dilemma, 6
process, 145–55
properties, 221–5, 234

propositional attitudes, 129–30, 220, 243–4
psychology, 115–17, 241
pure chance, 21, 31–2

quantum mechanics, 25–6, 56, 81, 106, 109, 127, 140–1, 159–60
Quine, W.V., 28, 54, 139, 165, 216, 220, 244
    and analytic–synthetic distinction, 2, 32
    and indeterminacy of translation, 87, 243
    and instrumentalism, 137
    and laws of nature, 164
    and mathematics, 121
    and natural kinds, 124
    and properties, 221–5
    and propositional attitudes, 129–30
    and reference, 94, 151–2
    and semantic ascent, 26
    and space-time, 63–6 *passim*, 147
    and theory of knowledge, 173
Quinton, Anthony, 33

Ramsey, F.P, 33, 112–13, 115, 301
Rashdall, Hastings, 284
Rawls, John, 294–6, 301–4
realism, 5–6, 132–42, 162–3, 168–84
reality, not a property, 92
reference, 91, 96, 97, 170
Regan, Donald, 6
Reichenbach, H., 51–2, 55, 75n, 128, 135, 231n
relativity
    general, 40, 72, 135, 153, 154, 182, 218
    special, 51, 53, 54, 61, 63, 68–70 *passim*, 82, 93–5 *passim*, 146
Rescher, Nicholas, 173, 299
Rietdijk, C.W., 95
rights, 303, 304n
Robb, A.A., 58
Robinson, Abraham, 304n
Romney, Gillian, 99
Rorty, Richard, 215
Rosen, N., 27

Ross, David, 277, 288
Routley, R., 46n
rule-following, 206–7
Ruse, Michael, 122
Russell, Bertrand, 15, 185n, 203
Ryle, Gilbert, 2, 29–30, 93, 103–18, 146, 189

Salmon, Wesley, 115, 135, 136
Santillana, G. de, 47n
satisfaction, 136
Schilpp, P.A., 63
Schlesinger, G., 41, 42, 47n
Schrödinger's cat paradox, 81–2
science
    extensional language for, 221
    and Ockham's Razor, 38–46
    progress of, 103–4
    and properties, 222–3
    Ryle on, 103–18
scientific knowledge, 11–13, 137–8
scientific plausibility, 2, 11–22, 30–2
secondary qualities, 33, 125–6, 194–5, 204–5
self-love, 284, 289
Sellars, Wilfrid, 5, 74, 145–55, 213n, 251
semantic ascent, 26
sensations, 189–200, 218
    see also brain processes
Shaffer, Jerome, 213n
Shimony, Abner, 143n
Sidgwick, H., 259, 263–4, 266–7, 277, 292, 297, 299–300, 304n
simplicity, 40–6, 134, 142n, 158, 165–6, 200
simultaneity, 68–70, 73, 82, 85
Singer, Peter, 280, 301, 304n
Skyrms, Brian, 81
Smythies, J.R., 201
Sober, Elliot, 40, 142n
space-time, 5, 51–8 *passim*, 61–76, 82–8, 95–6, 127, 153–5 *passim*, 218
special relativity, 51, 53, 54, 61, 63, 68–70 *passim*, 82, 93–5 *passim*, 146
Sperry, R., 246, 248–54 *passim*

Spinoza, Baruch, 7*n*, 33, 121
Stannard, F.R., 34
Stein, Howard, 95–6
Stock, Guy, 171
Stocker, Michael, 272, 273, 278
Stopes-Roe, H.V., 118*n*
Stout, A.K., 261, 266–7
Stove, David, 164
Strawson, P.F., 15, 36*n*, 62, 64, 91, 213*n*
'Strawsono-Aristotelian' conceptual scheme, 61–7, 72, 73, 219, 220
Strehlow, T.G.H., 75*n*
synonymy, 129, 220–2 *passim*, 225, 243, 244
Swinburne, R., 33

Tarski truth-theory, 177
Taylor, Richard, 78, 80, 85
Tennant, Neil, 173
tenses, 65–7, 75, 86–7, 89*n*, 95, 126–7, 130, 152–3, 218
Thales problem, 181
Tichý, Pavel, 138
time
    causal theories of, 51–9, 155
    and identity theory, 218
    and memory, 66, 87–8, 127
    motion of time, 5, 78–88, 127–9
    and theory of truth, 173–4
    see also indexical expressions, space-time, tenses
Thomson, J.J., 135
Thorburn, W.M., 38
Thorpe, W.H., 253
Tooley, Michael, 99, 167*n*
topic neutral analysis, 4, 156*n*, 196, 234
Toulmin, S.E., 260, 270
Townsend, Aubrey, 156*n*
truth, degrees of, 169–84
truth conditions, 149, 177
truth in a model, 136, 141
two worlds myth, 116

Ullian, J.S., 160, 173
universalization principle, 261
Urmson, J.O., 260, 264, 270
use–mention fallacy, 171–2
utilitarianism, 1, 6, 34, 180
    act (extreme), 259–70, 274, 289, 292
    actions, 259–60
    and distributive justice, 292–305
    and generalized benevolence, 283–90
    ideal, 289–90, 296
    and integrity, 278–80
    and over-riding desires, 272–81, 284
    rule (restricted), 259–70, 273
    satisfaction, 290
Van Fraassen, B., 133, 142*n*, 143*n*, 158–61 *passim*, 166
variable hypotheticals, 112–13, 115
veridical paradox, 164
verificationism, 3, 30, 97, 137
verisimilitude, 137–8, 140, 142, 143*n*
Vigier, J.P., 12
virtues, artificial and natural, 285–8
Vogt, Karl, 208

Waismann, F., 30
warranted assertibility, 169, 173–84
Weyl, H., 66
Wheeler, J.A., 203
Williams, B.A., 74–6*n*, 213*n*, 272, 275, 276, 278
Wisdom, J., 209
Wittgenstein, L., 11, 15, 20, 22*n*, 87, 113, 189, 198, 206–10 *passim*
Wittgensteinianism, 30
Woodger, J.H., 192
Wright, Crispin, 173

Young, J.Z., 124

Zeno's paradox of the stadium, 56

Index compiled by Joyce Kerr